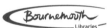

GREAT BRITISH FOOD

Great British Menu is an Optomen Television Production

LONDON, NEW YORK, MUNICH, MELBOURNE, DELHI

Executive Managing Editor Adèle Hayward
Managing Art Editor Kat Mead
Production Editor Jenny Woodcock
Production controller Elizabeth Warman
Art Director Peter Luff
Publisher Stephanie Jackson

This edition was produced for
Dorling Kindersley Limited by
splinter-group.net
Design Rebecca Painter
Editorial Jonathan Hilton

This edition first published in Great Britain in
2008 by Dorling Kindersley Limited
80 Strand, London WC2R ORL

A Penguin Company
2 4 6 8 10 9 7 5 3 1

By arrangement with Optomen Television
Optomen logo © Optomen Television 2006, 2007
Optomen Television Production Team: Executive Producer Nicola Moody
Series 1
Series Producer Bernice Daly, Researcher Annina Vogel, Studio Producer
Sophie Seiden, Assistant Producer Jackie Baker, Personal Assistant
Vanessa Land, Home Economist Lisa Harrison.
Series 2
Series Producer Gary Broadhurst, Production Manager Raewyn Dickson,
Assistant Producer Ross Blair, Researchers Christopher Monk and Sam Knowles,
Personal Assistant Vanessa Land, Home Economist Karen Taylor.

A CIP catalogue record for this book is available from The British Library.
ISBN-13: 978 1 4053 3318 4

Printed by Tien Wah Press, Singapore

See our complete catalogue at **www.dk.com**

CONTENTS

Great British Food is a compilation of the very best recipes from *Great British Menu* and *Great British Menu Cookbook* – two earlier books that were produced to accompany BBC TWO's television series Great British Menu. The first outing of the television series gathered together some of the country's finest chefs to compete for the chance to be part of the team creating a very special lunch indeed – a banquet to celebrate the Queen's 80th birthday.

The competition celebrated not only this personal milestone, but also the United Kingdom's remarkable culinary renaissance. The recipes created by the chefs for the competition, many of which are reproduced here, reflect brilliantly the range and quality of the ingredients, produce and cuisine found in these diverse and bountiful islands.

We have come a long way. When Queen Elizabeth II succeeded to the throne in 1952 the end of food rationing was still two years away. Britain, broken and impoverished by the sacrifices of the Second World War, and in retreat from its once mighty Empire, was a grey, austere place, where food and drink were widely regarded as little more than a necessity endured. The puritan was in the ascendant during those years of austerity; the cavalier within us would have to wait.

The pleasures of the table were never entirely neglected. Elizabeth David raised sights with her magisterial paeans to unpretentious and honest food, albeit conjured from the then elusive produce of the Mediterranean, those "blessed lands of sun and sea and olive trees". But in many ways, this celebration of all things distant only encouraged the further diminution of Britain's culinary heritage, though a few lonely voices could be heard in the wilderness. Among them was that of Jane Grigson, whose boundless,

brilliantly articulated love for the food of these islands fed an optimism that refused to lie down "even when confronted with perceived realities".

Her optimism was not misplaced. For, over a quarter of a century after she penned those words, Britain is a serious food nation once more. Greater affluence has seen many more of us dining out with regularity, celebrating our palates, taking pleasure in food, demanding ever higher quality. A remarkable openness to new ideas, encouraged by widespread travel and postwar immigration, has seen the people of Britain embrace cuisines from every corner of the world, which, in turn, have fused with native traditions to create a vibrant food culture, peopled by world-class chefs, entrepreneurs and producers, people who are making the most of Britain's extraordinarily diverse larder.

There is another important ingredient in the mix – a new-found passion for our past, the rediscovery of the very best of Britain's regional dishes and produce. Some politicians have tried – and failed – to present Britain as a young country. It is not. It is an ancient one and it is at its best when it embraces both the past and the future, seeking the best of both worlds. Nowhere is this more evident than in the way food producers, many of them featured in these pages, have used the internet to market the finest traditional products, from choice cuts of Aberdeen Angus beef, to the revival of mutton, to the every growing array of artisanal cheeses, to the varieties of fruit and vegetables we had turned our back on in the sterile pursuit of conformity.

The realm over which Queen Elizabeth II still reigns has undergone a revolution in its eating habits, marked by the marriage of technology and tradition. Escaping its puritan past, the United Kingdom is now a land of plenty, peopled by culinary cavaliers, a "blessed plot" indeed.

INTRODUCING THE CHEFS

SAT BAINS

Sat Bains' food philosophy is all about giving diners a completely unique experience. As he says, "Why bother coming to a restaurant and spending good money if you can do better yourself at home?" This bold, forward-thinking attitude has already reaped considerable professional rewards: he is the only chef in Nottingham to be awarded a Michelin star and his restaurant won the coveted AA 'Restaurant of the Year' award for 2007.

Born into a Punjabi family in Derby, Sat admits his main reason for joining catering college was "to meet girls". But whilst there he discovered a love of cooking too, and quickly developed into a hugely talented and passionate chef.

Sat got his big break when he became part of the team that opened the first of Raymond Blanc's brasseries, Le Petit Blanc, in Oxford in 1996. He then moved to a Head Chef's job at the Martin's Arms in Nottingham. Building on his growing successes, in 1999 Sat won the prestigious Roux Scholarship, and was awarded the chance to flex his culinary muscles at the world-renowned, three Michelin-starred Le Jardin de Sens in the south of France. This moulded him into the chef he is today: contemporary and cutting edge.

But despite the lofty heights of his culinary achievements, Sat has never lost sight of his roots in the Midlands, and the rich variety of produce it offers. "We need to back the artisan producers and keep the food bloodline of the Midlands going," he says. And through his much-lauded Restaurant Sat Bains, that's exactly what he's doing. "I'm very excited about modern British cooking. It's on par with any country in the world right now and we need to all celebrate that." We're sure all his Great British Menu competitors would agree.

GALTON BLACKISTON

Galton Blackiston's career began as a cash-strapped 17-year-old selling his own culinary creations on a market stall in Rye. After failing his A-levels he focused his attention on selling a home-made range of biscuits, cakes and preserves known as 'Galton's Goodies'. It proved such a success he turned his attentions to a career as a chef. Though not the most orthodox route into the industry, it proved a wise choice.

Honing his talents at work rather than in the classroom, he got his break under the guidance of TV chef John Tovey whilst working at the Miller Howe hotel in the Lake District. Steadily he progressed up to being Head Chef there before work experience overseas helped him develop even further.

In 1992 Galton and wife Tracey took a gamble and turned an 18th-century manor house in Norfolk into 'Morston Hall'. As well as a Michelin star it also showcases the best local produce around. In Galton's eyes, its style represents the best of modern British cuisine. "I love the tradition in British cooking, be it fish, chips and gravy or roast beef and Yorkshire pudding. These are unique parts of British cooking that can be modernised but never lost."

Galton has twice been named 'East Anglian Chef of the Year', and also honoured as 'Craft Guild of Chefs' Chef of the Year'. Not content with these accolades he has also written two cookery books – *Cooking at Morston Hall* and *A Return to Real Cooking*.

He is a great ambassador of seasonal produce and grows plenty of it in his own garden. "Just about all the produce I use comes from my 'backyard', when it is in season – from mussels when there's an 'r' in the month to asparagus for just six weeks in the year."

MARK BROADBENT

Rochdale-born Mark Broadbent has been Executive Head Chef at Conran Bluebird restaurant since 2003. His career began at age 17, when he became a Commis Chef at The Rembrandt in Knightsbridge. A natural in the kitchen, Mark quickly moved on to work at the five-star Britannia Intercontinental. There he met his mentor, David Nicholls, and spent three years learning as much as he could with David's support.

Mark wanted to experience new cultures and environments, so he took a year out and went travelling around India, Australia and the US, working shifts in various restaurants to gain inside knowledge and experience of international cuisine. However, his travelling didn't shake his passionate commitment to British food and he wants people to rediscover British flavours. "What excites me is revisiting and redefining traditional dishes that have faded from our culinary consciousness, while caring deeply about the husbandry and provenance of the ingredients."

After returning to the UK in 1991, Mark put his new-found recipes and techniques to work, becoming a master of modern British cooking. His rise through the ranks – from Sous Chef at Restaurant 192 to Head Chef at Morton's Members Club & Restaurant – in just a decade is testament to his skill. Mark doesn't believe in combining international cuisines just for the sake of it, complaining that, "Our tastebuds have become jaded through an excess of lemongrass and a compulsion to embrace only what's new. Fusion? More like con-fusion." In 2003 his skilful use of flavours impressed Great British Menu judge Oliver Peyton enough to ask him to be the Head Chef at Isola in Knightsbridge. There, Mark revolutionised their menu of traditional regional Italian cuisine by integrating British produce.

JOHN BURTON RACE

"When I first moved here, I got in the car, drove around and was amazed at what I found. Fantastic fish, lamb, quail and duck, as good as anywhere." John Burton Race moved to Dartmouth in 2003, following the success of his television programme and book, *French Leave*, in which he took his substantial family over to France to get back to his culinary roots.

"In France I discovered simplicity. For years, I had been chasing Michelin stars, but France was a clean slate. I put the emphasis on the plate rather than the garnish. I call it progress."

His "progress" to a more simple culinary philosophy continues back on this side of the Channel, with the dishes he prepares at his Dartmouth restaurant, the New Angel.

"I aim to cook with local produce, in season. That's my philosophy. It's all about taste. That can be difficult as there's no continuous supply. The area's not big enough. But there are just enough 'little nutcases' round here to make sure the produce never dries up. So far, so good. I am sure everyone says this about their own area, but I can honestly say, this region's got the lot."

MICHAEL CAINES MBE

Adopted into a large family in Exeter, Michael Caines grew up surrounded by good food. "Mum was a good English cook who used fresh, seasonal ingredients and baked great cakes, whilst Dad cultivated vegetables and apples. Meals were always a big family affair."

With a passion for all things culinary instilled at a young age, Michael quickly developed a real flair for cooking, winning the 'Student of the Year' award at Exeter Catering College in 1987. Raymond Blanc was impressed, and offered him a three-year mentorship at Le Manoir aux Quat'Saisons.

Michael went on to spend a number of years in France, sharpening his skills under the guidance of chefs Bernard Loiseau and Joël Robuchon. He returned to Britain in 1994 to take up the position of Head Chef at Gidleigh Park, on the edge of Dartmoor. It was here that he made his reputation, gaining two Michelin stars for his food, despite a car accident in which he lost his right arm.

Michael pairs his French training with the best regional ingredients. His enthusiasm for the quality and diversity of British produce is infectious. "In modern Britain it's impossible to define a typical British person; similarly, it is equally impossible to define exactly what is typical British cuisine."

But Michael is also keen to spread the gospel of good food beyond the trappings of haute cuisine: he formed Michael Caines Restaurants Ltd in 1999 and opened restaurants in Exeter and Bristol. He has also recently launched a boutique hotel chain called 'ABode', each hotel containing a Michael Caines restaurant. Locations so far include Exeter, Glasgow, Canterbury and Manchester. "The UK has a great larder. We need more good local restaurants, for a more relaxed experience that's real value for money."

Michael's position in the league of top chefs was cemented when he was awarded an MBE for services to the hospitality industry in 2006.

RICHARD CORRIGAN

Raised on a farm in County Meath in the Irish Midlands, Richard Corrigan was one of seven children. He was surrounded by food from the beginning. "We had no money, but no hunger," he recalls. "Father hunted, shot and poached everything we wanted. Regardless of the lack of money we ate like kings." Despite these humble beginnings Richard has become a world-renowned Michelin-starred chef.

Richard's career began earlier than most. Disillusioned with school, he began working at the local Kirwin Hotel with his father's friend, Ray Vaughan. At 21 he moved to London and worked under Michel Lorrain at the Meridian in Piccadilly and then at the Irish restaurant Mulligans. He went on to make a considerable impression at Searcy's in the Barbican Centre – an area of London that had hitherto been regarded as a culinary desert. In 1997 Richard bought his own restaurant, Lindsay House in Soho, and his first Michelin star soon followed. The restaurant remains a favourite for food lovers.

From opening a restaurant at the top of London's 'gherkin' building in 2004 to reviving the fortunes of the capital's iconic fish restaurant, Bentley's, a year later, it's little wonder Richard is known as 'the Irish chef in London'. As well as running his restaurants, Richard is also part of the select culinary council at British Airways, devising menus for long-haul and premier class flights.

Richard's food remains loyal to his Irish roots. In the first Great British Menu he skilfully demonstrated Irish food's earthy sophistication with dishes such as Venison Wellington with Pickled Cabbage and, of course, his overall winning starter of Wild Smoked Salmon, which wowed the judges. Passionate and committed, with an intense natural flair, Richard is now firmly established as one of the most remarkable chefs of his generation.

STUART GILLIES

Stuart Gillies is famed for bringing New York-style café dining to London. His combination of exceptional food and a relaxed informal atmosphere has proved a massive success amongst the capital's food lovers. He currently holds the prestigious title of Executive Chef of the Boxwood Café at the Berkeley Hotel, a joint venture with Gordon Ramsay.

Stuart grew up in Crawley, Sussex, a town that he describes as a "culinary desert". After graduating from catering college, he worked at a local hotel for a year as part of a YTS scheme. It was an inauspicious start to what has been a meteoric rise through the culinary ranks. Stuart made a huge step up with his arrival at the Michelin-starred Connaught, where he worked as Head Chef alongside Angela Hartnett. He then progressed to London's famous celebrity haunt, Le Caprice.

Stuart's cooking has a vibrant international flavour, influenced by his experiences in New York working with legendary chef Daniel Boulud. "Cooking in this country has evolved so quickly in the last 15 years," he says. "I think that's because a lot of chefs went abroad to learn to cook and brought the knowledge back with them." The Big Apple's influence is clear to see on the Boxwood's contemporary menu: the foie gras and veal burger is a favourite amongst the regulars.

Seasonality is key to Stuart's cooking, and his menu evolves throughout the year to reflect the availability of ingredients. Making the most of terrific local produce, he believes that British cooking is back on the map. "It would be arrogant to say that British food is the best in the world, but it's certainly as good as anywhere else."

ANGELA HARTNETT

Though born in Kent and raised in Essex, Angela Hartnett comes from a long line of Northern Italian immigrants – the 'Bracchi' – who arrived in South Wales at the beginning of the 20th century and ran the fish bars and cafés within which the miners of the Rhondda Valley were introduced to the delights of 'frothy coffee'. "I really got into food at my grandad's fish and chip shop," Hartnett recalls, "and Mum said I should go to France to learn about cooking. But I wanted to get an education first. So I studied history in Cambridge."

As commis chef to Hans Schweitzer at Midsummer House, "the best restaurant in Cambridge", she was schooled in classic French techniques. After six months in Barbados, she got a job at Gordon Ramsay's Aubergine. "That was so exciting. Gordon was always in the kitchen; there was a real buzz about it." She also spent time in Tuscany, and cooked alongside Giorgio Locatelli, at Zafferano, and Marcus Wareing at Pétrus. After a stretch in Dubai, she became Executive Chef at The Connaught, offering cuisine influenced by the flavours of Italy and the wider Mediterranean. She is now Chef Patron at York and Albany, and at Murano, both in London.

"We're getting better in this country, but we're still behind Italy, France and Spain for everyday eating," she judges. "Food is still a middle class thing here – in Italy the working class eat as well as anyone. We need a push on seasonality, a boycott on ready meals, and some regulation to support local producers."

MARK HIX

As a youngster growing up in Dorset, Mark Hix quickly realised that it was home economics rather than metal work that held his full attention. So after leaving school he studied catering and got a job at the staff canteen at the Hilton Hotel in London. He craved more experience, and when the opportunity arose to go to the Grosvenor House Hotel and work with legendary chef Anton Edelmann, he seized it with both hands.

Job offers continued to roll in and Mark found himself working at the Dorchester as a Commis Chef under Anton Mosimann, where he quickly got promoted to Chef De Partie. His big break came, at just 22, when he became Head Chef at the Candlewick Room. He then progressed to the position of Head Chef at Le Caprice, and soon after became Chef Director of the group overseeing all eight restaurants, which most recently included the launch of the already legendary Scotts in Mayfair. In December 2007, after seventeen years with the Caprice Group, Mark left to concentrate on his own projects. He is currently working with Rocco Forte's Mayfair hotel Brown's and opening his first independent restaurant Hix Oyster and Chop House in Smithfield Market, London.

Mark is also a cookery writer and in 2003 was awarded the 'Glenfiddich Newspaper Cookery Writer of the Year' prize for his column in the *Independent on Saturday*. On top of his day job, Mark spent two years researching his most recent books, *British Regional Food* and *British Seasonal Food*.

He is a champion of good British cuisine and lists one of his passions as discovering artisan food producers throughout the UK. "We're now out of the roast beef scenario and are finally getting respect from our overseas friends. There's great produce on our doorsteps and it's getting better, so there's no need to fly produce in from other parts of the globe anymore."

ATUL KOCHHAR

Renowned for his vibrant, exquisitely spiced food, Atul Kochhar became the first Indian chef to be awarded a coveted Michelin star as Head Chef of Tamarind in 2001. He opened his own restaurant, Benares, in London's exclusive Mayfair two years later and in 2007 it, too, was awarded a Michelin star. With such consistently excellent and innovative food it's no surprise Atul has been hailed as the best Indian chef in London.

Atul was born in eastern India in 1969 as one of six children. He started his cooking career at The Oberoi group of hotels, quickly progressing to Sous Chef at the much-fêted five-star Oberoi Deluxe in New Delhi. While cooking for these hotels, Atul learned the full spectrum of international cuisine, including French and Italian. It's this melding of Eastern and Western approaches that lies at the heart of all his cooking.

Always keen to reinvent and reinvigorate his food, Atul regularly returns to his homeland in order to research new recipes and discover new ingredients. Cooking for Atul is all about being faithful to the origins of each recipe: the presentation and execution may be modern, but the true foundation of each dish he prepares can be traced to households across India.

Atul's cutting edge approach to Indian cookery became evident in the first series of Great British Menu, and he continues to break conventional boundaries, opening our eyes and mouths to multicultural cuisine. As Atul puts it: "Multicultural cuisine hasn't happened overnight; it's been happening over centuries, and now its time has really come!"

JEREMY LEE

Jeremy Lee grew up in the village of Auchterhouse near Dundee, and his deceptively simple cooking retains the freshness of his first encounters with food. "The foods of the sea, the coast, the lowlands and highlands of Scotland are equally glorious."

After working as a waiter at The Old Mansion House Hotel in Auchterhouse, Jeremy soon realised his future lay in the kitchen instead. He stayed there for four years before moving to London, where his career began at Boodles restaurant, before progressing to caterers Duff & Trotter. A meal at Bidendum convinced him just how much he missed the buzz of the restaurant kitchen. He managed to get work at Bidendum where he stayed for three years, creating the seemingly simple but unforgettable dishes for which he is now famous.

In 1991 he joined Alastair Little as Head Chef at the Frith Street Restaurant. In 1995 Jeremy launched Euphorium in Islington, then moved to The Blueprint Café as Head Chef where he has been ever since. A glance at the Blueprint's menu shows Jeremy's unswerving faith in Scottish produce, with dishes showcasing ingredients like Galloway beef and Arbroath smokies.

Though he has worked in London for many years he has never forgotten the culinary joys that Scotland offers. "The produce of Scotland is of such quality and flavour that the respect it commands is great." It's this respect for fine ingredients that leads Jeremy to believe British cuisine is going through something of a renaissance. "It is wonderful to work with producers who remain true to their splendid ingredients. Indeed, so good are these ingredients, British cooking is harking back to seemingly gentler times while striving to make its mark on very fast-paced modern times."

TOM LEWIS

"We don't have the best climate in the world," admits Tom Lewis, head chef at Monachyle Mhor, a hotel that nestles alongside Loch Voil in the genteel highlands of Perthshire, "but we do have great flavours in Scotland. Lots of game in season [Lewis is an able shot], venison, pheasant, duck, fish, of course, and great beef. The thing is to keep it simple. I don't fanny about. I let the flavours do the talking."

Despite his love of Scotland, Lewis was born among a family of farmers near the Welsh market town of Abergavenny. Completely self-taught, he was inspired to cook by his mother, a copy of *Larousse*, and a broadcast of Desert Island Discs featuring Nico Ladenis. Despite having worked as a sheep-shearer in the Antipodes, he reckons that cooking is the hardest job in the world. But for Tom it's reaping rewards.

For over ten years now, he has been in the kitchen at Monachyle Mhor, picking up awards for his daily changing menu that's more reliant on the seasons than most. "What fish are cooked depends entiely on what fish are caught," he says. If he shoots one of the deer that roam his 800 hectares, that will make it on to the menu as well. The hotel's herb garden is kept in good shape by gardener Black Dan, and nearly everything else comes from within a 19km radius.

But it's not all haute cuisine. Lewis also runs a fish and chip shop in Callander. "Beef dripping for the chips, and fresh fish, a lot more variety than you usually see," Lewis proclaims. "Haddock, sea bass, lemon sole, coley, hake, it's all for sale in the fish and chip shop."

NOEL MCMEEL

Noel McMeel is Executive Head Chef of Castle Leslie in County Monaghan, Ireland. His unique cooking has helped Castle Leslie gain a spot among the top ten places to stay in the world.

Local produce is at the heart of Noel's cooking. Inspired by his farm upbringing, Noel strongly believes in using only the best local ingredients. However, his cooking is anything but parochial. It is his successful combination of traditional Irish ingredients and his extensive international professional experience that have cemented his reputation as one of the finest modern Irish chefs.

After training at the Northern Ireland Hotel and Catering College, Noel joined the kitchen at The Villager, in Crossgar, as an apprentice. He decided then to leave Ireland and worked in some of the most respected restaurants in the world, including a stint under Jean-Louis Palladin at the Watergate Hotel in Washington DC. In San Francisco he got the chance to work with his idol, Alice Waters, at Chez Panisse.

But Noel could not be away from his beloved Ireland forever, and so was delighted to take up the position of Head Chef at the Beech Hill Country House Hotel in Londonderry. In the late 1990s his dream of opening his own restaurant in his homeland finally came true. Trompets, his first venture, quickly received critical acclaim and soon he was in demand to cook at high-profile events around the world. He joined Castle Leslie in 2000 and subsequently had the honour of cooking for the wedding of Paul McCartney and Heather Mills.

Quality, passion and flair are at the heart of everything Noel does. Firmly believing that "life is what you make it – you have to go after it, get it and deal with it", his life philosophy perfectly reflects his cuisine.

NICK NAIRN

Not only is he Scotland's most famous chef, Nick Nairn was also the youngest chef north of the border ever to be awarded a coveted Michelin star – not bad for a self-taught cook who claimed that at the quite advanced age of 25 he couldn't even successfully boil an egg.

Nick developed his passion for food whilst travelling the world with the merchant navy, sampling delicious cuisine from all over the globe. Returning to his native Scotland he realised he wanted to open his own restaurant. The result was Braeval, which he opened close to his hometown of Stirling in 1986.

The year after its opening Nick was awarded the 'Scottish Field and Bollinger Newcomer' award. A key aspect of his success is using fresh Scottish produce, and he has campaigned vigorously to promote it. "Scottish food is all about the produce. We are in a bit of a melting pot at the moment and I think the true identity of modern Scottish food is in the process of being forged right now."

In 1997 Nick opened Nairn's Restaurant with Rooms in Glasgow. Never one to rest on his laurels, his next venture was Nairn's Anywhere in 2000, an event-catering business providing food to any location. That same year he continued to diversify and launched The Nick Nairn Cook School. It was so successful that Nick sold his acclaimed Glasgow restaurant to concentrate his energies on the school and his other ventures.

As his profile has grown, Nick has added TV chef to his already impressive CV. Since 1996 he has made regular appearances on the popular show Ready Steady Cook, though undoubtedly his finest achievement in front of the camera was having his roe deer main course presented to the Queen at her 80th birthday banquet.

PAUL RANKIN

A native of Ballywater, Co Down, Paul Rankin gained Northern Ireland's first ever Michelin star at his original Roscoff restaurant in Belfast city centre. He had fallen in love with cooking while travelling the world with his Canadian wife Jeanne. On returning to Europe, they both worked for three years under Albert Roux at Le Gavroche before heading for California's Napa Valley, which, Rankin recalls, "was like a Garden of Eden", where small producers provided him with baby greens, wild mushrooms, ten different types of tuna and line-caught wild salmon. "There was a freedom to mix things up." When he opened Roscoff in Belfast in 1989 he put culinary skills on display. Seeking a more casual "funky, fusion" experience, he refitted Roscoff as Cayenne (though he's found a new home for Roscoff in Belfast's Linenhall Street).

Paul Rankin is a keen advocate of the best Northern Irish produce. "Where you win or lose in this game is in the shopping. We've got quality food here, and there's been terrific progress over the past 15 years. But we still need more artisanal small producers. I think of Parmesan cheese as the model: fine food produced on a large scale to a high standard, a balance between quality and the market."

GARY RHODES

When a 13-year-old Gary Rhodes made a Sunday roast for his family, followed by a steamed lemon sponge pudding from a recipe by Marguerite Patten, he knew the path his life should take. "I felt like the lord of the manor," he recalls. "That was it. I wanted to cook." After training at Thanet technical college, he became commis chef at the Amsterdam Hilton and a sous chef at the Reform Club before developing his abiding passion for British food at the Castle Hotel, Taunton, where he retained, at the age of 26, its Michelin star. Another star followed when he became head chef at Mayfair's Greenhouse Restaurant. Alongside his broadcasting career, he has picked up Michelin stars for a further four of his restaurants, City Rhodes, Rhodes in the Square, Rhodes 24, and in 2008, Rhodes W1.

His passionate commitment to British produce is especially evident at Rhodes Twenty Four, located in the City of London's tallest building, where dishes like braised oxtail and bread and butter pudding are regular fixtures. "At Rhodes Twenty Four, we keep as close to the seasons as possible," he says. "Around 80 per cent of our produce is British. I'm very much for the return of the local greengrocer but you must give supermarkets some credit for the way they've introduced the public to a wider range of tastes."

To introduce seasonality back into the high street, Rhodes suggests that the first line of every supermarket should have a certain amount of local produce. "That way we would be supporting the nation's produce."

SIMON RIMMER

In 1990, when Simon Rimmer teamed up with his business partner to take over a vegetarian café in Manchester, they could not afford to hire a chef. So, with the aid of a couple of second-hand books, Rimmer taught himself to cook vegetarian dishes, and Green's, the re-named restaurant, proved an enormous hit. Unlike many of Britain's leading chefs, Rimmer never trained in rigorous classic French technique, developing instead a highly eclectic style influenced in particular by the flavours of Thailand and wider South East Asia. "I had always been a fan of Asian food," says Rimmer," and it offered a means of making exciting vegetarian food rather than the brown and stodgy version that was prevalent then."

Rimmer believes that concerns about BSE in 1992 proved a crucial factor in the success of Green's. "People began to take a greater interest in what they ate, and began to rethink their attitudes to food." Rimmer cites two recent developments in British food that he welcomes. "The introduction of vegetarian rennet by many cheesemakers has presented us with a whole new palate. I also welcome the world market. Though we do try to source a lot of ingredients locally, we've still benefitted from this explosion of new flavours."

Though he thinks Manchester still lacks "a really fantastic city centre restaurant", he's encouraged by the resurgence of high quality food production in the North West. "The success of new cheeses like Blacksticks Blue is incredibly exciting, as is the return of local cattle breeds."

Simon has opened a second restaurant, Earle, in Hale, Cheshire, and is presenter of the TV series Kitchen Millionaire.

MATT TEBBUTT

When Matt Tebbutt was six months old his family moved to Newport, South Wales, and he has always classified himself as an "honorary Welshman".

His path to culinary success began in 1995 when he moved to London to study a diploma course at Prue Leith's School of Food and Wine. He followed this with a baptism of fire: working under Marco-Pierre White at The Oak Room and The Criterion. It was at the latter that Matt met his great friend and fellow Welshman Bryn Williams, and though they remain close, they are hugely competitive.

In 1998 Matt moved into the kitchens of Chez Bruce under the watchful eye of Bruce Poole. But it was whilst working under Alastair Little that Matt's cooking style really began to take shape. His fresh and flavoursome food bears the marks of his time with Little, a period in his life that shaped his view on British cuisine. "British cooking can be a mish-mash of ill-conceived rubbish or it can highlight the very best elements from the diversity of cultures in Britain today."

In 2001 Matt returned to Wales, transforming the Foxhunter pub in Monmouthshire into the AA 'Welsh Restaurant of the Year' in just three years. He strives to use only the best, most seasonal produce, which means the Foxhunter menu changes at least once a day to accommodate Matt's quest for freshness.

Though he spent a lot of time in England, Matt has never lost his passion for Welsh produce. "Welsh cooking has always been seasonal, fresh and simple, which are three of the most important aspects of cooking."

MARCUS WAREING

Despite still being in his thirties, Marcus Wareing is the chef behind two of London's best restaurants – Banquette and Pétrus, the latter of which won its long-awaited second Michelin star in 2007. He is also Executive Chef of the Savoy Grill, reopening in early 2009 following its refurbishment. But Wareing's super chef status has never quelled his passion for honest Northern food. "The North has a fantastic tradition of cooking and farming, and I love the warm, earthy food that represents it as a region."

The son of a Merseyside fruit and veg merchant, Marcus trained at Southport College before starting at The Savoy in London at 18. A stint at Le Gavroche with Albert Roux followed, where he learned the art of classic French cuisine. Between 1991 and 1993 Marcus honed his skills at a number of famous restaurants, including The Point in New York and The Grand Hotel in Amsterdam, again with Albert Roux. In 1993 Marcus started working alongside Gordon Ramsay as Sous Chef at the newly opened Aubergine. In March 1999, with the backing of Gordon, Marcus opened Pétrus and within seven months it had won a Michelin star.

Even though his grounding is firmly in French cuisine, he has never lost his passion for British recipes and British ingredients. This was evident in Great British Menu, where he presented his own interpretation of the classic Northern dish, Lancashire Hot Pot. His legendary Custard Tart was also chosen as overall winner in the dessert category and went on to be presented to the Queen at her 80th birthday banquet.

Marcus considers his amazing success to be part of a wider cooking renaissance in this country. "British cuisine is in the best state ever. We have some of the world's best chefs and it's great that we are becoming more aware of our fantastic British producers."

BRYN WILLIAMS

In 2006 Bryn Williams became a high profile champion of Welsh food when he secured the Head Chef's position at Odette's in North London. By using the best seasonal produce from the area that first inspired him, he has succeeded in turning the fashionable Primrose Hill set on to his classic Welsh dishes. Born and raised in Denbigh, North Wales, Bryn has always felt that "Wales has a fantastic larder from land and sea" and "the pure land gives pure ingredients I love to work with".

Bryn first became interested in food at primary school when he went on a trip with his classmates to a local bakery and got to spend a day making bread. Whilst training at the Llandrillo College in North Wales he got invaluable work placements at several world-class restaurants, including the Michelin-starred Restaurant Chateau Neercame in Maastricht and the Hotel Negresco in Nice. On his return to Britain in 1997, Bryn headed to London, where he started out at Le Gavroche, training under two of the capital's greatest chefs – Marco Pierre White and Michel Roux Jr.

After three years at Le Gavroche, Bryn was ready to take up the position of Senior Sous Chef at The Orrery, Conran's flagship Michelin-starred restaurant. It was whilst working at The Orrery that Bryn triumphed over one of the UK's top female chefs, Angela Hartnett, in the first Great British Menu with his Salt-Marsh Lamb. This and other dishes he served up in the competition are now regular fixtures on his menu at Odette's.

Even though he's been based in London for ten years Bryn hasn't lost touch with his Welsh roots. He is a judge at the 'Taste of Wales' awards, and regularly appears at The Royal Welsh Show and Conwy Feast. Bryn believes British cooking is in many ways "more advanced than the French, with a lighter touch. We're more with the times."

ANTONY WORRALL THOMPSON

One of the most familiar chefs on British television, Antony Worrall Thompson was born in Stratford-upon-Avon to two Royal Shakespeare Company actors who, romantically, were performing in *Romeo and Juliet* at the time. After swimming the Channel at the age of 16, he turned his attention to cooking, and has been involved in a roster of celebrated London restaurants: Ménage à Trois (a favourite of the late Princess Diana), One Ninety Queen's Gate, dell'Ugo, Zoe, Atrium, Palio, Drones, De Cecco.

Today he runs Notting Grill in Holland Park, as well as Kew Grill, Barnes Grill and Windsor Grill, which specialise in organic meat, fish and vegetables, cooked simply, and according to the seasons. "We must get back to basics," he says. "We need local food for local people. People get used to soils around a particular region, and the fact that food is now imported from all over the place has led, I believe, to a rise in diseases such as psoriasis." Antony also has two pubs The Greyhound in Rotherfield Peppard and The Lamb Free House & Kitchen at Satwell, both in Oxfordshire.

Worrall Thompson is especially concerned with the increase in diabetes and obesity among children. "There's a feeling that we've mucked about too much with our food. That's why I'm keen that we buy the best British produce, especially organic food."

Worrall Thompson puts his preaching into practice, running a small organic garden where he rears Middle White pigs and grows herbs and vegetables for his Grills and pub interests. He also owns an avocado farm in Spain.

CHAPTER ONE STARTERS

20

CRAB AND TEA-SMOKED MACKEREL TARTS
WITH DUCK EGG MAYONNAISE

SERVES 8
250g puff pastry
2 duck eggs
2 tbsp vinegar (any kind)
2 tsp finely chopped chives
juice of ¼ lemon
150ml mayonnaise
250g white crab meat, picked over
    to remove all shell and cartilage
salt and pepper

TEA-SMOKED MACKEREL
olive oil
1 large mackerel, filleted and with skin,
    pin bones removed
45g chamomile tea leaves
30g demerara sugar
30g risotto rice

1 Preheat the oven to 220°C/gas 7.
2 To make the tea-smoked mackerel, you need a heavy roasting tin, a wire rack large enough to sit over the rim of the tin and an old wooden spoon. You will also need a sheet of foil folded double that is large enough to cover the rack and tuck in under the rim of the tin.
3 Dip a piece of kitchen paper in olive oil and lightly oil the rack and one side of the foil. Season the fish fillets and place skin-side down on the rack. Drape the foil oiled-side down over the fish, leaving the overhang loose.
4 Make the smoking mixture by mixing the tea, sugar and rice together in a bowl. Heat the roasting tin on the hob, moving it around to get an even heat. Scatter the smoking mixture over the bottom of the tin and stir it around with the wooden spoon. The sugar will melt and stick the tea to the rice, and then will start to burn. Immediately set the rack with the fish over the tin and remove from the heat. Protecting your hands with oven gloves or a tea towel, tuck the overhanging foil tightly all around the rim of the tin. When the foil is sealed really tight and no smoke is escaping from the sides, turn the heat back on and continue to move the tin around for 30 seconds. Then transfer to the oven to cook for 5 minutes.
5 Remove the tin from the oven and leave the fish to cool without unwrapping. Turn the oven down to 190°C/gas 5. Line a large, heavy baking tray with baking parchment.
6 Roll out the pastry on a lightly floured surface to a large, neat rectangle about 3mm thick. Place the pastry on the parchment-lined tray. Cover with another sheet of baking parchment, then set a second heavy baking tray on top to act as a weight. Bake for 8–10 minutes or until the pastry starts to turn a very light brown. Remove

from the oven and take off the top tray and paper. Cut out eight discs from the pastry using a 7cm plain cutter. Return the discs to the oven on the parchment-lined tray and bake uncovered for 3–4 minutes or until golden and crisp. Leave to cool on a rack.

7 Take eight metal rings, about 8cm in diameter and 1cm deep, and tightly cover one end of each ring with cling film like a drum skin. Set the rings on their covered ends on a tray, and put into the fridge to chill.

8 Break the duck eggs into two separate cups. Bring 1 litre water and the vinegar to a gentle simmer in a large saucepan. Stir the water clockwise, then carefully drop the eggs into the vortex and poach for 6 minutes. Lift out the eggs with a slotted spoon and place in a bowl of iced water. Leave to cool. When the eggs are totally cold, remove from the water and drain on kitchen paper. Chop the eggs coarsely and place in a bowl, then cover and keep in the fridge.

9 When the mackerel is cool, remove it from the rack and peel away the skin. Check for any small bones with your fingers, then flake the fish into a bowl. Add the chives, lemon juice and one-third of the mayonnaise, then add the crab and lightly fold everything together, taking care not to break up the fish (you want to see nice chunks). Stir in half the chopped eggs, and check for seasoning.

10 Divide the mixture into eight equal portions and press into the chilled metal rings. Mix the rest of the chopped eggs with just enough of the remaining mayonnaise to bind, then taste and adjust the seasoning if necessary.

11 To serve, dab a little mayonnaise in the middle of each plate. Place a pastry disc in the top of each metal ring and carefully turn the ring over onto the plate, so the pastry is on the bottom and secured in place by the mayonnaise. Remove the cling film, push the fish mixture down in the ring with a small spoon so that it presses onto the pastry and lift off the ring. Using two teaspoons, make small quenelles of the egg mayonnaise to garnish the tops of the tarts.

WARM SALAD OF LOBSTER
WITH SUMMER VEGETABLES AND HERBS
AND A WELSH WATER VINAIGRETTE

SERVES 4

VINAIGRETTE
125ml spring water
2 tbsp Chardonnay wine vinegar
200ml olive oil
1 bay leaf
½ bunch of tarragon
1 small garlic clove, crushed
pinch of caster sugar
salt and pepper

LOBSTERS
1 onion, halved
1 carrot, halved

1 head of garlic, halved crossways
10 white peppercorns
4 live lobsters, each 400g
olive oil

SUMMER VEGETABLES
12 baby carrots
12 asparagus tips
100g freshly shelled broad beans
12 baby leeks
50g samphire
50g wood sorrel (or use watercress)
50g pennywort (or use mustard cress
or rocket)

1 To make the vinaigrette, combine the spring water and vinegar in a bowl and season with salt and pepper. Whisk in the olive oil. When mixed and the seasoning is right, add the bay leaf, tarragon, garlic and sugar. Cover and leave to infuse at room temperature for 24 hours. After this, strain the vinaigrette and discard the herbs and garlic. Pour half the vinaigrette into a large bowl.

2 To cook the lobsters, three-quarters fill a heavy-bottomed pan with water and add the onion, carrot, garlic and white peppercorns. Bring to the boil and boil for 4–5 minutes. Season with a good handful of salt. Drop the lobsters into the boiling water and cook for 6 minutes.

3 Lift out the lobsters and place in iced water. Remove the claws, then put the lobsters back into the boiling water to cook for a further 2 minutes. Lift out into iced water again. When the lobsters are cold, crack the body/tail shells and remove the meat in one piece. Crack the claws and remove the meat. Set all the lobster meat aside.

4 To prepare the summer vegetables, blanch all the vegetables, including the samphire, in boiling salted water for 2–3 minutes. Drain. Slip the broad beans out of their skins, then add all the vegetables to the vinaigrette in the bowl. Leave to cool. As they are cooling the vegetables will absorb the flavours of the vinaigrette.

5 When ready to serve, cut the lobster meat into bite-sized pieces, season with salt and pepper, and pan-fry in a little olive oil to warm through. Drain the summer vegetables (discard the vinaigrette) and add to the frying pan to warm through. Remove from the heat and add the remaining vinaigrette just to warm it.

6 Spoon the warm lobster and vegetables onto four plates, scatter over the sorrel and pennywort, and drizzle with the warm vinaigrette. Serve immediately.

LIGHTLY CURED SEA TROUT
WITH PICKLED CUCUMBER

SERVES 4
50g sea salt
100g caster sugar
bunch of dill, roughly chopped
1 piece of sea trout fillet, about 1kg,
   skin on

CUCUMBER
2 cucumbers
sea salt
1 tbsp caster sugar
1 tbsp white wine vinegar
3 tbsp Dijon mustard
5 tbsp groundnut oil
1 tbsp chopped dill

1 Two days ahead of serving, rub the salt, sugar and roughly chopped dill together well. Rub this very well into the sea trout all over. Wrap the fish in a parcel of foil and place on a tray with a weight on top. Put the tray in the fridge and chill for 24 hours. Turn the parcel over and chill for a further 24 hours.

2 Early on the day of serving, peel the cucumbers. Cut them in half lengthways and remove all the seeds. Slice the cucumber diagonally across and not too thinly. Tip the slices into a colander, dredge liberally with sea salt and leave to drain for 2–3 hours. Rinse the cucumber very well, then drain thoroughly. Squeeze in a cloth until very dry.

3 Stir the sugar into the vinegar to dissolve. Add the mustard, then whisk in the oil a spoonful at a time. Use to dress the cucumber along with the chopped dill.

4 To serve, unwrap the fish and scrape away the dill, salt and sugar mixture on the surface. Cut slices, not too thin, from the trout and lay them on plates. Add a heaped spoonful of the cucumber salad on the side. (This makes more sea trout than you need for 4 servings, but it is good to cure more than you need as it keeps well for a week, and makes a delightful treat to have in the fridge.)

LOBSTER KE PANJE
TANDOORI LOBSTER CLAWS WITH
AUBERGINE FRITTERS AND PEAR CHUTNEY

SERVES 4

4 large lobster claws
mixture of vegetable oil and melted butter
chaat masala to sprinkle
1 tbsp finely chopped coriander leaves
½ tsp lime juice
coarsely crushed Szechuan pepper
salt

PEAR CHUTNEY

3 large pears, peeled, cored and sliced
1 large cooking apple, peeled, cored and sliced
1 tbsp raisins
1 small cinnamon stick
¼ tsp black peppercorns
½ tsp five spice powder
75g brown sugar
75ml rice wine vinegar

AUBERGINE FRITTERS

2 tbsp gram flour
¼ tsp each toasted cumin seeds, red
    chilli powder, garam masala, chaat
    masala and fenugreek leaf powder
½ tsp finely chopped fresh ginger
1 tbsp finely chopped coriander leaves
vegetable oil for deep frying
2 small, round baby aubergines

MARINADE

100g plain yoghurt
½ tsp each lightly toasted ajwain seeds,
    ginger-garlic paste and garam masala
¼ tsp each ground coriander, ground
    cinnamon and red chilli powder
50ml vegetable oil
1 tsp finely chopped fresh ginger

1 First make the chutney. Place all the ingredients in a pan with $^1/_4$ tsp salt and cook on a moderate heat for 30–40 minutes or until the pears and apple are reduced to a mushy consistency. Remove from the heat and leave to cool.

2 Next make the fritter batter. Mix together the gram flour, spices, coriander and $^1/_4$ tsp salt with enough water to make a dropping consistency. Set aside.

3 To prepare the lobster, wash well in running water and crack the shells lightly with a small hammer. Whisk together all the ingredients for the marinade with $^1/_4$ tsp salt and rub it on to the cracked lobster claws. Leave to marinate for 5–10 minutes.

4 Preheat a tandoor to hot or preheat the oven to 180°C/gas 4. Also heat oil for deep frying in a deep pan or wok to 180–190°C.

5 Skewer the lobster claws and cook in the tandoor for 3–4 minutes; baste with oil and butter, then cook for further 3 minutes. If cooking in the oven, place on a baking tray and cook for 2 minutes; turn over, baste and cook for another 2 minutes.

6 For the aubergine fritters, cut each aubergine into four wedges. Dip in the batter to coat well, then drop into the hot oil and fry until light golden and the aubergine is well cooked. Drain on kitchen paper.

7 To serve, place a lobster claw on each plate (rectangular if possible) and sprinkle with chaat masala, chopped coriander and lime juice. Arrange two aubergine fritters on each plate and add a spoonful of pear chutney. Sprinkle with Szechuan pepper.

SHELLFISH TIAN
WITH WHOLEMEAL TOAST

SERVES 4
120g picked white crab meat
50g peeled Southport brown shrimps
35g mayonnaise
½ bunch of chives, finely chopped
¼ bunch of chervil, finely chopped
pinch of mild paprika
juice of ¼ lemon
salt and pepper

GARNISH
1 hard-boiled egg, white and yolk separated and chopped
40 small capers, each cut in half
5 baby gherkins (cornichons), cut into rounds
1 shallot, finely diced
large sprig of parsley, chopped

TO FINISH
1 tbsp white wine vinegar
5 tbsp olive oil
small salad leaves
wholemeal toast and butter

1 In a cold mixing bowl combine the crab, shrimps, mayonnaise, herbs and paprika. When mixed, season with lemon juice, salt and pepper to taste.
2 Divide the crab mixture evenly among four 7.5cm metal rings set on a tray lined with cling film, filling the rings by about two-thirds. Press down with a spoon to compress, then refrigerate for at least 15 minutes.
3 Gently mix together the ingredients for the garnish.
4 Place a filled ring in the middle of each plate and gently push out the crab to form a tower. Neatly arrange the garnish in a circle around the crab.
5 To finish, whisk together the vinegar and oil, and season to taste. Lightly dress the salad leaves with this dressing, then arrange a small mound on the top of each of the crab tians. Serve immediately, with buttered wholemeal toast.

CRAB CAKES
AND MAYONNAISE

SERVES 6

CRAB CAKES
1 large live crab
400g floury potatoes, such as King Edward
grated zest of 1 lemon
small handful of flat-leaf parsley,
    stalks discarded
1 garlic clove, finely chopped
1 egg yolk
3–4 drops of Tabasco sauce
plain flour for coating
vegetable or groundnut oil for frying
sea salt and freshly ground white pepper

MAYONNAISE
3 egg yolks, at room temperature
1 rounded tbsp Dijon mustard, plus 1 tsp
1 tbsp lemon juice
400ml groundnut oil

TO SERVE
6 little bunches of watercress
lemon quarters

1 The most humane way to kill the crab is to put it to sleep in the freezer first for about 1 hour. If you don't have time, simply plunge a large spike through its purse.
2 Put a large saucepan of water on to boil and add enough salt to give the taste of the sea. Plunge the crab into the boiling water, place a lid on the pan and boil for 12 minutes. Remove the crab from the water and leave to cool on a tray.
3 Peel the potatoes and rinse them very well in a colander until the water runs clear. Cut the potatoes into even-sized large pieces and place in a pan of water. Lightly salt the water and bring to the boil over a high heat. Lower the heat to a simmer and cook the potatoes quite gently for 10–15 minutes or until tender. Drain well and mash. Cover and set aside.
4 Remove the meat from the crab. Reserve the brown meat for another dish (this can be used to make a pâté by mixing with some Tabasco and Worcestershire sauces and a pinch of ground mace, then covered with clarified butter). Once you have removed all the white meat, pick through it to remove and discard any bits of shell and cartilage. Put the crab meat in a large bowl.
5 Combine the lemon zest, parsley leaves and garlic in a heap on a board and chop together finely. Add to the white crab meat along with the mashed potato, egg yolk, Tabasco, salt and pepper, and beat well until thoroughly mixed. Taste to check the seasoning. Let the mixture sit in the fridge for an hour or so to settle.
6 Shape the crab mixture into 18 little cakes about 2.5cm in diameter. Lay them on a tray and keep cool until ready to cook.

7 To make the mayonnaise, beat the egg yolks with the heaped tbsp of mustard and lemon juice in a bowl, then slowly whisk in the oil. Season with salt and pepper. Stir in the remaining mustard to spike up the taste. Turn the mayonnaise into a serving bowl.

8 Lightly flour both sides of the crab cakes. Heat a heavy-based frying pan, then add a little oil and heat through. Gently sit the cakes in the hot oil and fry until pale golden on the base. Turn over and continue cooking for 2–3 minutes or until thoroughly heated, lowering the heat if they start to get too brown.

9 Place three crab cakes on each plate and put a small bunch of watercress and a lemon quarter alongside. Serve immediately, with the mayonnaise.

SALAD OF CRISP-FRIED SOUTH COAST SQUID
AND SPRING ONIONS IN SWEET CHILLI SAUCE

SERVES 4

SWEET CHILLI SAUCE
125g demerara sugar
2 tbsp red wine vinegar
½–1 tsp dried chilli flakes
2 tsp lime juice
2 tsp palm sugar
salt

SALAD
2 spring onions, diagonally sliced
1 medium red onion, thinly sliced
small bunch of rocket leaves
small bunch of bull's blood leaves
   or baby chard

SQUID
2 tbsp cornflour
½ tsp ground coriander
½ tsp chilli powder
½ tsp toasted cumin seeds
3 large squid, cleaned and tentacles kept,
   bodies cut into 1cm thick rings
vegetable oil for deep-frying

GARNISH
mixed micro salad leaves, or mustard cress
   mixed with coriander leaves

1 First make the sauce. Tip the demerara sugar into a heavy-based saucepan, mix in 2–3 tbsp cold water and let stand for 2 minutes (this helps dissolve the sugar). Heat slowly to dissolve the sugar, then bubble until lightly caramelised. Remove from the heat and slowly stir in 4 tbsp water. Return to the heat, add the vinegar and bring to a simmer. Stir in the chilli flakes, lime juice, palm sugar and salt. Simmer for 10–20 minutes, to a dipping consistency. Remove and cool to room temperature.

2 Mix all the salad ingredients together and keep wrapped in a wet cloth or damp kitchen paper in the refrigerator until required.

3 For the squid, stir the cornflour and spices together in a bowl, then mix in 5–6 tbsp water to make a batter. Add the pieces of squid and toss in the batter to coat. Set aside for 10 minutes.

4 Heat oil in a deep-fat fryer to about 180°C. Deep-fry the squid in batches for 3–4 minutes or until golden and crisp, reheating the oil in between each batch. Remove the squid with a slotted spoon and drain on kitchen paper.

5 Gently toss the fried squid with the salad. Drizzle 2 tbsp of the chilli sauce on top and lightly mix. (Any remaining chilli sauce will keep in the fridge for up to 3 weeks and is good as a dipping sauce or in salad dressings.) Place in a loose arrangement on each plate. Garnish with the mixed micro leaves, or mustard cress and coriander, and serve immediately.

SEARED SCALLOPS
WITH GRAPE AND MINT DRESSING

SERVES 4

12 king-size scallops, coral removed
1 tbsp black sesame seeds
1½ tsp each chilli and garlic flakes,
    mixed
½ tsp each ground coriander and
    cumin, mixed
3 tbsp olive or vegetable oil
100g unsalted butter
12 large black seedless grapes
12 large green seedless grapes
salt and pepper

GRAPE SAUCE

200g black and green seedless grapes
50g mint leaves
20g fresh ginger, chopped
1 small green chilli
1 tsp salt
1 tsp dried mango powder
    or chaat masala

GRAPE SAUCE DRESSING

20g unsalted butter
½ tsp black sesame seeds
½ tsp white sesame seeds
1 tbsp julienned fresh ginger
1 shallot, finely chopped
200ml Wickham Vineyard's 'special release
    fumé' or other dry white English wine
¼ tsp paprika
¼ tsp mango powder or chaat masala

GARAM MASALA CARAMEL

100g caster sugar
pinch of garam masala powder

GARNISH

1 young carrot, cut into julienne
micro salad leaves or pea shoots

1 Put all the ingredients for the grape sauce in a blender and blend until smooth. Set aside.

2 To make the grape sauce dressing, heat the butter in a pan, then add the black and white sesame seeds. As they pop, add the ginger and shallot. Sauté until translucent, then pour in the wine and reduce to one-third. Stir in 200ml of the grape sauce, the paprika, mango powder and salt to season. Remove from the heat and set aside.

3 Next make the caramel. Line a baking sheet with baking parchment. Place the sugar and 2 tbsp water in a heavy-based pan over a low heat and stir until the sugar has dissolved. Increase the heat to medium and boil, without stirring, until the syrup caramelises to a golden colour. Carefully pour the hot caramel onto the lined baking sheet, sprinkle immediately with the garam masala and place another parchment sheet on top. Carefully roll out with a rolling pin to make a thin sheet of caramel. Leave to set. Remove the caramel from the paper and break into small pieces. Set aside for the garnish.

4 Divide the scallops into three batches. Dip one batch, on one side only, in the sesame seeds; dip the second batch, on one side only, in the chilli and garlic flakes; and dip the third batch, on one side only, in the ground coriander and cumin. Cook the scallops in their separate batches. Heat 1 tbsp of the oil in a frying pan and add the sesame scallops, sesame-side down. Cook over a medium heat for 30 seconds, then add one-third of the butter. Cook for a further 30–60 seconds to give a golden colour, then turn and cook for 1 more minute. Transfer to a warm plate. Repeat with the remaining scallops, using fresh oil and butter for each batch.

5 After the last batch of scallops has been sautéed, add the grapes to the oil and butter mixture left in the pan (if there is too much fat, pour off a little). Sauté the grapes for 2 minutes. Add a spoonful of the grape sauce dressing to lightly deglaze the pan. Remove the pan from the heat and keep warm. Season the scallops lightly with salt and pepper.

6 To serve, warm the grape dressing, then spoon some into the centre of each plate. Drag the back of a spoon through the dressing and across the plate to make a long streak. Place three scallops, one of each spice flavour, on the streak. Place glazed grapes near the edge, then spoon over the grape sauce dressing and place small pieces of caramel leaning on the grapes. To garnish, sprinkle with the carrot julienne and micro salad leaves.

32

ROAST LANGOUSTINE
WITH SPICED AVOCADO

SERVES 4

12 live medium-sized langoustines

4 tbsp olive oil

salad leaves dressed with olive oil and
    lemon juice, to serve

salt and pepper

Langoustine oil (optional)

350g langoustine shells (heads and claws)

2 tbsp olive oil

1 celery stick, roughly chopped

40g bulb fennel, cut into small sections

50g carrots, cut into chunks

30g leek, cut into chunks

1 tsp tomato purée

80ml fish stock

250g tomatoes, roughly chopped

¼ tsp coriander seeds

½ tsp fennel seeds

¼ tsp cumin seeds

2 sprigs of thyme

2 large sprigs of basil

peeled zest of ½ lemon

about 500ml light fruity olive oil

SPICED AVOCADO

1 large, ripe Hass avocado, peeled,
    stoned and chopped

1 red lombok chilli, very finely chopped

2 tsp Thai fish sauce

grated zest and juice of ½ lime

3 tbsp chopped coriander

1 tbsp sunflower oil

1 Preheat the oven to 220°C/gas 7.

2 First make the langoustine oil. Roughly chop the langoustine shells. Place in a roasting tray along with the langoustine heads and toss with 1 tbsp of the olive oil. Roast for 12–15 minutes.

3 Meanwhile, put the vegetables in a saucepan with 1 tbsp olive oil and lightly brown over a moderate heat for 4–5 minutes, adding the tomato purée towards the end of cooking. Remove from the heat.

4 Add the shells to the vegetables. Set the roasting tray over a moderate heat. When hot, add the fish stock and stir to deglaze. Pour this liquid over the shells in the saucepan. Add the tomatoes, spices, herbs and lemon zest with enough fruity oil to almost cover the shells. Bring to a gentle simmer and cook for about 20 minutes. Allow to cool, then leave in the fridge overnight.

5 The following day, bring the oil to a simmer again over a moderate heat and cook for 15 minutes. Allow to cool slightly, then pass through a fine sieve or muslin. The oil can be kept in the fridge for 2–3 days or frozen for longer storage.

6 Combine the ingredients for the spiced avocado in a bowl. Cover and leave at room temperature for 1 hour to allow the flavours to merge and mingle.

7 Preheat the oven to 220°C/gas 7.

8 Rub the langoustines with some olive oil and place them in a roasting tin. Roast for 7–8 minutes. Allow to cool.

9 Carefully remove the tails and shell, then cut the langoustines in half lengthways. Scoop out all the soft brown meat from the heads (this is similar to the brown meat on a lobster). To do this, turn the heads upside down and lift off the pelvis and legs to leave a soft cup full of brown goo, which you can scrape out. Be careful not to scrape so hard that you remove the hard stomach as well. Add this brown meat to the spiced avocado and combine well.

10 To assemble, set a metal ring in the centre of each plate. Place two langoustine halves, flat-side down, at the bottom of each ring, then cover with a spoonful of spiced avocado. Add another two langoustine halves, more avocado and a final pair of langoustine halves. Press down gently so that it all merges together; the avocado acts like a cement to hold the langoustine together in a tower. Carefully remove the rings and top each tower with a small ball of salad. Finish with a drizzle of langoustine oil, if using.

PRAWN AND AVOCADO
'COCKTAIL'

SERVES 4
12–16 live Strangford prawns (langoustines)
4 tbsp home-made mayonnaise
2 tbsp chopped basil
salt and white pepper

AVOCADO LAYER
1 ripe avocado, peeled and diced
1 tsp finely chopped shallot
1 tsp finely snipped chives
1 tbsp lemon juice

CHERRY TOMATO VINAIGRETTE
2 tbsp sherry vinegar
½ tsp smooth Dijon mustard
pinch of caster sugar
120ml extra virgin olive oil
8 cherry tomatoes, very finely diced
1 tsp very finely chopped shallot

GARNISH
6 quail's eggs, boiled for 2 ½ minutes,
    peeled and quartered
mixed salad leaves
4 strips of home-made potato chips
    (optional)

1 Bring a large pot of water to the boil and season heavily with salt: it should taste like the sea. Add the langoustines, bring back to the boil and boil for 1 minute. Remove the langoustines and allow to cool. When they are cool enough to handle, peel them.

2 Cut each langoustine into two or three, then combine with the mayonnaise, basil and a little salt and pepper. Toss gently together, and set aside.

3 Mix the diced avocado with the shallot, chives and lemon juice and season with salt and pepper. Set aside.

4 To make the vinaigrette, whisk the sherry vinegar with the Dijon mustard, sugar and a pinch each of salt and pepper until dissolved. Stir in the oil. Reserve 2 tbsp vinaigrette, then toss the tomatoes and shallot into the rest. Taste for seasoning.

5 To assemble, place a 4–5cm metal ring in the centre of each plate. Put about 2 tbsp of the avocado mixture in each ring and push down well. Top with the langoustine mayonnaise, again pushing down well. Surround each ring with a few tablespoons of cherry tomato vinaigrette and set three quail's egg quarters on top of the tomatoes. Remove the rings.

6 Toss the salad leaves with the reserved vinaigrette, and carefully set a few leaves on the langoustines. Top each with a strip of potato chip and serve.

36

SMOKED SALMON WITH BLINIS
AND WOODLAND SORREL AND WILD CRESS

SERVES 4
50g woodland sorrel
50g wild cress
25ml olive oil
juice of ½ lemon
500g smoked wild salmon
salt and pepper

IRISH SODA BREAD
100g wholemeal flour
100g self-raising flour
1 tbsp bicarbonate of soda
50g jumbo oatmeal
25g wheat germ
25g wheat bran
10g salt
75g runny honey
25g black treacle
400ml buttermilk

BLINIS
85g plain flour
pinch of freshly grated nutmeg
1 whole egg
1 egg yolk
150ml milk
115g warm mashed potato
knob of butter

TO SERVE
St Killian cheese or other
    soft creamy cheese
a few snipped chives

1 Preheat the oven to 150°C/gas 2.

2 First make the soda bread. Put all the ingredients into a large bowl and mix by hand to make a soft dough.

3 Using floured hands, shape the dough into two oval shapes and place on a floured non-stick baking tray. Bake for 45 minutes or until the breads sound hollow when tapped on the base.

4 Meanwhile, make the blini batter. Put the flour in a bowl with 1 tsp salt and the nutmeg and stir in the egg and egg yolk. Whisk in the milk, then fold in the cooked warm potato. Cover and leave to rest in the fridge until ready to cook.

5 Pick the woodland sorrel and wild cress by removing just the soiled end and washing in a little salted water. Leave to dry on kitchen paper, then place in a bowl. Just before serving, dress with the olive oil, lemon juice and some seasoning.

6 To cook the blinis, heat a little butter in a non-stick frying pan. Add spoonfuls of the blini batter and fry for 1–2 minutes on each side or until golden brown. This will make eight blinis.

7 To serve, cut the smoked salmon into 2cm slices and arrange three slices on each serving plate. Add two blinis to each and a quenelle of cheese. Dress the plates with the sorrel and cress and garnish with some chives. Remove the bread from the oven and serve alongside.

HOME SMOKED SALMON
WITH OATMEAL PANCAKES, HORSERADISH
AND CHIVE CRÈME FRAÎCHE

SERVES 4
350g best quality smoked organic salmon,
   cut into 16 thin slices
salad leaves dressed with olive oil and
   lemon juice
4 tsp Avruga caviar
sprigs of chervil or dill
salt and pepper

OATMEAL PANCAKES
70g pinhead oatmeal
85g plain flour
10g caster sugar
170ml tepid milk
10g fresh yeast
2 egg whites
chopped soft herbs such as dill or chervil
olive oil

CHIVE CRÈME FRAÎCHE
60g good quality crème fraîche
2 tbsp creamed horseradish
chopped chives
lemon juice

1 To make the pancake batter, mix together the oatmeal, flour and a pinch of salt in a stainless steel bowl. Add the sugar to the warm milk and crumble in the yeast, mixing thoroughly, then pour the milk mixture into the flour mixture and gently stir together. When well mixed, cover with cling film and keep in a warm place until the batter has doubled in size.
2 Meanwhile, put the crème fraîche in a bowl and mix in the creamed horseradish. Add the chives and lemon juice and season to taste.
3 Whisk the egg whites to a soft peak, then fold a small amount into the batter to loosen it. Fold in the rest of the egg whites together with the herbs.
4 Heat an 8–10cm blini pan and add a little olive oil. Add a 50ml ladle of batter and cook for 3–4 minutes or until the thick pancake is golden on the base. Flip over, then cook until golden on the other side. Remove and keep warm in a low oven while you cooked the remaining pancakes (you will make five, so will have one extra to enjoy).
5 To serve, place a warm pancake on each plate. Top each pancake with a spoonful of chive crème fraîche and then with salad leaves. Carefully arrange four thin slices of smoked salmon on the leaves, then add a twist of black pepper and 1 tsp of Avruga caviar. Garnish with chervil or dill.

38

CURED SALMON
WITH SWEET CITRUS ASPARAGUS AND DILL HOLLANDAISE

SERVES 4
450g salmon fillet (preferably middle cut)
25g coarse sea salt
25g caster sugar
1 tsp crushed white peppercorns
finely grated zest of 1 lemon
salt and pepper

SWEET CITRUS DRESSING
50g caster sugar
juice of 2 lemons
strip of lemon zest
1 star anise
1 stick lemongrass, finely chopped
150ml olive oil

DILL HOLLANDAISE
2 tbsp white wine vinegar
2 tsp caster sugar
175g unsalted butter
2 egg yolks
juice of 1 lemon
2 tsp Dijon mustard
2 tbsp chopped dill

ASPARAGUS
8 asparagus spears, peeled
handful of watercress sprigs

1 Lay the salmon fillet skin side down on a large sheet of cling film. Remove any pin bones. Mix together the salt, sugar, pepper and lemon zest until well combined. Spread over the salmon, then wrap it in the cling film. Place the salmon on a tray, salted side up. Put another tray on top and place a weight on this roughly equal to the weight of the salmon. Refrigerate for 24 hours to complete the curing process: the salt and sugar will dissolve into the salmon, leaving a 'cooked' finish.

2 To make the sweet citrus dressing, boil together the sugar and 50ml water. Once the sugar has dissolved, add the lemon juice and zest, star anise and lemongrass. Simmer the syrup for several minutes. Remove from the heat and leave to infuse for several hours. Then strain and whisk in the olive oil and seasoning to taste. (This makes about 150ml; it can be kept in an airtight jar in the fridge for several weeks.)

3 For the hollandaise, rapidly simmer the vinegar and sugar until reduced by half. Set aside. Melt the butter in a saucepan and simmer for 2 minutes; cool until warm. It will separate into milky white solids at the bottom and clear clarified butter on top.

4 Place the yolks, lemon juice and 2 tbsp water in a blender and blend briefly. While blending, slowly add the warm clarified butter to make a thick, creamy consistency. Whisk in the reduced vinegar, mustard, dill and seasoning. Keep warm.

5 Plunge the asparagus into a pan of boiling salted water and cook until just tender. Drain and refresh quickly in iced water. Cut each spear into four or five pieces.

6 To serve, unwrap the salmon and wipe off any lemon zest, then cut into 12 slices. Season the asparagus and watercress with salt, pepper and a little citrus dressing. Arrange the salad and salmon on the plates. Add a small dish of hollandaise to each.

SMOKED SALMON
AND WHEATEN BREAD 'SANDWICH'

SERVES 4

100g cream cheese
4 tbsp crème fraîche
1 tsp freshly grated horseradish,
    or 2 tsp prepared horseradish
4 tbsp peeled and deseeded cucumber,
    diced into 1cm cubes
1–2 tbsp very finely chopped red onion
2 tbsp finely snipped chives

2 tbsp capers, rinsed and roughly chopped
lemon juice
4 slices brown Irish soda bread
120g smoked salmon, finely sliced
salt and white pepper

GARNISH

1–2 radishes, finely sliced
½ bunch of mustard cress

1 Mix together the cream cheese, crème fraîche, horseradish, cucumber, red onion, chives, capers and some salt and pepper. Taste for seasoning, and add some lemon juice if desired.

2 With a 5cm metal ring, cut a disc from each slice of soda bread. Set the 5cm ring in the centre of a plate and insert a disc of bread, pressing it down to the bottom of the ring. Top with 2 tbsp of the cream cheese mixture and push it down on to the bread. Top generously with smoked salmon. Remove the ring, and repeat with the remaining plates.

3 Garnish each 'sandwich' with two slices of radish and a little mustard cress.

In Northern Ireland, the brown soda bread is called 'wheaten bread' and is made, often at home, from a coarse wheatmeal flour. It's wonderful with smoked fish and hard cheese, and is the best bread to use with smoked salmon.

40

CURED SLICES OF SALMON TROUT
WITH ONION CONFIT AND SMOKED BACON

SERVES 6

1 side of salmon trout (sea trout),
   with skin, about 1kg, pin bones removed
200g rock salt
50g caster sugar
grated zest and juice of 3 limes
12 thin rashers of smoked bacon,
   preferably Cumbrian
4 tbsp extra virgin olive oil, plus extra
   for drizzling

2 tsp white wine vinegar
salt and pepper

ONION CONFIT
50g unsalted butter
3 small white-skinned onions,
   preferably new season's, halved
   and cut into 3mm slices
1 bay leaf
sprig of thyme

1 Lay the fish flat, skin-side down, on a tray with raised sides. Mix together the rock salt, sugar, and lime zest and juice. Press this mixture all over the flesh side of the fish. Cover with cling film and refrigerate for 8 hours. Don't leave for longer than this or the fish will over-cure and become solid.

2 Scrape off the salt and rinse the fish thoroughly under cold running water. Now put the fish in a large bowl, cover with cold water and leave in the sink with the cold tap trickling gently for 20 minutes. Lift the fish out and dry thoroughly with a cloth.

3 Remove the skin from the fish with a sharp knife. Cut the fish into thirty-six 1cm-thick slices, working from the tail to the head end. Arrange the slices, slightly overlapping in six groups of six, on a baking tray lined with baking parchment. Cover and keep in the fridge.

4 To make the confit, heat the butter in a large pan until it melts and starts to bubble. Add the onions and herbs, and season with a good pinch of fine salt. Cook over a medium heat for about 10 minutes or until the onions are very tender and have caramelised to a deep golden brown. Stir frequently and add a teaspoon of water from time to time, to prevent the onions from catching on the bottom of the pan. Remove from the heat, discard the herbs and keep the confit warm.

5 Preheat the oven to 200°C/gas 6.

6 Line a baking tray with baking parchment. Lay the bacon rashers in a single layer on the tray and cook in the oven for 6–8 minutes or until crisp. Remove the bacon and keep warm on kitchen paper.

7 Drizzle the slices of trout with a little olive oil and warm in the oven for 5–6 minutes.

8 Meanwhile, make a simple dressing by whisking the 4 tbsp olive oil with the vinegar and a little salt.

9 Season the fish with a light sprinkling of sea salt and a twist of pepper, then lay six slices neatly on each plate. Make a quenelle of the onion confit and place next to the fish. Place two rashers of bacon on the confit and finish with a drizzle of dressing.

42

CRISP SOFT SHELL CRAB
CRAB SALAD AND TANDOOR SMOKED SALMON MOUSSE
WITH KUMQUAT AND SPICY PLUM CHUTNEYS

SERVES 4

KUMQUAT CHUTNEY
100g kumquats, sliced
30g palm sugar
20ml white vinegar
½ tsp toasted cumin seeds
½ tsp toasted coriander seeds, crushed
1 red chilli
1 tsp melon seeds
salt

SPICY PLUM CHUTNEY
1kg red plums, stoned and roughly chopped
300g brown or palm sugar
500ml red wine vinegar
3 star anise
½ tsp garam masala
1 dried red chilli
½ tsp crushed black peppercorns

MARINADE FOR SALMON
20 garlic cloves, peeled
small bunch of coriander leaves
knob of fresh ginger, lightly crushed
4–5 lime leaves
1 tbsp grated lime zest
2 tbsp lime juice
1 tbsp red chilli powder
½ tbsp garam masala
50ml vegetable oil
1 tbsp gram flour
100g plain yoghurt

SALMON MOUSSE
400g salmon fillet with skin, cut into
    4cm cubes
knob of butter for smoking (optional)
2 tbsp melted butter for basting
2 tbsp single cream
1 tbsp set plain yoghurt
1 tbsp chopped mint leaves
1 lime leaf, finely chopped
1 tsp finely chopped fresh ginger
1 tsp lime juice
¼ tsp garam masala

SOFT SHELL CRAB FRITTERS
½ tbsp ginger-garlic paste
1 tsp ground turmeric
1 tsp ground coriander
½ tsp red chilli powder
1 tbsp finely chopped fresh ginger
2 tbsp chopped coriander leaves
1 tbsp lime juice
2 tbsp rice flour
4 small soft shell crabs
vegetable oil for deep frying

CRAB SALAD
3 tbsp vegetable oil or coconut oil
1 ½ tsp mustard seeds
10 curry leaves, chopped
1 tsp chopped fresh ginger
½ tsp chopped green chilli
100g chopped onions
300g white crab meat, flaked
1 tsp ground turmeric
3 tbsp coconut milk
1 tsp chopped coriander leaves
1 tbsp freshly grated coconut or
    desiccated coconut

GARNISH
mustard cress
julienne of plums tossed in oil

1 First make the kumquat chutney. Heat all the ingredients together with 1 tsp salt and cook to a thick chutney-like consistency, stirring from time to time. Remove from the heat and allow to cool.

2 Next make the plum chutney. Heat all the ingredients with 1 tsp salt and simmer for 30 minutes or until the plums are soft. Pass through a fine sieve. (This makes more chutney than you need for 4 servings; the remainder can be kept in the fridge for up to 3 months.) Warm through before serving.

3 To make the marinade for the salmon, blend together the garlic, coriander, ginger, lime leaves, lime zest and juice, the spices and 1/2 tbsp salt to make a fine paste. Heat the oil in a pan, add the gram flour and cook, stirring, to make a roux, without burning. Allow to cool, then mix the spice paste and roux with the yoghurt. Add the cubes of salmon, turning them to coat all over, then leave to marinate for 1 hour.

4 To prepare the soft shell crabs, mix together the spices, herbs, lime juice and rice flour, then marinate the crabs for 30 minutes.

5 While the salmon and crabs are marinating, make the crab salad. Heat the oil in a heavy-bottomed pan and sauté the mustard seeds until they splutter. Add the curry leaves and sauté, then stir in the ginger and green chilli. Add the chopped onions and sauté until translucent. Add the crab meat with the turmeric and 3/4 tsp salt and sauté for 2 minutes, then mix in the coconut milk, coriander and coconut. Remove from the heat and set aside to cool.

6 If you want to smoke the salmon before cooking it, you can use a special smoker, if you have one, or fashion a makeshift smoker with a deep bowl or saucepan that has a tight-fitting lid. Put the salmon in the bowl or pan and set a small metal bowl of burning charcoal in the middle. Drop a knob of butter on the charcoal and put on the lid so that no smoke can escape. Leave to smoke for 30–40 minutes. Remove the charcoal bowl and discard.

7 Preheat the oven to 200°C/gas 6 or the grill to high.

8 Cook the salmon in the oven or under the grill for 10–15 minutes, basting once or twice with melted butter to keep the fish moist. Allow to cool to room temperature. Remove the skin from the salmon and break up the flesh with a fork.

9 To finish the salmon mousse, whisk together the remaining ingredients, then lightly mix in the salmon. Keep in the fridge until required.

10 Just before serving, cook the soft shell crabs. Heat oil in a wok to 180°C, then deep fry the crabs until they are crisp and golden brown on both sides. Remove and drain on kitchen paper.

11 To serve, use rectangular plates if possible. Place a quenelle of salmon mousse, a neat mound of crab salad (shaped in a 4cm metal ring) and a crisp soft shell crab in a line on each plate. Drizzle the warm plum chutney on the plate and spoon the kumquat chutney near the salad. Garnish the plate with mustard cress and plums.

44

FLEETWOOD COCK CRAB
WITH POTATO DROP SCONES AND LAND CRESS

SERVES 4
1 large live crab, preferably a cock crab
200ml organic rapeseed oil
1 fennel bulb, sliced or chopped
2 carrots, roughly chopped
1 large onion, roughly chopped
4 ripe and juicy large tomatoes, chopped
1 star anise
strip of pared lemon zest
squeeze of lemon juice
good sprig of tarragon
120g land cress
salt and pepper

POTATO DROP SCONES
500g Maris Piper or King Edward potatoes
2½ tbsp plain flour
50ml full-fat milk
3 medium eggs
4 medium egg whites
2½ tbsp double cream
2 tbsp vegetable oil for shallow frying

1 Put the crab in the freezer for about an hour, to desensitize it, then plunge it into a large saucepan of boiling salted water. Boil for 12–18 minutes, depending on size (ask your fishmonger for advice on this when you buy the crab – cock crabs are larger than hen crabs, so they take longer to cook). Drain and leave until cool enough to handle, then crack the claws and prise open the body. Pick out all the white meat, keeping the chunks as large as possible; cover and keep the fridge. (The brown meat can be used for a soup or sauce.) Discard the dead man's fingers and crack the shells from the claws and body.

2 Preheat the oven to 180°C/gas 4.

3 Heat the oil in a large flameproof casserole until hot. Add the cracked crab shells and the fennel, carrots, onions and tomatoes. Fry over a medium heat until nicely coloured. Add the star anise. Transfer the casserole to the oven and roast for about 1¹/₂ hours, turning the ingredients occasionally. Remove from the oven and add the lemon zest and juice and the tarragon. Stir, then cover the pot and leave to infuse overnight. The next day, strain the infused oil through a fine sieve lined with muslin. Discard the contents of the sieve.

4 To make the drop scones, cook the potatoes in their skins in boiling water until soft. Drain and peel, then work through a potato ricer or food mill (mouli). When cool, transfer to a food processor and add all the other ingredients for the scones (except the oil). Blitz until smooth, but be careful not to overmix. Pour the batter into a bowl, cover and chill for 2–3 hours.

5 Heat a large non-stick frying pan until hot. Add the vegetable oil and heat it, then drop six dessertspoonfuls of the batter into the pan, keeping them far apart. Fry for about 2 minutes in total until the scones are puffed up and lightly browned on both

sides, turning once. Drain on kitchen paper and keep warm in the oven while frying
the remaining batter in the same way, to make 12 scones altogether.

6 To serve, dress the land cress with the crab oil and some salt and pepper. Arrange on plates with the white crab meat next to it, then place three scones alongside the crab. Drizzle a little crab oil on each plate to finish.

GALTON BLACKISTON

MOUSSE OF NORFOLK-GROWN PEAS
ON CREAMED CEPS WITH CRISP BACON

SERVES 6
25g salted butter, plus extra for greasing
   the ramekins
275g freshly shelled peas
1 medium egg, plus 1 medium egg yolk
200ml whipping cream
6 very thin slices smoked streaky bacon
salt and pepper

CREAMED CEPS
white truffle oil or olive oil
2 shallots, finely chopped
1 garlic clove, finely chopped
250g fresh ceps (porcini) or other wild
   mushrooms, sliced
120ml double cream

1 Generously butter six 7.5cm diameter ramekins, then set them aside in the fridge. Preheat the grill.

2 Melt the 25g butter in a saucepan. Add the peas and 2 tbsp water. Season lightly, then cover with a lid and cook gently for about 3 minutes or until the peas are just tender. Remove from the heat and whiz the peas in a food processor or blender to a smooth purée. With the machine running, add the egg, egg yolk and whipping cream. Season. Pass the mixture through a sieve into a jug, then pour it into the cold ramekins. The mixture will only half fill the dishes, but it puffs up during cooking.

3 Place the ramekins in the top of a double boiler or bain marie pan, cover and steam gently over simmering water for 8–10 minutes or until the mousses are just set but still wobble in the centre.

4 While the mousses are steaming, cook the bacon and ceps. Place the bacon slices on a baking tray and grill until crisp.

5 Heat a frying pan over a high heat. Add a splash of truffle or olive oil, then quickly fry the shallots and garlic until soft and translucent. Add the ceps and fry very briefly, seasoning as you go. Remove from the heat and keep warm.

6 To serve, stir the double cream into the ceps and place a spoonful in the centre of each plate. Run a small, sharp knife around the inside of each ramekin and turn the pea mousses out onto the creamed ceps. Top each mousse with a slice of crisp bacon.

SMOKED EEL AND CRISP PORK BELLY
WITH BABY BEETROOT AND HORSERADISH CREAM

SERVES 4

1 piece of good-quality pork belly on the bone, with skin intact, about 2kg
coarse sea salt
1 head of garlic, cut crossways in half
small bunch of thyme
6 bay leaves
about 500ml duck fat or rendered pork fat
14 raw baby beetroots
olive oil

4 fillets of smoked eel, each 50–75g, sliced at an angle into bite-sized pieces
salt and pepper
flat-leaf parsley leaves, young beetroot leaves or baby salad leaves to garnish

HORSERADISH CREAM

5 tbsp freshly grated horseradish
4 tbsp crème fraîche
squeeze of lemon juice

1 Rub the pork belly all over with coarse sea salt, then with the cut sides of the garlic. Scrunch the thyme and 3 of the bay leaves in your hands, and rub these all over the joint too. Now sit the joint skin-side up in a container with the garlic and herbs. Cover and leave in the fridge for 24 hours.

2 Preheat the oven to 140°C/gas 1.

3 Remove the garlic and herbs from the pork and reserve. Quickly rinse off the salt, then pat the joint dry. Warm the duck or pork fat in a roasting tin on top of the stove until it becomes liquid, then slip in the joint, skin-side up. It must be submerged in fat, so you may need to add more. Add the reserved garlic and herbs, and bring the fat to the boil. Cover with a heavy lid, put in the oven and cook for about 3 hours. To check if the pork is done, pierce it in the middle with a carving fork and try to pick it up – it should slip off the fork. Leave the joint to solidify in the liquid by letting it cool, then putting it in the fridge overnight.

4 The next day, wash the beetroots and place them in a pan of cold water with the remaining bay leaves. Bring to the boil and simmer for 40–50 minutes or until tender. Allow the beetroots to cool in the liquid, then lift them out and peel off the skins. Purée 2 of the beetroots in a blender, then work through a sieve into a bowl. Stir in about 50ml olive oil to give the purée a pouring consistency.

5 Make the horseradish cream by stirring all the ingredients together. Cover and refrigerate until needed.

6 Remove the solid pork belly from the tin and place skin-side down on a board. Prise away the bones with the tip of a sharp knife. Turn the pork over and trim into a block, discarding any fat and gristle. You should end up with a 7.5cm square of prime meat cut from the middle (the trimmings are good fried with eggs for breakfast, or cut into lardons and used in salads). Cut the block into 5mm-wide strips and pan-fry with a little olive oil (or use some of the duck or pork fat) in a very hot pan for 1–2 minutes on each side until brown and crisp.

7 To serve, spoon some horseradish cream onto each plate, add three beetroots (sliced if you like), a couple of slices of pork belly and some pieces of eel fillet. Finish by garnishing with your choice of leaves, and spooning beetroot purée around each plate.

SAT BAINS

HAM, EGG AND PEAS

SERVES 4
4 very fresh duck eggs
8 wafer-thin slices French stick
olive oil
3–4 tbsp good chicken stock
10g salted butter
100g freshly shelled peas
4 wafer-thin slices British air-dried ham,
   or similar, such as Serrano or Parma

100g fresh pea shoots, chilled
salt

PEA SORBET
40g liquid glucose, warmed
400g frozen petit pois
2 sprigs of mint, roughly chopped
caster sugar if needed

1 To make the pea sorbet, bring the liquid glucose and 200ml water to the boil in a saucepan to make a stock syrup. Add the frozen petit pois and mint. Pour into a blender and process on high speed to make a purée. Chill, then pour into your ice cream machine and churn for 20–30 minutes or until the sorbet looks like a soft scoop ice cream. Taste for seasoning and adjust with a pinch each of sugar and salt, if necessary. Transfer to a freezer container and freeze.

2 Next, poach the eggs. A rice cooker is the best thing to use, but if you don't have one, heat a pan of water to around 62°C, ideally monitoring the temperature with a digital probe. Carefully add the eggs in their shells and leave at 62°C for about 1^1/$_2$ hours – the whites will be just firm and the yolks runny. Remove the eggs with a slotted spoon and set aside.

3 Preheat the oven to 180°C/gas 4. Arrange the bread slices on a large baking sheet, brush with olive oil and bake for 12 minutes or until golden brown.

4 Pour the chicken stock into a medium saucepan and add the butter, shelled peas and a good pinch of salt. Simmer gently for 3–4 minutes or until the peas are tender.

5 To serve, carefully peel the shells from the duck eggs. Spoon the braised peas into the centre of warmed shallow soup bowls. Sit the eggs on top of the peas. Lay a slice of ham over each egg, and spoon a quenelle of pea sorbet to one side. Lay a couple of pieces of toast on top of the ham. Dress the pea shoots with a drizzle of olive oil and a sprinkling of salt, then scatter them all around.

48

ASPARAGUS AND WILD HERB SALAD
WITH DUCK EGGS

SERVES 4
250g asparagus
4 duck eggs
seasoned flour, beaten egg, crumbs
   and oil for deep-frying (optional)
50–60g wild herb leaves, such as
   nasturtium, wild chervil, bittercress,
   chickweed, etc
salt and pepper

CELERY SALT
1 head of celery with plenty of leaves
sea salt

VINAIGRETTE DRESSING
6 tbsp cold-pressed rapeseed oil
2 tbsp cider vinegar
1 tsp English grain mustard
1 garlic clove, halved
few sprigs of tarragon

1 First make the celery salt. Set your oven to its lowest temperature (the warming oven of an Aga is ideal for this). Remove all the leaves from the head of celery and roughly chop them (use the celery sticks themselves for a soup, stock or salad). Scatter the celery leaves over one or two baking trays lined with greaseproof paper, and leave in the oven overnight or until the pieces are dry and crisp. Don't let them go brown. Put them into a food processor with a handful of sea salt and grind to a powder-like consistency, as coarse or as fine as you wish. For a smaller amount of celery salt, spread the inner leaves of the celery head on kitchen paper, then microwave on Low for 5 minutes or until bright green and brittle. Cool, then blitz in a spice mill with some sea salt. Store in an airtight container or Kilner jar. (You'll have more celery salt than you need for this recipe, but it's great for gulls' eggs or other egg dishes – and in a Bloody Mary of course.)
2 Remove the woody ends from the asparagus, and cook the spears in boiling salted water for 5–6 minutes or until tender. Drain and leave to cool.
3 Lower the eggs into a saucepan of boiling water. Return to the boil and boil for 3–5 minutes, depending on their size (if yours are the size of hen's eggs, boil them for 3 minutes; if they are larger, which they usually are, allow 4–5 minutes). Drain and refresh under cold running water for a few minutes until they are cool enough to handle, then peel. If you like, you can then deep-fry the duck's eggs. Coat in seasoned flour and beaten egg, followed by fresh white breadcrumbs. Deep-fry in hot oil for 3–4 minutes or until golden, then drain on kitchen paper.
4 Make the vinaigrette dressing by shaking all the ingredients together in a bottle or jar with the lid on.
5 Cut each asparagus spear in half and arrange on plates with the herb leaves. Drizzle over the vinaigrette. Break the eggs in half crossways (or cut them if they have been deep-fried) and place two halves in the middle of each salad with their yolks facing up. Sprinkle each egg half with a pinch of celery salt, then serve.

CROWN OF
ENGLISH ASPARAGUS

SERVES 4

28 asparagus spears

1 leek, white and pale green part only,
   halved lengthways and leaves separated

175g Vulscombe goat's cheese or other
   very soft, creamy goat's cheese

100ml single cream

¼ garlic clove, crushed

cayenne pepper

2 gelatine leaves, soaked in cold water
   for at least 10 minutes

1 small raw beetroot

150ml cider vinegar

40g sugar

4 sprigs of chervil

salt

TARRAGON VINAIGRETTE

juice of ½ lemon

120ml white wine vinegar

pinch of caster sugar

500ml olive oil

2 garlic cloves, cut in half

3 sprigs of tarragon

1 First make the tarragon vinaigrette. Put the lemon juice, wine vinegar, sugar and a little salt and pepper in a bowl. Whisk in the olive oil. Using a small funnel, pour into a jar or bottle and add the garlic cloves and sprigs of tarragon. Put a lid or cork on the bottle or jar and set aside to infuse while you make the crowns. Shake the vinaigrette well before using. (This makes more vinaigrette than you need for this dish; keep it for salads and other preparations.)

2 For the crowns, you need four stainless steel rings, each 6cm wide and 3.5cm deep. Place the rings on a tray lined with cling film.

3 Peel the asparagus stalks and trim the ends so the spears will stand upright inside the rings with the tips above the rim. Plunge the asparagus into a pan of boiling salted water and cook for 1–2 minutes or until tender, then remove to iced water to refresh. Drain and set aside.

4 In the same water cook the leek leaves until tender, then refresh in iced water and drain. Dry on paper towels.

5 In a food processor work the goat's cheese until smooth. Add the cream, garlic, a tiny pinch of salt and a speck of cayenne pepper. Mix for 1 minute or until smooth.

6 Gently squeeze dry one of the gelatine leaves and melt it in a little warm liquid, then add to the cheese mixture and stir to mix thoroughly.

7 Place the cheese mixture in a piping bag and pipe a small amount into the bottom of each ring. Stand the asparagus in the cheese, seven spears to each ring. Pipe the rest of the cheese into the rings, filling them up and securing the asparagus. Place in the refrigerator to set.

8 Meanwhile, peel the beetroot, rinse it and grate on a coarse blade. Put in a saucepan, cover with the vinegar and 150ml water and add the sugar. Bring to the boil and simmer for 15 minutes.

9 Strain through a fine sieve into a clean pan, pressing well to extract all the juice. Discard the beetroot in the sieve. Bring the juice back to the boil and reduce by half. Squeeze dry the second gelatine leaf and add to the juice, stirring until it has completely melted. Set the pan over iced water to cool, stirring often, until a thick, oil-like consistency is achieved.

10 Remove the asparagus moulds from the fridge and carefully spoon the beetroot jelly on top. Return to the fridge to set.

11 To serve, lift off the rings from the asparagus moulds, using the warmth of your hands around the rings to loosen, if required. Wrap a leek leaf around each mould to look like a band. Carefully transfer the asparagus moulds to four plates. Sprinkle with tarragon vinaigrette and garnish with chervil.

No food is quite as delicate and fragile as asparagus. The sugar stored in its spears – which gives it its distinctive sweet and grassy flavour – begins to turn to starch as soon as the asparagus is plucked from the earth. Buying locally and seasonally is a must – do not even consider imported varieties.

52

ENGLISH ASPARAGUS
WITH A WARM LEEK PURÉE, PUFF PASTRY CASE, HOLLANDAISE AND QUAIL REDUCTION

SERVES 4
400g puff pastry
12 asparagus spears, peeled and trimmed
8 quail's eggs
butter
4 sprigs of chervil
50ml truffle oil (optional)
salt and pepper

LEEK PURÉE
50g unsalted butter
4 medium leeks, cut into 1cm dice
1 bouquet garni
500ml chicken stock

QUAIL REDUCTION
400g quail bones, chopped
200g chicken wings, chopped
40ml vegetable oil
40ml white wine vinegar
300ml white wine
1 litre chicken stock
sprig of thyme
¼ bay leaf
1 shallot, chopped

½ carrot, chopped
1 celery stick, chopped
1 medium leek, chopped
2 garlic cloves, chopped
35g dried morels, powdered

HOLLANDAISE SAUCE
25g unsalted butter
1 shallot, finely chopped
1 garlic clove, finely chopped
½ tsp crushed black peppercorns
sprig of tarragon
sprig of thyme
½ bay leaf
1 parsley stalk
25ml white wine vinegar
25ml dry white wine
2 egg yolks
75ml warm clarified butter
pinch of cayenne pepper
juice of ½ lemon

1 First make the puff pastry boxes. Preheat the oven to 200°C/gas 6. Roll out the pastry 1cm thick and cut out four 8 x 5cm rectangles. Place on a baking tray. Bake for 20 minutes or until golden brown. Remove the lid and scoop out the soft centre. Set the boxes and lids aside.

2 Blanch the asparagus spears in boiling, slightly salted water for 3 minutes. Refresh in iced water, drain and set aside.

3 Add a cap of white wine vinegar to a wide pan of boiling, slightly salted water and poach the quail's eggs for 2 minutes or until softly poached. Refresh immediately in iced water. Drain and reserve until needed.

4 To make the leek purée, melt the butter in a saucepan over a moderate heat, add the leeks and bouquet garni and sweat for 6–8 minutes to start the release of their flavour. Do not allow them to colour at all, as this will discolour the finished purée. Cover with the chicken stock, bring to the boil and skim. Simmer for 20 minutes or until the leeks are very tender.

5 Discard the bouquet garni, then blitz the leeks in a blender until smooth and velvety. Pass through a fine chinois, then season with salt and pepper and set aside.
6 Next make the quail reduction. Preheat the oven to 200°C/gas 6. Put the quail bones and chicken wings in a roasting tray with half the vegetable oil. Place in the oven and roast until golden in colour. Remove the bones and wings to a saucepan and reserve. Discard the excess fat.
7 Add the white wine vinegar to the roasting tray, bring to the boil and stir to deglaze. Over a moderate heat reduce down to a syrup. Add the white wine and reduce by half. Pour into the saucepan with the bones. Cover with the stock, bring to the boil and skim. Reduce the heat slightly, add the herbs and leave to simmer.
8 Meanwhile, heat the rest of the vegetable oil and brown the vegetables and garlic until evenly caramelised. Drain thoroughly and add to the quail stock. Stir in the morel powder and reduce the liquid by two-thirds. Strain through a fine chinois and reduce down again until syrupy in consistency. Keep warm.
9 Next make the hollandaise sauce. Melt the butter in a saucepan, then add the shallot, garlic, peppercorns and herbs. Cook over a moderate heat for 5 minutes, without colouring. Pour the vinegar into the pan and boil until it has completely evaporated. Add the wine and boil until reduced to a syrup. Take the pan off the heat, remove the herbs and discard.
10 Put the egg yolks and 2 tsp cold water in a stainless steel bowl set over a saucepan of almost boiling water. Whisk the yolks until they thicken and form soft peaks. Gradually add the warm clarified butter, whisking rapidly until the sauce becomes smooth. Add the wine and shallot reduction and continue whisking vigorously. Season with the cayenne, a little salt and the lemon juice. Remove from the heat but leave over the pan of water to keep hot.
11 Heat the puff pastry cases in the oven for 3–4 minutes. Reheat the leek purée and check seasoning. Reheat the asparagus spears in a little butter and season to taste. Reheat the quail's eggs in boiling water for 30 seconds, then drain on kitchen paper.
12 To assemble, place a pastry box on each of four warmed plates and fill with a spoonful of leek purée. Place three asparagus spears in each box and top with two quail's eggs. Spoon the hollandaise over the quail's eggs and replace the pastry lids on a slant. Dress the plates with the quail reduction, garnish with sprigs of chervil, drizzle over a little truffle oil to intensify the flavours and serve immediately.

BELLY PORK, LANGOUSTINES AND LARDO
WITH GRANNY SMITH APPLES

54

SERVES 4

1 piece boned belly pork, about 500g,
    skin and rind removed
2–3kg duck fat, or you can use lard
    or 2 litres groundnut oil
pared zest of 2 oranges
pared zest of 2 lemons
2 vanilla pods, split lengthways
big bunch of lemon thyme
8 live langoustines
5g lardo (Italian cured back fat),
    plus 8 wafer-thin slices to serve

SALT MIX

10 white peppercorns, crushed
20 coriander seeds
5 green cardamom pods

5 whole cloves
2 cinnamon sticks, broken in pieces
100g wet sea salt, such as fleur de sel
2 sprigs of rosemary
10 sprigs of lemon thyme
2 garlic cloves, crushed

SHERRY SYRUP

100ml good quality sweet sherry

APPLE PUREE

3 Granny Smith apples, thinly sliced
200ml apple juice

APPLE SALAD

1 Granny Smith apple
squeeze of lemon juice
sea salt

1 You need to start 2 days ahead. To make the salt mix, put the peppercorns and all the dry spices in a frying pan and toast over a medium heat for about 2 minutes, shaking the pan often so they don't burn. Remove the cardamom seeds from the pods and put into a spice mill or a small electric blender with the remaining toasted spices. Blitz for about 30 seconds to make a coarse mix. Add the wet salt, rosemary, thyme and garlic, and blitz again for 30 seconds.

2 Rub the salt mix into the flesh side of the pork belly. (If you don't use all the salt mix, keep in a jar for using another time.) Sit the pork on a tray, cover and refrigerate for 24 hours.

3 The next day, rinse off the salt mix and pat the pork very dry with kitchen paper. Put the fat of your choice in a deep roasting tin or other deep pan and add the orange and lemon zests, vanilla pods and thyme. Heat the fat on top of the stove to 70°C (use a thermometer to check), then carefully add the pork. Cover and leave to cook very gently until the meat is very tender – this can take up to 10 hours. During this time, check regularly to be sure the temperature remains at 70°C. (A temperature of 70°C is ideal, but if you have trouble keeping it that low, cook at 100°C for 5 hours.) To test if the meat is done, push a large two-pronged fork into the centre; it should come out clean and do so as easily and smoothly as if it were coming out of a piece of butter. If not done, continue to cook.

4 While the meat cooks, make the sherry syrup and apple purée. Bubble the sherry in a small pan until reduced to a thick balsamic-vinegar consistency, then set aside. Put the apple slices in a pan with the apple juice. Bring to a simmer and cook for about 5 minutes. Strain off some of the liquid (leave the apples moist enough to purée, but not too wet). Purée the apples in a blender until smooth, then pass through a sieve. Chill.

5 Preheat the oven to 190°C/gas 5.

6 When the pork is done, lift it from its cooking fat and lay it on a rack to drain. Then place it on a tray, set another tray on top and press down with a heavy weight. Leave in the fridge overnight to flatten.

7 The next day, remove the heads and the middle tail bits (waste pipe) from the langoustines. Blanch the langoustines in boiling salted water for 5 seconds, then plunge into a big bowl of iced water to cool for a few minutes. Remove the shells and dry the langoustines. Keep chilled until needed.

8 When ready to serve, trim the pork into a square, then cut into four 5cm cubes. Lay the cubes fat-side down in a dry non-stick ovenproof frying pan and cook for about 5 minutes or until caramelised. Turn the cubes of pork over and transfer the pan to the oven to cook for 5 minutes. Remove from the oven but leave in the pan.

9 While the pork is cooking, make the apple salad. Slice the apple very thinly, preferably using a mandolin. Sprinkle the slices with lemon juice and a little sea salt.

10 To cook the langoustines, melt the 5g of lardo in a non-stick frying pan, add the langoustines and fry for 30 seconds on each side.

11 To serve, cut each cube of pork into four slices. Lay four slices on each warmed plate, sit two langoustines on top and drape a slice of lardo over the langoustines so it starts to melt and look translucent. Drop little spoonfuls of apple purée around the pork and finish with a scattering of the apple salad over the langoustines and pork. Finish with a drizzle of sherry syrup.

56

SMOKED VENISON LOIN
WITH PICKLES AND CUMBERLAND SAUCE

SERVES 4
250g loin of smoked Tatton venison
selection of exotic baby salad leaves
salt and pepper

PICKLING VEGETABLES
12 baby beetroots
12 baby carrots
12 baby turnips
12 pickled walnuts

PICKLING LIQUOR
200ml sherry vinegar
200ml Cabernet Sauvignon vinegar
200ml groundnut oil
200ml extra virgin olive oil

CUMBERLAND SAUCE
shreds of zest and juice of 2 oranges
shreds of zest and juice of 1 lemon
1 shallot, finely chopped
25g piece peeled fresh ginger, grated
25g butter
4 tbsp Port
1 tsp Dijon mustard
200g redcurrant jelly

1 Preheat the oven to 200°C/gas 6. Wrap the beetroots in a foil packet, then roast for 10 minutes. Allow to cool. Peel the beetroots if necessary.

2 Blanch the carrots and turnips separately in a pan of boiling water for 3 minutes; drain and refresh.

3 Combine all the ingredients for the pickling liquor. Taste and add a little sugar if too bitter. Divide among four separate containers. Put the beetroots in one, the turnips in another, the carrots in the third and the walnuts in the last. Cover and leave to marinate for at least 2 hours, but ideally for 24 hours.

4 To make the Cumberland sauce, blanch the orange and lemon zests in boiling water for 1 minute; drain. Gently fry the shallot and grated ginger in the butter for 3–4 minutes or until soft. Add the blanched zest, juices, Port and mustard, stirring, and bring to the boil. Reduce by half. Add the redcurrant jelly and simmer gently for 4–5 minutes or until it melts into the sauce. Allow to cool.

5 To serve, slice the venison into medallions. Pile a few leaves on each plate, fan the venison on top and add three pieces of each pickle around the meat. Drizzle around the sauce or serve it separately.

CARPACCIO OF CURED VENISON
WITH HORSERADISH, CHIVE AND
ROASTED WALNUT CREAM

SERVES 4

1 boneless loin of venison, about 1kg
rapeseed oil
150g sea salt
10 juniper berries, very finely crushed
3 star anise, very finely crushed
1 tbsp cracked black pepper
leaves of 1 sprig of rosemary,
   very finely chopped
leaves of 2 sprigs of thyme,
   very finely chopped
1 tbsp coriander seeds, crushed
1 tsp grated orange zest
1 tsp grated lemon zest
salt and pepper

ROASTED WALNUT CREAM

8 walnuts, shelled
300ml whipping cream
1 tsp freshly grated horseradish
1 tsp wholegrain mustard, preferably
   Castle Leslie
5 chives, finely chopped

GARNISH

olive oil
a few chives

1 Heat a heavy pan until very hot, then sear the venison in a little oil over a high heat until nicely coloured on all sides. This should take about 3 minutes. Remove from the pan.

2 Mix together the sea salt, juniper berries, star anise, pepper, rosemary, thyme, coriander seeds, and orange and lemon zests on a baking tray, then spread out in a 3mm-thick layer.

3 Roll the warm venison in the spice mixture, making sure it is well coated all over. Wrap tightly in cling film and leave to infuse at room temperature for about 2 hours, then freeze for at least 4 hours until solid.

4 Preheat the oven to 180°C/gas 4.

5 For the roasted walnut cream, spread the walnuts out on a baking tray and roast for 5 minutes. Rub off the excess skin while the nuts are warm, then chop the nuts roughly and leave to cool. Whip the cream until it holds a peak. Mix in the walnuts, horseradish, mustard and chives. Add seasoning to taste. Keep in a covered bowl in the fridge until serving time.

6 To serve, unwrap the venison and slice very finely on a meat slicer or with a very sharp knife. Arrange the slices in a semi-circle on each plate and glaze with a little olive oil. Spoon the roasted walnut cream in the middle, in a quenelle shape if you like, and garnish with chives.

58

GALANTINE OF QUAIL
SPIKED WITH RAISINS, SERVED
WITH A SALAD OF WALNUTS

SERVES 4
4 boned quails
mixed salad leaves to serve
salt and pepper

RAISINS
15g jasmine tea leaves
250ml boiling water
100g raisins
1 shallot, finely chopped

QUAIL MOUSSE
75g skinned quail breast meat
   (2-3 breasts)
75g skinned chicken breast meat
   (1 very small breast)
80ml double cream
50g chopped onion
½ garlic clove, crushed
50g unsalted butter

50g wild mushrooms, finely chopped
20g raisins
20g toasted walnuts, finely chopped
50g toasted pistachio nuts
1 tsp chopped tarragon

CARAMELISED WALNUTS
100g caster sugar
100g walnuts halves
vegetable oil for deep-frying

WALNUT VINAIGRETTE
150ml walnut oil
50ml Champagne vinegar or white
wine vinegar
small sprig of thyme
½ garlic clove, lightly bashed

1 Stir the tea into the boiling hot water, then leave to steep until the water is warm. Put the raisins in a jar or plastic container and strain in the tea through a fine sieve. Leave to soak for 12 hours.

2 To make the quail mousse, blend the quail and chicken breast meat in a blender three times for about 3 minutes each time, leaving to cool in the fridge between each blending. (This stops the mousse over-heating.) Add the cream, then remove from the blender and transfer to a bowl. Set the bowl on a bowl of ice.

3 Sweat the onion and garlic in the butter until soft and translucent, but with no colour. Add the mushrooms and continue cooking until all the moisture has gone. Allow to cool, then fold into the quail and chicken purée along with the raisins, toasted walnuts and pistachios, and tarragon. Season with salt and pepper.

4 Open out one of the boned quails skin-side down on a large piece of cling film. Season lightly with salt and pepper, then pipe (using a piping bag fitted with a small round nozzle) or spoon one-quarter of the quail mousse down the middle. Roll the quail around the mousse, keeping the mousse in the centre, then roll up in the cling film so the quail encircles the mousse neatly in a sausage shape. Make sure the quail is well wrapped in the cling film, then twist the ends like a cracker and fold them back on themselves to seal. Repeat with the remaining quails and mousse.

5 Poach the quail parcels in a bain-marie with the water at 80°C (or in a large saucepan, making sure they are well submerged while cooking) for 30–35 minutes. Remove from the hot water and place in iced water. Leave until cold, then drain and chill overnight in the fridge, still wrapped in cling film.

6 To make the caramelised walnuts, pour 100ml water into a saucepan, stir in the sugar and bring to the boil. When the sugar has dissolved, add the walnuts and cook until the sugar syrup reaches 110°C. Meanwhile, heat oil in a deep-fat fryer to 180°C.

7 Using a slotted spoon, remove the walnuts from the sugar syrup, letting any excess syrup drain off, then place carefully in the hot oil and fry for about 2 minutes or until golden brown. Remove with a slotted spoon to a metal tray. Season with a pinch of salt.

8 To make the vinaigrette, mix all the ingredients together in a bowl and pour into a jar or plastic bottle. Shake well before using.

9 When ready to serve, drain the tea-soaked raisins and season with some of the vinaigrette and the chopped shallot. Remove the cling film from each quail and cut 4–6 slices, leaving the rest of the quail whole (or slice the whole quail).

10 Place the quail on the plates, fanning the slices. Dress the salad leaves with some vinaigrette and arrange a little in the centre of each plate. Break up a few caramelised nuts and scatter around the outside of the plate along with the dressed raisins. Serve.

SOUSED MONACHYLE ROE DEER
WITH A ROASTED BEETROOT AND
HORSERADISH CREAM

SERVES 4
loin of roe deer (see method)
olive oil
1 tbsp tarragon vinegar
salt and pepper
mixed peppery leaves

MARINADE
equal parts red and white wine to cover meat
600g coarse sea salt
bunch of thyme
10 bay leaves
good pinch of ground cloves
3 garlic cloves, crushed
small handful of black peppercorns (20-30)
small handful of small dried chillies (10-12)
4 good strips of orange zest

OATCAKES
350g pinhead oatmeal
350g porridge oats
400g brown flour
125ml extra virgin olive oil
125ml light olive oil

**ROASTED BEETROOT AND
HORSERADISH CREAM**
2 beetroots
1 tbsp olive oil
sprig of thyme
1 good tbsp home-made horseradish
    cream (freshly grated horseradish
    mixed with mayonnaise or
    crème fraîche)
1 shallot, finely chopped

1 To make the marinade, put all the ingredients in a pot and bring to the boil, then remove from the heat and leave until cold. Place the meat in the marinade and leave in a cool place or the fridge for 5–7 days or until the meat feels firm. Drain and pat dry, then wrap in muslin and air dry in a cool place (not the fridge) for 1 week. The venison will serve 15–20 portions; it can be kept in the fridge for up to 2 weeks.
2 Preheat the oven to 170°C/gas 3.
3 To make the oatcakes, mix together all the ingredients with a good pinch of salt, then add about 300ml water until it binds. With a floured rolling pin, roll out the dough to 2–3mm thick. Cut out square shapes and place on a non-stick baking tray. Fold the trimmings back together and roll out and cut again. Bake for 25 minutes or until a pale colour. Cool on a wire rack. This will make quite a lot of oatcakes; they can be kept in an airtight container for up to 2 weeks.
4 Turn the oven up to 180°C/gas 4. Put the beetroots in a small roasting tray and toss with the olive oil, a splash of water and the thyme. Roast for 35–45 minutes, depending on size. When cold, peel and chop. Fold the beetroot into the horseradish cream together with the shallot and add salt and pepper to taste.
5 Mix the tarragon vinegar with 4–5 tbsp olive oil and seasoning to taste.
6 To serve, slice the roe deer very thinly and arrange on the plates. Drizzle with olive oil and add a small grinding of black pepper. Spoon the beetroot cream on top. Toss the salad leaves with the vinaigrette and serve on the side together with the oatcakes.

62

PEA AND LEEK TARTS
WITH GLAZED ASPARAGUS AND HERB SALAD

SERVES 6

18 spears of young, tender English
    asparagus, woody ends cut off and
    peeled if necessary
leaves of 24 sprigs of tarragon, finely chopped
leaves of 24 sprigs of chervil, finely chopped
24 chives, finely chopped
100g baby salad leaves
salt and pepper

TART CASES

250g plain flour
pinch of caster sugar
160g chilled unsalted butter, diced
1 medium egg, lightly beaten
few drops of cold milk, if needed
2 medium egg yolks, beaten, for sealing

FILLING

1 small leek, finely shredded
2 tbsp olive oil
½ tsp very finely chopped rosemary
250ml whipping cream
125g frozen English petits pois
10g Parmesan, finely grated
pinch of caster sugar

GLAZE

100g unsalted butter
2 medium egg yolks
10g Parmesan, finely grated
1 tsp double cream, lightly whipped

WHITE WINE VINAIGRETTE

1 tbsp white wine vinegar
4 tbsp olive oil

1 First make the tart cases. Sift the flour into a bowl with the sugar and a pinch of salt. Rub in the butter until the mixture looks like breadcrumbs, then mix in half the beaten egg. Add the remaining egg a little at a time until you can bring everything together to form a dough. If it starts to get sticky, don't add all of the egg; if it feels dry, add a drop or two of cold milk as well as the egg. Turn the dough onto a floured surface and knead very lightly into a rough ball. Wrap the ball in cling film and chill for about 30 minutes.

2 Butter and flour six metal rings, about 7.5cm in diameter and 1.6cm deep. Stand the rings on a baking sheet lined with a non-stick mat or baking parchment, and chill with the dough.

3 Preheat the oven to 170°C/gas 3.

4 Roll out the dough on a floured surface until 3mm thick. Cut out six discs about 11cm in diameter. Line each metal ring with a pastry disc, pushing it firmly into the bottom inside edge and letting the surplus hang loosely over the top. Prick the bottoms all over with a fork, then line each tart case with greaseproof paper or a double layer of cling film and fill with baking beans. Bake the tart cases blind for 12–14 minutes or until the pastry is fully cooked. Remove from the oven, and turn the oven down to 140°C/gas 1.

5 Remove the paper and beans while the pastry is warm. Cool slightly, then brush all over the inside of the tart cases with the beaten egg yolks, sealing any cracks. Return to the oven to bake for 4 minutes to set the egg, then cool slightly. Trim off

the overhanging pastry by gently sawing with a small serrated knife at a 30° angle. Set the cases aside, still in their rings on the mat or paper.

6 To make the filling, gently sweat the leek in the olive oil with the rosemary and 2 tbsp water in a covered pan for 10–15 minutes or until very soft but not coloured. Cool. Bring the cream to the boil in a separate pan. Add the frozen peas and simmer for 1–2 minutes or until soft, then immediately purée in a blender until smooth and thick. Leave until cold, then mix with the leek, Parmesan, sugar and seasoning.

7 Fill the tart cases three-quarters full with the creamy pea mixture. Bake for about 16 minutes or until the filling is almost set but still has a slight wobble in the centre. Remove from the oven and cool slightly until just warm.

8 Meanwhile, plunge the asparagus spears into a pan of boiling salted water and simmer for 4–5 minutes or until just tender. Drain and refresh in iced water. Drain again, cool and dry on a cloth.

9 For the glaze, gently melt the butter in a heavy saucepan. Pour off the clear butter into a bowl, leaving the whey in the bottom of the pan. Keep both warm. Put the egg yolks in a bowl with $1/2$ tbsp cold water. Set over a pan of gently simmering water and whisk until thick and aerated – the mixture should triple in volume and hold a ribbon trail when the whisk is lifted. Transfer the bowl to an empty saucepan and slowly whisk in the clear butter until all is incorporated, adding some of the whey to help prevent the sauce from splitting, if necessary. Fold in the Parmesan and cream, and season to taste.

10 Preheat the grill so that it is warm, not hot. Remove the metal rings from the tarts. Arrange three asparagus spears on the top of each tart, with their tips resting on the edge of the pastry case. Spoon the glaze over the top in a smooth, even layer, then slide the tarts under the grill to warm them through for 2–3 minutes and lightly colour the glaze.

11 Meanwhile, make the dressing by whisking the vinegar and oil with salt and pepper, then toss with the tarragon, chervil, chives, and baby leaves.

12 To serve, place the warm tarts on individual plates, and pile the salad on the side in a little mound.

SALAD OF DUCK LIVERS, HEARTS, SNAILS AND BACON
WITH DANDELION AND APPLE

SERVES 4

100g slab of streaky bacon, skin removed

75g duck fat

12 duck hearts, trimmed

16 duck livers, cleaned

24 fresh snails, poached in court bouillon
and drained, or ready prepared snails,
thawed if frozen or drained and rinsed
if canned

best-quality sherry vinegar, preferable Xerez,
for deglazing

4 tbsp duck jus (below), or 4 tbsp rich
chicken jus or gravy

hazelnut oil

salt and pepper

DUCK JUS

1 uncooked duck carcass, chopped

mirepoix of finely diced vegetables (2 onions,
2 carrots, ½ head celery and 1 leek)

organic rapeseed oil

red wine

sprig of thyme

1 bay leaf

SALAD

2 tbsp organic rapeseed oil

1 tsp cider vinegar

150g mixed fresh salad leaves, such
as dandelion, onion cress, land cress,
watercress, purslane, red amaranth
and flat-leaf parsley

3 crisp, tart eating apples, peeled and
cut into 1cm dice

1 If making the duck jus, brown the carcass and mirepoix in a little oil in a large saucepan over a high heat, then deglaze with a good splash of red wine. Add the thyme and bay leaf, and cover the carcass with cold water. Bring to the boil, then simmer gently for 1¹/₂ hours. Strain the stock into a clean pan and boil to reduce to a gravy-like consistency. Taste for seasoning, taking care not to over-salt as the jus will be reduced further when it is used for deglazing later. Set aside.

2 Put the slab of bacon in a saucepan of cold water and bring to the boil. Take off the heat and leave for about 5 minutes or until you see the bacon puff up a little, then drain. Cut into strips about 2cm long and 1cm wide and thick.

3 Heat a large, heavy or non-stick frying pan until hot. Add the duck fat and sauté the hearts and bacon over a high heat for 2–3 minutes. Add the livers and sauté for about 30 seconds on each side until well caramelised. Now add the snails, and deglaze the pan with a splash of vinegar and the duck jus (or chicken jus or gravy). Cook for a minute until reduced to a light sauce. Check the seasoning, and adjust if necessary.

4 Make a vinaigrette dressing for the salad with the rapeseed oil, cider vinegar and seasoning. Dress the salad leaves with the vinaigrette, and toss with the apple cubes.

5 To serve, pile the salad in a small heap in the centre of each plate, then arrange the livers, hearts, bacon and snails around. Spoon the sauce over and finish with a drizzle of hazelnut oil.

CURED DUCK, DUCK LIVER LOAF
AND PICKLED PEARS WITH
GRILLED WALNUT BREAD

SERVES 4

PICKLED PEARS
1cm piece fresh ginger
½ tsp whole cloves
½ tsp allspice berries
2 sticks cinnamon
thinly peeled rind of ½ lemon
350ml red wine vinegar
350ml red wine
375g soft brown sugar
1kg Conference pears, peeled, cored
   and each cut into 6 lengthways

CURED DUCK
1 tsp crushed toasted white peppercorns
1 tsp crushed toasted coriander seeds
½ tsp bay leaf powder
½ tsp crushed toasted cumin seeds
85g Maldon sea salt
85g caster sugar
2 large duck breasts
300ml light chicken stock

DUCK LIVER 'LOAF'
450g duck livers, trimmed of any white
   skin and bile stains
2 garlic cloves, crushed to a paste with salt
1 shallot, finely chopped and sweated
   in a little butter until soft
3 tbsp Port
1 tbsp brandy
225g unsalted butter, melted
salt and white pepper

1 First prepare the pickled pears. Bruise the ginger with a rolling pin, and crush the cloves and allspice with the back of a firm knife. Tie the ginger, cloves, allspice, cinnamon and lemon rind in a piece of muslin. Put the red wine vinegar, red wine and sugar in a non-reactive saucepan and add the spice bag. Bring to the boil, stirring to dissolve the sugar, then simmer gently for 10 minutes.

2 Add the pears and continue simmering very gently for 10–15 minutes. With a slotted spoon remove the pears to two warm, clean 1 litre kilner jars. Allow the syrup to cool, then remove and discard the spice bag. Pour the cold syrup over the pears and seal the jars. Leave in a cool, dark place for at least 1 month before using. The pears can be kept for up to a year.

3 Next prepare the cured duck. Mix together all the ingredients except the duck breasts and stock. Scatter half the cure mixture in a shallow tray lined with overhanging cling film. Place the duck breasts, flesh side down, in the tray and cover with the remaining cure. Wrap up in the cling film, place a weight on top and refrigerate for 24 hours, turning the duck parcel over from time to time.

4 Once the duck breasts are in the fridge, make the duck liver loaf. Preheat the oven to 120°C/gas ¹/2. Place the duck livers, 1 tsp salt, ¹/4 tsp white pepper, the garlic, shallot and its butter, Port and brandy in a liquidiser and blend for 1 minute or until smooth. Pulse in the melted butter, then pass the mixture twice through a fine drum sieve into a bowl.

5 Line a small terrine mould with cling film. Spoon in the liver mixture and cover with oiled cling film. Set the mould in a roasting tray and add nearly boiling water to come three-quarters of the way up the sides of the mould. Place in the oven and cook for 45 minutes to 1¹/2 hours or until firm.

6 Remove the mould from the roasting tray and allow to cool, then remove the oiled cling film. Re-cover with fresh cling film to keep out the air. Chill overnight.

7 Rinse the cure from the duck breasts, then place them skin side down in a non-stick frying pan. Cook over a low heat for about 10 minutes to release some fat; remove and allow to cool.

8 Preheat the oven to 160°C/gas 3. Place the duck breasts in a snug-fitting roasting tray and add the stock. Cook them in the oven for 15–20 minutes or until the internal temperature of the duck reaches 60°C (use a meat probe or instant-read thermometer to check). Remove from the roasting tray and allow to cool.

9 To assemble, cut the duck breasts lengthways on the diagonal into thin slices. Arrange two or three slices to one side of each of four cold plates. Slice the duck liver loaf and place one slice almost opposite the sliced duck. Create a food triangle on the plate by adding the pear pickle. Put a little Maldon salt and crushed white pepper on the duck liver loaf. Serve with grilled walnut bread.

Pickled pears are traditionally served as a Boxing Day treat with leftover turkey or capon. Rich, spicy and with a complex texture, they are the perfect foil for cold meats.

SALT DUCK SALAD

SERVES 4
4 duck breasts
rock salt
1 carrot, roughly chopped
1 leek, roughly chopped
1 celery stick, roughly chopped
1 onion, roughly chopped
sprig of thyme
1 bay leaf
salt and pepper

VINAIGRETTE
100ml olive oil
10ml red wine vinegar
½ tsp honey

VEGETABLE SALAD
1 bulb fennel, finely sliced
2 celery sticks, finely sliced
6 radishes, finely sliced
bunch of watercress, stalks discarded

TO FINISH
toasted sesame seeds
flat-leaf parsley leaves, deep-fried
    until crisp

1 Rub the duck breasts all over with rock salt, then leave in the fridge for 3 days, turning them from time to time. Rinse to remove the salt.

2 Combine the carrot, leek, celery, onion, thyme and bay leaf in a large saucepan and cover with water. Add the duck breasts and bring to the boil. Reduce the heat and cook for 15 minutes at a simmer, skimming when necessary. Leave the duck breasts to cool in the liquid.

3 Mix together the vinaigrette ingredients with salt and pepper to taste.

4 Put all of the ingredients for the vegetable salad in a bowl and season with the vinaigrette, tossing to mix.

5 To serve, slice the duck thinly and arrange on plates with the salad. Finish with toasted sesame seeds and deep-fried parsley.

70

POACHED GOOSNARGH
CHICKEN SALAD WITH LENTILS

SERVES 4
2 chicken breasts, each 200g, skinned
1 tbsp parsley stalks
1 tbsp black peppercorns
4 spring onions
1 garlic clove, peeled
salt and pepper

LENTILS
200g Puy lentils, washed
1 red onion, finely chopped
1 red pepper, diced
olive oil for frying
50ml groundnut oil
50ml extra virgin olive oil
50ml sherry vinegar
juice of ½ lemon
1 tbsp chopped parsley

1 To shape the breasts into neat cylinders, wrap them individually in cling film. Put the chicken breasts, parsley stalks, 1 tsp salt, the peppercorns, onions and garlic in a pan. Cover with water and bring to the boil. Remove from the heat, cover and leave to poach in the residual heat for 2 hours.

2 Meanwhile, cook the lentils in water until al dente; drain. Gently fry the onion and red pepper in a little olive oil until soft. Tip into a bowl and add the lentils. Stir together, then allow to cool.

3 Make a dressing by whisking together the groundnut and extra virgin olive oils, vinegar and lemon juice. Season well. Toss the lentils in the dressing. Add the parsley just before serving.

4 Drain the chicken breasts. When they are cold, unwrap them and slice into neat medallions. Divide into four portions.

5 To serve, spoon the lentil salad on to plates and sit the chicken medallions on top.

72

SALAD OF SLOW-ROASTED WOOD PIGEON
WITH HAZELNUTS AND APPLES

SERVES 4
4 wood pigeons, oven ready
olive oil
1 garlic clove, sliced
sprig of thyme
1 bay leaf
25g butter
salt and pepper

HAZELNUT VINAIGRETTE
150ml hazelnut oil
3 tbsp Champagne vinegar or white
   wine vinegar
sprig of thyme
½ small garlic clove, lightly bashed

PIGEON SAUCE
3 tbsp groundnut or vegetable oil
20g unsalted butter
50g shallots, sliced

½ head of garlic, cut crossways
100g button mushrooms, sliced
1 tbsp sherry vinegar
150ml Madeira
500ml chicken stock
100ml veal glacé
3 tbsp double cream
5 black peppercorns
2 sprigs of thyme

TO SERVE
2 Cox's apples, peeled and diced
mixed baby salad leaves
handful of toasted and skinned hazelnuts,
   halved
3 shallots, finely chopped
mixed herbs, such as chervil, chives
   and marjoram

1 Remove the breasts from the pigeons (reserve the carcasses) and tie each into a cylinder shape using a fine string. Place on a deep tray, cover with olive oil and add the garlic, thyme and bay leaf. Cover and marinate overnight in the fridge.
2 Meanwhile, to make the vinaigrette, mix all the ingredients together in a bowl and transfer to a bottle. Set aside.
3 For the pigeon sauce, chop the reserved pigeon carcasses into small pieces. Heat the oil in a roasting tin on top of the stove. Add the pigeon carcasses and fry to colour lightly, then add the butter and continue to colour. Stir in the shallots and garlic, and lightly colour the shallots. Add the mushrooms and sweat for 5 minutes. Pour in the sherry vinegar and stir to deglaze the pan, then cook until reduced to nothing. Pour in the Madeira and bring to the boil, then boil to reduce by two-thirds. Stir in the chicken stock, veal glacé, cream, peppercorns, thyme and salt. Bring to the boil and skim the scum, then reduce to a gentle simmer and cook for 30 minutes. Pass through a colander, then a fine sieve into a clean saucepan. Boil to reduce to a sauce consistency. Finish by whisking in a little of the hazelnut vinaigrette, enough to taste. Set aside.
4 When ready to serve, remove the pigeon breasts from the olive oil and season with salt and pepper. Heat the 25g butter in a frying pan, add the pigeon breasts and fry

for 4–6 minutes to colour; they will be medium rare. Remove from the heat and leave to rest for about 5 minutes.

5 To serve, reheat the pigeon sauce. Toss the apples with some of the remaining vinaigrette. Do the same with the mixed salad, then the hazelnuts, shallots and herbs. Carve each pigeon breast into three slices and place on serving plates. Pile the mixed salad on top. Scatter the apple dice and hazelnut mixture around the plate and finish with a drizzle of the pigeon sauce.

GALTON BLACKISTON

TERRINE OF HAM HOCK
WITH PICCALILLI AND TOASTED
SPELT BREAD WITH ENGLISH MUSTARD BUTTER

SERVES 8

PICCALILLI
600ml white wine vinegar
250g caster sugar
50g freshly grated horseradish
  (or creamed horseradish sauce)
2–3 sprigs of thyme
1 bay leaf
2 large red chillies, deseeded and diced
300g red peppers, deseeded
200g yellow peppers, deseeded
200g cucumber, peeled and deseeded
200g courgettes
200g fennel bulb
200g celery sticks
200g button or pickling onions
50g salt
40g cornflour
15g turmeric (2 tbsp)
75g Dijon mustard (6 tbsp)

TERRINE
3 green (unsmoked) ham hocks on the
  bone, each about 1.2kg
2 pig's trotters, split lengthways
1 tsp coriander seeds
1 tsp black peppercorns
bouquet garni (2 bay leaves, few sprigs of
  thyme, 2 sprigs of parsley and few
  optional sprigs of tarragon, tied together)
2 shallots, chopped
1 bottle (75cl) white wine
4 tbsp white wine vinegar
2 tbsp small capers, rinsed and drained
50g gherkins, rinsed and chopped
generous handful of parsley, finely chopped
salt and pepper

NORFOLK SPELT BREAD
350g Letheringsett spelt flour, sifted
1 tsp salt
1 tsp English mustard powder
40g soft salted butter
50g chopped walnuts
25g sultanas (optional)
10g fresh yeast
1 tsp caster sugar
60–75ml lukewarm milk
60–75ml lukewarm water
1 egg, beaten

ENGLISH MUSTARD BUTTER
50g very soft unsalted butter
1 heaped tsp English mustard powder

1 Make the piccalilli well ahead as it improves with keeping. Combine the vinegar, sugar, horseradish, thyme, bay leaf and half of the chilli in a saucepan. Heat gently until the sugar has dissolved, then bring to the boil. Simmer gently for a couple of minutes. Set aside to cool, then strain and set aside.

2 Meanwhile, cut all the vegetables into small cubes (the onions can either be left whole or cut into halves or quarters). Pour 2 litres of water into a large bowl and stir in the salt. Immerse all the vegetables in the salted water and leave to soak overnight. The next morning, rinse the vegetables and drain well, then place in a large bowl.

3 Put the remaining chilli, the cornflour, turmeric and mustard in a bowl and mix to a runny paste with about 150ml of the cold strained vinegar. Bring the rest of the strained vinegar to the boil in a clean saucepan over a moderate heat, then stir in the paste mixture. Cook for 2–3 minutes, stirring, until thickened.

4 Pour the hot mixture over the vegetables and mix thoroughly. Fill five sterilised 450g jam jars with the piccalilli. When cool, cover and seal. (The piccalilli will keep for up to a month in a cool place. Keep in the fridge once opened. It's good to make plenty, as it goes well with a lot of snacky foods.)

5 To make the terrine, put the ham hocks and pig's trotters in a large saucepan and cover with cold water. Bring to the boil and boil steadily for 10 minutes, skimming off any scum from the surface. Remove the hocks and trotters, and discard the water.

6 Return the hocks and trotters to the cleaned pan. Add the coriander seeds, peppercorns, bouquet garni and shallots. Pour in the wine and vinegar, and add enough cold water to just cover the ingredients. Bring to the boil, then simmer very, very gently (no need to cover the pan) for a minimum of 2 hours or until the hocks are tender and the meat flakes easily.

7 Leave the hocks and trotters to cool in the liquid for about an hour. Remove the hocks, cover with cling film and set aside. Discard the trotters.

8 Strain the cooking liquid through a muslin-lined sieve into a clean pan. Place the pan on a high heat and bring the liquid to a rapid boil. Boil to reduce down to 650ml, then pass it once again through a sieve lined with a clean piece of muslin into a jug. Set aside.

9 Line a 1.5-litre terrine with a double layer of cling film, leaving some film draping over the sides.

10 Peel the skin off the hocks, then shred the meat into nuggets. Place in a large bowl with the capers, gherkins and parsley. Mix well. Taste and season with pepper (add salt only if really necessary). Pile the mixture into the lined terrine and press down firmly. Slowly pour in the reduced liquid, adding just enough to cover the meat. As you pour, tap down well to ensure the liquid is spread throughout the terrine. Cover with the overhanging cling film and chill overnight.

11 To make the spelt bread, put the flour, salt, mustard powder, butter, chopped walnuts and sultanas (if using) in the bowl of a food mixer. Using the dough hook, mix thoroughly together.

12 Combine the yeast and sugar in a bowl, mixing with your fingertips so that the yeast breaks down and becomes smooth and almost liquid. Mix in 60ml each of the warm milk and water and the egg. With the mixer running, slowly pour the yeast mixture into the flour to make quite a soft dough (it will become firmer on kneading), adding a little more warm liquid if needed. Allow the machine to knead the dough for 5–8 minutes or until it comes away from the sides of the bowl and does not stick to your fingers. Remove the bowl from the mixer and cover with a damp tea towel. Leave in a warm place for 1–1½ hours or until the dough has doubled in volume.

13 Line a large baking tray with greaseproof paper. Turn the dough out onto a lightly floured surface and knead well with the palm of your hand, then shape the dough into a plump rectangle. Place it on the baking tray and leave in a warm place for 45 minutes (no need to cover) to prove and double in size again.

14 Preheat the oven to 220°C/gas 7. Bake the bread for 20–25 minutes or until golden and it sounds hollow when you tap your knuckles on the top. Cool on a wire rack.

15 For the mustard butter, beat together the butter and mustard powder in a bowl until thoroughly mixed. Taste and season with salt and pepper. Press into small pots and firm up in the fridge.

16 The terrine is best eaten at room temperature. Serve it sliced, with the piccalilli, slices of toasted spelt bread and English mustard butter.

FILLET OF PERTHSHIRE LAMB
SEARED KIDNEY AND BALSAMIC ONIONS
ROCKET AND BROAD BEANS
WITH ARRAN MUSTARD DRESSING

SERVES 4
4 fillets of lamb
4 lamb kidneys, cut in half and veins
   and skin removed
olive oil
salt and pepper

BALSAMIC ONIONS
6 red onions, sliced
20ml olive oil
about 200ml balsamic vinegar

ARRAN MUSTARD DRESSING
100ml lamb stock
1–2 tsp coarse grain Arran mustard
   (or other good quality wholegrain
   mustard)

BROAD BEAN AND ROCKET SALAD
2 handfuls of baby broad beans
2 handfuls of rocket

1 Preheat the oven to 230°C/gas 8.

2 First prepare the balsamic onions. Sweat the onions in the olive oil, then pour over enough vinegar just to cover the onions. Slowly cook until the vinegar is almost completely reduced. Season before serving.

3 Meanwhile, sear the lamb fillets and kidneys in a little hot oil in a frying pan for 1–2 minutes on each side. Place in the oven and cook for 2 minutes. Remove and leave to rest before slicing.

4 While the lamb is cooking, make the Arran mustard dressing and salad. Reduce the lamb stock by half, then stir in the mustard. Reduce a little more. Meanwhile, blanch the broad beans in boiling salted water for 2 minutes. Drain and refresh, then pop the beans from their skins. Toss the beans with the rocket and a drizzle of the mustard dressing.

5 To serve, slice each lamb fillet at a 45° angle into three pieces. Spoon the balsamic onions on to each warm plate, arrange the pieces of lamb fillet on the onions and top with the kidneys. Add the broad bean and rocket salad and pour the mustard dressing over or around.

CRUBEENS AND BEETROOT
WITH SALAD LEAVES AND SALAD CREAM

SERVES 4

BRINE
900g sea salt
450g light soft brown sugar
1 tbsp saltpetre (optional – it isn't essential,
    but it improves the colour of the meat)
1 clove
10 black peppercorns
6 juniper berries
4 garlic cloves, split in half
1 bay leaf
3 sprigs of thyme

CRUBEENS
6 pig's trotters, well cleaned and
    hairs removed
bouquet garni
mirepoix of diced vegetables (1 carrot,
    2 celery sticks, 1 leek and 1 onion)
1 small ham hock
1 bottle (75cl) dry white wine
olive oil
2 shallots, finely chopped
1 cup chopped parsley
2 tbsp made English mustard
100g fine fresh white breadcrumbs
2 tsp English mustard powder

75g plain flour
2 large eggs, beaten
corn oil for shallow-frying
salt and pepper

SALAD CREAM
1 tsp made English mustard
1 tsp caster sugar
2–3 tbsp white wine vinegar
¼ tsp white pepper
150ml evaporated milk
150ml organic rapeseed oil

BEETROOT RELISH
4 small raw beetroots
1 onion, finely sliced
olive oil
2 tbsp red wine vinegar
50ml red wine
1 tbsp freshly grated horseradish
sugar to taste

TO SERVE
4 small raw beetroots
2 sprigs of thyme
1 garlic clove, unpeeled, pounded flat
organic salad leaves and herbs in season,
    such as frisée, flat-leaf parsley, wood
    sorrel, pea shoots and dandelion

1 Put all the ingredients for the brine in a large saucepan with 3 litres cold water. Bring to the boil, stirring until the sugar has dissolved and skimming off the foam that rises to the surface. Simmer for 10 minutes, then remove from the heat and leave to cool.

2 Put the trotters in a large bowl and pour over the cold brine. Cover the trotters with a plate to keep them submerged, then cover the bowl and leave in the fridge for 24 hours.

3 Drain the trotters and put them in a large saucepan. Cover with cold water, add the bouquet garni and bring to the boil. Reduce the heat, cover and simmer for 3 hours.

4 Preheat the oven to 160°C/gas 3.

5 Make a bed of the vegetable mirepoix on the bottom of a heavy casserole. Set the ham hock on top and pour over the white wine. Cover the pan with cling film, then tie a sheet of foil tightly over the top with string and cover with a tight-fitting lid. Braise in the oven for 3^1/$_2$ hours.

6 Leave both trotters and ham hock to cool in their pans, then remove. Using a very sharp knife, score through the skin and split the trotters in half lengthways. Carefully take out the meat, discarding the bones and gristle but keeping the fat with the meat. Reserve the skins. Shred the trotter meat, and the meat from the ham hock.

7 Heat a splash of olive oil in a heavy frying pan and sweat the shallots, stirring frequently, over a low to medium heat for 8–9 minutes or until softened but not coloured. Remove from the heat and stir in the parsley, then mix with the shredded meats and fat, and the made mustard. Season lightly with salt and pepper. Divide the mixture into four portions.

8 Lay two large (catering-size) sheets of cling film on top of each other on a board and smooth out any wrinkles. Place the trotter skins on the cling film, opening them out and laying them flat. Arrange them close to each other in pairs so you have three rows that make a 'blanket' of skins. Put the meat mixture in the middle of the skins and form into a long sausage, then roll up the sausage so that it is completely encased in the skins. Now roll the sausage in the cling film and twist the ends to seal. Chill overnight.

9 The next day, make the salad cream. Whisk the mustard, sugar and vinegar with the white pepper and ^{1}/$_2$ tsp salt. Add the evaporated milk and continue to whisk. Gradually whisk in the oil to make a cream consistency. Check the seasoning. Keep cool.

10 To make the beetroot relish, peel and grate the raw beetroots, sprinkle with salt and leave to stand for 30 minutes. Rinse off the salt. Sweat the onion in a splash of hot olive oil with some salt and pepper until softened but not coloured. Add the wine vinegar, wine and grated beetroot, and stir. Cover and cook until reduced. Uncover and fold in the horseradish with sugar, salt and pepper to taste. Set aside.

11 Preheat the oven to 180°C/gas 4.

12 Place the whole raw beetroots on a large sheet of oiled foil, add the thyme and garlic, and sprinkle with olive oil, salt and pepper. Close the foil to make a parcel and place on a baking tray. Roast for 30–35 minutes or until the beetroots are tender. Cool, then peel and halve.

13 Remove the cling film from the sausage and cut it in half lengthways. Place each half cut-side down on a board and cut in half lengthways again. Now cut each quarter crossways into five 3–4cm nuggets or crubeens. Mix the breadcrumbs and mustard powder together on a plate. Coat the crubeens in the flour, then in the beaten eggs and finally in the crumbs. Shallow-fry in hot corn oil for 2–3 minutes or until crisp and golden brown. Drain well.

14 To serve, put five crubeens and two beetroot halves on each plate with a spoonful of beetroot relish. Lightly dress the salad leaves with olive oil and seasoning, then put a pile of leaves on each plate. Serve the salad cream in a bowl.

80

POTTED SALT BEEF
WITH LAND CRESS AND RYE TOAST

SERVES 8

1 piece of salted beef brisket, 500–600g
1 carrot
½ onion
¼ leek
½ celery stick
½ head garlic, cut crossways
large sprig each of rosemary and thyme
200g mayonnaise, preferably home-made
25g fresh horseradish, very finely grated
   on a Microplane
1 crisp red-skinned English apple, peeled
   and finely diced
salt and pepper

TO SERVE

4 small handfuls of land cress
   (or other cress)
2 tbsp white wine vinaigrette
dill pickles, cut into wedges
rye sourdough bread, thickly sliced
   and toasted

1 If necessary, soak the brisket in a bowl of cold water for 24 hours in the fridge (ask your butcher for advice on this when you buy the beef).

2 Place the brisket in a large saucepan, cover generously with fresh cold water and bring to the boil over a high heat. When almost boiling, skim off any scum from the surface, and add the vegetables, garlic and herbs. Cover and bring back to the boil, then remove the lid and simmer gently for 3–3¹/₂ hours. The brisket must be submerged all the time during cooking, so check regularly and pour in more water if necessary.

3 At the end of cooking, the brisket should feel very tender when pierced in the middle with the tip of a small sharp knife. Remove the pan from the heat and leave the meat to cool in the liquid for 30 minutes, then remove to a tray and leave until cold. Cover with cling film and chill overnight.

4 The next day, remove any fat and sinews from the meat, then pull the meat into long strands with your fingers. Cut the strands across into 2–3cm strips and place in a bowl. Add the mayonnaise, horseradish and diced apple. Gently fold together until evenly mixed, then add seasoning to taste.

5 For each serving, place a metal ring measuring 5cm in diameter and 4cm deep on an individual serving plate. Fill the ring with potted beef and level it off, then lift the ring up and off while gently pressing down on the mix. Toss the land cress in the dressing and arrange in a small mound next to the potted beef along with wedges of dill pickle. Serve with rye toast.

82

HOME-CURED
SOUTH DEVON BEEF
WITH WHOLEGRAIN MUSTARD VINAIGRETTE

SERVES 4

600g salt

150g sugar

2 litres red wine (Cabernet Sauvignon)

25g whole black peppercorns

1 heaped tsp juniper berries

15g thyme leaves

15g rosemary

1 beef topside or silverside joint,
about 800g

WHOLEGRAIN MUSTARD VINAIGRETTE

75g wholegrain mustard

50ml white wine vinegar

200ml olive oil

salt and white pepper

TO SERVE

olive oil

young mixed salad leaves

picked mixed herbs (chive flowers, chervil,
baby purple basil and mustard cress)

1 Combine the salt, sugar and 2 litres water in a saucepan and bring to the boil, stirring until dissolved. Remove from the heat and allow to cool.

2 In another pan, bring the wine to the boil. Flambé to burn off the alcohol completely. Once there are no more flames, remove from the heat and allow to cool slightly, then add the peppercorns, juniper berries and herbs. Cool completely.

3 Combine the two mixtures in a bowl and put in the beef. Cover and leave to marinate in the fridge for 10 days.

4 Remove the beef from the marinade (discard the marinade) and wrap it in a muslin cloth. Hang in a cool, airy place for 4–8 days, depending on the environment and humidity. When ready, the surface of the meat will be dry.

5 Unwrap the beef and cut away the dry meat. Wrap the joint in cling film and put it into the freezer. The beef is best kept frozen to prevent it from discolouring; the meat will discolour if left in the freezer for longer than 3 months.

6 To make the vinaigrette, place the mustard in a bowl and whisk in the vinegar and 50ml water, then the olive oil. Season with salt and pepper. Emulsify using a whisk or a hand blender. (This vinaigrette will keep well in the fridge.)

7 To serve, slice the beef from frozen and arrange on the plates. Brush lightly with olive oil to prevent the beef from oxidising, then leave until the beef is at room temperature At the last minute brush with the mustard vinaigrette. Toss the mixed salad leaves with vinaigrette and use with the herbs to dress the beef.

MIXED BEETS AND ASPARAGUS
WITH WOOLSERY GOAT'S CHEESE

SERVES 4

250g raw beetroots, preferably mixed
   varieties and colours, such as white,
   golden and red
250g asparagus
handful of silver sorrel leaves
150–200g Woolsery goat's cheese,
   broken into small nuggets
2–3 pickled walnuts, diced
salt and pepper

DRESSING

1 tbsp cider vinegar
3 tbsp cold-pressed rapeseed oil

1 Cook the beetroots in their skins in boiling salted water for about an hour or until tender. (If using different colours, cook them separately.) Drain and leave to cool, then rub off the skins.

2 Remove the woody ends from the asparagus, and cook the spears in boiling salted water for 5–6 minutes or until tender. Drain and leave to cool.

3 Cut the beetroots into bite-sized pieces (a mixture of slices and wedges). Cut the asparagus spears in half.

4 Make the dressing by whisking the vinegar and oil with seasoning to taste.

5 To serve, carefully arrange the beetroots and asparagus on plates with the sorrel leaves, then scatter the goat's cheese and pickled walnuts over the top. Drizzle over the dressing just before serving.

84

ENGLISH SALAD PLATE

SERVES 4

BEETROOT DRESSING
200ml ruby Port
2 tbsp red wine vinegar
1 medium raw beetroot, peeled and
   finely grated
50ml groundnut oil
50ml walnut oil
salt and pepper

BEETROOT SALAD WITH PORT
3–4 medium to large raw beetroots
50g soft goat's cheese
1 tbsp single cream or crème fraîche
   (optional)
whole or snipped chives

CELERIAC AND PEAR SALAD
1 small celeriac
1 large or 2 small pears
juice of 1 lime
2 heaped tbsp mayonnaise
1–2 tsp wholegrain mustard

BLUE CHEESE CAESAR GEM SALAD
50ml mayonnaise
100ml crème fraîche
100g blue cheese, at room temperature,
   broken into small nuggets
1 small garlic clove, crushed
1 tsp Dijon mustard
1 tsp capers
1 tbsp lemon or lime juice
2 Little Gem lettuces

GARNISH (OPTIONAL)
rocket, watercress or chives
olive or walnut oil

1 First make the beetroot dressing. Boil the ruby Port until reduced to 50ml.
Whisk together the reduced Port, red wine vinegar, 2 tbsp water and the grated
beetroot. Mix the two oils, then whisk them into the beetroot mixture. Season
with salt and pepper. Leave to infuse while you cook the beetroots for the salad.
Before using the dressing, pass it through a sieve.
2 Cook the beetroots either by boiling for 1 hour until tender, or by wrapping in
foil and baking on sea salt in a preheated 180°C/gas 4 oven for up to 2 hours. Once
cooked, leave to cool. Peel the beetroots and cut each into four or five slices. The
slices can now be shaped into neat rounds of the same size using a round cutter.
Place in a bowl, season and top with the beetroot dressing. Set aside.
3 Beat the goat's cheese until smooth. If still slightly grainy and dry, stir in the
chosen cream and season with salt and pepper, if needed. Add the chives. Mould
the cheese between two spoons to create four oval 'quenelle' shapes. Keep in a cool
place until serving time.
4 To serve the beetroot salad, lift the beetroot slices from the dressing and layer
them into four stacks, set on the plates and drizzle with a little more dressing.
Place the cheese quenelles on top just before serving.

5 Next prepare the celeriac and pear salad. Peel the celeriac and thinly slice, then cut each slice into matchsticks. Peel and grate the pear, stirring in the lime juice to prevent discoloration. Mix with the celeriac and season with coarse sea salt and pepper. Mix the mayonnaise with the preferred quantity of mustard, then stir into the celeriac and pear mixture to bind. Refrigerate until required. The celeriac and pear flavour will become stronger as it rests.

6 Finally, prepare the blue cheese Caesar Gem salad. In a small food processor, blitz together all of the ingredients, except 50g of the cheese and the lettuces, until smooth. Season with a twist of pepper. The dressing can be left with a slight coarse consistency, or blitzed for a smooth finish. If too thick, whisk in water to loosen.

7 Discard the outer leaves of the lettuces and separate the remaining leaves. To serve, mix the remaining blue cheese nuggets amongst the leaves and arrange in piles on the plates. Drizzle with the dressing.

8 To assemble, arrange a portion of each salad on the four plates. Scatter rocket, watercress or chive sticks on top and finish with a trickle or two of olive or walnut oil.

Long-neglected, beetroot is now a fashionable 'superfood'. Low in fat and rich in vitamins and minerals such as zinc and iron, it even contains a compound – betaine – which is said to fight depression.

LEEK AND WILD MUSHROOM TART
WITH HOLLANDAISE

SERVES 4
250g shortcrust pastry
2 leeks, finely sliced
butter
200g wild mushrooms
olive oil
finely chopped flat-leaf parsley
green salad to serve

HOLLANDAISE SAUCE
8 tbsp white wine vinegar
1 shallot, finely sliced
sprig of thyme
1 bay leaf
4 black peppercorns
3 egg yolks
150g unsalted butter, melted
1 tsp lemon juice

OPTIONAL ADDITIONS
fried quail's eggs
sliced fresh truffle

1 Preheat the oven to 180°C/gas 4. Roll out the pastry and use to line four 10cm tart rings placed on a baking tray. Line them with greaseproof paper and weight down with dried beans, then bake blind for 12–15 minutes or until golden brown. Leave to cool until needed. Remove from the rings before filling.

2 To make the hollandaise, put the vinegar, shallot, herbs and peppercorns in a pan and reduce by two-thirds. Strain the mixture into a bowl and whisk in the egg yolks. Set the bowl over another bowl of warm water and slowly add the butter, whisking well after each addition. When all the butter has all been incorporated add the lemon juice and 2 tsp water. Taste and season if necessary. Cover with cling film and set aside in a warm place.

3 Lightly sauté the leeks in butter until soft.

4 Meanwhile, sauté the mushrooms in olive oil, then toss with some parsley.

5 Fill the pastry cases with the leeks and mushrooms. To make them extra special you can add some fried quail's eggs or sliced truffle. Heat in the oven for 10 minutes.

6 Cover the tarts with the hollandaise, then flash under a hot grill to glaze. Serve with a crisp green salad.

88

GLAZED
GOAT'S CHEESE AND BEETROOT
WITH A SALAD OF WELSH HERBS
AND BEETROOT DRESSING

SERVES 4

4 Welsh goat's cheeses, each 120g

sprigs of thyme

olive oil

120g sugar

3 large beetroots, cooked, peeled and roughly diced

2 tsp balsamic vinegar

12 or more raw baby beetroots

150g Snowdon mountain herbs, such as wood sorrel,
    hairy bittercress, pennywort or whatever is in season

20g toasted pine nuts

salt and pepper

1 Put the cheeses in a bowl with some thyme and olive oil to cover. Leave to marinate while you prepare the beetroot dressing.

2 Melt the sugar in a heavy-bottomed pan on a moderate heat, then cook until the sugar has turned golden brown. Add the cooked beetroot and cook for a further 3 minutes, stirring until the beetroot is completely coated with the caramel. Remove from the heat and add the balsamic vinegar. Transfer to a food processor and blend to a smooth consistency.

3 Pour the purée into a muslin-lined colander set in a bowl and allow the liquid to drain through. Season the liquid to taste and double the volume with olive oil to create a dressing. Season the purée. Set both dressing and purée aside.

4 Preheat the oven to 140°C/gas 1.

5 Wrap the baby beetroots in a foil envelope with some sprigs of thyme. Place in the oven and bake for 10–12 minutes. Peel the beetroots and leave to cool.

6 Remove the cheeses from the marinade and blot off any excess oil with kitchen paper. Glaze the tops of the cheeses using a blow torch (or under a hot grill) until golden brown.

7 Dress the Welsh herbs in the beetroot dressing.

8 To assemble, spread a tablespoon of beetroot purée on each plate. Add the dressed herbs and position the glazed cheeses on top. Drizzle round the remainder of the beetroot dressing, add the baby beetroots and sprinkle with toasted pine nuts. Serve with warm laver bread.

90

TERRINE OF CAPRICORN
GOAT'S CHEESE, APPLES AND CELERY
AND A SALAD WITH TOASTED WALNUTS
AND RAISINS

SERVES 4

TERRINE OF GOAT'S CHEESE
300g Capricorn goat's cheese, or other mild
    but mature goat's cheese that isn't too soft
200g plain Greek yoghurt
200ml whipping or double cream
4 gelatine leaves, soaked in cold water for
    at least 10 minutes
60g finely diced celery
60g finely diced apple
100g goat's cheese log (plain, not covered
    with ash or herbs), cut into lengths
salt and white pepper

MARINATED RAISINS
40g raisins
100ml Down St Mary sparkling wine,
    or other sparkling or still wine

WALNUT VINAIGRETTE
100ml walnut oil
75ml groundnut oil
50ml Champagne or white wine vinegar

TO SERVE
80g walnut halves
milk
1 Cox's apple
mixed salad leaves

1 First put the raisins to soak in the wine for 24 hours.

2 To make the terrine, place the 300g goat's cheese in a food processor and blend until a smooth purée. Blend in the Greek yoghurt, then remove from the food processor and place in a bowl.

3 Heat the cream until hot but not boiling. Gently squeeze the softened gelatine dry, then add to the hot cream and stir until completely melted. Cool slightly, then whisk this into the yoghurt and goat's cheese purée. Add the diced celery and apple, and season with a little salt and pepper.

4 Line a terrine mould or small loaf tin with cling film (or you can use individual moulds), then fill halfway with the cheese and yoghurt mixture, spreading it evenly into the corners. Place the goat's cheese lengths down the middle. Top with the remaining cheese and yoghurt mixture, smoothing the surface flat. Tap the terrine on the work surface to ensure there are no air pockets. Cover and leave to set in the refrigerator for 1 hour.

5 Mix all the ingredients for the vinaigrette together, with salt and pepper to taste, and place in a bottle or plastic pourer. Before using the vinaigrette, shake it well.

6 To prepare the walnuts, put them in a small pan and cover with a mixture of half water and half milk. Bring to the boil, then remove from the heat and leave to soak for a few minutes. Drain and peel off the thin brown skins, using a small paring knife. This is a bit fiddly, but takes away any bitterness in the nuts. Toast the walnuts in a dry pan, or in the oven, then set aside.

7 When ready to serve, drain some of the raisins from the wine and place in a bowl with some of the walnuts. Add a little vinaigrette and toss to coat. Slice the Cox's apple finely, then cut into thin batons. Toss with some vinaigrette.

8 Combine the salad leaves with the remaining drained raisins and toasted walnuts in another bowl and dress with vinaigrette.

9 Turn the terrine out of the mould and slice using a hot knife.

10 To assemble, place the terrine at one end of each plate (ideally use long or oval plates). Pile the salad at the other end of the plate. Put the raisins and walnuts into the middle and place the apple batons on top, or sprinkle them around the terrine.

PASTRY LAYERS WITH
WILD MUSHROOMS AND NORFOLK ASPARAGUS
BLUE CHEESE DRESSING AND SALAD LEAVES

SERVES 4
2 shallots, finely chopped
1 garlic clove, finely chopped
3 tbsp olive oil
225g mixed wild mushrooms
2 tbsp chopped parsley
16 asparagus spears, trimmed to 7.5cm long
young salad leaves
salt and pepper

PASTRY
110g soft plain flour
pinch of cayenne pepper

110g salted butter
175g mature Cheddar, finely grated
1 egg yolk

BLUE CHEESE DRESSING
1 tsp runny honey
1 tsp Dijon mustard
1 tsp red wine vinegar
150ml groundnut or extra virgin olive oil
2 tsp lemon juice
1 shallot, very finely chopped
50g firm Binham Blue cheese, crumbled

1 Begin by making the pastry. Put all the ingredients, with the exception of the egg yolk, in the bowl of a food processor and whiz quickly to combine, then add the egg yolk and process again until the pastry comes together. Divide in half, shape into two balls and wrap individually in cling film. Leave to rest in the fridge for an hour.
2 Preheat the oven to 180°C/gas 4.
3 Roll out one of the pastry balls on a lightly floured surface as thinly as you dare (about 3mm thick is ideal). Make sure you keep moving the pastry to prevent it from sticking. Cut into 12 neat rectangles 7.5cm long and 5cm wide (re-roll any trimmings). Transfer the rectangles to a baking tray lined with baking parchment, leaving a little space between them. Cover with another sheet of baking parchment and place another baking tray on top. I set a couple of bricks on this to weight it down even more. Bake for 20 minutes or until the pastry is golden and crisp. Leave the biscuits to cool and firm on the tray, then transfer to a wire rack and set aside.
4 Next make the dressing. In a bowl whisk together the honey, mustard and a good pinch each of salt and pepper, then whisk in the vinegar. Slowly pour in the oil and lemon juice, whisking constantly. Add the shallot and blue cheese.
5 Heat a frying pan and quickly fry the shallots and garlic in the oil until soft, then add the wild mushrooms and season. Continue cooking over a high heat until the mushrooms soften. Transfer to a bowl and add the chopped parsley. Leave to cool.
6 Cook the asparagus in a pan of boiling water until just tender. Drain and refresh.
7 To serve, lay a biscuit on each plate. Spoon some mushrooms along the biscuit and top with two asparagus spears. Cover with another biscuit and add the remaining mushrooms and asparagus. Put the final biscuit on top. Spoon the dressing around and garnish with some young salad leaves.

HAM HOCK TERRINE
PICKLED MUSHROOMS AND APPLE COMPOTE

SERVES 4
4 ham hocks
2 large carrots, chopped
2 large onions, chopped
4 sprigs of thyme
1 bulb garlic, cut in half crossways
large bunch of parsley, chopped
salt and pepper

PICKLED MUSHROOMS
4 shallots, finely chopped
100ml white wine vinegar
250g girolles, stalks scraped

APPLE COMPOTE
4 Cox's apples, peeled, cored and
   chopped
knob of butter

1 Put the ham hocks in a large pan and cover with water. Bring to the boil and skim. Add the carrots, onions, thyme and garlic and simmer for 3 hours or until the meat comes away from the bone. Remove from the heat and allow to cool.
2 Drain the hocks, reserving the liquid, and pick the meat from the bone. Place the meat in a large bowl and season with salt, pepper and chopped parsley.
3 Pass the liquid through a sieve into a saucepan and reduce it by one-third over a high heat. Add the liquid to the meat and mix together, then place in a 30cm long terrine mould lined with cling film. Put the terrine in the fridge to set.
4 To prepare the pickled mushrooms, cook the shallots in the vinegar and 100ml water for a few minutes, then pour the hot liquid on to the mushrooms in a bowl. Leave to cool.
5 Cook the apples with the butter until soft, then crush with a fork and season with salt and pepper.
6 To serve, cut the terrine into slices 1cm thick and place on the plates. Drain the mushrooms and sprinkle around the terrine. Finish with a quenelle of apple compote on top of the terrine.

Ham hock, the small joint at the lower portion of a pig's hind leg, is a traditional ingredient of cawl, a slow-cooked Welsh broth.

CULLEN SKINK

SERVES 4
20g unsalted butter
2 banana shallots, finely diced
100g leek, white only, finely diced
2 medium garlic cloves, crushed
    then finely diced
200g Ratte potatoes, boiled until soft
    then peeled
2 Arbroath smokies, skin and bones removed
100ml whole milk
100ml double cream
pepper

FISH STOCK
2 tbsp olive oil
100g chopped white vegetables, such as
white of leeks, fennel and onion
100ml dry white wine
2 Arbroath smokies, roughly chopped

GARNISH
1 Arbroath smokie, skin and bones removed
chopped chives

1 To make the fish stock, put the oil into a heavy saucepan and heat, then add the vegetables and stir well to coat with the oil. Cover and sweat over a low heat for about 10 minutes; do not allow them to colour. Take the lid off the pan and pour in the white wine. Boil for 1 minute. Now add 1.2 litres of water and the smokies. Bring up almost to the boil, then skim well. Reduce the heat and simmer very gently for about 20 minutes. Allow to cool. Once cold, strain the stock through a very fine sieve, preferably lined with a double layer of muslin. (The stock can be made 2 days ahead, then kept chilled until needed.)

2 To make the soup, put a large saucepan over a medium heat. Add the butter and, when it has melted, throw in the shallots, leek and garlic. Cover and sweat for 5–10 minutes, but don't allow the vegetables to colour.

3 Add the cooked potatoes. Flake the smokies and add to the pan. Cover and sweat for a further 2 minutes, then add 1 litre of the stock and season with pepper. Bring to the boil and simmer for 8–10 minutes.

4 Take the pan off the heat and allow to cool slightly. Carefully pour the mixture into a blender and put on the lid. Take the stopper out of the hole in the lid and cover the hole with a tea towel to stop the hot mix splattering. Blitz for a few seconds, then slowly add the milk and cream through the hole. When it's all added and the mixture is smooth, pass through a chinois to give a fine, velvety texture.

5 To serve, pour the soup into a clean pan and heat gently to avoid burning. Flake the remaining smokie and divide among four warmed shallow bowls. Ladle in the soup and garnish with chopped chives.

96

WARM SEARED PIGEON
WITH A CARAMELISED RED ONION TART
AND WILD GARLIC DRESSING

SERVES 4
4 pigeon crowns, boned and halved to
   make 8 suprêmes (boneless breasts with
   wing bones attached)
olive oil
4 small handfuls of mixed salad leaves
salt and pepper

RED ONION TARTS
25g salted butter
25g light soft brown sugar
2 red onions, sliced into half rings
75ml red wine

75ml red wine vinegar
1 star anise
½ x 375g sheet of ready-rolled puff pastry
1 medium egg yolk mixed with 1 tsp water

WILD GARLIC DRESSING
large handful of young wild garlic leaves
4 tbsp olive oil
juice of ½ orange
juice of ½ lemon

1 Ask your poulterer or butcher to make the pigeon suprêmes, and to scrape the wing bones clean for an attractive presentation.

2 For the tarts, melt the butter in a saucepan, add the sugar and cook over a medium heat for 3–5 minutes until becoming golden brown and caramelised. Mix in the onions. The sugar will go into lumps, but don't worry. Add the wine, vinegar and star anise, put the lid on and cook over a medium heat for 15–20 minutes or until the onions soften and reduce down. Remove from the heat.

3 Preheat the oven to 160°C/gas 3.

4 Lay the sheet of puff pastry on a floured surface and brush with the egg yolk wash. Working from top to bottom, mark wavy lines across the pastry using the tines of a fork. Cut out four 10cm squares and place them on a non-stick baking sheet. Press a 5cm plain, round pastry cutter into the middle of one of the squares. Spoon in some of the onions, allowing about 1 tbsp per square, then carefully remove the cutter. Repeat with the remaining pastry squares and onions.

5 Bake the onion tarts for 10–15 minutes or until golden brown. Remove from the oven and leave to cool. Increase the oven temperature to 200°C/gas 6.

6 To make the dressing, plunge the wild garlic leaves into a saucepan of boiling salted water and blanch for 1–2 seconds. Drain and refresh in iced water, then drain again and squeeze out as much water as possible. Work the blanched garlic to a purée in a blender with the oil, orange and lemon juices, and salt and pepper. Pass through a sieve and set aside.

7 Season the pigeon suprêmes. Heat a heavy ovenproof frying pan until hot, then add a little olive oil and put in the suprêmes, skin-side down. Sear for 1 minute or until the skin is golden and crisp, then transfer the pan to the oven to roast for 3 minutes. Remove the pan from the oven and place the pigeon suprêmes on a wire rack to rest for 5 minutes.

8 Meanwhile, reheat the onion tarts in the oven for a few minutes, and toss the salad leaves with the dressing.

9 To serve, set the warm onion tarts on the plates. Link two pigeon suprêmes together with their wing bones and place skin-side up on top of each tart. Arrange the dressed salad leaves alongside.

RICHARD CORRIGAN

COLCANNON SOUP

SERVES 4
2 tbsp unsalted butter
1 large onion, chopped
4 garlic cloves, chopped
250g potatoes, preferably Romano or
   Desirée, peeled and thinly sliced
ham stock or chicken stock
bouquet garni

1 Hispi cabbage, shredded
300ml double cream
salt and pepper

TO SERVE
8 rashers of bacon, preferably O'Doherty's
   Black Bacon, grilled
slices of toasted wheaten bread

1 Heat the butter in a large saucepan and sweat the onion, garlic and potato slices for 5 minutes without colouring. Pour over enough stock to cover all the vegetables, and add the bouquet garni and seasoning. Bring to the boil, then cover and simmer for about 15 minutes.

2 Add the cabbage and bring back to the boil, then remove from the heat right away. Pour into a sieve set in a bowl and immediately chill the stock and vegetables separately in the fridge.

3 When both stock and vegetables are chilled, purée together in a blender until smooth, then pass through a sieve into a clean saucepan. (If you prefer a more rustic texture, don't blend or pass.)

4 To serve, reheat the soup, enrich with the cream and check the seasoning. Serve piping hot in earthenware bowls, with grilled bacon on slices of toasted wheaten bread.

98

MUSSEL BREE

SERVES 4

1.5kg fresh mussels in the shell
175ml dry white wine
50g butter
2 shallots, chopped
2 celery sticks, finely chopped
1 carrot, finely chopped
1 garlic clove, crushed and finely chopped

200ml double cream
1 tsp lemon juice
pinch of cayenne
50g cooked basmati rice (you need
about 20g raw rice)
2 tbsp finely chopped chives
olive oil for drizzling (optional)

1 To prepare the mussels, place them in a bowl of cold water and scrub well to remove any dirt or barnacles. Tip the water out and repeat this process until the water is clear. Pull out the beards, which are the tough fibres protruding from between the shells. Discard any open mussels that don't close when tapped on the work surface.

2 Heat a large pan with a lid until hot. Have the wine close at hand. Lift the mussels into the pan, add the wine and slam on the lid. Cook over a high temperature, shaking the pan from time to time, until all the mussels have opened. This should take 3–4 minutes. Discard any mussels that don't open during cooking.

3 Pour the mussels into a colander lined with muslin and set over a bowl. Reserve the liquid that drains into the bowl (you should have about 300ml). When cool enough to handle, shell the mussels, leaving a few in their shells to garnish. Set the mussels and the strained cooking liquid aside.

4 In a large pan, melt the butter over a medium heat and add the vegetables and garlic. Cook until soft; don't allow them to brown. Add 300ml of the mussel cooking liquid and bring to the boil. Add the cream and stir in, then add the lemon juice, cayenne and rice. Simmer for a couple of minutes.

5 Purée in a blender, then pass through a fine sieve. Pour the soup into a clean pan.

6 To serve, reheat the soup gently, then add the mussels and allow them to warm through. Divide among four warmed bowls and garnish with a sprinkling of chopped chives and an optional drizzle of olive oil.

100

UNCLE ARWYN'S
BEETROOT SOUP

SERVES 4
1 medium onion, sliced
olive oil
4 large raw beetroots, about 500g total weight
600ml vegetable stock
12 raw baby beetroots
sprig of thyme
150ml crème fraîche
salt and pepper

1 Cook the onion with a little olive oil in a heavy-bottomed saucepan for about 5 minutes or until just softened. While the onions are cooking, peel the large beetroots and cut into small dice. Add to the onions and cook for another 5 minutes. Pour in the vegetable stock, season and bring to the boil. Lower the heat and leave to simmer for 20–30 minutes or until the beetroot is tender.

2 Preheat the oven to 160°C/gas 3.

3 While the soup is cooking, season the baby beetroots with salt and pepper, and place in a small roasting tin with the sprig of thyme. Roast for 20–25 minutes or until soft. Remove from the oven and peel off the skin.

4 When the soup is done, tip the contents of the pan into a blender or food processor and process to a smooth purée.

5 To serve, reheat the soup if necessary. Place the whole roasted baby beetroots in soup bowls. Ladle the soup over and finish each serving with a spoonful of crème fraîche.

102

FIELD MUSHROOM SOUP
WITH RED MULLET

SERVES 4
1kg wide cap field mushrooms
150ml olive oil
3 large shallots, finely sliced
2 garlic cloves, crushed
juice of ½ lemon
1 litre hot vegetable or chicken stock
250ml cream
150g unsalted butter, diced (optional)
salt and pepper

GARNISH
100g mixed wild mushrooms
olive oil
4 small fillets of fresh red mullet,
   scaled

1 First make the soup. Remove the dark gills from the field mushrooms and discard. Wash and dry the mushrooms, then slice 2mm thick.
2 Heat the oil in a large heavy-bottomed pan, add the shallots and cook until lightly coloured. Add the garlic and cook until a little soft, then add the sliced mushrooms and season with salt and a few turns of fresh black pepper. Cook for 5–8 minutes or until lightly coloured. Add the lemon juice and reduce a little, then add the stock and bring to a rapid simmer. Turn to a low heat and simmer for 15 minutes.
3 Check the seasoning is correct, then ladle the soup into a blender or food processor and purée until smooth. Pass the soup through a fine sieve into a clean pan and stir in the cream. Set aside. Before serving, heat the soup and stir in the optional butter to make it really silky.
4 Heat some olive oil in a non-stick pan, add the wild mushrooms and quickly stir fry until wilted. Season with salt, then remove the mushrooms from the pan and reserve on kitchen paper.
5 Wipe out the pan, then heat some more olive oil in it. Season both sides of the fish fillets with salt, then place gently in the pan, skin side down. Give the pan a little shake to ensure that the fish doesn't stick. The fillets may curl up, but do not press them down as this will zip back the skin; simply leave them and they should flatten out naturally. Cook for about 1¹/₂ minutes, then turn over and cook for a further 1 minute. Take the fish out of the pan and drain briefly on kitchen paper.
6 To assemble, put a small mound of wild mushrooms in the middle of each warm, wide-rimmed soup bowl, place the red mullet on top and pour the soup around. To finish you can drizzle some nice olive oil in a ring on the soup. Serve immediately.

104

CAWL CENNIN
WITH CAERPHILLY CHEESE

SERVES 4
5–6 leeks, finely sliced
200g Caerphilly cheese
fresh crusty bread to serve

STOCK
1 piece of uncooked bacon (hock or collar),
    about 1kg
2 onions, cut in half
2 carrots, cut into rough chunks
4–5 celery sticks, cut into rough chunks
1 head of garlic, halved crossways
small bunch of thyme
3–4 bay leaves
1 tsp black peppercorns

1 To make the stock, put all the ingredients in a large saucepan, cover with cold water and bring to the boil. Turn the heat down to a gentle simmer and cook uncovered for 2–3 hours, skimming frequently.

2 Remove the pan from the heat and allow to settle, then pass the liquid through a very fine sieve into a bowl. Chill the stock overnight. Reserve the cooked bacon.

3 The next day, remove the fat from the surface of the stock, then reheat and taste it. If you prefer a stronger flavour, you can reduce and concentrate the stock, but be careful not to make it too salty.

4 Strain the stock into a clean pan, throw in the sliced leeks and simmer for about 5 minutes or until tender. At this point, you can add some chunks of the cooked bacon (this is optional, as all the flavour is now in the stock). Taste for seasoning, and season only if necessary.

5 To serve, ladle the soup into individual bowls and crumble the cheese over the top. Serve hot, with fresh crusty bread.

LEEK AND POTATO SOUP
WITH POACHED OYSTERS

SERVES 4
25g butter
1 tbsp olive oil
1 small white onion, finely chopped
4 large leeks, about 300g total weight,
    finely sliced
2 large potatoes, peeled and cut into cubes
1 bouquet garni
8 small rock oysters
fish stock
snipped chives

CHICKEN STOCK
4 chickens, cut into portions
1 leek, roughly chopped
1 celery stick, roughly chopped
1 onion, roughly chopped
1 head of garlic, cut in half crossways
sprigs of thyme
1 bay leaf

1 First make the chicken stock. Place the chickens, chopped vegetables, garlic and herbs in a large pan, cover with cold water and bring to the boil. Skim off any fat that rises to the surface, then leave to simmer for $1^1/2$–2 hours. Strain the stock through a colander set in a bowl, then pass through a sieve. You need 700ml stock for the soup; keep the remainder for another use.

2 Remove the 'oysters' from the chicken portions in the colander and leave to one side for use later as a garnish. Discard all the remaining contents of the colander.

3 Melt the butter with the olive oil in a saucepan. Add the onion and slowly cook without colouring. After a couple of minutes add the leeks, then sweat for about 5 minutes over a low heat. Do not allow the vegetables to colour.

4 Add the potatoes and bouquet garni and cook uncovered for 2 minutes, then pour in the hot chicken stock. Bring to the boil and cook until the potatoes are soft.

5 Remove the bouquet garni, then blitz the soup in a food processor or blender. Pour into a bowl and set over ice to cool. Chill in the fridge until ready to serve.

6 Remove the oysters from their shells and lightly poach in a touch of fish stock. Drain and allow to cool.

7 To serve, place the sea oysters and chicken 'oysters' in large soup bowls and ladle the soup on top. Finish with a sprinkling of chives.

106

CHILLED POTATO SOUP
WITH WATERCRESS PESTO AND
GOAT'S CHEESE CREAM CROSTINI

SERVES 4-6

2 tbsp olive oil

2 leeks, white and pale green parts
only, sliced

2 onions, finely chopped

2 garlic cloves, finely chopped

½ tsp soft thyme leaves

4 King Edward potatoes, peeled and cubed

1 bay leaf

2 litres chicken or vegetable stock

pinch of freshly grated nutmeg

300ml double cream

3 tbsp snipped chives

salt and white pepper

GOAT'S CHEESE CREAM CROSTINI

1 baguette

3 tbsp extra virgin olive oil

1 garlic clove, peeled

125g very soft, young goat's cheese

3 tbsp double cream

WATERCRESS PESTO

4 garlic cloves

1 tsp Maldon sea salt

1 bag or large bunch of watercress,
chopped

5 tbsp olive oil

4 tbsp freshly grated Parmesan

lemon juice to taste

1 Heat the olive oil in a saucepan, add the leeks, onions, garlic and thyme, and cook over a moderate heat for 15 minutes or until the vegetables are soft but not coloured.

2 Add the potatoes and bay leaf and cook until the potatoes start to stick to the bottom of the pan. Add the stock and nutmeg and stir. Bring to the boil, then reduce the heat and simmer for 15–20 minutes or until the potatoes are cooked.

3 Purée the soup in a blender until smooth, then pass through a fine sieve into a clean saucepan. Season to taste. Thin down with more stock, if necessary. Allow the soup to cool, then chill in the fridge.

4 For the crostini, preheat the oven to 160°C/gas 3. Slice the baguette on the diagonal into 5–10mm slices. Use 2 tbsp of the olive oil to brush over the slices, then place them on a baking tray and bake until crispy and golden, turning halfway through the time. Remove from the oven and rub each slice with the garlic clove to flavour. Set aside.

5 Place the goat's cheese in a bowl with the double cream and remaining olive oil. Mash to combine, then season with salt and pepper. Keep in the refrigerator until half an hour before use.

6 To make the pesto, crush the garlic cloves with the sea salt in a mini food processor until you have a fine paste. Add a little of the watercress and work together vigorously, then stir in the olive oil, Parmesan and remaining watercress. Add lemon juice and seasoning to taste.

7 To serve, stir the double cream into the soup, then fold in the chives and top with the watercress pesto. Spread the goat's cheese cream on the crostini.

108 SOUP OF
JERUSALEM ARTICHOKES
WITH NORFOLK PHEASANT

SERVES 4

175g onions, finely sliced
50g salted butter
600ml chicken stock
450g Jerusalem artichokes, peeled
    and finely sliced
pinch of ground mace

600ml milk
2 pheasant breasts, skinned
2 pheasant legs, skinned
½ egg white
6 tbsp double cream
4 slices of smoked streaky bacon
salt and pepper

1 Begin by making the soup. In a large heavy-based saucepan sweat the onions in the butter until softened. Add the stock, artichokes and mace, bring to the boil and simmer until the artichokes are soft. Add the milk and simmer for a few minutes longer, then remove from the heat. Purée the soup in a blender or food processor until smooth, then pass through a sieve into another saucepan. Check the seasoning and set aside.

2 Remove the fillets from the underside of each pheasant breast and set aside. Place the breasts between two pieces of cling film and bash gently with a rolling pin into fairly thin and even rectangular shapes. Set aside.

3 Take the meat from the pheasant legs and blitz with the egg white in a food processor until smooth. I like to push this through a sieve to get rid of any sinews. This isn't essential, but you get a smoother result. Place the puréed meat in a bowl and lightly season, then slowly add the cream, beating well after each addition. Add enough cream to achieve a dolloping consistency. Spoon half the purée along the centre of each flattened breast, then place the reserved fillets on top of this. Roll each flattened breast firmly around the purée to make a sausage, then roll these tightly in cling film and tie each end tightly with string. You can prepare ahead to this stage.

4 Half an hour before you are ready to serve, place the pheasant rolls in a steamer or a saucepan of boiling water and cook for 20–30 minutes. When ready the rolled breast should feel firm to the touch.

5 While the pheasant is cooking grill the bacon until crisp; set aside.

6 Remove the pheasant from the steamer or boiling water and allow to rest for a few minutes. Meanwhile, gently reheat the soup and spoon it into bowls.

7 Slice the pheasant 'sausages' while still in their cling film wrappers, then slip off the film as you arrange the slices on top of the soup. Top each bowl with a piece of crisply grilled bacon and serve immediately.

ULSTER VEGETABLE SOUP
WITH BACON DUMPLINGS

SERVES 4
600ml vegetable stock
small bunch of fresh thyme
olive oil
50g onion, chopped
1½ garlic cloves, chopped
2 carrots, neatly chopped
1 celery stick, neatly chopped
1 courgette, neatly chopped
1 small leek, neatly chopped
pepper
freshly grated Parmesan to serve

DUMPLINGS
4 rashers of good unsmoked bacon
olive oil
50g finely chopped onion
1 large garlic clove, chopped
25g parsley, chopped
25g tarragon, chopped

1 First make the dumplings. Cut the rind off the bacon rashers; reserve the rinds for the soup. Mince the bacon very finely in a food processor – if the bacon is minced too coarsely it will not roll into dumplings and bind properly and the dumplings will break up. Transfer to a bowl.

2 Heat a little olive oil in a frying pan, add the onion and garlic and sweat over a low heat until soft but not coloured. Remove from the heat and stir in the parsley and tarragon. Leave to cool, then add to the minced bacon. Season to taste with pepper. Roll the mixture into walnut-sized dumplings, pressing firmly together. Keep covered in the fridge until ready to use.

3 For the soup, put the vegetable stock in a saucepan and add the bacon rinds and thyme. Bring to the boil and simmer for 15 minutes. Strain.

4 Heat a little olive oil in the saucepan, add the onion and garlic and sauté over a moderate heat for about 2 minutes, stirring frequently. Add the carrots and sauté for 2 minutes. Add the celery and courgette and sauté for another 2 minutes. Finally, add the leek and sauté for 2 more minutes. Pour the stock into the pan and bring to the boil. Simmer for 7–8 minutes or until the vegetables are just tender but still a little crunchy.

5 Remove the pan from the heat and add the dumplings. Return to the heat and bring the soup almost to the boil. Simmer gently for 7 minutes.

6 Check the seasoning, then serve, sprinkled with Parmesan.

CHAPTER TWO **FISH COURSE**

112

WARM SALAD OF

HOT-SMOKED SEA TROUT, ASPARAGUS AND CUCUMBER
WITH CAPER AND EGG DRESSING

SERVES 4

10 spears of English asparagus, peeled
  and woody ends cut off
250g hot-smoked sea trout fillets
olive oil for drizzling
60g lamb's lettuce
¼ cucumber, peeled and shaved into strips
¼ bunch of chives, finely chopped

CAPER AND EGG DRESSING

100g cornichons (baby gherkins),
  finely chopped
100g baby capers
1 shallot, finely chopped
1 hard-boiled egg, grated
50ml olive oil
1 tbsp coarsely cut tarragon leaves
1 tbsp chopped chives
1 tsp sherry vinegar
1 tsp Dijon mustard

1 Preheat the oven to 180°C/gas 4.

2 Plunge the asparagus into boiling salted water and simmer for 4–5 minutes or until just tender. Drain and refresh in iced water. Drain again, cool and dry, then cut each spear across in half at an angle. Cut the trout into four equal pieces.

3 Make the dressing by mixing all the ingredients together.

4 Line a baking tray with baking parchment. Place the trout and asparagus on the baking tray, drizzle with olive oil and warm through in the oven for 2–3 minutes. Meanwhile, mix the lamb's lettuce and cucumber in a bowl.

5 Break the warm fish into large flakes. Add to the salad with 2 tbsp of the dressing and fold gently together.

6 To serve, arrange five pieces of asparagus on each plate like the spokes of a wheel. Carefully spoon the salad into the middle. Sprinkle with chopped chives and serve immediately, while the trout is still warm. The remaining dressing can be handed separately in a jug.

CRISP-FRIED SPICY JOHN DORY
WITH GRILLED TOMATO CHUTNEY,
CUCUMBER SALAD AND CRUSHED PEAS

SERVES 4
4 john dory fillets, each 100–120g, skin on
1 tbsp lime juice
groundnut oil for deep-frying
1 tsp chaat masala
salt and pepper

CUCUMBER SALAD
1 small cucumber, peeled, deseeded
    and cut into julienne
2 medium tomatoes, deseeded and
    cut into julienne
½ medium red onion, halved and
    thinly sliced
10 sprigs of coriander

DRESSING
2 tbsp chilli jam
about 2 tsp lime juice
about 2 tsp vegetable or olive oil

GRILLED TOMATO CHUTNEY
4 medium tomatoes
2 garlic cloves, unpeeled
about 1 tbsp olive oil
1 small green chilli
3 tbsp chopped coriander leaves
1 tsp finely chopped fresh ginger
½ tsp toasted cumin seeds, crushed
2 tbsp lime juice

BATTER
1½ tsp each ginger and garlic pastes,
    mixed together
½ tsp ground turmeric
½ tsp red chilli powder or crushed
    black pepper
¼ tsp garam masala powder
½ tsp mango powder
¼ tsp ajwain seeds (optional)
100g gram flour
1 tbsp cornflour
120ml sparkling water

CRUSHED PEAS
100g freshly shelled peas
15g unsalted butter
2 tsp vegetable oil
pinch of asafoetida
½ tsp cumin seeds
½ tsp red chilli flakes
1 tbsp vegetable stock or water
1 tbsp single cream

1 Mix together all the ingredients for the cucumber salad. In a separate bowl, mix the dressing, adding just enough lime juice and oil to slacken the jam, and to your taste. Chill the salad and dressing.

2 Preheat the grill. To make the tomato chutney, lay the whole tomatoes and garlic on a baking tray and drizzle with a little oil. Grill until well charred. Peel the garlic, then place on a large board with the grilled tomatoes and the rest of the chutney ingredients. Chop together finely to combine. (Or pulse in a food processor to a chutney consistency.) Keep chilled until required.

3 Marinate the fish in the lime juice with a pinch of salt for 20 minutes.

4 To make the batter, mix all the dry ingredients in a bowl, then slowly pour in the sparkling water, whisking as you do so. Wipe the fish with kitchen paper to remove excess moisture, then add to the batter. Leave for 10 minutes.

5 Meanwhile, make the crushed peas. Lightly blanch the peas in boiling salted water for 1 minute, then drain. Heat the butter and oil in a frying pan. Add the asafoetida and, as it foams, add the cumin seeds. When the cumin seeds crackle, add the chilli flakes and the blanched peas. Cook for 3–4 minutes, then stir in the stock and cream, and season. Remove from heat and, with a wooden spoon, crush the peas. Keep warm while you fry the fish.

6 Heat some groundnut oil in a large wok over a medium heat, then deep-fry the fillets for 3–5 minutes or until golden and crisp on both sides. Remove and drain on kitchen paper. Sprinkle with the chaat masala.

7 To serve, toss the cucumber salad with dressing to taste. Spoon the crushed peas onto large warm plates. Place the fish on top, then pile some of the cucumber salad on the fish. Spoon a little tomato chutney around the plate.

GALTON BLACKISTON

MOUSSE AND GRILLED FILLET OF WILD SEA BASS,
SERVED ON SAMPHIRE WITH A BROWN SHRIMP AND TARRAGON SAUCE

SERVES 8
8 small wild sea bass fillets, each just over 100g, skin on, scaled and pin bones removed
250g samphire, well rinsed
1 tsp caster sugar
25g unsalted butter
salt and pepper

WILD SEA BASS MOUSSE
350g wild sea bass fillet, pin bones removed, skinned and cubed
½ egg white
330ml double cream

BROWN SHRIMP AND TARRAGON SAUCE
1 tbsp lemon juice
1 tbsp white wine
1 tbsp white wine vinegar
1 medium shallot, finely sliced
175g salted butter
3 medium egg yolks
pinch of caster sugar
175g peeled brown shrimps
2 tbsp chopped tarragon

1 To make the mousse, place the sea bass in a food processor and blitz at high speed to purée. Add the egg white and blitz again. Scrape the purée out of the food processor and, using the back of a ladle, push the mixture through a coarse sieve (or tamis) into a bowl.

2 Season the purée with salt and pepper. Add the cream little by little, stirring well between each addition. The finished mixture should be smooth and of a dolloping consistency.

3 Next make up eight little parcels of the mousse. For each parcel, place a square of cling film on your work surface and put a spoonful of mousse into the centre. Bring the four corners up and tie together firmly as if you were tying up a balloon. Set the parcels aside in the fridge. (They can be prepared up to a day ahead.)

4 To make the brown shrimp and tarragon sauce, combine the lemon juice, wine, vinegar and shallot in a small pan and reduce by half. In another pan, melt the butter and allow it to bubble.

5 Put the egg yolks, sugar and a pinch of salt in a food processor and give them a quick whiz to blend. With the processor running, strain in the hot reduced shallot mixture, followed slowly by the hot butter. When all the butter has been added, pour the sauce into a bowl. Stir in the brown shrimps. (The sauce can be made up to 1 hour ahead and left in a bowl set over warm, but not too hot, water.) Add the tarragon at the last minute.

6 When ready to serve, place the cling film parcels in the top of a double boiler and steam over a gentle heat for about 10 minutes. The mousses are ready when they feel firmish to the touch.

7 Meanwhile, preheat the grill to high and bring a large saucepan of water to the boil, ready for cooking the sea bass and samphire. Score the skin of the sea bass fillets, being careful not to cut too deeply into the flesh. Season the flesh side, then arrange, skin-side up, on an oiled baking tray. Brush the scored skin with olive oil. Grill for about 4 minutes or until the skin has blackened and the flesh is just cooked. There is no need to turn the fillets.

8 While the fish cooks, drop the samphire into the pan of boiling water and add the sugar. Boil for 2 minutes, then test a sprig to see if it is cooked (the fleshy end should slip off the stem easily). Drain the samphire thoroughly and smear with the butter.

9 When the mousses are cooked, remove from the steamer. Place some samphire in the centre of each ovenproof plate. Set the grilled fillets of sea bass, skin-side up, on the samphire, then carefully peel off the blackened skin. Snip open the little mousse parcels with scissors, slip off the cling film and place a fish mousse on top of each fillet. Stir the tarragon into the brown shrimp sauce and spoon a little over each mousse. Place the plates under the still hot grill briefly to glaze the sauce (watching carefully), then serve immediately.

116

LEMON SOLE AND OYSTERS
WITH MUSCOVADO JELLY AND
SWEET AND SOUR CHICORY

SERVES 4

8 fresh oysters in their shells

4 tsp agar-agar

50g dark muscovado sugar, plus
a little extra for sprinkling

125g salted butter

juice of ½ lemon

50ml good chicken stock

50ml good fish stock

2–3 drops of sherry or balsamic vinegar

2 whole lemon soles (ask your fishmonger
to remove the head, fins and black skin,
and cut lengthways down through the
central spine, to give you 4 long pieces
– the fish is still on the bone)

olive or groundnut oil for shallow frying

1 tsp chopped parsley

SWEET AND SOUR CHICORY

1 head chicory

lemon juice

pinch of caster sugar

sea salt

olive oil

1 tsp chopped chives

1 Remove the oysters from their shells. Strain the juices and reserve. Chop each oyster into three and keep chilled until needed.

2 To make the muscovado jelly, mix the agar-agar with 100ml cold water in a pan and leave (off the heat) for a few minutes until softened, then stir in the muscovado sugar and boil for 1 minute. Pour in one-third of the reserved oyster juices. Strain through a fine sieve into a small container and leave to set at room temperature (this should take about 20 minutes).

3 Put 100g of the butter into a small pan. Melt, then heat until almost nut brown and starting to sizzle and caramelise on the bottom of the pan. As the butter foams, quickly mix in the lemon juice and the two stocks to create an emulsion. Add the vinegar for a touch of acidity. Remove from the heat and whiz with a stick blender to make a creamy sauce. Add half of the remaining oyster juices and whiz again with the stick blender. Drop in the chopped oysters. Set aside at room temperature.

4 Pat the pieces of lemon sole dry with kitchen paper. Add a smear of oil to a large non-stick frying pan and heat until you can feel the heat rising when you place your hand above the surface. Lay the fish pieces in the pan, white skin-side down, and cook gently for 2 minutes. Drop in the remaining 25g butter, which will melt and foam straightaway. Turn the fish over and cook gently for 1 more minute. Remove from the heat and leave the fish to continue to cook in the residual heat of the pan for a couple of minutes.

5 Meanwhile, finely slice the head of chicory lengthways on a mandolin. Put into a bowl and squeeze over a little lemon juice. Add the sugar, some sea salt, a drizzle of olive oil and the chives, then toss everything together and taste for seasoning. Add the chopped parsley to the oyster butter sauce.

6 To serve, drain the lemon sole on kitchen paper and carefully remove the bone from each piece. Place a piece of fish on each plate and brush with the remaining oyster juices (or spray on using an atomiser).

7 Spoon the warm oysters over the fish with some of the butter sauce, then dot tiny scoops of the muscovado jelly, taken with the tip of a teaspoon, between the chopped oysters. Sprinkle the jelly with just a little muscovado sugar. Scatter the chicory alongside the fish.

RICHARD CORRIGAN

WHOLE POACHED WILD SALMON AND DUCK EGG DRESSING
WITH WHEATEN BREAD AND COUNTRY BUTTER

SERVES 6-8
1 whole wild salmon, 3-3.5kg, gutted
   and scaled
salt and pepper

WHEATEN BREAD
250g plain flour, plus extra for dusting
10g salt
10g bicarbonate of soda
250g wholemeal flour
150g jumbo oatmeal
2 tsp clear honey
1 tsp black treacle
375ml buttermilk
125ml full-fat milk

CUCUMBER SALAD
1 cucumber, peeled, deseeded and
   finely sliced
100ml white wine vinegar
25g caster sugar

½ tbsp mustard seeds
handful of dill, chopped

COURT BOUILLON
1 bottle (75cl) dry white wine
bunch of flat-leaf parsley
2 small leeks, sliced
2 celery sticks, sliced
2 onions, sliced
1 tbsp sea salt
6 black peppercorns
2 bay leaves

DRESSING
150g good-quality organic unsalted butter
4 duck eggs
4 tbsp capers
small handful of flat-leaf parsley, chopped
2 tbsp chopped chives
lemon juice

1 First make the bread. Preheat the oven to 200°C/gas 6. Line a baking sheet with baking parchment.

2 Sift the plain flour, salt and soda into a large bowl and mix in the wholemeal flour and oatmeal. Mix the honey and treacle into the buttermilk, then quickly and lightly fold the buttermilk and milk into the dry ingredients. Use five folds of the hand and do not overwork – when the ingredients are heavy, the action should be light.

3 Divide the dough into quarters with floured hands, then mould each into a round and place on the baking sheet. Dust lightly with plain flour and mark a cross in the top of each loaf. Bake for 20–30 minutes or until the loaves sound hollow when tapped on the base. Transfer to a wire rack, drape a damp cloth over the loaves and leave to cool. (Wheaten bread should be eaten on the day of baking, or toasted the next. This will make four loaves, but the bread freezes well.) Turn the oven down to 100°C/gas ¹/4.

4 While the bread is baking, make the cucumber salad. Sprinkle the cucumber slices with salt and leave to stand. Put the wine vinegar in a heavy pan with 100ml water, the sugar and mustard seeds. Heat gently until the sugar has dissolved, then boil to reduce by half. Remove from the heat. Rinse and drain the cucumber, then mix into the pickling liquid with the dill. Set aside.

5 Put all the ingredients for the court bouillon in a large fish kettle with 6 litres cold water. Bring to the boil and simmer for 20 minutes.

6 Lower the salmon into the court bouillon. Bring back to the boil, then cover the kettle tightly so no steam can escape. Transfer to the oven and poach for 25 minutes with the oven door ajar.

7 Meanwhile, make the dressing. Melt the butter and keep warm. Lower the duck eggs into a pan of boiling water and simmer for 4 minutes. Lift the eggs out of the water and cool a little under the cold tap, then carefully peel off the shells. Mash the eggs in a bowl with a fork, then mix in the capers, herbs and warm melted butter. Season with lemon juice, salt and pepper to taste. Keep the dressing warm.

8 Remove the salmon from the court bouillon as soon as the poaching time is up. Serve with the cucumber salad and warm dressing, with slices of wheaten bread and country butter on the side.

120

PAN-FRIED JOHN DORY
WITH LOBSTER MASH, BROAD BEANS,
SAMPHIRE AND COURGETTE FLOWERS

SERVES 4

2 live lobsters, preferably native South
    Coast, each 500–600g
200g freshly shelled broad beans
4 baby courgettes, with flowers attached
200g samphire
4 large fillets of john dory, each
    about 150g, skinned
200ml olive oil
50g butter
salt and pepper

LOBSTER SAUCE

mirepoix of finely diced vegetables
    (½ onion, 1 carrot, 2 celery sticks,
    ¼ fennel bulb)
4 garlic cloves, finely diced
2 tbsp olive oil
1 tbsp tomato purée

large sprig of thyme
large sprig of basil
½ star anise
6 fennel seeds
6 coriander seeds
6 black peppercorns
4 tbsp white wine
2 tbsp brandy
500ml home-made chicken stock

LOBSTER MASH

4 large Desirée potatoes, peeled
    and quartered
125ml double cream
about 100g unsalted butter, diced
freshly grated nutmeg
8 basil leaves, coarsely chopped
6 tarragon leaves, coarsely chopped

1 Put the lobsters in the freezer for an hour to desensitize them (no longer than this or the meat will become frozen), then cut them in half lengthways and separate the heads, claws and tails. Cut the heads into about six pieces, reserving all the liquid that comes out. (If there are any corals, freeze them to use in another dish.) Blanch the claws and tails in boiling salted water for 4 minutes. Drain and leave on a tray until cool enough to handle, then remove the shells while still warm. Cut the meat into 1cm dice and set aside. Reserve all the shells and heads.

2 To make the lobster sauce, cook the mirepoix and garlic in the oil over a high heat for 10–15 minutes or until lightly browned. Add the lobster shells and heads with all the liquid, and mix well. Cook for 2 minutes, then add the tomato purée and cook for 1 more minute before adding the herbs, spices, wine and brandy. Cover with the stock and 500ml water and bring to the boil, then simmer for 45 minutes. Strain through a muslin-lined sieve into a clean pan and boil until reduced to 100ml. Keep the sauce warm.

3 Plunge the broad beans into boiling salted water and simmer for 3–5 minutes or until tender. Drain and refresh in iced water, then drain again and peel off the skins.

4 Remove the flowers from the courgettes and set aside. Cut each courgette lengthways into quarters, then dice each length into 1cm pieces. Cook in boiling salted water for 2 minutes only. Drain, refresh in iced water and drain again. Split the courgette flowers lengthways in half and pick out the stamens, then split the flowers in half again.

5 Pick the roots off the samphire and blanch the stems in boiling water for 1 minute. Drain, refresh in iced water and drain again.

6 To make the mash, put the potatoes in a pan of cold salted water and bring to the boil. Turn the heat down and simmer gently for about 25 minutes or until the potatoes are just cooked. Meanwhile, boil the cream in a separate pan until reduced by half. Drain the potatoes, then dry off slightly and mash. Work the mash through a food mill (mouli), ricer or sieve into a clean pan and beat in 50g butter, a few pieces at a time, followed by three-quarters of the reduced cream. Now beat in another 50g butter, and season to taste with nutmeg, salt and pepper. If you think the mash needs it, you can add more butter at this stage.

7 Reheat the mash until hot, then gently fold in half the diced lobster meat along with the chopped basil and tarragon. Taste for seasoning and fold in the remaining cream. Cover the surface of the mash with greaseproof paper or cling film and keep warm by the side of the stove.

8 Cut each john dory fillet lengthways into three pieces. Season. Heat 150ml of the olive oil in a large heavy frying pan until hot but not smoking. Lower in the pieces of fish, skinned side up, and pan-fry for 1–1$^1/_2$ minutes or until golden underneath. Turn the pieces over and repeat on the other side. When the fish is almost done, add the butter in small pieces and let it start to turn golden brown and foam around the fish. Remove the fish and drain well on kitchen paper.

9 In a small saucepan, gently reheat the blanched broad beans, courgette dice and samphire with all but 2 tsp of the remaining olive oil and 1 tsp water. When hot, add the lobster sauce and the courgette flower pieces, then the remaining diced lobster meat and oil. Taste and add seasoning if necessary.

10 To serve, quickly reheat the mash for 20 seconds or so, then spoon onto the centre of each plate. Top each serving with three pieces of fish and drizzle the lobster and vegetable dressing over and around.

FILLET OF TURBOT
IN RED WINE
WITH ARTICHOKE PURÉE AND PICKLED BABY BEETS

SERVES 6
6 thick turbot fillets, each 125–150g, skinned
salt and pepper
18 small sprigs of lovage or very fine flat-leaf
  parsley to garnish

POACHING LIQUOR
2 litres red wine
2 sprigs of thyme
½ bay leaf
1 garlic clove, peeled

PICKLED BABY BEETS
9 raw baby beetroots
1 tsp demerara sugar
4 tsp balsamic vinegar

ARTICHOKE PUREE
25g unsalted butter
500g Jerusalem artichokes, peeled
  and very finely sliced
2 sprigs of thyme
½ bay leaf
1 garlic clove, peeled
50ml double cream

1 For the poaching liquor, pour the wine into a large saucepan and add the thyme, bay leaf, garlic clove and 1/2 tsp salt. Boil over a medium-high heat until reduced to 750ml. Strain through a fine sieve, preferably lined with muslin, into a large wide pan and set aside.

2 To make the pickled baby beets, peel the beetroots with a small, sharp knife or a very fine potato peeler, then place in a pan with 150ml water, the sugar, balsamic vinegar and a pinch of salt. Bring just to the boil. Cover the pan and simmer for 8–10 minutes or until tender. Remove the beetroots. Pass the cooking liquid through a fine sieve, then return to the pan and reduce to a nice glaze over a medium heat. Cut the beetroots in half and add to the glaze. Set aside.

3 Next, make the artichoke purée. Melt the butter in a heavy pan. Add the artichokes, season with a pinch of salt and add the thyme, bay leaf and garlic clove. Stir well. Cover with a sheet of greaseproof paper and sweat the artichokes for 10–15 minutes or until they are very soft. Stir regularly during cooking, and add a little water if they start to colour. Add the cream and boil for 3 minutes, then remove the thyme, bay leaf and garlic. Purée the artichokes in a blender until silky smooth. Check for seasoning, and keep warm.

4 Bring the poaching liquor to the boil, then remove from the heat. Carefully lower in the fish fillets, making sure they are submerged in a single layer and not sitting on top of each other. Leave the turbot off the heat like this for 7–8 minutes or until the fish is just cooked through, only returning the pan to a low heat if the liquor cools down too much before the fish is cooked.

5 While the fish is cooking, gently reheat the beetroots and the artichoke purée. When the fish is cooked, remove it very gently from the poaching liquor using a fish slice and drain on kitchen paper. Season each fillet with a pinch of sea salt.

6 To serve, place a piece of fish on each plate and garnish with a neat spoonful of artichoke purée and beetroot halves. Drizzle a little of the beetroot glaze around the fish, and finish with the lovage or parsley.

MATT TEBBUTT

SEWIN AND SOUSED VEGETABLES
WITH COCKLES AND WOOD SORREL

SERVES 4
4 sewin (sea trout) fillets, each
   about 175g, skin on
400g live cockles in their shells
100g wood sorrel
50ml extra virgin olive oil

POACHING LIQUOR
4 celery sticks
4 carrots
2 large onions
2 bay leaves
1 tsp black peppercorns
1 tsp coriander seeds
400ml dry white wine
200ml white wine vinegar

1 To make the poaching liquor, slice the celery and carrots on the diagonal, to the same thickness. Halve the onions, place the halves cut-side down and slice into semi-circles. Throw these vegetables into a wide saucepan and add the remaining ingredients and 100ml cold water. Bring to the boil and simmer for 30 minutes. Remove from the heat.

2 Slip the sewin into the poaching liquor. Return the pan to a gentle heat and cook, uncovered, for 6–7 minutes. Do not allow the liquid to boil. Remove the fish and keep warm. Lift the vegetables out of the poaching liquor with a slotted spoon and keep warm.

3 Pour most of the poaching liquor out of the pan, leaving behind just enough to cover the bottom. Bring this to the boil and throw in the cockles. Cover with the lid and cook, shaking the pan from time to time, until the cockles open – this should take 2–3 minutes. Drain the cockles and remove them from their shells, keeping some in the shell for the garnish.

4 To serve, place some soused vegetables on warm plates with the sewin on top, and scatter the cockles around. Finish with the wood sorrel, a splash of olive oil and the cockles in their shells.

SKATE WING,
NUT BROWN BUTTER, PARSLEY JELLY, CAPERS AND LEMON CONFIT

SERVES 4

4 skate wings, each 500g, skinned and
    filleted (ask the fishmonger to do this)
3 tbsp olive oil
knob of butter
squeeze of lemon juice
salt and white pepper

PARSLEY JELLY
100g parsley, stalks and leaves
2 tsp agar-agar powder

LEMON CONFIT
2 unwaxed lemons
50g caster sugar

BUTTER SAUCE
100g salted butter
juice of 1 lemon
5 tbsp chicken stock
50g small capers, rinsed and dried

1 To make the parsley jelly, put the parsley through a juicer, then pour immediately into an airtight container and chill. Sprinkle the agar-agar and a pinch of salt over 4 tbsp cold water in a small saucepan. Leave to soak for 2–3 minutes. Bring to the boil and boil for 1 minute, then pour in the parsley juice. Pour into a clean container and chill for about 1 hour or until softly set. Purée the jelly in a blender and pass it through a sieve. Keep in a plastic squeezy bottle in the fridge until ready to use.

2 For the lemon confit, wash the lemons, then thinly slice on a mandolin. Put the sugar in a saucepan with 200ml water. When the sugar has dissolved, bring to the boil. Carefully lay the lemon slices in the syrup. Remove from the heat and cool. (These are best made a day ahead; any extras will keep in the fridge for 2–3 weeks.)

3 To make the butter sauce, melt the butter in a saucepan until it foams and then turns to a nut-brown colour. Add the lemon juice, a pinch of salt and the chicken stock. Remove from the heat and blend with a stick blender to create an emulsified sauce. Throw in the capers and keep warm.

4 Cut each skate fillet in half lengthways. Roll each up into a long roll, rolling from the long side so you get a cigar shape that is plump in the middle and tapers off at the ends. Secure each with a wooden cocktail stick.

5 Heat the olive oil and butter in a non-stick frying pan. When the butter is foaming, add the rolls of skate and spoon over the oil and foaming butter as they cook. Allow about 5 minutes, turning occasionally. Remove, drain on kitchen paper and let rest for a few minutes.

6 To serve, season the skate with the lemon juice and some salt and white pepper. Place in warm bowls, spoon the butter sauce over and arrange some lemon slices on top of the fish. Dot the parsley jelly around the fish and into the sauce to give you bursts of fresh green colour and flavour.

PAN-FRIED BLACK BREAM
WITH MADRAS CURRY SAUCE AND
SEMOLINA POLENTA

SERVES 4

4 medium-sized black bream fillets, skin on

2 tbsp vegetable oil

15g butter

salt and pepper

mustard cress to garnish

MADRAS SAUCE

2 tbsp vegetable oil

2 cloves

1 tsp finely chopped fresh ginger

1 green chilli, deseeded and finely chopped

6 curry leaves (fresh or freeze-dried)

2 medium onions, thinly sliced

½ tsp ground turmeric

½ tsp ground coriander

½ tsp black pepper

1 large tomato, chopped

1 medium-sized, just ripe mango,
    flesh puréed

300ml coconut milk

SEMOLINA POLENTA

200g coarse semolina

3 tbsp vegetable oil

1 tsp black mustard seeds

1 tbsp unroasted peanuts, roughly crushed

1 red chilli, split

6 curry leaves

1 tbsp finely chopped fresh ginger

1 medium onion, finely sliced

1 tsp lime juice

1 tbsp chopped coriander leaves

4 tbsp dry breadcrumbs

butter and a splash of vegetable oil
    for frying

1 First make the sauce. Heat the oil in a wok, add the cloves, ginger, chilli and curry leaves, and sauté for 1 minute. Add the sliced onions and sauté for 2–3 minutes or until translucent, then add the turmeric, coriander and black pepper and sauté for 1 more minute. Add the tomato and sauté for 2 minutes, then add the mango purée. Cook for a further 2–3 minutes. Pour in the coconut milk and simmer gently for 2–3 minutes. Set aside. If the sauce goes a bit thick, add 1 tbsp warm water.

2 For the polenta, tip the semolina into a frying pan and toast over a medium heat, shaking the pan often, until lightly browned. Set aside. Heat the oil in a wok and add the mustard seeds, peanuts, whole chilli and curry leaves. Fry for 1 minute, then add the ginger. Stir in the onion and sauté until translucent. Pour in 450ml hot water and bring to the boil. Slowly add the toasted semolina, beating briskly as you pour to prevent any lumps from forming. If the mix seems a bit stiff to beat, add a little more boiling water. Mix well together, then stir in the lime juice, chopped coriander and salt to taste. Cook for a further 3–4 minutes. Discard the chilli. Spread the mixture in a 17cm square tin that is about 2.5cm deep. Leave to cool and set.

3 Cut the set semolina cake into 3 x 4cm rectangles and dust them lightly with the breadcrumbs on both sides. Melt a big knob of butter in a frying pan with a splash of oil, add the polenta cakes and fry to make a golden crust, adding more butter as needed. Keep warm. (Extra polenta cakes can be reheated for another time.)

4 For the bream, season the fillets with salt and pepper. Heat the oil in a non-stick pan, add the fillets, skin-side down, and fry for 2–3 minutes or until golden. Turn the fillets over, add the butter and fry on a medium heat for a further 1–2 minutes. Meanwhile, reheat the sauce.

5 To serve, place the fish on large plates. Pour some of the sauce over and around the fish, place a polenta cake alongside and top with some mustard cress.

MARK BROADBENT

POACHED TURBOT AND COCKLES
WITH ASPARAGUS AND BROWN SHRIMP BUTTER

SERVES 4

20 asparagus spears, preferably Formby
4 skinless pieces of turbot fillet, each
    about 200g
very finely shredded flat-leaf parsley
    to garnish

SOUSED COCKLES

125ml Chardonnay vinegar, preferably
    Forum
1 banana shallot, sliced into rings
sprig of thyme
2 bay leaves
5 black peppercorns
1 tsp pickling spice
450g live cockles in their shells, preferably
    from Morecambe Bay

BROWN SHRIMP BUTTER

450g cooked brown shrimps in their shells,
    preferably from Morecambe Bay
525g good salted butter, preferably
    Longley Farm Yorkshire, clarified
1 tsp blade mace
pinch of celery salt
2 pinches of cayenne pepper
pinch of grated nutmeg
black pepper
lemon juice

COURT BOUILLON

dry white wine, preferably English
1 tsp white peppercorns
large bouquet garni (1 large sprig of thyme,
    3 celery sticks, a few parsley stalks,
    ½ leek, 2 bay leaves and pared zest of
    ¼ lemon, tied together)

1 To souse the cockles, pour the vinegar into a heavy saucepan, add the shallot, herbs and spices, and bring to the boil. Simmer for 10 minutes, then add the cockles and cover the pan. Cook for 3–5 minutes only, just until the cockles open. Do not overcook. Drain the cockles, reserving the sousing liquor, and remove them from their shells. Set both cockles and liquor aside.

2 Trim the ends off the asparagus at an angle, and peel away any woody bits. Plunge the spears into a pan of boiling salted water to cook for 2 minutes. Drain and refresh in iced water, and drain again. Set aside.

3 Preheat the oven to 180°C/gas 4.

4 For the shrimp butter, peel the shrimps and put the shells in a roasting tin with 125g of the butter. Roast for about 1 hour or until golden brown. Leave to infuse until cool, then pass the butter through a fine sieve lined with muslin into a clean pan. Add the remaining clarified butter, the mace, celery salt, cayenne and nutmeg. Simmer for 15 minutes. Take off the heat. Taste and balance the flavours with black pepper and a squeeze of lemon juice. If you've used a good salted butter, it won't be necessary to add any salt. Reserve in the pan.

5 To make the court bouillon, bring 1.2 litres water to the boil in a large saucepan with a healthy splash of wine, the peppercorns and bouquet garni. Lower the heat and simmer for 20–25 minutes, then remove from the heat and cover the pan. Leave to infuse until cold.

6 Strain the cold court bouillon into a straight-sided pan and bring to a simmer. Gently lower in the turbot fillets, arranging them in a single layer. Poach gently for 4–5 minutes.

7 While the fish is poaching, gently warm the asparagus in the reserved sousing liquor, then add the cockles and warm for no more than 30 seconds. Taste for seasoning. Warm the shrimp butter, add the peeled shrimps and gently warm through (do not cook). Taste for seasoning.

8 To serve, place a turbot fillet to the right side of each plate, and place the asparagus on the left. Spoon the cockles and a little of the sousing liquor over the asparagus and sprinkle with shredded parsley. Top the turbot with the shrimps and spoon the shrimp butter over and around.

PAN-FRIED WILD SALMON
WITH CONWY MUSSELS, CRUSHED NEW
POTATOES AND A HORSERADISH SAUCE

130

SERVES 4

500g fresh mussels in their shells
2 shallots, finely sliced
olive oil
250ml white wine
250ml single cream
lemon juice
5cm piece of fresh horseradish

200g Charlotte potatoes
bunch of chives, chopped
4 pieces of wild salmon fillet, each 120g,
    skin on
100g freshly shelled peas
50g pea shoots
salt and pepper

1 Prepare the mussels by washing them under cold water and removing the beards. Drain. In a heavy-bottomed pan, cook the shallots in a little olive oil until translucent. Add the mussels and pour on the wine. Place a lid on the pan and cook for 3–4 minutes or until the mussels have opened. (Discard any that do not open.) Drain the mussels in a colander set over a bowl. Pour the liquid from the bowl into a small pan and set aside. Pick the mussels out of their shells and keep, covered, in the fridge.

2 To make the sauce, bring the reserved mussel liquid to the boil. Add the cream and simmer for 5–6 minutes until reduced slightly. It should not be too thick, but more soupy. Season with salt, pepper and a squeeze of lemon juice. Remove from the heat, then grate in the fresh horseradish and leave to cool. When cool, taste the sauce. If the horseradish flavour is strong enough, strain through a fine sieve and leave to one side. If not, leave a little longer for the flavour to develop before straining.

3 Cook the whole potatoes in boiling salted water for 10–12 minutes or until tender. Drain and leave to cool. When cool, peel off the skins and put the potatoes back into the pan. Crush the potatoes with a fork. Season and add the chives. Keep warm.

4 Preheat the oven to 180°C/gas 4.

5 Season the salmon with salt and pepper. Heat a non-stick, ovenproof frying pan, then add a splash of olive oil and cook the salmon skin-side down for 2 minutes, without turning. Place the pan in the oven to cook for 3–4 minutes.

6 Meanwhile, heat a little of the horseradish sauce in a pan. Add the peas and cook for 1 minute, then add the mussels just to warm through. Heat the remaining sauce in another pan. Season the pea shoots with salt, pepper, lemon juice and olive oil.

7 For each serving, place a ring, about 4cm diameter, in the middle of a shallow bowl. Spoon the crushed potatoes into the ring, lightly packing them. Remove the ring. Scatter the mussels and peas around the potato and place a salmon fillet, skin-side up, on top. Scatter the pea shoots on top of the mussels and peas, then finish with a light drizzle of the warm horseradish cream sauce all around.

132

BRAISED FILLET OF WILD HALIBUT
WITH TRUFFLE AND WHITE BEAN SAUCE

SERVES 6

50ml good olive oil, plus extra for drizzling

3 skinless halibut fillets, preferably wild,
   each about 150g

2 tsp chopped chervil

20g unsalted butter

salt

fresh black truffles to serve (optional)

VEGETABLE NAGE

½ leek, outside leaves discarded, cut
   into 3cm lengths

2 carrots, cut into 2cm lengths

1 white-skinned onion, cut lengthways
   into eighths

1 celery stick, cut into 3cm lengths

1 large garlic clove, peeled

½ star anise, crushed

¼ tsp coriander seeds, crushed

large pinch of white peppercorns, crushed

few mixed sprigs of herbs (eg parsley, basil,
   chives and chervil)

lemon wedge

50ml dry white wine

SAUCE

100g dried white beans (haricots blancs),
   soaked in cold water overnight

300ml home-made chicken stock

¼ carrot

¼ celery stick

¼ white-skinned onion

1 garlic clove, peeled

50g piece of smoked bacon

250ml Madeira

500ml reduced home-made beef stock

10g fresh black truffles, chopped

white truffle oil to taste

1 First make the vegetable nage. Put the vegetables and garlic into a heavy saucepan and pour in cold water until it reaches the same level as the vegetables. Bring to the boil over a high heat. Skim, then simmer over a medium heat for 8 minutes.
2 Add the crushed spices with the herbs and lemon wedge. Simmer for a further 2 minutes, then take the pan off the heat and pour in the wine. Stir. Leave until cold, then refrigerate in a sealed glass or plastic container for 24 hours.
3 The next day, strain the liquid through a fine sieve. Keep, covered, in the fridge until ready to use. Discard the vegetables and flavourings.
4 To make the sauce, drain and rinse the beans, then put them in a pan of fresh water and bring to the boil. Drain and rinse under cold running water. Put the beans back into the pan and add the chicken stock, 200ml water, the carrot, celery, onion, garlic, bacon and a pinch of salt. Bring to the boil. Turn down to a simmer, then cover and cook for 15–20 minutes. The beans need to be tender, but should still have some

bite. Drain the beans in a colander. Remove the vegetables, garlic and bacon. Leave the beans to cool, then chop them roughly with a sharp knife.

5 Boil the Madeira in a pan until reduced to 100ml. Add the reduced beef stock with the chopped beans and truffles, and continue to cook over a low heat for 20 minutes. Add truffle oil to taste and season with salt if needed. Set aside.

6 Now cook the halibut. Measure 150ml vegetable nage into a saucepan and heat until hot, then set aside in a warm place. Heat the olive oil in a non-stick frying pan over a medium-high heat. Season the halibut with fine salt and place skinned-side down in the pan. Fry for 3–4 minutes or until nicely coloured, then gently turn the fish over with a palette knife and cook for 1 more minute. Take the pan off the heat. Cover the top of the fish with the chopped chervil, then put the butter in the pan followed by the hot vegetable nage. Cover the pan with baking parchment and return to the heat to cook for 2 minutes.

7 Remove the fish from the nage and set aside in a warm place. Leave the pan on the heat and boil the nage, stirring all the time, until it is reduced to a thick emulsion. At the same time, reheat the bean sauce.

8 To serve, cut each piece of fish in half with a sharp knife, then place the fish in bowls and spoon a little of the reduced nage over each piece to glaze. Spoon the bean sauce over and around, and drizzle with olive oil. If you want to be really extravagant, slice fresh black truffles over the top just before serving.

SMOKED EEL MOUSSE

WITH BOXTY PANCAKES, HORSERADISH AND MUSTARD GRAIN CREAM, AND FRESH HERB SALAD

SERVES 4

500g fresh eel fillet, skinned

1 medium egg white

olive oil

125ml chilled double cream

250g smoked eel fillet, preferably Lough
    Neagh, diced

small handful each of coriander, basil,
    chervil and rocket leaves

salt and pepper

BOXTY PANCAKES

125g raw peeled potato (a floury variety such
    as Dunbar Standard or Maris Piper), grated

125g mashed potato, made from 200g floury
    potatoes, peeled and cooked

125g plain flour, plus extra for dusting

½ tsp baking powder

½ tsp salt

large knob of salted butter, melted and
    cooled

a little milk if needed

HORSERADISH AND MUSTARD GRAIN CREAM

300ml whipping cream

1 tsp freshly grated horseradish

1 tsp wholegrain mustard, preferably
    Castle Leslie

1 First make the smoked eel mousse. Check the fresh eel for any stray bones or skin, then work the flesh to a fine purée in a blender. Add the egg white and a pinch of salt, and purée again. Press the mixture through a very fine sieve into a bowl, checking again that there are no bones. Place the bowl over a bowl of ice and put into the fridge to chill for 10–15 minutes.

2 Preheat the oven to 150°C/gas 2. Lightly brush four 7.5–10cm non-stick moulds with olive oil (or use oiled ramekins lined with discs of baking parchment).

3 Remove the purée from the fridge and gradually mix in the cream using a rubber spatula. Do this very slowly or the mixture may curdle. Fold in the diced smoked eel and season. Spoon into the moulds. Cover them closely with cling film and then with foil. Set them in a roasting tin and pour enough warm water into the tin to come halfway up the sides of the moulds. Bake for 8 minutes or until a knife inserted in the centre comes out clean. Remove from the oven and leave to cool.

4 For the boxty pancakes, put the grated raw potato on a cloth and wring over a bowl, to catch the liquid. This will separate into a clear fluid with starch at the bottom. Pour off and discard the fluid. Add the grated and mashed potato to the starch left in the bowl and mix well. Sift the dry ingredients and mix into the potatoes along with the melted butter, adding a little milk if necessary to make a pliable dough.

5 Knead the dough lightly on a floured surface. Divide into four and form each portion into a flat round cake about 1cm larger than the moulds used for the eel mousse. With the back of a knife, mark each pancake into quarters without cutting right through.

6 Heat a large griddle or heavy frying pan until hot. Dust with flour, then place a pancake marked-side down on the griddle. Cook over a medium heat for 3–5 minutes or until browned. Turn the pancake over and repeat on the other side. Remove from the griddle and keep warm while you cook the remaining pancakes in the same way.

7 Meanwhile, make the horseradish cream. Whip the cream until it holds a peak, then fold in the horseradish, mustard, and salt and pepper to taste. Mix the herb leaves together, and season with sea salt and a small drop of olive oil.

8 To serve, put a pancake, marked-side up, on each plate, and unmould an eel mousse onto it. Garnish with the herb salad and a quenelle of horseradish cream.

JEREMY LEE

SALAD OF POTATOES, ARBROATH SMOKIE, AYRSHIRE BACON AND A SOFT-BOILED EGG

SERVES 4

500g little new potatoes
5 tbsp olive oil
2 tsp red wine vinegar
4 fresh organic eggs

8 thin rashers of streaky bacon
a brace of Arbroath smokies
2 knobs of butter
1 tsp Dijon mustard
salt and pepper

1 Cook the potatoes in a pan of plenty of lightly salted water for 12–15 minutes or until tender. Drain and, while still hot, peel and toss them with 1 tbsp of the oil and 1 tsp of the vinegar. Keep warm.

2 Preheat the oven to 170°C/gas 3.

3 Fill a small pan with water and set to a furious boil. Lay in the eggs with a spoon and cook for 4–4¹/₂ minutes. Remove the eggs swiftly and plunge into iced water to arrest the cooking. Peel and let sit in cold water until required.

4 Place the rashers of bacon on a wire rack and sit this on a baking sheet. Cook in the preheated oven for about 10 minutes or until the bacon is golden and crisp, cooking for longer if necessary.

5 Meanwhile, butter the smokies with a knob of the butter, then warm them briefly in a dish in the oven. Remove the skin and as many bones as possible. Flake the fish into a heatproof dish. Just before serving, lightly butter the flakes with the remaining knob of butter and warm gently in the oven.

6 Stir sea salt and freshly ground pepper into the remaining 1 tsp vinegar to dissolve, then add the mustard and whisk well. Gradually whisk in the remaining oil.

7 To serve, heap the potatoes onto plates. Scatter the warmed flaked smokies over. Cut the eggs in half and lay two halves on each serving. Lay the bacon rashers on top and spoon over the vinaigrette.

SOUSED MACKEREL
WITH POTATO SALAD

SERVES 4

4 mackerel fillets, each about 100g,
 as fresh as possible
35g fine sea salt
¼ cucumber
4 tsp freshly grated horseradish (or strong
 horseradish relish)
2 banana shallots, very finely sliced

MARINADE

400ml white wine vinegar
200g caster sugar
1 star anise
sprig of thyme
8 black peppercorns

POTATO SALAD

200g new potatoes, boiled in their skins
 until tender, then roughly chopped
3 tbsp mayonnaise
finely chopped chives

1 You need to start curing the mackerel 4–7 days ahead. First, check the fillets for pin bones with your fingertips and pull out any stray bones with tweezers. Lay the fish skin-side down in a shallow dish and sprinkle the salt liberally over the top. Cover and leave for about 6 hours or overnight in the fridge. You will find salty fish juices leach out and the flesh firms – this is all fine.

2 To make the marinade, pour the vinegar into a medium-sized pan. Put it over a low heat and add the sugar, star anise, thyme and peppercorns. Bring slowly to the boil, then take off the heat, cover and allow to cool.

3 Meanwhile, peel the piece of cucumber, halve lengthways and scoop out the seeds. Cut the cucumber into matchsticks and divide into four equal bundles.

4 Rinse the fish well in cold water, then pat dry with kitchen paper. Spread the horseradish thinly over the flesh side of the fillets. Lay a cucumber bundle at one end of each fillet and carefully roll up the fish around it. Secure the rolls with a wooden cocktail stick.

5 Take a smallish dish (not too shallow) that's just big enough to hold the mackerel side by side, and sprinkle some of the shallot slices over the bottom. Place the mackerel on top of the shallots, packing the fillets tightly together. Scatter the rest of the shallots on top, then pour the cooled vinegar marinade over the fish, making sure that the fillets are immersed. Cover tightly with cling film or with an airtight lid and refrigerate for at least 4 days, but no longer than 7 days.

6 When ready to serve, make up the potato salad by mixing all the ingredients together. Serve each mackerel fillet with a little pile of potato salad alongside.

BUTTERED TURBOT
WITH LEEKS AND WHITSTABLE CHAMPAGNE OYSTERS

SERVES 4

8 oysters
1 shallot, shredded
200ml Champagne
2 tbsp double cream
100g butter
squeeze of lemon juice
4 portions of turbot fillet, each 75–100g,
   skinned

1 large or 2 small leeks, finely
   shredded
1 heaped tbsp chopped chervil
salt and pepper

1 First open the oysters, saving all the juices. In a small saucepan, gently warm the oysters in their juices for a minute or two, then remove from the heat.

2 Put the shallot and Champagne into a saucepan, bring to the boil and reduce by half. Strain the oyster juices into the pan and continue to boil until once again reduced by half.

3 Add the cream and, once simmering, whisk in 75g of the butter, in small pieces, a few at a time. Finish with a squeeze of lemon juice and a seasoning of salt and pepper. Keep the sauce to one side.

4 Divide the remaining butter between two frying pans. Once sizzling, place the turbot in one pan and the shredded leeks in the other. Season both with salt and pepper. Gently fry both for a few minutes, allowing the turbot to take on a light golden colour before turning, and softening the leeks.

5 Warm the sauce, adding the oysters and chervil.

6 To serve, divide the leeks among four bowls and add an oyster to each. Place the turbot on top and finish with a second oyster, then spoon the sauce over.

SEARED RED MULLET
WITH ROSEMARY-SCENTED MUSSELS

SERVES 4

200ml white wine

1 onion, sliced

a few sprigs of rosemary

1kg fresh mussels, debearded and washed

100ml double or whipping cream

squeeze of lemon juice

4 fillets of red mullet

2 tbsp olive oil

knob of butter + 25g butter, diced

salt and pepper

MASHED POTATOES (OPTIONAL)

2 large, floury potatoes, preferably
  Maris Piper, peeled and quartered

25g unsalted butter

a few tbsp single cream or milk to loosen

1 Boil together the white wine, onion and some rosemary sprigs. Add the mussels. Cover with a tight-fitting lid and cook for 4–5 minutes, shaking the pan occasionally, until the mussels have opened. Drain in a colander set over a large bowl or saucepan. Discard any mussels that have not opened. Remove the mussels from their shells and keep to one side.

2 Simmer the mussel cooking liquor, whisking in the cream with a fresh sprig of rosemary, and cook for a few minutes. Season with salt, pepper and a squeeze of lemon juice. Pass the sauce through a fine sieve or muslin cloth. Set aside.

3 If serving the fish with mashed potatoes, cook the potatoes in boiling salted water for 20–25 minutes, depending on size. When the potatoes are tender, drain off all water and replace the lid. Shake the pan vigorously, which will start to break up the boiled potatoes. Add the butter and cream or milk, a little at a time, while mashing the potatoes to a smooth consistency. Season with salt and pepper to taste. Keep hot.

4 Remove any pin bones from the mullet fillets, then season with salt and pepper. Heat the olive oil in a frying pan. Once hot, add the mullet fillets, skin side down, and fry for several minutes or until golden brown and crisp. Add the knob of butter to the pan and turn the fillets. Baste with the frothy butter, then remove from the heat and allow the fish to continue its cooking with the residual heat left in the pan.

5 Meanwhile, warm the mussel sauce, whisking in the diced butter until totally absorbed. Add the mussels to the sauce and warm gently.

6 To serve, spoon or pipe mashed potato into the centre of each warm large bowl or plate. Spoon the mussels and creamy sauce around the potatoes and arrange the red mullet fillets on top.

OMELETTE ARNOLD BENNETT

SERVES 4
250g naturally smoked haddock fillet, skinned
milk for poaching
6 large eggs
50g unsalted butter
small bunch of chives, chopped
40g mature Cheddar or Gruyère, grated
salt and pepper

HOLLANDAISE SAUCE
100ml white wine vinegar
a few herb stalks (parsley, tarragon)
1 shallot, finely sliced
2 egg yolks
250g butter, melted and clarified
juice of ½ lemon

GARNISH
chopped chives or sprigs of chervil

1 First make the hollandaise. Heat the vinegar, herb stalks and shallot in a small pan and reduce by half. Remove from the heat and leave to infuse for at least 4 hours. Strain through a sieve into a bowl. Discard the contents of the sieve.

2 Put the egg yolks and 50ml water into another bowl set over a pan of simmering water and whisk until thick ribbons will form. Gradually whisk in the vinegar reduction and carry on whisking until thick ribbons will form again.

3 Very slowly pour in the warm (not hot) clarified butter, whisking the whole time. When all of the butter has been incorporated, you should have a nice thick emulsion. Pass through a fine sieve to remove any bits of cooked egg. Season with the lemon juice and salt, then cover with cling film and keep in a warm place.

4 Gently poach the haddock in milk to cover for about 5 minutes. Drain and flake into large chunks, discarding any bones. Set aside in a warm place.

5 Preheat the grill to high.

6 Beat the eggs in a bowl and season with salt and freshly milled black pepper. Melt the butter in a large non-stick frying pan. When foaming add the eggs. Allow to set on the base, then mix with a fork until half cooked. Allow to set on the base again.

7 Put the fish, chives and cheese on to the omelette and fold the edges into the middle. Divide the omelette among four small dishes (ramekins or flat ovenproof bowls). This can be a bit messy, so clean the sides of the dishes before you cover the top of the omelettes with hollandaise sauce. Glaze under the grill.

8 Garnish each omelette with chives or a sprig of chervil and serve straight away.

142

PAN-FRIED TURBOT
WITH COCKLES AND OXTAIL

SERVES 4
12oz sea beet, stalks removed
olive oil
freshly grated nutmeg
squeeze of lemon juice
4 pieces of skinned turbot fillet,
    each 120g
butter
salt and pepper

OXTAIL
1kg Welsh Black Beef oxtail, cut into pieces
1 litre red wine

1 large onion, chopped
1 large carrot, chopped
1 bay leaf
vegetable oil
seasoned flour
1 litre veal stock
2 litres chicken stock

COCKLES
400g cockles, cleaned
1 glass of white wine
2 tbsp crème fraîche

1 Put the oxtail in a bowl with the red wine, onion, carrot and bay leaf. Cover and leave to marinate in a cool place for 24 hours.

2 Preheat the oven to 140°C/gas 1.

3 Strain off the red wine from the oxtail and vegetables and place in a saucepan. Bring to the boil, skimming off any scum that rises to the surface. Meanwhile, heat some vegetable oil in a heavy-bottomed pan that can be put into the oven. Dust the oxtail in seasoned flour, then add to the pan and colour a golden brown on all sides. Remove from the pan and set aside. Add the marinated vegetables to the pan and cook until golden brown. Deglaze the pan with the hot red wine, then reduce by half.

4 Return the oxtail to the pan. Cover with the veal and chicken stocks and bring to the boil. Skim, then cover and place in the oven to cook for $2^1/_2$ hours.

5 Remove from the oven and leave to cool. When cooled, remove the oxtail and pick the meat from the bones, retaining the meat in large pieces; discard the bones. Strain the liquid into a saucepan and reduce by half. Keep the meat and sauce warm.

6 To cook the cockles place them in a warm pan with the white wine, cover and cook on a high heat for 1–2 minutes or until they open. Drain in a colander set in a bowl. Set the liquid to one side. Pick the cockles from their shells (leaving a few in shell).

7 Warm some olive oil in a deep pan and add the sea beet. Season with salt, pepper, nutmeg and lemon juice. Cook for 30 seconds to wilt. Keep hot.

8 Heat a little olive oil in a non-stick pan. Place the turbot in the pan and cook until the underside is brown. Turn the turbot pieces over and lower the heat. Cook for a further 2–3 minutes maximum. Add a knob of butter to finish.

9 To serve, place the sea beet on warm plates and arrange the cockles and picked oxtail around. Drizzle with the oxtail sauce. Position the turbot on the sea beet. Bring the cockle liquid to the boil, whisk in the crème fraîche and pour on to the plates.

SALAD OF SEA TROUT
WITH LAVER BREAD

SERVES 4
2 whole sea trout, filleted
8–12 baby violet artichokes
lemon juice
1 small carrot, diced
1 small bulb fennel, diced
1 garlic clove, crushed
olive oil

sprig of thyme
100ml white wine
rock salt and pepper

LAVER BREAD
100g laver bread
100g fine oatmeal
butter and vegetable oil

1 Remove any pin bones from the trout fillets, then score the skin. Set aside.

2 Prepare the artichokes by pulling off any large leaves, trimming and peeling them, then scooping out the chokes. As each one is prepared, drop immediately into a bowl of water and lemon juice to prevent discoloration.

3 Cook the carrot, fennel and garlic in a little olive oil with the thyme and a pinch of salt until lightly coloured. Add the artichokes and cover with the white wine and 100ml water. Cook for about 10 minutes or until the artichokes are tender (test with the tip of a sharp knife).

4 Meanwhile, mix together the laver bread and oatmeal with some salt and pepper and shape into four little cakes. Fry in butter with a touch of vegetable oil until golden brown on both sides. Remove from the pan and keep hot.

5 Pan-fry the trout fillets in a little hot olive oil, skin side down first, for about 2 minutes on each side.

6 To serve, place a laver bread cake in the centre of each plate and spoon the warm artichokes on top. Place the trout fillets on the vegetables.

Laver bread, or 'bara lawr' in Welsh, is an edible seaweed common to Wales's south west coast. Traditionally, it's boiled for up to 5 hours, reduced to a jelly and served with bacon.

144

WILD SEA BASS
GLAZED WITH A PINE NUT CRUST
WITH RED WINE SHALLOTS,
PARSNIP PURÉE AND BABY TURNIPS

SERVES 4
2 wild sea bass, 400–600g total weight,
    filleted and skinned
olive oil
salt and pepper

PINE NUT CRUST
100g toasted pine nuts
65g softened butter
1 tsp chopped chervil
½ garlic clove, chopped

RED WINE SHALLOTS
40g long shallots, finely diced
olive oil
30g caster sugar
30ml Cabernet Sauvignon vinegar
50ml Port
100ml red wine

PARSNIP PURÉE
75g butter
3 large parsnips, diced
1 tsp mild curry powder
50ml double cream

TURNIPS
8 or more leafy baby turnips
pinch of caster sugar
sprig of thyme
knob of butter

1 First make the pine nut crust. Roughly chop the pine nuts, then mix very well with all the other ingredients plus a pinch of salt. Place the mixture between two sheets of baking parchment on a tray and spread out evenly using a rolling pin until about 2mm thick. Place in the freezer. Once frozen, cut the crust to the same size as the sea bass fillets and return to the freezer.

2 Next prepare the red wine shallots. Fry the shallots in a little olive oil until slightly softened, without colouring them. Season with salt, then add the sugar and stir to dissolve. Add the vinegar and reduce until sticky. Add the Port and red wine, and reduce slowly. Before the sauce becomes thick, spoon out a little and reserve, then continue reducing the remainder until quite thick. Set aside.

3 To make the parsnip purée, melt the butter in a heavy-bottomed pan. When foaming add the parsnips and season with the curry powder and a little salt. Cook until very soft. If the parsnips look like they are becoming too dark or are sticking to the pan, add a little water from time to time. Add the cream, then purée in a food processor until very smooth. Correct the seasoning and set aside.

4 To prepare the turnips, take off the leaves, wash and reserve. Blanch the turnips in boiling salted water for 30 seconds, then cool in iced water. When cold, peel by

rubbing off the skin. Return to the pan, cover well with cold water and add the sugar, thyme and a pinch of salt. Bring to the boil and simmer until tender. Pour off most of the cooking liquid, then set aside.

5 When ready to serve, preheat the grill. Season the fish on both sides. Heat a little olive oil in a non-stick pan and fry the fish for 1 minute on each side. Transfer to a baking sheet and place the pine nut crust on top of the fish. Glaze under the grill until an even golden brown.

6 Meanwhile, warm the shallots. Add the butter to the turnips and warm through, then add the reserved turnip leaves and heat until wilted. Heat the parsnip purée in a small non-stick pot.

7 To serve, arrange the parsnip purée and shallots side by side on warm plates. Place the fish on the purée, and the turnips with their leaves around the fish. Drizzle round the reserved red wine sauce and a little olive oil.

Morecambe Bay is famous for wild sea bass, which thrive in its waters between May and October, reaching over 4kg in weight. It's a wonderfully adaptable fish, often at its best simply barbecued. Here it makes a brilliant though unlikely foil for the earthy, robust taste of turnip and parsnip.

INDIAN SPICED HALIBUT
WITH SOUTHPORT SHRIMP BIRYANI
AND MINI BHAJIS

SERVES 4
4 halibut fillets, each 100g
butter
salt and pepper

SPICED OIL
200ml vegetable oil
4 red chillies, puréed
1 tsp each coriander seeds, cumin seeds
    and black mustard seeds
2 star anise
1 garlic clove, peeled

BIRYANI
250g Basmati rice
½ onion
2 garlic cloves

2.5cm piece fresh ginger
4 red chillies
50g butter
1 tsp turmeric
15g garam masala
2 bay leaves
150g peeled brown shrimps
50ml rose water
juice of 1 lime

BHAJIS
150g gram flour
2 shallots, finely sliced
1 red chilli, finely chopped
oil for deep frying

1 First make the spiced oil. Combine all the ingredients, pop into a bottle and leave to infuse for at least 1 week.

2 To make the biryani, wash the rice in a colander, then leave to soak in water to cover for 30 minutes. Meanwhile, purée the onion, garlic, ginger and chillies in a food processor, then fry in the butter for about 20 minutes or until golden.

3 Preheat the oven to 200°C/gas 6.

4 Drain the rice, then add to the pan together with the turmeric, garam masala, bay leaves and just enough water to cover. Bring to the boil, then cook until the rice is just done. Fold in the shrimps. Transfer to a baking dish, cover with foil and bake for 10 minutes. Just before serving stir in the rose water and lime juice.

5 For the bhajis, make a batter by combining the flour with a little water, then add the shallots and chilli. Shape into tiny rounds and deep fry until crisp and golden. Drain on kitchen paper and keep hot.

6 To finish, season the fish fillets well and fry in butter for 1 minute on each side.

7 To serve, spoon the biryani on to the centre of the warm plates, sit the fish on top, drizzle with spiced oil and garnish with mini bhajis.

148

SEA BASS IN COCONUT MILK
AND GINGER SAUCE WITH CURRY LEAF POTATOES
TOPPED WITH ASPARAGUS CRESS

SERVES 4

4 small fillets of sea bass or sea bream,
  each 80–100g
vegetable oil
salt and pepper

COCONUT AND GINGER SAUCE

1 tbsp coconut or vegetable oil
¼ tsp mustard seeds
10 curry leaves
1 tsp finely chopped fresh ginger
3 garlic cloves, sliced into fine strips
2 green chillies, slit lengthways
2 onions, finely sliced
1½ tsp ground turmeric
1 tsp ground coriander
¼ tsp ground black pepper

2 tbsp freshly prepared tamarind extract
  (made by soaking tamarind slab in
  water and passing through a sieve)
400ml coconut milk

CURRY LEAF POTATOES

200g Jersey Royal potatoes, peeled
1 tbsp vegetable oil
¼ tsp finely chopped fresh ginger
¼ tsp black gram lentil
¼ tsp mustard seeds
10 curry leaves, deep fried and crushed
1 tbsp finely chopped coriander leaves

ASPARAGUS CRESS SALAD

asparagus cress
mustard cress
coriander cress
curry leaf oil

1 First make the sauce. Heat the oil in a flat pan and sauté the mustard seeds and curry leaves until they splutter. Add the ginger, garlic, green chillies and sliced onions and sauté until the onions are translucent. Reduce the heat to low and stir in the ground spices. Pour in 120ml water and add the tamarind extract. Once the sauce comes to a simmer, add the coconut milk and $1^1/2$ tsp salt. Simmer until the sauce is thick. Remove from the heat and set aside. Reheat for serving.

2 Cook the potatoes in boiling salted water until just tender; drain. Heat the oil and sauté the ginger, gram lentil and mustard seeds until spluttering. Add the potatoes and stir well to mix, crushing them roughly, then add the curry leaves and $^1/4$ tsp salt. Cook for a further 2–3 minutes. Remove from the heat and keep warm. Add the chopped coriander just before serving.

3 Pan fry the fish in some hot oil, making the skin very crisp.

4 Meanwhile, mix all the cresses together and dress with a little curry leaf oil.

5 To serve, place the potatoes in the centre of the warm plates and spoon the sauce around them. Place the fish on top of the potatoes and garnish with the cress salad. Drizzle with a little more curry leaf oil.

WILD TROUT
WITH ASPARAGUS, PEAS AND A CITRUS BUTTER VINAIGRETTE

SERVES 4

1 large fillet of wild trout, about 500g
2 tbsp light olive oil
125g shelled fresh peas
8 asparagus spears, peeled and cut into 1cm dice
1 leek, cut into 1cm slices
handful of pea shoots (optional)
salt and white pepper

CITRUS BUTTER VINAIGRETTE

2 tbsp finely chopped shallots
150ml dry white wine
1 tsp grated lemon zest
150g butter

1 Check the fish for bones and carefully scale the skin side with a blunt serrated knife. Rinse and pat dry. Cut into four portions and carefully make four or five shallow incisions in the skin of each portion using a very sharp knife. Brush with the olive oil and season, then place skin side up on a baking sheet. Set aside.

2 To make the vinaigrette, boil the shallots with the white wine in a small saucepan until reduced by half. Remove from the heat. Add the lemon zest and allow to infuse while you clarify the butter.

3 Melt the butter in another saucepan, bring to the boil and boil for 3–4 minutes. Remove from the heat and allow to settle, then skim off any foam or scum from the top. Pour the clear butter into the shallot reduction, leaving any milky residue behind in the pan (discard the milky residue). Season the vinaigrette and set aside. Warm through for serving.

4 Preheat the grill to high.

5 Place the trout fillets under the grill. Cook, without turning, until the skin is nicely crisp and the fish is just cooked. This should take 5–8 minutes, depending on the heat of the grill and the thickness of the fillets.

6 While the fish is grilling, cook the vegetables. Drop the peas and diced asparagus into a pan of boiling salted water and cook for 3 minutes, then add the leeks and cook for a further 2 minutes or until just tender. Drain thoroughly, then toss with the optional pea shoots.

7 To serve, spoon the hot vegetables into the centre of each warmed plate. Spoon over the warm citrus butter vinaigrette and top with the fillets of fish.

PAN-FRIED WILD SALMON
WITH SPICED SHELLFISH BUTTER

SERVES 4

150ml dry white wine

2 shallots, finely chopped

1 garlic clove, finely chopped

½ tsp soft thyme leaves

350g each small mussels and cockles
   or small clams

1 tsp olive oil

4 fillets of wild salmon, each about 175g,
   skinned

25g unsalted butter

1 tbsp reduced tomato passata or
   thinned tomato purée

115g peeled cooked brown shrimps, peeled

2 large diver-caught scallops, diced

8 Ratte or Pink Fir Apple potatoes, steamed
   until tender and peeled

salt and pepper

CAFÉ DE PARIS BUTTER

35ml tomato ketchup

25g English mustard

25g capers

2 shallots, finely chopped

handful of parsley, finely chopped

1 tbsp snipped chives

½ tsp chopped marjoram

½ tsp thyme leaves

6 tarragon leaves, finely chopped

½ tsp chopped rosemary

1 garlic clove, finely chopped

6 anchovy fillets, finely chopped

1 tbsp brandy

1 tbsp Madeira

½ tsp Worcestershire sauce

1 tbsp paprika

½ tsp curry powder

½ tsp cayenne

grated zest and juice of 1 lemon

grated zest of 1 orange

450g butter, at room temperature,
   cut into small cubes

1 First make the Café de Paris butter. Combine all the ingredients, except the butter, and add 1 tsp salt. Set aside for 4 hours. Beat the butter until fluffy, then mix in the other ingredients. Transfer to a sheet of cling film and shape into a neat log about 2.5cm in diameter. Wrap in the film and chill. (This will make more butter than you need for this recipe, but it can be kept in the freezer for up to 6 months; it is good on steaks, chicken and fish.)

2 Heat the wine with the shallots, garlic and thyme in a large saucepan over a low heat for 3 minutes. Increase the heat and add the mussels and cockles. Cover with a lid and give the pan a good shake, then cook for about 3 minutes or until all the shells have just opened. Discard any that don't open.

3 Tip into a sieve or colander set over a bowl so you can retain the juices. When cool enough to handle, remove the mussels and cockles from their shells and set aside. Retain a few in shell for garnish.

4 Return the juices to the pan and reduce over a high heat until you have 4 tbsp left. Remove from the heat and keep warm.

5 Heat a large frying pan until very hot. Add 1 tbsp of the Café de Paris butter and the oil. Season the salmon and place in the pan. Cook for 2–3 minutes on each side, depending on the thickness; remove and keep warm in a low oven.

6 Pour the shellfish juices into the hot fish pan and stir to combine with the pan juices. Add 2 tbsp Café de Paris butter, the unsalted butter and the reduced passata and cook until emulsified. Check the seasoning. Add the shelled mussels and cockles, shrimps and scallops to the shellfish butter and warm through.

7 To serve, place the salmon fillets on four warmed plates and spoon the shellfish and shellfish butter mixture over the fish. Garnish with the mussels and cockles in shell and the steamed potatoes.

Wild salmon, now rare, was once abundant in the Wye and Severn. One 19th-century chef at London's Reform Club had his salmon sent from Shrewsbury to London in time for that evening's dinner. In the Middle Ages, wild salmon was so common that apprentices insisted they should be fed it no more than three times a week.

BLACKENED
FILLET OF MACKEREL
ROOT VEGETABLES AND HORSERADISH CREAM

SERVES 4

1 tsp black peppercorns, crushed

pinch of cayenne pepper

1 tsp cumin seeds, toasted and crushed

½ tsp fennel seeds, crushed

1 tsp coriander seeds, crushed

4 large fillets of mackerel, all tiny bones removed

50ml olive oil

salt and pepper

ROOT VEGETABLES

100g diced cooked celeriac

60g diced cooked beetroot

10g coriander leaves, chopped

50ml tarragon vinaigrette

2 tsp lime juice

5g caster sugar

HORSERADISH CREAM

200ml whipping cream

55g freshly grated horseradish

½ bunch of chives, chopped

TO FINISH

25ml balsamic vinegar

salad leaves tossed in a little vinaigrette

juice of 1 lemon

1 Mix together the peppercorns and spices on a plate. Place the mackerel fillets, skin side down, in the spice mixture. Set aside.

2 Combine the celeriac and beetroot in a bowl. Add the remaining ingredients for the root vegetables, with $1/3$ tsp salt and pepper to taste.

3 Make the horseradish cream by combining the cream with the horseradish, chives and seasoning to taste, passing through a sieve and then whipping until thick.

4 On four plates, make lines of horseradish cream alternating with lines of balsamic vinegar. Dress each plate with a bouquet of salad leaves tossed in vinaigrette.

5 Heat the oil in a heavy-bottomed frying pan until it is smoking. Carefully place the mackerel fillets in the pan, skin side down. Reduce the heat slightly and cook for 2 minutes on each side.

6 Spoon the root vegetables on to the warm plates in a mound.

7 Flip the mackerel fillets and cook for a further 1 minute. Sprinkle with lemon juice, then carefully place the fillets over the vegetable dice. Serve at once.

154

SEARED HOME SMOKED SALMON
WITH AN APPLE AND WATERCRESS SALAD
AND HORSERADISH CREAM

SERVES 4

4 thick pieces of best quality smoked organic
    salmon, each 85-90g (look for a darker
    smoke and fish that has not been brined)
sunflower oil
salt

**NICK NAIRN COOK SCHOOL OATMEAL BREAD
(OPTIONAL)**

21g milk powder
610ml lukewarm water
40g fresh yeast
21g caster sugar
500g strong white flour
500g brown flour
100g pinhead oatmeal
18g salt
50ml virgin olive oil

APPLE AND WATERCRESS SALAD

125g white cabbage, very finely shredded
2 tbsp rice wine vinegar
1 tsp caster sugar
½ red chilli, finely sliced
2 spring onions, finely sliced at an angle
½ apple (we use James Grieve), skin on,
    grated
lime juice to taste
80g watercress, thick stalks removed,
    or organic mustard greens

HORSERADISH CREAM

3 tbsp mayonnaise (shop bought is fine)
3 tbsp freshly grated horseradish
2 tbsp crème fraîche
1 tsp freshly squeezed lemon juice

1 If making the oatmeal bread, whisk the milk powder into the warm water, then
add the yeast and sugar and stir gently. Leave to stand for 10 minutes to give the
yeast time to activate.

2 Sift the flours, oatmeal and salt into a large bowl and mix lightly. Add the yeast
mixture, stirring all the time. Add the oil, again stirring constantly, and mix into
a dough. Knead for 10 minutes (6–8 minutes in a mixer).

3 Lightly oil a big bowl. Place the dough in the bowl, cover with cling film or
a damp cloth and leave to prove at room temperature until doubled in size.

4 Remove from the bowl and re-mix, knocking the air out. Form into individual
loaves. You should get about four. Place these loaves on a baking sheet lined with
baking parchment. Place the baking sheet in a bin bag and blow air into it. Scrunch
up the end, catching the air inside, to make a sort of tent for your loaves to sit in.
Allow them to double in size once more.

5 Preheat the oven to 200°C/gas 6.

6 Remove the bin bag. Lightly score the tops of the loaves and dust with flour. Bake
for 40–50 minutes or until the bread sounds hollow when tapped on the base. Cool.

7 For the salad, mix the shredded cabbage with the rice wine vinegar, sugar and
a pinch of salt. Leave to marinate for 40 minutes at room temperature.

8 Then add the chilli, spring onions, apple, lime juice and salt to taste, and stir
in well. Using a fork will help to mix all the components evenly together. Divide

the salad into four portions and arrange on the left side of each of four plates.
9 Prepare the horseradish cream by combining all the ingredients in a bowl
and mixing well.
10 At the last minute, flash fry the smoked salmon in a little hot sunflower oil
for about 30 seconds on each side. Place the watercress on the cabbage salad and
top with the smoked salmon. Place a blob of horseradish cream to the side. Serve
immediately, with the oatmeal bread.

SIMON RIMMER

FILLET OF TROUT
WITH GIROLLE MUSHROOMS AND ALMONDS

SERVES 4
4 trout fillets, each 100g
lemon juice
melted butter
salt and pepper

MUSHROOM AND ALMOND MIXTURE
1 shallot, finely chopped
50g butter
125g girolles
75g toasted flaked almonds
1 tbsp aged sherry vinegar
1 tsp chopped flat-leaf parsley
75g fresh brown breadcrumbs

1 Preheat the grill.
2 To make the mushroom and almond mixture, gently fry the shallot in the butter
until soft but not coloured. Chuck in the mushrooms and crank up the heat, then
cook for about 1 minute. Drop the heat right down and stir in the almonds, vinegar,
parsley and seasoning. Finally, fold in the crumbs. Keep warm.
3 Season the fish, brush with a mix of lemon juice and butter and grill for a couple
of minutes on each side.
4 Serve each fillet of trout on top of a spoonful of the delicious mushroom mix.

POACHED SALMON
WITH FENNEL PURÉE AND ALMOND AND SHRIMP BUTTER

SERVES 4
1 whole fillet of salmon
court bouillon
salt and pepper

ALMOND AND SHRIMP BUTTER
50g chopped shallots
100g unsalted butter, softened
70g blanched almonds, sliced
250g peeled brown shrimps
20g dill, chopped
20g chives, chopped
10ml Pernod
juice of ½ lemon

FENNEL PUREE
2 bulbs fennel, finely sliced on
    a mandolin
75g chopped shallots
10g unsalted butter
5g fennel seeds
5g coriander seeds
150ml chicken stock
50ml double cream
20ml Pernod
100g fennel tops, chopped

1 First make the almond and shrimp butter. Sweat the shallots in a little of the butter, to soften. Transfer to a bowl and add the remaining softened butter. Mix in the almonds, shrimps, dill, chives, Pernod, lemon juice and salt and pepper to taste. Place the butter mixture in the centre of a piece of cling film and wrap up tightly to form a neat cylinder shape. Secure the ends and place in the fridge (or in the freezer) to harden.

2 To make the fennel purée, sauté the sliced fennel and shallots in the butter with the fennel and coriander seeds for 12–15 minutes, to soften. Add the stock and reduce by half.

3 Pour in the cream and add the Pernod, fennel tops and salt and pepper to taste. Transfer the mixture to a food processor and blend until smooth. If not serving straight away, pour the purée into a bowl set over a bowl of iced water, to cool (this will preserve the colour); reheat for serving.

4 Cut the salmon fillet into four pieces. Poach in the court bouillon for 6 minutes. Remove from the bouillon and allow to rest for 2–3 minutes.

5 To serve, spoon the warm fennel purée on to the plates and place the poached salmon on top. Remove the almond and shrimp butter from the cling film and cut into discs. Place on top of the salmon.

SEARED HERRING IN OATMEAL
WITH CELERIAC RÉMOULADE, GARDEN CRESS AND CHAMPAGNE CHIVE BUTTER SAUCE

SERVES 4

4 plump fillets of herring
100g oatmeal to coat
butter
handful of garden cress lightly dressed
    with a tarragon vinaigrette
salt and pepper

CELERIAC RÉMOULADE

½ head of celeriac
2 heaped tbsp coarse grain Arran mustard
2–3 tbsp mayonnaise to bind

CHAMPAGNE AND CHIVE BUTTER SAUCE

1 large shallot, finely chopped
1 tsp butter
150ml Champagne
1 good tbsp Champagne vinegar
1 tbsp double cream
200g cold unsalted butter, diced
1 tbsp finely chopped chives

1 First make the celeriac rémoulade. Peel and shred the celeriac, then mix with the mustard, salt and pepper and enough mayonnaise to bind. Leave overnight.
2 For the Champagne and chive butter sauce, sweat the shallot in 1 tsp butter, then pour in the Champagne and vinegar. Reduce until almost all the liquid has evaporated. Add the cream and bring back to the boil, then whisk in the diced cold butter, a few pieces at a time. Keep the sauce warm but do not boil. Just before serving add the chives.
3 Fold each herring fillet in half, skin side in, and coat with oatmeal. Pan fry gently in a little bit of butter for 2–3 minutes on each side.
4 To serve, spoon the celeriac rémoulade on the warm plates and top with the cress. Place the fish on this and pour over the butter sauce.

For centuries, oatmeal and herring – the silver darlings – have been staples of the Scottish diet. Together, rich in fibre and Omega-3 oils, they make a delicious dish that's good for heart and brain.

HARI MACHCHI
PAN-FRIED JOHN DORY MARINATED IN GREEN SPICE PASTE WITH OVEN-ROASTED BABY TOMATOES

SERVES 4
4 fillets of john dory
2 tbsp lemon juice
4 tbsp vegetable oil
salt and pepper

CORIANDER OIL
small bunch of coriander leaves
100ml olive oil

GREEN SPICE PASTE
50g mint leaves
50g coriander leaves
10g peeled fresh ginger
2 green chillies
1½ tsp fenugreek leaf powder
2 tsp chaat masala
1 tsp red chilli powder
2 tbsp gram flour

CORIANDER-INFUSED MUSHROOMS
1 tbsp vegetable oil
2 tbsp finely chopped onion
½ tsp coriander seeds, lightly crushed

100g shiitake mushrooms, thinly sliced
¼ tsp red chilli powder
¼ tsp ground turmeric
1 tbsp finely diced tomatoes
1 tbsp finely chopped coriander leaves

OVEN-ROASTED TOMATOES
1 tbsp vegetable oil
½ tsp each onion seeds, cumin seeds,
  sesame seeds, finely chopped fresh
  ginger and green chilli
24-30 baby plum or cherry tomatoes
  on the vine, separated into 4 portions
  on the vine
¼ tsp each fenugreek leaf powder, red
  chilli powder, ground coriander and
  ground turmeric
coarsely crushed black pepper

GARNISH
lemon juice
50g asparagus cress or mustard cress
12-16 sprigs of coriander

1 First make the coriander oil. Shock-blanch the coriander in boiling water, then drain and refresh. Squeeze dry in kitchen paper. Blend the coriander with the oil until smooth. Strain through a muslin cloth, then set aside. The oil can be kept in the fridge for 2 days. (You can make other herb oils in the same way.)
2 Place the fish fillets in a colander and sprinkle with the lemon juice and $^1/_2$ tsp salt. Leave for 15 minutes to drain the excess moisture.
3 Meanwhile, make the green spice paste. Blend all the ingredients together with $^1/_2$ tsp salt in a blender or food processor. Transfer to a shallow dish.
4 Pat the fish dry and put into the spice paste. Leave to marinate for 40 minutes.
5 Next prepare the mushrooms. Heat the oil in a pan and sauté the onion with the coriander seeds until translucent. Add the mushrooms and sauté for 2–3 minutes. Stir in the spices and sauté for 2 minutes, then add the tomatoes and $^1/_4$ tsp salt. Cook for 1–2 minutes. Remove from the heat and set aside, ready to reheat. Stir in the chopped coriander before serving.
6 Preheat the oven to 180°C/gas 4.
7 To prepare the tomatoes, heat the oil in a heavy-bottomed pan and sauté the onion,

cumin and sesame seeds with the ginger and green chilli until the seeds begin to pop. Add the tomatoes and sauté until they are slightly bruised by the heat and the skins burst open. Sprinkle with the spices, $^1/_4$ tsp salt and coarse pepper to taste, then transfer to the oven to roast for 3–4 minutes.

8 Meanwhile, cook the fish. Heat the oil in a flat pan. Shake off excess paste from the fillets, then place in the hot oil, flesh side down. Shallow fry for 3–4 minutes, then turn the fillets and fry the other side until the fish is cooked. Remove the fish from the pan and place on kitchen paper to remove the excess oil. Keep warm.

9 Make a dressing by mixing 2 tbsp of the coriander oil with lemon juice and seasoning to taste. Toss the cress and coriander sprigs in some of the dressing.

10 To serve, place the roasted tomatoes (still on the vine) in the centre of the warm plates. Place the pan-fried fish on the tomatoes and top with the mushrooms. Garnish with the cress salad and drizzle over the remaining coriander oil dressing.

BRYN WILLIAMS

GRILLED AND SMOKED MACKEREL
WITH CITRUS FRUITS

SERVES 4
4 mackerel, each 350g
pinch of turmeric (optional)
olive oil
salt and pepper

SAUCE
1 carrot, chopped
1 onion, chopped
2 garlic cloves, crushed
1 lemon, sliced
6 black peppercorns
1 bay leaf
1 star anise
bunch of basil

100ml dry white wine
100ml olive oil
50g butter

CITRUS FRUITS
1 orange
1 pink grapefruit
100ml sugar
50ml white wine vinegar

GARNISH
12 Charlotte potatoes
50ml olive oil
2 celery sticks
1 small celeriac
butter

1 To make the sauce, put the carrot and onion in a large pan with garlic, lemon slices, peppercorns, bay leaf and star anise. Add water to cover and bring to the boil. Reduce the heat and simmer for 8 minutes. Add the basil stalks and cook for a further 2 minutes. Remove the pan from the heat. Add the white wine and leave to infuse until needed.

2 When ready to serve, strain the stock, bring back to the boil and whisk in the olive oil and julienned basil leaves. Finish by incorporating the butter.

3 To prepare the citrus fruits, thinly peel the zest from the orange and grapefruit and cut into julienne. Place in a small pan of water and bring to the boil, then drain and refresh. Repeat this blanching procedure three times. In another pan dissolve the sugar in 100ml water and bring to the boil. Add the zest and simmer for 40 minutes or until tender. Remove from the heat and add the vinegar to give a balance of sweet and sour flavours. Set aside.

4 Peel and segment the citrus fruits, keeping all the juices, and place to one side.

5 Prepare the mackerel by gutting and washing it. Dry with kitchen paper. For the optional garnish, cut off 6cm of the tail end, keeping it on the bone. (This is for the smoking part of the dish.) Fillet the fish. Remove all pin bones from the fillets, then wash the fillets and pat dry. Trim the edges to neaten and leave to one side.

6 If you are going to prepare the optional smoked fish garnish, score the tail skin, then mix the tails with half of the citrus juice and the turmeric. Leave for 30 minutes. Before serving, smoke on the stove for 4–5 minutes and keep warm.

7 For the garnish, 'turn' the potatoes (or just peel them and cut into neat shapes), then cook in boiling salted water until almost tender. When nearly ready drain them and place in the remaining fruit juice with the olive oil. Leave to cool so they can take on the citrus flavours. Before serving bring the potatoes up to the boil in the juice and oil mixture.

8 Peel the celery and celeriac, then cut into equal-sized batons (12 of each). Cook in just enough seasoned water to cover with a knob of butter until just tender but not soft. Drain and keep hot.

9 Preheat the grill to high.

10 Place the mackerel fillets, skin side up, on an oiled baking tray. Brush the skin with oil and season. Place under the grill and cook for 3–4 minutes, without turning.

11 Meanwhile, make a bed of the hot batons of celery and celeriac on the warm plates. When the mackerel is ready place two fillets on each bed, skin side up. Place the warm mackerel tail standing up on top of the plate.

12 Add the hot potatoes to the side of the grilled mackerel and garnish the fish with segments of orange and pink grapefruit. Sprinkle the drained zest on the fish and spoon the sauce around the dish. Serve immediately.

ROAST TURBOT
WITH A LOBSTER, TOMATO AND TARRAGON VINAIGRETTE

SERVES 4
1 live lobster, about 500g
4 skinned fillets of turbot, each 120g
1 tbsp light olive oil
15g butter
salt and white pepper

LOBSTER CREAM SAUCE
1 tbsp light olive oil
1 tbsp each chopped carrot and onion
1 garlic clove, crushed
½ tbsp tomato paste
1 tbsp brandy
75ml white wine
150ml double cream

TOMATO AND TARRAGON VINAIGRETTE
½ tsp Dijon mustard
1½ tbsp white wine vinegar
90ml extra virgin olive oil
½ tsp crushed garlic
1 tsp chopped tarragon
½ tbsp chopped parsley
½ tbsp snipped chives
1 plum tomato, skinned, halved,
   deseeded and cut into 5mm dice

GARNISH
few sprigs of tarragon and chervil

1 Bring a large pan of salted water to a vigorous boil. Kill the lobster, then put into the boiling water. Cook for 12 minutes. Lift it out and plunge into a sink or bowl of cold water to stop the cooking process.

2 When cool enough to handle, pull off the claws, crack them and remove the meat. Pull the head and body section from the lobster tail, then cut the tail in half along the length. Discard the intestinal tract. Remove the tail meat and slice it up neatly, along with the claw meat. Set the meat aside.

3 To make the sauce, heat the oil in a very large pot until smoking. Roughly chop the lobster shells and head and body section, toss into the pot and sauté over a high heat for 3 minutes. Add the vegetables and garlic and cook for a further 2 minutes. Add the tomato paste, brandy and white wine. Allow the wine to reduce by half. Add 1 litre of water, reduce the heat and simmer for 20 minutes.

4 Strain the lobster stock through a fine sieve into a clean pan, then reduce to about 250ml. Add the cream and boil until thick and creamy. Set aside. Reheat for serving.

5 For the vinaigrette, whisk together the mustard, vinegar and some seasoning. Whisk in the oil, then the garlic and herbs. Stir in the tomato dice. Transfer to a pan.

6 Season the turbot with salt and pepper. Heat the oil in a large, heavy frying pan until it is almost smoking. Add the butter and, as it begins to foam, put the fillets in the pan. Sauté for about 3 minutes on each side. Test for doneness by pressing the fillets. If they want to flake apart, they are cooked and ready.

7 While the fish is cooking, gently heat the lobster in the vinaigrette.

8 To serve, spoon the lobster and vinaigrette on to warmed plates and drizzle round the lobster sauce. Place a fillet in the middle and garnish with tarragon and chervil.

LOBSTER MACARONI
WITH ROCKET AND PARMESAN

SERVES 4
2 large cooked lobsters, each about 400g
200g macaroni or similar pasta shape
250g rocket leaves
50g Parmesan, freshly grated
Maldon sea salt and pepper
extra freshly grated Parmesan or
   Parmesan shavings, to serve

LOBSTER SAUCE
olive oil
1 tbsp tomato purée
2 tbsp brandy
600ml lobster or langoustine stock
200ml double cream

1 To prepare the lobsters, pull off the large claws and set aside. Place the lobster on a chopping board and uncurl the tail so that the lobster is straight. Using a large sharp knife split the lobster in half, cutting through the head towards the tail. Open out and remove the little 'plastic' stomach sac in the head; discard. Carefully remove the tail meat and dice it. Crack the claws, fish out the meat and pull out the cartilage. Dice the meat and add to the tail meat. (You can add any coral or roe you find and the brownish head meat to the sauce.)

2 Preheat the oven to 220°C/gas 7.

3 To make the lobster sauce, chop the lobster legs into two or three sections and place them in a roasting tray with all of the shells. Toss the legs and shells in a little olive oil, then roast in the oven for 10 minutes.

4 Remove the tray from the oven and set over a moderate heat. Add the tomato purée to the shells and stir well, then brown for a minute or so. Add the brandy and flame it to toast the shells a little more. Pour the lobster stock over the shells, stirring and scraping with a wooden spoon to lift any sediment. Simmer for 10 minutes.

5 Strain the stock through a fine sieve into a saucepan. Bring to a simmer and allow the stock to reduce by four-fifths. Stir in the cream and return to a simmer, then let the sauce reduce by half. It will be really thick and intense at this stage. Keep warm or reduce a bit more if you think it needs it.

6 Cook the pasta in plenty of boiling salted water for 8–12 minutes or until al dente, depending on the pasta size.

7 Meanwhile, roughly chop half the rocket and stir into the sauce together with the Parmesan. Taste and season with salt and pepper, then fold in the diced lobster.

8 Drain the pasta really well, return to the hot pan and mix with the lobster sauce.

9 To serve, spoon the lobster macaroni into warm soup plates and top each serving with a handful of the remaining rocket leaves and a sprinkling of Parmesan.

MORSTON HALL CRAB CAKES
AND TARTARE SAUCE

SERVES 4

225g white crab meat
1 egg yolk, beaten
½ lobe of fresh ginger, finely grated
1 small, mild red chilli, finely chopped
2 tbsp chopped coriander
seasoned plain flour
1 egg, beaten with 80ml milk
Japanese or fine white breadcrumbs
splash of olive oil
knob of butter
salt and pepper
salad leaves, tossed at the very last minute
   with a splash of lemon juice, a small drizzle
   of olive oil and seasoning

TARTARE SAUCE

1 egg
pinch of caster sugar
pinch of English mustard powder
Maldon sea salt
150ml sunflower oil
150ml olive oil
1 tbsp white wine vinegar
1 tbsp lemon juice
2 small shallots, finely chopped
2 tbsp chopped flat-leaf parsley
1 tbsp chopped tarragon
3 small cornichons or 1 small gherkin,
   finely diced

1 In a bowl combine the white crab meat with the beaten egg yolk, ginger, chilli and coriander. Season to taste with salt and pepper. Divide the mixture into eight or 12 equal portions and shape each into a cake. Place the crab cakes on a tray, then put into the freezer for 30 minutes to firm up.

2 Meanwhile, set out three separate bowls, one with seasoned flour, the second with the egg and milk mixture (egg wash) and the third with the breadcrumbs.

3 Remove the crab cakes from the freezer and, one at a time, drop first into the seasoned flour to coat all over; shake off excess flour and dip into the egg wash; shake off any excess egg and turn in the breadcrumbs. Make sure the crab cake is lightly and evenly coated with breadcrumbs before placing it on a tray lined with greaseproof paper. Cover with cling film and refrigerate.

4 To make the tartare sauce, place the egg, sugar, mustard powder and a pinch each of Maldon salt and freshly ground black pepper in a bowl and, using an electric hand mixer on high speed, beat together thoroughly. While beating, slowly drizzle in the sunflower oil, followed by the olive oil and white wine vinegar. Turn off the mixer and stir in the rest of the ingredients, mixing well. Check the seasoning (I prefer flakes of Maldon sea salt and coarsely ground black pepper). This will make more sauce than you need for the dish; keep the remainder in the fridge for up to 5 days.

5 When you are ready to serve, heat a large heavy-based frying pan over a moderate heat. Add a splash of olive oil and a knob of butter, which should foam gently. Place the crab cakes in the pan and fry gently for 4 minutes on each side or until golden.

6 Serve the crab cakes with some tartare sauce and lightly dressed salad leaves.

166

LASAGNE OF MORSTON LOBSTER
WITH GRUYÈRE CREAM SAUCE

SERVES 4
2 live lobsters, each 700g
1 onion, chopped
large bouquet of soft herbs
   (tarragon, parsley, chervil, dill)
1 lemon, quartered
salt and pepper

LOBSTER SAUCE
a little olive oil and butter
1 large leek, roughly chopped
4 large shallots, roughly chopped
bunch of parsley stalks
lemon juice
250g baby plum tomatoes
1.2 litres fish stock or white chicken stock
100ml double cream
bunch of chives, snipped

PASTA
110g '00' pasta flour or strong
   plain flour
6 egg yolks
1 tsp truffle oil or olive oil

GRUYÈRE CREAM SAUCE
1 shallot, sliced
1 tbsp olive oil
a strip of lemon peel
25ml Noilly Prat vermouth
120ml whipping cream
50g Gruyère cheese, grated

1 First cook the lobsters. Bring a large saucepan of water to the boil with the onion, bouquet garni, lemon and 1 tsp salt. Once boiling, lower in the lobsters (first take off the rubber bands that keep the large claws closed). When the water boils again, cook for 6 minutes. Take the lobsters out and immediately plunge into iced water.

2 Place a lobster on a chopping board. Twist off the large claws and the body and head section from the tail. Using a pair of sturdy scissors carefully snip along the length of the tail shell, then ease the meat away from the shell. Using either the back of a knife or a rolling pin, gently break the shell of the claws, then extract the meat. Once you are satisfied you have extracted everything edible from the first lobster, repeat the procedure with the other lobster. Set all the meat aside. Keep the tail shells and body/head sections (not the claw shells) for the lobster sauce. By the way, if the lobsters have any dark green jelly (coral) in their heads, keep this as it is wonderful added to sauces for colour and flavour.

3 Next make the lobster sauce. Preheat the oven to 150°C/gas 2. Place the lobster tail shells and body/head sections in a roasting tin and roast for about 20 minutes to allow the shells to dry out a little.

4 Meanwhile, heat a little olive oil and butter in a saucepan and sweat the leek and shallots with the parsley stalks over a moderate heat. Add the roasted lobster shells together with some lemon juice, the tomatoes and enough stock to cover. Bring slowly to the boil and simmer gently for 1 hour. Remove from the heat and blitz the whole lot (heads included) in a blender or food processor, then pass the mixture through a sieve into a clean saucepan.

5 Bring to the boil again and simmer to reduce by about half, skimming off any scum. Keep tasting. When the sauce has reached the desired consistency and flavour, whisk in the cream. Check the seasoning. Set aside. Just before serving stir in plenty of snipped chives.

6 To make the pasta, sift the flour and a good pinch of salt into the bowl of a food processor. Lightly beat all the egg yolks with the truffle oil in a jug. Turn on the processor and quickly pour in the egg and oil mixture. As soon as the ingredients come together as a crumbly textured dough, remove from the machine and knead into a ball. Wrap in cling film and leave to rest in the fridge for at least an hour.

7 The next stage requires a pasta machine. Cut the pasta dough into two pieces. Take one of the pieces of dough and, on a lightly floured surface, flatten with your hands. Set the pasta machine on its widest setting and roll through the piece of dough. Fold in half and roll it through the machine again, still on its widest setting. Do this seven times in all. Now set the machine on the next setting and roll through once. Repeat on the next setting, then continue the process up to two notches from the thinnest setting. Lay the resulting long strip of pasta on your work surface. Using a 7.5cm round cutter, cut out discs. Repeat with the other piece of pasta dough. You need 12 discs for the lasagne, although I always cut a couple of extra. Allow the pasta discs to dry out while you make the Gruyère cream sauce.

8 Fry the shallot in the olive oil until softened, then add the lemon peel and Noilly Prat and bring to the boil. Simmer to reduce the liquid by half. Add the cream, bring back to the boil and simmer again to reduce and thicken. Pass through a sieve into another saucepan. Set aside, ready to reheat. Just before serving stir in the Gruyère.

9 Now you are ready to assemble the lasagne. Preheat the oven to 140°C/gas 1. Divide the lobster meat into eight equal portions on a buttered baking tray, giving each one a little claw meat as well as tail meat. Cover each portion of lobster with 3 tbsp of lobster sauce, then cover the tray with cling film. Place in the oven to warm through while you cook the pasta.

10 Drop the pasta discs into a pan of gently boiling salted water. Cook for about 3 minutes, then lift them out with a draining spoon. Quickly season and give them a splash of olive oil.

11 To serve, place a pasta disc in the centre of each warm plate. Place a portion of lobster on top, then cover with another pasta disc. Repeat the lobster and pasta layers, then spoon over the remaining lobster sauce and the Gruyère cream sauce.

WEST COAST SCALLOPS
QUINOA AND SMOKED HADDOCK KEDGEREE
WITH MUSTARD LEAVES
AND A LIGHT CURRY DRESSING

SERVES 4
8 scallops, shelled
olive oil
12 mustard leaves or rocket

KEDGEREE
125g quinoa
½ vegetable stock cube
2 fillets of pale-smoked Scrabster haddock
milk
2 bay leaves
few black peppercorns
4 free range eggs, hard-boiled and chopped
2 shallots, finely chopped
good sprig of parsley, chopped

1 small tsp curry powder
butter
cream
juice of 1 lemon

CURRY DRESSING
1 shallot, finely chopped
1 garlic clove, crushed
1 tsp curry powder
vegetable oil
100ml poaching liquid from the
    haddock, or fish stock
½ glass of white wine
bunch of flat-leaf parsley
2 tbsp double cream

1 First cook the quinoa for the kedgeree in water to cover, with the stock cube, for 8–10 minutes or until tender. Drain and reserve.

2 Poach the haddock in milk to cover with the bay leaves and peppercorns for 3–4 minutes. Drain the fish, reserving the liquid. When it is cool enough to handle, flake the fish, discarding skin and bones. Strain the liquid and make up to 100ml with fish stock or water if necessary. Set the fish and liquid aside.

3 To make the dressing, sweat the shallot with the garlic and curry powder in a little vegetable oil until soft but not brown. Pour over the haddock poaching liquid and add a good glug of white wine and the parsley stalks. Bring to the boil, then reduce by two-thirds. Add the cream and reduce to a sauce consistency. Pass through a sieve into a clean pan and add the chopped parsley tops. Set aside, and reheat for serving.

4 To make the kedgeree, combine the quinoa, haddock, eggs, shallots, parsley and curry powder in a bowl and fold together. Season with salt and pepper. Gently warm through in a pan in some butter, adding enough cream to bind and a good squeeze of lemon to taste. Keep warm.

5 If the scallops are large you can cut them across in half. Heat some olive oil in a frying pan, add the scallops and sear for 1–2 minutes on each side.

6 To serve, spoon some kedgeree into the centre of each warm plate, moulding it in a metal ring. Lift off the ring. Arrange the mustard leaves on the kedgeree. Place a scallop on top with the rest to the side. Drizzle the dressing around.

POACHED TURBOT
WITH OYSTERS AND SEAWEED SALAD

SERVES 4
1 leek, finely shredded
unsalted butter
1 fillet of turbot, about 600g, cut
    into 4 portions
8 rock oysters from Loch Leagh
splash of soy sauce
25g shallots, chopped
20g chives, chopped
salt and pepper

SEAWEED SALAD
500g mixed dried and wet seaweed
2 tsp olive oil
1 tsp white wine vinegar
25g shallots, finely chopped

COURT BOUILLON
knob of unsalted butter
2 carrots, diced
3 celery sticks, diced
2 leeks, diced
2 onions, diced
1 bay leaf
sprig of thyme
1 tsp coriander seeds
1 tsp fennels seeds
100ml white wine
50ml white wine vinegar

1 The night before, soak the dried seaweed for the salad in water to cover, to rehydrate. Next morning, drain and rinse well in cold water. Set aside.

2 To make the court bouillon, heat the butter in a large pan and sauté the carrots, celery, leeks and onions for a few minutes. Add the bay leaf with the thyme and stir in the coriander and fennel seeds. Pour in the white wine and vinegar and cook down for few minutes. Cover with water and bring to the boil, then simmer for 30 minutes. Strain into a clean pan and leave to simmer gently until required.

3 Place the leek in a buttered flameproof dish. Season the turbot fillets with salt and pepper, then place on the leek. Spoon over some of the court bouillon and cook for 3–4 minutes. Remove the fish using a slotted spoon and keep hot. (You can keep the court bouillon in the fridge or freezer to use for poaching other fish.)

4 Open the oysters, retaining the juices. Place the oysters in a sieve set in a bowl and drain, reserving the juices. Heat the oyster juices in a pan, add the oysters and poach for 1 minute. Add the soy sauce, a knob of butter and the shallots, then stir in the chopped chives. Heat for a further 2–3 minutes.

5 Meanwhile, make the seaweed salad. Whisk the olive oil and vinegar in a bowl and add the shallots. Place the seaweed in a separate bowl and add the vinaigrette. Toss together to coat.

6 To serve, place the turbot on the warm plates, arrange the dressed seaweed alongside and place the drained oysters on top.

TIAN OF BRIXHAM
SCALLOP AND CRAB MOUSSE
WITH LEMONGRASS AND GINGER SAUCE

SERVES 4
150g shelled scallops
50g brown crab meat
1 egg yolk
250ml whipping cream
150g white crab meat
10g fresh ginger, finely diced
pinch of cayenne pepper
juice of 1 lemon
2 large courgettes, sliced lengthways
salt and pepper

LEMONGRASS AND GINGER SAUCE
75g shallots, chopped
25g fresh ginger, chopped
50g fresh lemongrass, chopped
175g unsalted butter
5g white peppercorns
5g coriander seeds
75g brown crab meat
250g crab carcasses
250ml fish stock
chopped fresh coriander (optional)

GARNISH (OPTIONAL)
grapefruit segments
batons of fresh ginger

1 First prepare the sauce. In a stainless steel saucepan sweat the shallots, ginger and lemongrass in 75g of the butter for 5 minutes, without colouring. Add the peppercorns and coriander seeds and sweat for a further 2 minutes. Add the brown crabmeat and crab carcasses and sweat for 5 minutes longer. Pour in the fish stock, bring to the boil and cook for 20 minutes. Pass through a colander set over a bowl and then through a fine sieve. Reserve in a saucepan for later use.
2 To make the mousse, combine the scallops, brown crab meat, egg yolk and cream in a blender or food processor and blend until very fine and smooth. Remove from the blender and place in a bowl. Set over ice and mix in the white crab meat and ginger, then season with salt, pepper, cayenne and a dash of lemon juice. Set aside.
3 Preheat the oven to 180°C/gas 4.
4 Warm six 6cm diameter metal rings, then wrap cling film tightly around the bottom half. Allow the rings to cool, then butter the insides with softened butter.
5 Blanch the courgettes in boiling water, then drain and pat dry on a cloth. Line the sides of the metal rings with the courgette ribbons. Set them in a baking tray. Fill the moulds with the mousse.
6 Pour some hot water into the baking tray (no higher than the cling film wrapping) and cook in the oven for 8–10 minutes.
7 Meanwhile, to finish the sauce, warm it through, then whisk in the remaining butter and season with salt, pepper and a drop of lemon juice. Add the coriander.
8 To serve, turn out the mousses into the centre of the warm plates, garnish with grapefruit segments and batons of ginger, if using, and drizzle the sauce around.

ASSORTMENT OF CRAB

SERVES 4
2 carrots, roughly chopped
2 onions, roughly chopped
2 celery sticks, roughly chopped
1 live crab, about 2kg
1 tbsp olive oil
1 tbsp tomato purée
250ml brandy
bunch of basil, stalks reserved and
    leaves cut into julienne
3 tomatoes
1 shallot, diced
knob of butter
250ml double cream
squeeze of lemon juice
2 tsp rice wine vinegar
about 3 tbsp toasted sesame oil
squeeze of lime juice
salt and pepper

RAVIOLI
225g Italian 'oo' flour
2 eggs
1 tbsp saffron olive oil (steep a few strands
    of saffron in the oil, then strain)
bunch of basil, finely shredded
drop of lemon juice

CRAB TUILES
50g butter
50g plain flour
50g egg whites (about 2 medium
    egg whites)
sesame seeds

CRAB ROYALE
2 egg yolks
80ml double cream
freshly grated nutmeg

1 To cook the crab, put half the roughly chopped vegetables in a pan of salted water, bring to the boil and simmer for 5 minutes. Add the crab and cook for 9 minutes. When the crab is ready, lift it out and leave to cool. Discard the water and vegetables.
2 Preheat the oven to 140°C/gas 1. Put a roasting tin in the oven to heat.
3 Crack the crab body and claw shells and pick out the meat, keeping the brown and white meat separate. Check through the white crab meat to ensure all of the shell and cartilage are taken out. Chill the crab meat until needed. Bash the crab shells, then place in the hot roasting tin. Cook in the oven for 10–15 minutes or until dry.
4 While the shells are in the oven, make the stock. Sauté the remaining chopped vegetables in the olive oil in a large saucepan over a high heat for about 5 minutes or until golden. Stir in the tomato purée and cook for 2 minutes, stirring. Pour in the brandy, stirring to deglaze the pan. Add the crab shells. Deglaze the roasting tin with a little water to catch up all the flavoursome bits, then pour into the saucepan. Top up with more water (about 1 litre) to cover the vegetables and crab shells. Bring to the boil, skimming frequently. Add the basil stalks and simmer for 40 minutes.
5 Strain the stock through a muslin-lined sieve into a clean pan. Reduce by half over a high heat. Take out 250ml of this stock and reduce in a small pan for 3–4 minutes, to a thick glaze. This will be used later for the dressing and in the crab tuiles. Set the rest of the stock and the glaze aside.

6 To make the crab sauce, blanch the tomatoes, then remove and reserve the skins and seeds. Set the tomatoes aside. Sweat the shallot in the butter in a medium saucepan until translucent. Add the tomato skins and seeds, and cook until they are soft. Pour in the cream and bring to the boil. Add enough of the crab stock to give a sauce consistency and bring back to the boil. Season with lemon juice, salt and pepper to taste. Pass the sauce through a fine sieve and set aside.

7 For the ravioli dough, sift the flour into a bowl. Add the eggs, saffron oil and a pinch of salt. Knead until the dough is smooth, then wrap and leave to rest in the fridge for 1 hour.

8 Meanwhile, to make the mixture for the crab tuiles, heat the butter until it starts to turn brown, then let it cool. Sift the flour into a bowl. Add the browned butter, then the egg whites. Finally, gently mix in enough of the cold crab glaze to bind to a paste. Cover and leave to rest for 1 hour.

9 Preheat the oven to 140°C/gas 1.

10 Pass the reserved brown crab meat through a fine sieve. Weigh out 80g of this sieved meat into a separate bowl and set aside for the crab royale. To make the ravioli filling, mix 50g of the picked white crab meat with the remaining sieved brown crab meat. Add a handful of the shredded basil and season with salt, pepper and a drop of lemon juice. Set aside.

11 To finish the crab royale, add the egg yolks and cream to the 80g sieved brown crab meat. Season with salt, pepper and nutmeg. Mix well and pass through a fine sieve. Divide the mixture among four heatproof shot glasses and stand them in a small deep tin. Pour enough hot water into the tin to come halfway up the glasses. Bake for about 15 minutes or until set like a custard. Remove from the oven and set aside in the tin of hot water. Turn the oven up to 200°C/gas 6.

12 Roll out the ravioli dough as thinly as possible using a pasta machine, then divide into two rectangles, each about 20cm long and 14cm wide. (Keep any remaining dough for another pasta dish.) Lay one rectangle flat on the work surface and mark it into quarters. Divide the ravioli filling into four and pile a portion in the middle of each quarter of the dough sheet, with equal spaces between. Brush the dough around the filling with water and place the second sheet of dough on top, gently pressing to seal. Cut to make four square ravioli. Cover and set aside.

13 Use a palette knife to spread the tuile mixture as thinly as possible into eight oval shapes on one or two baking sheets. Sprinkle with sesame seeds and bake for 5–8 minutes or until golden and crisp. Cool on a wire rack.

14 Add the rice wine vinegar and sesame oil to the remaining crab glaze. Season with salt and pepper and keep this dressing to one side. Finely chop the reserved tomatoes and add to the remaining white crab meat along with the julienned basil. Season with salt, pepper, lime juice and extra sesame oil if needed, and mix well.

15 Cook the ravioli in boiling salted water for 4 minutes; drain.

16 To serve, spoon the white crab meat salad into four 4cm rings set on four plates. Remove the rings. Position the crab tuiles on top. Season the ravioli with salt, place next to the crab salad and drizzle with some of the dressing. Lift the warm shot glasses of crab royale from the water, dry them and put one on each plate. Gently reheat the crab sauce, then foam it using a stick blender and spoon a little foam into each glass on top of the crab royale.

MICHAEL CAINES

PAN-ROASTED SCALLOPS
WITH CRISP SMOKED BELLY PORK,
PEA PURÉE AND A SHALLOT AND BACON FOAM

SERVES 4
8 large scallops
olive oil for frying
lemon juice
salt and pepper
pea shoots to serve

BRAISED BELLY PORK
1 onion, halved
6 cloves
1 piece of smoked, boned pork belly, about 500g, preferably Gloucestershire Old Spot or another traditional breed
6 shallots, peeled
1 carrot, halved lengthways
4 garlic cloves, peeled
about 1 tbsp fresh ginger peelings
2 tsp black peppercorns
1 tsp chicken bouillon powder
1 star anise
10 juniper berries
1 strip of orange zest, oven-dried or fresh
bouquet garni

OLIVE OIL VINAIGRETTE
150ml olive oil
3 tbsp Champagne vinegar or white wine vinegar
1 small garlic clove, lightly crushed
small sprig of fresh thyme

SHALLOT AND BACON FOAM
200g smoked bacon, chopped
250ml milk
70g unsalted butter, plus a knob to finish
250g shallots, sliced
large sprig of thyme
1 bay leaf
300ml fish stock
3 tbsp double cream

PEA PURÉE
300g frozen peas
100g unsalted butter, cut into pieces

1 For the belly pork, stud each onion half with 3 cloves and place in a saucepan with the belly pork, the rest of the pork ingredients and 1.5 litres water. Bring to the boil, then immediately reduce the heat so the water is at 80–90°C (use a thermometer to check). The water must not boil while the belly cooks. Cook for 2–3 hours or until cooked and tender. Allow to cool in the liquid.

2 Remove the belly pork, place on a tray and set another tray on top. Wrap completely in cling film, ensuring the pork is pressed flat. Chill for 6 hours. Strain the cooking liquid and reserve.

3 Meanwhile, mix all the ingredients for the vinaigrette in a bowl. Pour into a bottle or plastic pourer and set aside. Shake well before using.

4 To make the shallot and bacon foam, place the chopped bacon and milk in a saucepan and bring to the boil. Set aside to infuse. Meanwhile, heat the 70g of butter in a pan, add the shallots and a pinch of salt, and sweat until softened but not coloured. Add the thyme and bay leaf, and continue to sweat for 2 minutes. Pour in the fish stock, cream and the infused milk with the bacon. Bring to the boil and simmer gently for 20 minutes. Remove the bacon, thyme and bay leaf, and pour the liquid and shallots into a blender. Blend until very smooth, then pass through fine sieve into a clean pan. Season with salt and pepper and set aside.

5 For the pea purée, cook the peas in boiling salted water until tender. Drain and refresh in iced water, then purée in a food processor. Pass the purée through a sieve into a heavy-based pan. Warm through, gradually adding the butter while stirring. Season with salt and pepper. Keep warm.

6 Remove the pressed pork from the fridge and cut into four 1cm-thick slices. Remove the thick rind. Cut the slices into 6cm lengths and put them in a pan with some of the reserved cooking liquid. Reheat, but be careful not to boil.

7 Meanwhile, season the scallops with salt and pepper. Heat a little olive oil in a non-stick pan. Add the scallops and cook until golden brown, then turn over and gently finish cooking until the centres are warm. Season with lemon juice and keep warm.

8 To serve, dress the pea shoots with a little of the vinaigrette (any extra can be used another time). Spoon the pea purée onto each plate, then drag a spoon across to create a tear shape. Place the pork in the middle and set two scallops on top of each serving. Gently reheat the shallot and bacon foam, add a knob of butter and blend with a hand blender to create a cappuccino effect. Spoon this over the scallops and top with the pea shoots.

PAN-ROASTED
DUBLIN BAY PRAWNS

SERVES 4

75g unsalted butter
good handful of wild garlic leaves
24 large raw Dublin Bay prawns
   (langoustines), in shell

200g organic green salad leaves
squeeze of lemon juice
salt and pepper

1 Heat the butter in a heavy pan until hot. Add the wild garlic leaves followed by the langoustines, and pan-roast over a high heat for 3–5 minutes. Season.
2 To serve, dress the salad leaves with the lemon juice and the juices from the pan. Serve immediately, with the cooked langoustines.

A BROTH OF
SCOTTISH SHELLFISH

SERVES 4

2 live lobsters, each about 500g
at least 16 good-sized live langoustines
   in shell
4 big handfuls of fresh mussels in shell,
   about 800g total weight
4 smaller handfuls of fresh clams in shell

a few fresh razor clams in shell
50g unsalted butter
1 small onion, finely chopped
glass of white wine
squeeze of lemon juice
big handful of chopped parsley
salt and pepper

1 Fill a large saucepan with water and bring to a furious boil. Season with as much salt as needed to make the water taste of the sea. Drop in the lobsters, put the lid on the pan and bring back to the boil as quickly as possible. After 1–2 minutes, remove the lobsters to a tray and leave them to cool. Return the water to the boil, drop in the langoustines and cook for 45 seconds. Remove these to a tray.
2 Remove the beards from the mussels, then wash well under cold, running water. Wash the clams in a similar fashion.
3 Melt the butter in a large pan, add the onion and cook gently until softened but not coloured. Turn up the heat. Tip in the mussels, add the white wine and season with salt and pepper. Place the lid on the pan, shake gently and let the mussels steam

open. Discard any that remain firmly shut. Once opened, remove the mussels with a slotted spoon to a bowl and cover with a damp cloth.

4 Place the clams in the liquid in the pot and steam open in the same way, then remove to a bowl and cover. Do the same with the razor clams.

5 Pour the cooking liquid from the mussels and clams into a medium pan, checking closely for any grit and straining if required. Add 150ml water and bring to the boil, then set aside. This is your broth.

6 Pull the claws from the lobsters and crack well to remove the meat. Split the tail lengthways and remove the meat from the shell. Remove the langoustines from their shells. Slice the lobster and langoustine meat. Take all the clams and mussels from their shells.

7 To serve, bring the broth to the boil and add a squeeze of lemon juice and the parsley. Check the seasoning, then stir in all the shelled shellfish. Ladle into bowls.

MARK BROADBENT

ROAST SCALLOPS
WITH ENGLISH PEAS,
CRISP AIR-DRIED HAM AND PEA SHOOTS

SERVES 4

8 slices of air-dried ham, preferably
    Peter Gott's Cumbrian ham
12 diver-caught scallops
80g soft unsalted butter
vegetable oil
4 punnets of pea shoots (available from
    Chinese shops)
salt and pepper

PEA BLANCMANGE

1 tbsp caster sugar
20g mint leaves
650g freshly shelled peas
3 large gelatine leaves
200ml double cream
grated zest and juice of ¼ lemon

PEA DRESSING

2 tsp double cream
organic rapeseed oil
2 tbsp shredded mint

1 First make the pea blancmange. Bring a saucepan of salted water to the boil. Add the sugar and half the mint leaves, then the peas. Bring back to the boil and simmer for 1–1^1/$_2$ minutes or until the peas are soft. Drain and refresh the peas in iced water, then drain again. Set 50g peas aside for the dressing. Blitz the remaining peas in a food processor until just smooth.

2 Soften the gelatine in warm water for about 10 minutes. Lift the gelatine out, drop into a small heavy pan and add just enough water to cover the bottom of the pan. Heat very gently until the gelatine has melted, then stir into the cream. Strain the gelatine cream through a fine sieve into a large bowl, then whip to a soft peak.

3 Fold the cream and pea purée gently together. Fold in the remaining chopped mint and the lemon zest and juice. Season to taste. Transfer the blancmange to a smaller bowl, cover and chill in the fridge for about 3 hours or until set firm yet still delicate.

4 For the pea dressing, blend the reserved 50g peas with the cream and a splash each of rapeseed oil and water using a hand blender or small mixer. The dressing should be loose enough to drizzle but still retaining some texture. Season, then add the shredded mint. Set aside.

5 Preheat the oven to 140°C/gas 1. Put the slices of ham on a baking sheet and set another baking sheet on top so the ham is kept flat. Roast for 20–30 minutes or until the ham is crisp.

6 Meanwhile, smear one face of each scallop with softened butter. Keep the scallops cool, not chilled, until ready to cook.

7 Heat a heavy frying pan until very hot, then add a splash of vegetable oil and put in the scallops butter-side down. Sear, without moving them, for 1 minute. Turn them over and sear the other side for 1 minute. Remove to kitchen paper to drain. Season with salt and pepper.

8 To serve, place a generous quenelle of pea blancmange in the middle of each plate. Arrange three scallops around, then place two pieces of ham in the pea blancmange. Spoon the pea shoots and pea dressing decoratively around the plate.

TOMATO AND FENNEL ESSENCE
WITH OYSTERS, DUBLIN BAY PRAWNS AND CRAB

SERVES 4
12 raw Dublin Bay prawns (langoustines)
   in their shells
4 fresh oysters in their shells
1 cooked crab
fresh soda bread to serve

ESSENCE
1.5kg dark red, over-ripe tomatoes,
   coarsely chopped
1 fennel bulb, chopped
5 celery sticks, chopped
2 large shallots, finely chopped
3 garlic cloves, thinly sliced
100g light soft brown sugar

1 tsp each chopped basil, chervil
   and coriander
50ml Pernod
1 tbsp Tabasco sauce
2 tsp Worcestershire sauce
salt
cayenne pepper

GARNISH
4 basil leaves
leaves of 1 sprig of coriander
1 ripe tomato, skinned, deseeded
   and diced

1 To make the essence, put all the ingredients in a blender with 1.5 litres cold water and a pinch each of salt and cayenne. Purée, then transfer to a chinois or very fine sieve placed over a bowl. Leave to strain overnight in the fridge.

2 When ready to serve the next day, preheat the oven to 150°C/gas 2. Drop the prawns into a saucepan of boiling salted water. Return to the boil and cook for 2–3 minutes or until all the shells turn pink. Drain the prawns and leave them to cool, then peel off the shells.

3 Open the oysters using an oyster knife. Keep them refrigerated in their liquor in a covered container until required.

4 Remove the claws from the crab, crack open with a rolling pin or small hammer and remove the white meat. Remove the white meat from the body. Flake all the white meat (do not use any brown meat – save it for another dish).

5 Divide the white crab meat among four ovenproof bowls and top with the prawns followed by the drained oysters. Put the bowls in the oven and warm the shellfish through for 5–10 minutes. Meanwhile, pour the strained tomato essence into a saucepan and heat gently.

6 Ladle the hot essence over the warm shellfish, and garnish with the herb leaves and diced tomato. Serve immediately, with fresh soda bread.

CRAB AND WILD CRESS SALAD
WITH COCKLE DRESSING

SERVES 4
400g live cockles in their shells
dry white wine
400g fresh white crab meat
1 tbsp chopped chervil
1 tsp chopped tarragon
1 tsp extra virgin olive oil
4 handfuls of wild watercress
salt and white pepper

SAFFRON VINAIGRETTE
50ml white wine vinegar
pinch of saffron strands
200ml olive oil

1 To make the vinaigrette, warm the vinegar with 100ml water in a small pan. Drop in the saffron and leave to infuse off the heat for 30 minutes. Stir in the olive oil and season with a pinch each of salt and pepper. (This makes more than you need for this recipe, but it keeps well in a screw-top jar in the fridge.)

2 Put the cockles in a saucepan, splash in some wine and cover the pan. Cook over a strong heat for 1–2 minutes or until the shells open, shaking the pan from time to time. Pour the cockles into a colander to drain and leave until cool enough to handle, then pick out the cockle meat, reserving some cockles in their shells for the garnish.

3 Mix the crab meat with the chervil and tarragon, and season with a pinch each of salt and pepper. Add the olive oil.

4 To serve, pile a generous amount of crab meat on each plate and place some watercress alongside. In a small bowl, stir the shelled cockles with as much saffron vinaigrette as you like, then spoon over the watercress. Garnish with the reserved cockles in their shells.

184 # CROMER CRAB TART

SERVES 6
300g shortcrust pastry
2 tbsp olive oil
2 small bunches of spring onions,
    finely sliced
450g white crab meat
40g Parmesan cheese, freshly grated
salt and pepper
lightly dressed salad leaves to serve

CUSTARD
3 medium eggs, plus 2 medium egg yolks
425ml double cream
pinch of freshly grated nutmeg

1 Preheat the oven to 180°C/gas 4. Place a 23cm round, 4cm deep flan ring or loose-bottomed tart tin on a baking tray.

2 Roll out the pastry and use to line the flan ring or tin, then line the pastry case with baking parchment and fill with baking beans. Bake blind for about 25 minutes or until the pastry just starts to colour. Carefully remove the baking beans and parchment. If there are any cracks in the pastry, use leftover pieces of pastry or beaten egg to fill them. Return the pastry case to the oven to finish cooking the base for 3–5 minutes. Leave to cool.

3 Meanwhile, make the custard. Place the eggs, egg yolks and cream in a bowl and beat gently, seasoning with nutmeg and salt and pepper to taste. Pass through a sieve into a jug. (The pastry and custard can be prepared ahead to this stage. Keep the custard in the fridge.)

4 Heat the olive oil in a frying pan, then quickly fry the spring onions until just softened. Scatter them in the pastry case. Stir the white crab meat and Parmesan into the custard mixture and lightly season, then carefully pour it onto the spring onions.

5 Bake the tart for about 50 minutes or until the filling is just set. Leave to cool for a few minutes before serving, with some lightly dressed salad leaves.

HOT SPIDER CRAB PÂTÉ

SERVES 4-6
1 large cooked spider crab, 1.5–2kg
4 shallots, finely chopped
1 garlic clove, crushed
½ tsp cayenne pepper
100g unsalted butter
40ml dry sherry
100g brown crab meat
50g fresh white breadcrumbs
juice of ½ lemon, or to taste
salt and pepper
thin slices of toast to serve

1 To get the meat out of the crab, twist the legs and claws off, then crack them open and remove the white meat. Now turn the main body on its back and twist off the pointed flap. Push the tip of a table knife between the main shell and the part to which the legs were attached, twist the blade to separate the two, then push it up and remove. Scoop out the brown meat from the well of the shell and put with the leg and claw meat.

2 On the other part of the body, remove the dead man's fingers (the feather-like, grey gills attached to the body) and discard. Split the body in half with a heavy knife. Now you need to be patient and pick out the white meat from the little cavities in the body. Add this to the rest of the meat. Scrub and reserve the shell for serving, if you like.

3 Gently cook the shallots, garlic and cayenne pepper in the butter for 3–4 minutes or until soft. Add the sherry, 100ml water and 100g brown crab meat as well as the brown crab meat from the spider crab. Stir well, then add the breadcrumbs, half the lemon juice and seasoning to taste. Simmer for 7–8 minutes, stirring occasionally.

4 Whiz one-third of this mixture in a blender, then stir it back into the main mixture in the pan along with the white crab meat. Taste and add more lemon juice and seasoning, if necessary.

5 Spoon the mixture into the crab shell, if using, or into a serving dish. Serve hot, with thin slices of toast.

DARTMOUTH CRAB PLATE

SERVES 4

SPIDER CRAB CONSOMMÉ
100ml olive oil
3 carrots, sliced
2 onions, sliced
1 bulb fennel, sliced
40g sea salt
15g black peppercorns
1 tsp coriander seeds
4 slivers of orange peel
5 garlic cloves
sprig of thyme
½ bay leaf
sprig of basil
6 tomatoes, halved and deseeded
20g fresh ginger
1 star anise
pinch of fennel seeds
1.5 litres fish stock
750ml dry white wine
50ml white wine vinegar
2 large or 3 small live spider crabs,
    2kg total weight, scrubbed clean

CLARIFICATION
50g diced celery
50g diced onions
50g diced leeks
25g diced carrots
225g white fish trimmings
50g tomato purée
5 egg whites

POTTED BROWN CRAB
1 live brown crab, about 1kg
court bouillon (or fish stock or very salty water)
1 tbsp mayonnaise
juice of 1 lemon
2 tbsp chopped parsley
4 hard-boiled eggs, yolks and whites
    separated
tarragon vinaigrette
4 tbsp clarified butter
freshly grated nutmeg
cayenne pepper
1 tsp brandy
2 tomatoes, skinned, deseeded and
    each cut into 4 'petals'
salt and pepper

GARNISH (OPTIONAL)
diced pickled cucumber or finely
    shredded lettuce

1 First make the consommé. Warm the oil in a large pan and gently sweat the sliced vegetables until soft, without colouring. Add the sea salt, peppercorns, coriander, orange, garlic, thyme, bay leaf, basil, tomatoes, ginger, star anise and fennel seeds. Cook for 10 minutes.

2 Pour in the fish stock and bring to the boil. Simmer for 20 minutes. Add the white wine and vinegar, and simmer for a further 10 minutes. Kill the crabs, then carefully add to the pan. Cook for 15 minutes. Leave to cool.

3 Mix together the ingredients for the clarification. Strain the cooled consommé into a clean pan. Add the clarification mixture. Bring to the boil, stirring often to prevent sticking. Once at boiling point, turn down the heat to simmer for 20 minutes. Finally, pass through a piece of clean muslin to trap any fine particles. Check the consommé for seasoning, then set aside.

4 For the potted brown crab you need four 5cm metal rings. Place them on a tray lined with cling film.

5 Cook the crab in court bouillon for 18 minutes. Remove and allow to cool. Pull off the large claws and legs. Break open the 'box' and scoop out the brown meat into a sieve; drain. Crack open the large claws and pick out the white meat into a bowl. Combine the white crab meat with the mayonnaise. Combine the brown meat with the parsley, 1 tsp lemon juice, salt and pepper.

6 Pass the egg whites and yolks separately through a sieve. Season with salt, pepper and tarragon vinaigrette.

7 Melt the clarified butter. Add the remaining lemon juice, a little nutmeg, a tiny pinch of cayenne pepper, salt and the brandy.

8 Dry the tomato petals on a cloth, then cut them to the size of the rings. Season with salt and pepper and place two petals in the bottom of each ring. Add a layer of white crab meat, then the sieved egg yolk, followed by the egg white. Top with the brown crab, then add another layer of white crab. Finish with the remaining tomato petals and seal with the spiced butter. Chill to set.

9 To serve, warm the spider crab consommé. Turn out the potted crab on to one end of four rectangular plates. Place a small soup cup of spider crab consommé opposite. In between you could garnish with a little pickled cucumber or finely shredded lettuce. Melba toast is a nice addition.

188 TROUT AND LEEK PIE
WITH SORREL HOLLANDAISE

SERVES 4

4 fillets of brown trout, each about 125g,
pin bones removed
4 discs of puff pastry, each 9cm diameter
4 discs of puff pastry, each 14.5cm diameter
beaten egg yolk
salt and pepper
rocket and sorrel leaves to serve

LEEK FILLING

55g unsalted butter
900g leeks, white and pale green parts only,
thinly sliced
1 garlic clove, crushed to a paste with
Maldon sea salt

1 tsp soft thyme leaves
1 bay leaf
3 tbsp vegetable stock
150g cream cheese
1 tbsp anchovy essence
4 tbsp double cream

QUICK SORREL HOLLANDAISE SAUCE

2 large free range egg yolks
juice of ½ lemon
250g unsalted butter, melted
pinch of cayenne pepper
25g unsalted butter
2 handfuls of sorrel leaves

1 First make the filling. Melt the butter in a non-stick saucepan, add the leeks, garlic, thyme, bay leaf and stock, and cook over a gentle heat for 15–20 minutes or until all the liquid has evaporated and the leeks are soft and tender. Allow to cool, then beat in the cream cheese, anchovy essence and cream. Season to taste.
2 Preheat the oven to 200°C/gas 6.
3 Cut each trout fillet into three equal pieces. Poach them in boiling salted water for 2 minutes; drain and cool.
4 Lay the four smaller pastry discs on a work surface and prick them with a fork. Arrange some of the leek filling on the pastry, leaving a 2cm border. Add three pieces of trout to each, then cover with the rest of the leek mixture. Lay the larger pastry discs on top. Crimp the edges, brush the dome with egg yolk and trim the border. Use the point of a knife to make a light crescent-shaped indentation on the dome of each pastry. Bake for 30 minutes or until golden brown and crusty.
5 Meanwhile, make the hollandaise. Put the egg yolks in a food processor and add the lemon juice and 1 tbsp cold water. With the motor running, gradually add the melted butter through the feed tube. Add cayenne pepper and salt to taste. You may want to add a little more lemon juice. Keep warm over a pan of hot water.
6 Melt the 25g butter in a shallow pan. When it is hot and foaming add the sorrel leaves and gently heat until the leaves have wilted. Stir the wilted sorrel into the hollandaise sauce.
7 Serve the pies with the sorrel hollandaise and a small salad of rocket and sorrel.

190

PAN-FRIED CORNISH LOBSTER
WITH YOUNG SUMMER VEGETABLES
AND HERBS IN A SAFFRON BISQUE

SERVES 4

4 live Cornish lobsters, each 500g
12 baby carrots
12 bulbs baby fennel
12 asparagus tips
4 small leaves spring cabbage, cut into
    small batons
50g shelled broad beans
50g shelled peas
olive oil
chopped tarragon
salt and pepper
picked tarragon, chervil and chives
    to garnish

SAFFRON BISQUE

500ml extra virgin olive oil
50ml Cognac
100g carrots, finely chopped
100g onion, finely chopped
100g fennel, finely chopped
½ garlic clove, chopped
1 tsp white peppercorns
1 tsp coriander seeds, crushed
1 tsp cumin seeds, crushed
1 tsp cardamom seeds, crushed
good pinch of saffron strands
1 star anise, crushed
1 bay leaf
5 sprigs of thyme
30g tomato purée
250g plum tomatoes, chopped
100g unsalted butter
a little lemon juice

1 Kill the lobsters, then pull off the claws and separate the tail from the body and head section. Drop the tails into boiling water and cook for 30 seconds only, then place in iced water. Bring the water back up to the boil and add the lobster claws. When boiling again, cook for 3 minutes. Place in the iced water.

2 Remove the meat from the lobster tails in one piece. Crack the claws to remove the meat, keeping it as whole as possible. Place the lobster meat on a tray for later use.

3 Next make the bisque using the lobster carcasses (tail shells and body and head sections). Preheat the oven to 200°C/gas 6. Pour 400ml of the olive oil into a roasting tray and place in the oven to heat, then add the lobster carcasses. Roast for 30 minutes (do not let the shells burn). Remove from the oven and deglaze the roasting tray with the Cognac.

4 While the lobster carcasses are roasting, sweat the carrots, onions, fennel and garlic in the remaining olive oil in a stainless steel saucepan for 10 minutes without colouring. Add the spices and herbs and sweat for a further 5 minutes. Now add the tomato purée, fresh tomatoes and 200ml water, and cook for 10 minutes.

5 Add the roasted lobster carcasses and the juices from the tray. Pour in enough water almost to cover the lobster carcasses and bring to the boil. Simmer for 20 minutes. Pour into a colander set in a bowl and leave to drain, then pass the resulting liquid through a fine sieve. Add 5g salt, then taste and adjust seasoning. Put 200ml of the bisque in a saucepan with the butter and set aside, ready to reheat. (This recipe makes more bisque than you need; serve the remainder as a soup.)

6 When ready to serve, preheat the oven to 200°C/gas 6. Cook all the vegetables separately in boiling salted water, or in a steamer, until just tender; drain and refresh. Peel the broad beans to remove the tough skins. Set aside.

7 Heat some olive oil in two non-stick frying pans (one for the lobster tails and the other for the claw meat). Carefully add the lobster, then place in the oven to heat for 2 minutes. Turn the lobster meat over, add some chopped tarragon and heat for a further 2 minutes.

8 Meanwhile, heat the lobster bisque. Reheat the vegetables in a steamer.

9 Slice each lobster tail into six pieces and arrange around the warm bowls or plates. Place the claw meat in the middle and scatter the vegetables around.

10 Froth the bisque using a hand blender and season with salt, pepper and a drop of lemon juice. Spoon around the dish. Drizzle some of the cooking oil from the lobsters around and sprinkle over the picked herbs to finish.

DEVON CRAB AND GINGER DUMPLINGS
WITH A LEMON THYME AND GINGER SAUCE

SERVES 4

VEGETABLE STOCK
1 onion
1 leek
3 carrots
4 celery sticks
3 garlic cloves, unpeeled, lightly crushed
2 star anise
1 tsp white pepper
1 bay leaf
5 cloves
250ml white wine
sprig each of thyme, tarragon, chervil
and coriander

SAFFRON DUMPLING DOUGH
1 (0.25g) packet saffron
2 tsp olive oil
1 egg
3 egg yolks
250g plain flour, sifted with 1 tsp salt

CRAB, SCALLOP AND GINGER MOUSSE
75g scallops
1 egg yolk
100ml double cream
75g brown crab meat, free of any
cartilage or shell

20g very finely diced fresh ginger
250g white crab meat, free of any
cartilage or shell
cayenne pepper
lemon juice
salt and pepper

LEMON THYME AND GINGER SAUCE
175g unsalted butter
75g shallots, sliced
25g fresh ginger, chopped
40g lemon thyme
1 tsp white peppercorns
1 tsp coriander seeds
75g brown crab meat, free of any
cartilage or shell
250g crab shells
200ml fish stock
lemon juice

GARNISH
5cm piece of fresh ginger, peeled
squeeze of lemon juice
pink grapefruit segments, cut into
small pieces
finely shredded coriander leaves

1 To make the stock, cut the vegetables into medium rough dice. Put them into a stainless steel saucepan with the garlic, star anise, pepper, bay leaf, cloves and enough water just to cover. Bring to the boil and cook until the vegetables are soft. Add the wine and bring back to the boil. Remove from the heat, add the herbs and leave to cool. Strain and reserve for the sauce.

2 To make the dumpling dough, put 1 tbsp water in a small saucepan with the saffron and olive oil, and bring to the boil. Leave to cool. Lightly beat the egg and egg yolks, and mix into the saffron liquid. Place the flour in a food processor. With the machine running, slowly add the egg mixture to make a dough with a grainy texture that just starts to cling together but is not too wet. The amount of liquid absorbed by the flour will vary, so be careful not to make the dough too dry or wet. Remove the dough and bring together into a ball. Wrap in cling film and leave to rest at room temperature for 30 minutes.

3 Meanwhile, make the mousse. Put the scallops, egg yolk, cream and brown crab meat in a blender and blend to a fine purée. Turn into a bowl and set in another bowl of iced water to cool. Put the diced ginger in a small pan of cold water, bring to the boil and boil for 1 minute, then refresh in cold water. Repeat this blanching twice. Add the ginger and white crab meat to the scallop purée, then season with a pinch of cayenne, a few drops of lemon juice, salt and pepper. Put the mousse mixture into a piping bag fitted with a small round nozzle (or keep in the bowl if you would prefer to spoon the mousse). Chill while you make the sauce.

4 Melt 75g of the butter in a stainless steel saucepan, add the shallots, ginger and lemon thyme, and sweat for 5 minutes, without colouring. Add the peppercorns and coriander seeds, and sweat for 2 more minutes. Add the brown crab meat and crab shells, and sweat for a further 5 minutes. Pour in 300ml of the vegetable stock and the fish stock and bring to the boil. Simmer for 20 minutes. Strain through a colander, then a fine sieve.

5 Measure 100ml of this flavoured stock (any remaining stock can be frozen) into a small pan, heat and then whisk in the remaining butter, a small piece at a time. Season with salt and pepper and a drop of lemon juice. This is the sauce for the dumplings. Set aside.

6 Using a mandolin, carefully cut the piece of ginger for garnishing into thin slices, then into fine strips. Put in a saucepan with a squeeze of lemon juice and enough water to cover. Bring to the boil, then refresh in cold water. Repeat this blanching three times. Set the ginger aside in a small pan of cold water.

7 Using a pasta machine (take it down to the last number), roll out the dumpling dough until it is smooth and fine. Using a 6–8cm round cutter, cut out discs of dough and place on a cling film-lined tray. You need 12 discs.

8 Make one dumpling at a time. Drop a disc of dumpling dough into boiling water and cook for 30 seconds, then refresh in iced water. Remove and dry on a towel, then place on a piece of cling film that is bigger than the disc. Pipe or spoon a ball of crab mousse into the middle. Lift up the cling film and mould the dough around the mousse into a ball. Twist the end of the film to seal like a money bag. Repeat to make 12 dumplings in all. (You may have extra mousse.)

9 Drop the wrapped dumplings into a pan of simmering water and cook them for 6 minutes. While they are cooking, reheat the dumpling sauce, the ginger garnish (in the water) and the pink grapefruit (in their own juice). Remove the dumplings from the water with a slotted spoon, then carefully unwrap them.

10 To serve, arrange three dumplings in each serving bowl, garnish with the ginger strips and the grapefruit, and pour in the sauce. Finish with a scattering of coriander.

194
LANGOUSTINES
WITH SUMMER VEGETABLE STEW

SERVES 4
12 live langoustines
4 sticks of rosemary

VEGETABLE NAGE
1 large onion, chopped
1 leek, chopped
2 celery sticks, chopped
1 fennel bulb, chopped
4 large carrots, chopped
1 head of garlic, cut in half crossways
8 white peppercorns, crushed
1 tsp coriander seeds
1 star anise
1 bay leaf
40g mixed herbs, such as chervil,
tarragon, parsley, chives and basil
300ml dry white wine

TOMATO WATER
1½ tsp white wine vinegar
1½ tsp caster sugar
10 ripe plum tomatoes, quartered

pinch of Maldon salt
¼ tsp Tabasco sauce
½ tsp Worcestershire sauce
8 basil leaves

VEGETABLE STEW
50g butter
2 small carrots, diced
⅓ garlic clove, very finely chopped
2 baby leeks, very finely sliced
1 small courgette, diced
75g mange tout, chopped
3 tbsp freshly shelled peas
2 tbsp finely chopped flat-leafed parsley
3 spring onions, sliced
12 cherry tomatoes, quartered
grated zest of ½ lemon

TO FINISH
4 chervil leaves
a few chives, sliced into big sticks
4 basil leaves, scrunched up and shredded
  finely into a chiffonade

1 To make the nage, put all the chopped vegetables into a large pan and cover with water (about 1 litre). Add the garlic, peppercorns, coriander seeds, star anise and bay leaf. Bring to the boil and simmer for about 8 minutes. Add the fresh herbs and simmer for a further 3 minutes. Now add the white wine, stir and remove from the heat. Cover and leave to infuse for 48 hours in a cool place.

2 For the tomato water, put the vinegar and sugar in a small saucepan and mix well. Simmer over a medium heat for $1^1/_2$–2 minutes to produce a syrup. Remove from the heat and stir in 180ml water. Add the tomatoes, along with any tomato juice, and the remaining ingredients. Purée the mixture, in batches, in a blender, then pour into a colander lined with a sterilised linen cloth or muslin set over a bowl. Allow to drain in the fridge overnight. The next day, discard the solid material in the colander, and set the liquid aside.

3 Strain the nage through a fine sieve and discard the vegetables and herbs. Set the nage aside. (You don't need all the nage for this recipe; that left over can be frozen and used as a stock for sauces, soups and so on.)

4 Put a large pan of water on to boil over a high heat. Pull the heads off the langoustines. If the gut has remained in the body, find the middle segment of the tail and fold it backwards. Break it and pull away from the body. The gut should come away with it.

5 When the water is boiling, use a slotted spoon to lower in the langoustines, then blanch for 30 seconds. (Do this in two batches.) Lift them out and plunge straight into a bowl of iced water to stop them cooking further. Leave for a few seconds, then remove and drain. Crush each langoustine gently in your hand to break the shell. It should then peel off easily.

6 Strip the rosemary leaves off the sticks, retaining about 2cm at the top (growing) end. Skewer three langoustines onto each stick of rosemary and set aside.

7 To make the vegetable stew, place a large pan over a medium heat and add 30g of the butter and 300ml of the vegetable nage. Whisk together into an emulsion. Add the carrots and garlic and cook for $1^1/2$ minutes. Add the baby leeks. You may need to add a little boiling water if the sauce has reduced right down – it should be like a soupy butter emulsion. Stir the leeks for a few seconds, then stir in the courgette. Add the mange tout and peas. Cook for about 30 seconds. Add the parsley, spring onions, cherry tomatoes and lemon zest. Stir, then take off the heat.

8 Melt the remaining 20g of butter in a large frying pan. Add 75ml of the tomato water and whisk to emulsify. (The remaining tomato water can be frozen, or used as the base for a savoury jelly.) Remove from the heat. Add the skewers of langoustine to the tomato emulsion and allow them to sit in it for a few minutes to take on the flavour, turning them once.

9 To serve, arrange the vegetables in shallow bowls and spoon over some of their saucy liquid. Remove the langoustine skewers from their emulsion, place a skewer in the centre of each bowl and sprinkle with the chervil, chives and basil.

SCALLOPS, LOBSTER AND SPIDER CRAB
WITH WILD SEASHORE VEGETABLES AND OYSTER BUTTER

SERVES 4

1 small cooked lobster
1 medium cooked spider crab
couple of handfuls of wild seashore
    vegetables, such as samphire, sea beet,
    rock samphire, sea purslane and sea peas,
    trimmed of any thick or woody stalks
4 scallops, with or without corals
good knob of unsalted butter
salt and pepper

OYSTER BUTTER

2 shallots, roughly chopped
½ glass English white wine
2 shucked oysters
150g cold unsalted butter, diced
juice of ½ lemon, or to taste

1 For the oyster butter, put the shallots in a saucepan with the wine and the same amount of water and simmer until reduced by two-thirds. Add the oysters, remove from the heat and whiz in a blender until smooth. Return to the pan over a low heat and whisk in the butter to form a smooth sauce. Add lemon juice, salt and pepper to taste. Remove from the heat, cover the surface of the oyster butter with cling film and keep in a warm place.

2 Preheat the oven to 160°C/gas 3.

3 Remove the meat from the tail and claws of the lobster, and cut into 1cm-thick slices. Remove the white meat from the body and claws of the crab. (Don't throw the lobster and crab shells and the brown meat away – use them for a soup, stock or sauce.) Heat the lobster and crab meat in a covered dish in the oven for 6–7 minutes.

4 Meanwhile, bring a saucepan of water to the boil and quickly blanch the sea vegetables (except sea peas) for 10–15 seconds or until just tender. Keep the different types separate. Drain and keep warm.

5 Cut the scallops horizontally in half and season with salt and pepper. Melt the butter in a frying pan until almost browned, then quickly cook the scallops for just 10 seconds on each side.

6 To serve, arrange the blanched sea vegetables on plates with the scallops, lobster and crab on top, then spoon the oyster butter around. If you've got some sea peas, scatter them on raw at the end.

ROAST RIB OF WELSH BLACK BEEF
WITH ONION PURÉE

SERVES 4

1 rib-eye joint of Welsh Black beef,
   about 800g
olive oil for frying
300g white onions, very thinly sliced
butter for frying
300g fresh ceps, cut in half
100g green beans
1 small shallot, finely diced
salt and pepper

OXTAIL

300g oxtail, in one piece
500ml red wine
1 large onion, chopped
1 large carrot, chopped
1 bay leaf
50g plain flour
2–3 tbsp vegetable oil
2 litres chicken stock

BONE MARROW

4 pieces bone marrow, each 5cm thick
25g coarse dry breadcrumbs
25g dried onion
50g plain flour
2 eggs, beaten
oil for deep-frying

1 Put the oxtail in a glass dish, cover with the red wine and add the onion, carrot and bay leaf. Leave to marinate in a cool place for 24 hours.

2 Preheat the oven to 160°C/gas 3.

3 Strain the red wine marinade from the oxtail and pour into a pan. Reserve the oxtail and vegetables. Bring the marinade to the boil and skim off any scum that rises to the surface. Remove from the heat and set aside.

4 Mix the flour with a little salt and pepper to season. Heat the vegetable oil in a flameproof casserole on a medium heat. Dust the oxtail in the seasoned flour, then add to the hot oil and fry until golden brown. Remove from the casserole and set aside. Add the marinated vegetables to the casserole and fry until golden brown. Deglaze with the reserved red wine marinade and reduce by half.

5 Return the oxtail to the casserole and pour in the chicken stock. Bring to the boil. Skim, then cover and transfer to the oven to cook for 2^1/$_2$ hours. Remove and leave to cool. (The oxtail can be cooked a day ahead and refrigerated overnight.)

6 When the oxtail has cooled, remove it from the liquid and pick the meat from the bones, keeping the meat in large pieces. Strain the liquid and reduce by half. Set the meat and liquid aside (this is the sauce).

7 Take the marrow out of the bones, either by pushing it through or breaking the bones. Rinse the marrow under cold water, then leave to soak for 30 minutes to remove all the blood. Drain and pat dry. Mix the breadcrumbs with the dried onion. Season the marrow and roll in the flour, then coat in the eggs and finish by rolling in the breadcrumbs. Keep chilled until ready to cook.

8 Turn the oven up to 190°C/gas 5. Season the rib of beef with salt and pepper. Heat a heavy roasting tin with a little olive oil and sear the beef until golden brown on all sides. Transfer to the oven and roast for 25 minutes for medium rare, or 35 minutes for medium. Remove from the oven and leave to rest for 25 minutes.

9 While the beef is roasting and resting, make the onion purée. Cook the white onions in a heavy-bottomed pan over a low heat with a large knob of butter until translucent (this takes about 20 minutes). Season with salt and pepper, then blend in a food processor until smooth. Set aside.

10 Deep-fry the marrow in oil heated to 170°C for 45–60 seconds or until golden brown and crisp. Drain on kitchen paper and keep warm.

11 Season the ceps with salt and pepper. Heat a splash of olive oil and a knob of butter in a warm frying pan, add the ceps, placing them face down, and fry briefly until they are golden. Keep warm.

12 Cook the green beans in boiling salted water for 2–3 minutes. Remove from the pan with a slotted spoon and place in iced water to stop the cooking process, then drain. Cook the shallot with a small knob of butter in a frying pan until soft. Add the green beans, season with salt and pepper, and toss to warm through.

13 To serve, reheat the sauce, and the oxtail in a little of the sauce. Place the green beans to one side of each warmed plate. Carve the beef into slices of 1cm thickness and lay on top of the beans. Spoon the onion purée on one side of the beef, then arrange the bone marrow, oxtail and ceps on the other side. Drizzle over the sauce.

FILLET STEAK
PICKLED WALNUTS AND HORSERADISH

SERVES 4

4 fillet steaks, each 250g, trimmed
    of any sinew
4 tbsp groundnut oil
80ml Madeira
225ml good beef stock
9–12 pickled walnuts, plus 1 tbsp
    of the pickle
50g unsalted butter
salt and pepper

HORSERADISH CREAM

good-sized stick of fresh horseradish,
    about 1.5cm wide x 5cm long (make
    it longer if you like things hot)
2–3 tsp caster sugar
2 tbsp white wine vinegar
200ml double cream

1 To make the horseradish cream, peel the horseradish swiftly and then grate finely. The tears will flow, but grate with fury, so it will be done quickly. The heat of fresh horseradish is vital for this dish. Stir the sugar into the vinegar to dissolve, then heap in the horseradish. Let sit for half an hour or so. Very lightly whip the cream, then stir into the horseradish. Cover the bowl well – then dry your eyes. (The sauce can be made a few hours ahead and chilled, but not too far ahead or the horseradish flavour will fade dramatically.)

2 Place the steaks cut-side up and season liberally and evenly with sea salt and freshly ground pepper. Warm a heavy-bottomed frying pan, then pour in the oil. When gently smoking, carefully sit the steaks in the pan and do not touch – at all. Let the meat cook gently until the edges turn a good rich, dark brown, moving the pan if the steaks are cooking unevenly. After 7–8 minutes, turn the steaks onto the other side and you should reveal a splendid crust. Continue to cook for a few minutes further, then remove the steaks to warm plates and set aside.

3 Stir the Madeira into the pan and boil until only a teaspoonful remains. Add the stock and the spoonful of pickle from the walnuts, simmering gently until slightly thickened. Add the butter all at once. Return to the boil, then pour the sauce through a fine sieve into a small pan and keep warm.

4 To serve, slice the pickled walnuts in half and heap over the steaks. Pour the sauce over and add a dollop of horseradish cream alongside.

204

POACHED
FILLET OF HEREFORD BEEF
WITH BABY VEGETABLES
WILD MUSHROOM BROTH AND HERB SAUCE

SERVES 4

2 pieces of beef fillet, centre cut, each 325g, fat removed and tied
8 French beans, blanched
8 strips of peeled roasted red pepper
6 long strips of canned anchovy
1 tbsp olive oil
salt and pepper

WILD MUSHROOM BROTH

85g dried ceps (porcini), soaked in boiling water for 30 minutes
450g leeks
225g carrots, peeled
225g turnips, peeled
½ head celery, cut in half lengthways
1 head garlic, cut in half crossways
¼ Savoy cabbage
450g tomatoes, skinned, quartered and deseeded
2 onions, 1 stuck with 2 bay leaves and 2 cloves
3 sprigs of thyme
½ bunch of chervil
2 bay leaves
15g Maldon sea salt
12 white peppercorns
3 litres beef stock or water
1 bottle red wine

BABY VEGETABLES

4 baby leeks
4 asparagus tips
4 baby turnips, scraped, leaving 2.5cm of green top
4 baby carrots, scraped, leaving 2.5cm of green top
4 baby Jersey Royal potatoes, scraped
8 sugar snaps
8 French beans
4 broccoli florets
4 best quality, small fresh ceps, lightly pan fried in butter
4 cherry tomatoes, peeled
55g unsalted butter

HERB SAUCE

2 handfuls of flat-leaf parsley leaves
2 pickled cucumbers, roughly chopped
3 garlic cloves, roughly chopped
2 tbsp capers, rinsed
4 canned anchovy fillets, rinsed
1 tbsp red wine vinegar
1 tbsp lemon juice
8 tbsp good extra virgin olive oil
1 tbsp Dijon mustard

1 First prepare the broth. Drain the dried ceps, reserving the soaking liquid, and put them in a saucepan with the remaining broth ingredients. Simmer very gently for $1^1/_2$ hours. Strain the broth and pour into a clean, wide saucepan. Add the mushroom soaking liquid and simmer gently for 30 minutes.

2 While the broth is cooking, prepare the baby vegetables (excluding the ceps and tomatoes). Bring a pan of salted water to the boil and cook each vegetable separately, removing when cooked, plunging into iced water and draining.

3 Next make the herb sauce. Chop together the parsley, cucumbers, garlic, capers and anchovies until medium coarse. Or, pulse in a food processor, although you get a better product if you hand chop this salsa. Transfer to a non-reactive bowl and slowly whisk in the remaining ingredients. Season with salt and pepper. Set aside.

4 Lard each beef fillet with four French beans, four strips of roasted pepper and three anchovy strips by threading the ingredients through the beef with a larding needle. Heat the oil in a large frying pan. Season the beef and sear all over until golden brown. Place the meat into the simmering broth. Cook for 12 minutes (do not allow the liquid to boil) for a wonderfully rosy interior. When the meat is cooked to your satisfaction, remove and set aside to rest for 10 minutes.

5 Meanwhile, make the vegetable parcels by dividing all the vegetables (including the ceps and tomatoes) equally among four sheets of cling film. Season with salt and pepper and dot with the butter. About 5 minutes before serving place the vegetable parcels in a steamer to reheat.

6 To serve, carve each fillet into four slices. Place the vegetables in the bottom of four large bowls, top with a little broth and then add two slices of steak, pink side up. Serve the herb sauce separately or drizzle a little over the steaks.

206

PEPPERED FILLET OF BEEF
WITH WHISKY AND MUSHROOM SAUCE

SERVES 4
3 tbsp black peppercorns
4 fillet steaks, each about 175g
4 tsp Dijon mustard
2 tbsp sunflower oil
50g butter

200g fresh ceps, sliced into chunks
50ml blended whisky
8 tbsp beef stock
4 tbsp double cream
Maldon sea salt and pepper

1 Crush the peppercorns coarsely in a mortar and pestle or grind using a pepper grinder on a coarse setting. Alternatively, you can grind the pepper in a spice mill, but you must then tip the pepper into a fine sieve and shake out all the powder. This is very important because the powder will make the steaks far too spicy.

2 Spread the peppercorns over a small plate. Smear both sides of the steaks with the Dijon mustard, then coat them in the crushed peppercorns. Season the steaks with salt. If you add the salt before this stage it draws out the moisture, preventing the pepper from sticking to the meat.

3 Heat a large, heavy-bottomed frying pan until nice and hot. Add the sunflower oil and then the steaks, and brown both sides, turning once only. Don't fiddle with the steaks once they are in the pan or the peppercorn crust will fall off – the aim is to produce a good crusty coating on each surface.

4 Now add the butter and allow it to colour a nut brown, but don't let it burn. Add the ceps and work around in the butter. As the mushrooms start to absorb the juices, turn the steaks again and allow them to cook for 3–4 more minutes on each side, turning once or twice and moving them around the pan to make sure the whole surface has plenty of colour and the edges of the meat are well seared. Transfer the steaks to a baking tray and set aside in a warm place.

5 Add the whisky to the pan and cook over a very high heat for 1 minute to boil off the alcohol. A word of warning – the whisky is likely to burst into flames. If this worries you, have a large lid handy to whack on the pan. Add the stock and reduce until really thick, then pour in the cream. Reduce again, scraping and stirring together any gooey bits from the bottom of the pan. When it boils fiercely, it's ready.

6 To serve, pour any juices from the resting meat back into the sauce and place a steak on each warm plate. Spoon the sauce with the mushrooms over the steak.

DRY-AGED BEEF
WITH TEXTURES OF THE ONION FAMILY

SERVES 4

15 large banana shallots

olive oil

few sprigs of thyme and rosemary

100g salted butter

500ml good chicken stock, plus extra
for the sauce

2kg chicken wings, each chopped into thirds

groundnut oil

200g firm, small button mushrooms,
very thinly sliced

2 bay leaves

2 very ripe plum tomatoes, halved

1 garlic clove, squashed

150g small baby onions

1 piece boned well-aged beef sirloin, such
as Dexter or other rare breed, about 800g

about 100ml milk

20 spring onions, trimmed

1 white onion, thinly sliced in rings

soy sauce

1 egg, beaten with salt and pepper for
an egg wash

about 100g fresh white breadcrumbs

salt and crushed white pepper

1 Preheat the oven to 160°C/gas 3. Set 2 of the shallots (skin on) on a sheet of foil.
Drizzle with olive oil, then scatter over a thyme sprig and some salt. Wrap up in the
foil and bake for 45 minutes or until soft. Leave to cool, still wrapped.

2 Peel and very thinly slice 8 more of the shallots. Melt 75g of the butter in a pan,
add the sliced shallots and fry over a low to medium heat for about 1 hour or until
well caramelised. Pour in the 500ml chicken stock, scrape the bottom of the pan to
deglaze it and simmer for 2 minutes. Pour everything into a blender and blend to a
purée, which will be like a thick soup. Sieve the purée into a clean pan and set aside.

3 To make the sauce, lay the chopped chicken wings in a large roasting tin and roast
for 1–1¹/₂ hours or until golden brown and well caramelised, turning them every
10 minutes so they don't catch. Meanwhile, heat a little groundnut oil in a small
pan with the remaining 25g of butter, add the sliced mushrooms and another 3 thinly
sliced shallots, and cook over a low heat for about 45 minutes or until softened and
caramelised. Drain on kitchen paper.

4 Tip the chicken wings into a large colander set over a bowl. Reserve the fat and
juices that drain into the bowl. Put the chicken wings and the caramelised
mushrooms and shallots into a pressure cooker. Add a sprig each of rosemary and
thyme, the bay leaves, tomatoes, garlic and a pinch of salt. Pour in enough chicken
stock so the chicken wings are barely covered, then pressure cook for 45 minutes.
(If you don't have a pressure cooker, put everything into a large heavy pan instead,
wrap three layers of cling film over the top of the pan and place the lid on top. Bring
slowly to the boil, then simmer gently for 1¹/₂ hours.)

5 Meanwhile, bake the baby onions. Turn the oven temperature up to 200°C/gas 6.
Lay the baby onions (skins on) in a small casserole and add enough salt to cover

them. Cover with a lid and bake for 1 hour or until soft and the salt has created a crust. Remove and cool slightly, then peel off the skins and set aside.

6 While the baby onions are cooking, cook the beef (see note on page 230). Heat a little groundnut oil in a pan, add the beef and sear to caramelise it the outside. Transfer the beef to a vacuum-sealed, airtight bag. Heat a pan of water to 58°C. Put the beef in the pan and poach, uncovered, for $1^1/4$ hours, keeping the water at a constant 58°C. Remove the beef from the water and leave to rest in the bag.

7 Peel and very thinly slice another of the shallots, preferably using a mandolin. Put in a shallow dish and pour over enough milk to cover. Leave to soak for about 1 hour.

8 When the pressure cooking is done, allow everything to cool, then strain the stock through muslin into a clean saucepan. Reduce over a high heat to a light sauce consistency, not too thick.

9 Finely chop the remaining shallot. Whisk 1 tbsp of the reserved fat and juices from the chicken into the reduced stock and stir in the shallot. Set the sauce aside.

10 Drop the spring onions into a pan of boiling salted water to blanch for 2 minutes, then remove with a slotted spoon into a bowl of seasoned iced water. Dress the white onion slices with a little olive oil, soy sauce and salt. Set aside.

11 Drain the milk-soaked shallots and pat them dry, then dip in the beaten egg. Season the breadcrumbs with salt and pepper and use to coat the onions. Heat oil in a deep-fat fryer to 140°C, add the breaded shallots and fry for 4–5 minutes or until golden and bubbles stop coming to the surface of the oil. Drain the shallots on kitchen paper and keep hot.

12 Take the shallots from the foil parcel and split down the middle (skin still on). Heat a splash of olive oil in a non-stick frying pan and lay the shallots in the pan, cut-side down. Fry for about 4 minutes or until caramelised. Keep warm. Drain the spring onions well, then fry in a little hot oil for 2–3 minutes. Keep warm.

13 Remove the beef from its bag. Heat a little olive oil in a large frying pan, add the beef and cook for no more than 1 minute, rolling it around in the hot fat. It should be well caramelised on the outside but still pink all through.

14 To serve, season the beef with salt and pepper, then carve into four slices and lay a slice on each serving plate. Scatter the dressed white onion slices over the beef. Arrange the 'textures of the onion' around the plate – the caramelised shallots, fried spring onions, deep-fried shallots, baked baby onions and a dollop of the warmed shallot purée. Reheat the sauce gently, then drizzle over and around the whole dish.

BRAISED FEATHERBLADE AND
PAN-ROASTED FILLET OF BEEF
WITH BROAD BEANS, PEAS
AND BABY SPINACH

SERVES 4

1 piece of boneless beef featherblade
(shoulder), about 800g
vegetable oil
250g shallots, quartered
mirepoix of finely chopped vegetables
(1 onion, 1 carrot, 2 celery sticks and ½ leek)
4 tbsp tomato purée
½ head of garlic, cut in half crossways
small bunch of thyme
75ml Port
500ml red wine
750ml home-made veal or beef stock

1 centre-cut piece of beef fillet, about 180g
50g salted butter
1 quantity mash (see Pan-fried John Dory
on page 120; make without the lobster
and herbs)
salt and pepper

VEGETABLE GARNISH

100g freshly shelled broad beans
100g freshly shelled peas
2 tbsp olive oil
250g baby spinach

1 Preheat the oven to 120°C/gas $^1/_2$.

2 If there is a lot of fat still attached to the beef shoulder, trim it off until the piece is just lightly covered all over in fat. Season the meat, then sear in a little hot vegetable oil in a large, heavy flameproof casserole over a high heat until coloured on all sides. Remove the meat from the pot and set aside.

3 Drain the fat from the casserole. Splash in a little more oil and heat until hot. Add the shallots and the mirepoix, and fry until lightly coloured. Stir in the tomato purée and cook for 2 minutes, then add the garlic, thyme, Port and wine. Bring to the boil. Pour in the stock and return the beef shoulder to the pot. Cover with greaseproof paper, then transfer the casserole to the oven to braise for 3–3$^1/_2$ hours or until the meat is tender. Remove the beef to a wire rack and set aside until cold. Strain the sauce into a clean pan and boil until reduced by half. When the beef and sauce are cold, chill in the fridge overnight.

4 The next day, prepare the vegetable garnish. Blanch the broad beans in boiling salted water for 3–5 minutes or until tender. Drain and refresh in iced water, then drain again and peel off the thin skins. Blanch the peas for 1–2 minutes or until tender. Drain and refresh in iced water, then drain again.

5 Preheat the oven to 200°C/gas 6.

6 Cut the chilled beef shoulder into four pieces, each weighing about 120g. Place the pieces in a heavy pan, pour over enough of the reduced sauce to half cover the meat and add 50ml water. Cover and bring slowly to the boil, then transfer to the oven to heat for 15 minutes. At the end of this time the beef should be hot and tender, and the sauce should have reduced by half again and be thick enough to coat and glaze the beef. If the sauce is too thin, pour half of it into another pan and boil it until reduced, then return to the pan of beef. Set aside in a warm place.

7 Stand the fillet of beef on one of its cut ends and slice downwards with the grain into four equal pieces. Season the pieces on all sides. Heat a large, heavy frying pan until hot. Add the butter and melt until the foam starts to turn golden brown, then add the pieces of fillet and sear over a high heat for about 3 minutes or until evenly coloured on all sides. Baste constantly during cooking, watching that the butter remains golden – if it gets too hot and starts to turn dark, remove the pan from the heat to cool. Transfer the pieces of fillet to a wire rack and leave to rest while you finish the vegetables.

8 Heat the olive oil in a saucepan, add the beans and peas, and warm through gently for 1 minute. Add the spinach, mix well and season lightly, then remove from the heat and let the spinach wilt, stirring occasionally. Reheat the mash, and the glazed beef if necessary.

9 To serve, put a piece of glazed braised beef on each plate and top with an upturned piece of fillet, which has been cut in half at a 45° angle. Put a quenelle of mash next to the meat with a spoonful of green vegetables. Spoon some of the sauce over the meat and serve the rest separately.

NOEL MCMEEL

FILLET OF BEEF
WITH TRADITIONAL CHAMP, SLOW-ROASTED MUSHROOMS, AND CABBAGE AND BACON, SERVED WITH STOUT GRAVY

SERVES 4

1 tightly packed Savoy cabbage, about 600g
rapeseed oil
4 rashers of back bacon, preferably
    Pat O'Doherty's black bacon, rinds
    removed, cut into lardons
4 fillet steaks, preferably Kettyle Northern
    Irish, each 150–200g
salt and pepper

SLOW-ROASTED MUSHROOMS

50ml rapeseed oil
4 garlic cloves, crushed
leaves of 1 sprig of rosemary, finely chopped
leaves of 3 sprigs of thyme, finely chopped

4 flat cap mushrooms, stems removed
    and caps peeled

CHAMP

1.5kg potatoes, preferably British Queens,
    peeled
100ml whipping cream
4 spring onions, chopped
50g salted butter

GRAVY

350ml Irish stout
3 tbsp redcurrant jelly
sprig each of rosemary and thyme
2 garlic cloves, roughly chopped

1 Preheat the oven to 130°C/gas ¹/₂.

2 First prepare the mushrooms. Mix together the oil, garlic, rosemary and thyme. Arrange the mushrooms gill-side up on a non-stick baking tray, pour over the oil and herb mixture, and season with sea salt and freshly cracked black pepper. Roast the mushrooms for 1 hour.

3 Meanwhile, cook the potatoes for the champ in boiling salted water for about 20 minutes until soft, then drain and mash until all lumps are eliminated. Bring the cream and spring onions to the boil in the pan, add the mash and beat until smooth. Season and add the butter. Set aside in a warm place.

4 Cut the cabbage into six or eight wedges. Discard the thickest part of the core, but leave a little to help hold the leaves together. Heat a little oil in a frying pan until it is very hot and fry the bacon until crisp. Add the cabbage and mix with the bacon, then reduce the heat, cover the pan with a lid and cook slowly for 5–10 minutes or until the cabbage is tender. Season and set aside in a warm place.

5 Remove the mushrooms from the oven and keep warm. Increase the oven temperature to 200°C/gas 6 and place a baking tray inside to heat up.

6 Season the steaks all over. Heat a heavy frying pan until red hot, then add a little oil. Place the steaks in the pan and sear all over (top, bottom and sides). Transfer the steaks to the hot tray and finish cooking in the oven, allowing 4–5 minutes for medium-rare meat. Remove the steaks from the oven and leave to rest in a warm place while you make the gravy.

7 Deglaze the steak juices in the frying pan with the stout, then boil to reduce by about three-quarters. Add the redcurrant jelly, rosemary, thyme and garlic, and simmer for 5 minutes. Strain and season, then keep hot.

8 To serve, put a mushroom in the middle of each warmed plate. Top with cabbage and bacon, and then a steak. Spoon a quenelle of champ on top of each steak, and drizzle the gravy around the plate.

SLOW-COOKED
HEREFORD OXTAIL
WITH STOUT AND PRUNES
HORSERADISH MASH

SERVES 4

6 pieces of oxtail, each 5cm, about 1.5kg
    total weight
2 tbsp olive oil
85g unsalted butter
3 onions, finely sliced
½ tbsp chopped sage
10 pitted prunes
6 canned anchovies, cut in half lengthways
500ml Young's luxury double chocolate stout
    or equivalent local beer
450ml chicken stock
4 pickled walnuts, quartered
4 sheets of caul fat

MARINADE

4 tsp coarsely ground black peppercorns
2 tsp Maldon sea salt
2 tsp dried oregano
1 tsp thyme leaves
4 garlic cloves
6 tbsp soft brown sugar
2 tbsp olive oil
2 tbsp wine vinegar

ROAST VEGETABLES

12 baby onions, peeled
12 baby carrots, trimmed
12 button mushrooms
12 garlic cloves, unpeeled
1 tbsp olive oil
40g unsalted butter
2 tsp aged vinegar
2 tbsp chopped parsley

HORSERADISH MASH

1kg floury potatoes, peeled and chopped
115g unsalted butter
6 tbsp strong horseradish cream
225ml hot milk

1 For the marinade, blend the peppercorns, salt, herbs, garlic and sugar in a food processor, then gradually add the oil and vinegar.
2 Rub the oxtail with the marinade, then leave to marinate in a cool place for at least 3 hours or, ideally, overnight.
3 Preheat the oven to 150°C/gas 2.
4 Wipe off the marinade and retain. Fry the oxtail in half of the oil and butter in a flameproof casserole until browned on both sides; remove and set aside.
5 Add the remaining oil and butter to the casserole and heat gently until foaming, then add the onions and chopped sage. Allow the onions to cook over a gentle heat until they are caramelised. This will take about 20 minutes. Add six of the prunes and the anchovies.

6 Place the oxtail back on top of the onions in the casserole. Add the reserved marinade, the stout and chicken stock and bring to the boil. Cover the casserole and transfer to the oven to cook for about 3 hours or until the meat is very tender and almost falling off the bone. Allow to cool.

7 Remove the oxtail from the pot and set aside. Pour all the pan juices with the onions and prunes into a food processor and blend until smooth. Pour into a clean saucepan and add the pickled walnuts; cook until the sauce has reached a coating consistency. Remove 4 tbsp of sauce to a large bowl and allow to cool. Set the pan of remaining sauce aside, to reheat for serving.

8 Remove the oxtail meat from the bone, shred it with two forks and place in the bowl with the 4 tbsp sauce. Season the mixture and divide into four 'burgers'. Lay the four sheets of caul fat on a work surface and place an oxtail burger in the centre of each one. Make an indentation in each burger and push in a prune, enclosing it in the oxtail, then wrap the burgers neatly in the caul fat. Pan fry the parcels until they are lightly golden all over.

9 Place the oxtail parcels in a roasting tray. Add the baby onions and carrots, mushrooms and garlic with the oil and butter. Set over a moderate heat and shake the pan to brown the vegetables all over. Increase the oven heat to 200°C/gas 6 and pop the roasting tray into the oven. Roast for 30 minutes.

10 Meanwhile, make the horseradish mash. Cook the potatoes in boiling salted water until tender. Drain and pass through a potato ricer or food mill into a medium bowl. Add the butter, horseradish cream and half the milk and stir to combine. Add the remaining milk if the mash is too stiff. Season to taste. Keep hot.

11 Remove the oxtail parcels and keep hot. Add the vinegar and parsley to the roast vegetables and season with salt and pepper to taste. Serve the oxtail with the roast vegetables, a little sauce and the horseradish mash.

GRILLED
FILLET OF SOUTH DEVON BEEF
WITH A SHALLOT AND TOMATO SAUCE

SERVES 4
4 fillet steaks of mature beef, each 150g
Maldon sea salt
2 tbsp groundnut oil
salt and pepper

SHALLOT AND TOMATO SAUCE
6 shallots, chopped
1 garlic clove, chopped
35g unsalted butter
8 tomatoes, deseeded and roughly chopped
sprig of tarragon
sprig of thyme
1 bay leaf
250ml white wine
200ml dry Madeira
100ml Port
200ml chicken stock

HERB BUTTER SAUCE
60g shallots, chopped
½ garlic clove, chopped
sprig of tarragon
2 tbsp white wine vinegar
3 tbsp dry white wine
1 tbsp double cream
200g cold unsalted butter, diced
lemon juice
cayenne pepper
2 tomatoes, skinned, deseeded and diced
1 tbsp chopped parsley
1 tbsp chopped chervil
½ tbsp chopped tarragon, blanched
½ tbsp chopped chives

1 First make the shallot and tomato sauce. Gently cook the shallots and garlic in 20g of the butter until very soft. Purée in a blender. Put the purée in a clean pan and add the tomatoes, tarragon, thyme and bay leaf. Cook gently for 5 minutes or until the tomatoes start to break down.

2 Add the white wine, bring to the boil and reduce by half. Pour in the Madeira and Port, boil and reduce by half. Add the chicken stock and bring to the boil. Skim and simmer for 30 minutes.

3 Pass through a fine sieve, then let the sauce drip through a clean piece of muslin, leaving quite a heavy residue behind; discard the residue. Pour into a clean pan, bring to the boil and cook for about 2 minutes or until the desired consistency is achieved. Whisk in the remaining butter and check seasoning. Set aside.

4 For the herb butter sauce, combine the shallots, garlic, tarragon sprig, vinegar and wine in a small heavy-bottomed saucepan. Boil until you have 1 tbsp syrupy liquid. Add the cream, then over a gentle heat whisk in the diced butter a little at a time. The finished sauce will be creamy and a delicate yellow. Do not allow to boil. Season with lemon juice, salt, cayenne and freshly ground pepper. Pass through a fine sieve into a bowl and set in a saucepan of hot water to keep warm.

5 Preheat the grill to high. Season the fillet steaks with sea salt. Heat the oil in a heavy-bottomed frying pan, then brown the fillets on all sides. Place under the hot

grill and cook to your taste: 5 minutes for medium rare, 6 minutes for medium etc. Remove from the heat and allow to rest for 5 minutes.

6 Meanwhile, warm the shallot and tomato sauce. Add the diced tomatoes and chopped herbs to the butter sauce.

7 To serve, place the fillets on warm plates. Pour a pool of shallot and tomato sauce close to each fillet, then carefully spoon the herb butter sauce over the top of the steaks. As an optional garnish, if serving this in the summer, add seasonal produce such as broad beans and new potatoes.

BRYN WILLIAMS

WELSH BLACK BEEF
CARAMELISED ONIONS AND RED WINE SAUCE

SERVES 4
4 fillet steaks of Welsh Black Beef, each 180g
vegetable oil
20 baby onions, peeled
butter
2 leeks, finely chopped
100ml double cream
250g girolles, stalks scraped

olive oil
salt and pepper

RED WINE SAUCE
3 shallots, sliced
butter
sprig of thyme
300ml Port
300ml red wine
750ml veal stock

1 Preheat the oven to 180°C/gas 4.

2 First make the sauce. Sweat the shallots in a little butter with the thyme, then add the Port and red wine and bring to the boil. Reduce by one-third. Add the veal stock and reduce to a good sauce consistency. Check the seasoning.

3 Meanwhile, season the fillet steaks and sear on all sides in a little vegetable oil in a hot ovenproof pan. Place in the oven and roast for 7–9 minutes. When ready, leave to rest in a warm place.

4 While the fillets are cooking, roast the whole baby onions in a frying pan in some oil and butter until soft and golden brown.

5 Blanch the leeks in boiling salted water for 30 seconds, then drain. Bring the double cream to the boil and add the blanched leeks. Cook together for 4–5 minutes or until leeks are coated by the cream.

6 Pan-fry the mushrooms in olive oil with some salt and pepper.

7 To serve, position the creamed leeks in the centre of each warm plate and place a fillet of beef on top. Assemble the mushrooms and onions around the beef and pour on the red wine sauce.

POACHED FILLET
OF WELSH BLACK BEEF WITH SAUTÉED SNAILS
AND ASPARAGUS ON CAULIFLOWER PURÉE

SERVES 4

24 spears of young asparagus
1 litre beef consommé or beef stock
olive oil
4 fillet steaks, preferably Welsh Black
   beef, each about 250g
knob of unsalted butter
salt and pepper

CAULIFLOWER PURÉE

1 large white onion, sliced
50g unsalted butter
1 large or 2 small heads of cauliflower,
   trimmed and chopped
about 250ml full-fat milk

SNAILS

20 ready prepared snails (see note below)
knob of unsalted butter
100g fresh wild garlic leaves, or 1 wild garlic
   root, chopped, or 1 garlic clove, chopped
25g finely chopped shallots
leaves ripped from a few sprigs of thyme
1 tbsp chopped flat-leaf parsley

1 First make the cauliflower purée. Sweat the onion in half the butter until soft. Add the cauliflower and stir briefly, then cover the pan and cook gently for 20–25 minutes or until the cauliflower is soft but not brown. Add the milk and bring back to the boil. Purée in a food processor with the remaining butter, which should be cold. Push the purée through a fine sieve into a bowl. Check the consistency – it should just hold its shape. If it is too stiff, let it down with a little milk. Set aside in a warm place.

2 Plunge the asparagus spears into a pan of boiling salted water and blanch for 1–2 minutes, then drain and refresh in iced water. Drain again and set aside.

3 Bring the consommé to a gentle simmer in a wide pan. Meanwhile, heat a little olive oil in a large heavy frying pan until very hot, and sear the steaks over a high heat until nicely coloured on all sides. Transfer the steaks to the consommé, reserving the meat juices in the frying pan. Simmer gently for 8 minutes for rare beef. Do not let the liquid boil. Remove the steaks from the consommé and let rest for 5 minutes.

4 While the steaks are resting, add a ladleful of the consommé and a knob of butter to the meat juices in the frying pan and simmer until reduced. At the same time, sauté the snails in a knob of butter in another frying pan with the garlic leaves, shallots and thyme leaves. Throw in the blanched asparagus spears and parsley, and season to taste. Reheat the cauliflower purée, if necessary.

5 To serve, spoon some cauliflower purée onto each plate and place a steak on top. Garnish with snails, garlic and asparagus, and drizzle over the reduced sauce. Note: Buy ready prepared frozen snails in bags and thaw them before use. Or use canned snails: drain and rinse, then blanch briefly by dipping in boiling water.

220

ROAST SIRLOIN OF
PERTHSHIRE HIGHLAND BEEF
WITH AYRSHIRE POTATOES, ROASTED GLAMIS ASPARAGUS AND A RADISH RELISH

SERVES 4
12 small new potatoes
duck fat
1kg boned sirloin or ribeye of beef
½ glass of red wine
100ml beef stock
2 tbsp unsalted butter
2 tbsp plain flour
20 asparagus spears
olive oil
12 baby carrots

12 baby turnips
300g fresh peas
salt and pepper

RADISH RELISH
12 red radishes, finely chopped
2 shallots, finely chopped
1 tbsp good-quality aged sherry vinegar
4 tbsp light olive oil, not too peppery

PARSLEY BUTTER
knob of butter
1 heaped tbsp chopped parsley

1 First make the radish relish. Mix all the ingredients together, season with salt and pepper and leave overnight in the fridge.

2 Preheat the oven to 120°C/gas ¼.

3 Cut the top and bottom off each potato to make a barrel shape, then put them in a roasting tray and cover with duck fat. Place in the oven to cook for 25–30 minutes.

4 Meanwhile, make the parsley butter by mashing the ingredients together.

5 When the potatoes are done, remove them from the oven and keep warm. Turn up the oven temperature to 230°C/gas 8.

6 Season the beef, then sear in a hot roasting tin on top of the cooker. Add the red wine. Transfer to the oven and roast for 30–40 minutes, then leave to rest in a warm place for at least 15 minutes. Meanwhile, prepare the gravy and vegetables.

7 Skim excess fat from the juices in the roasting tin, then add the stock. Bring to the boil. Mash the butter with the flour to make a beurre manié. Add this in small pieces to the hot juices, whisking to thicken. Check the seasoning.

8 Put the asparagus in another roasting tin, drizzle with olive oil and season with salt and pepper, then roast for 5–7 minutes. Pop the potatoes into the oven to reheat for about 8 minutes. Cook the carrots, turnips and peas, separately, in boiling salted water until just tender; drain, then toss with the parsley butter.

9 To serve, spoon the mixed vegetables into the centre of the warm plates and arrange the asparagus to the side. Slice the beef and fold over to give height, then place on the vegetables. Stand the potatoes alongside. Pour over the gravy and finish with a good spoonful of radish relish.

RACK OF LAMB, SAUTÉED TONGUE AND SWEETBREADS
WITH SAMPHIRE AND BROAD BEANS

SERVES 4

2 lambs' tongues
700g lambs' sweetbreads
white wine vinegar
1 rack of lamb with 8 rib bones, chined
150g freshly podded young broad beans
seasoned plain flour for dusting
50g unsalted butter

150g samphire
300ml lamb stock
salt and pepper

GARNISH
mint leaves
flat-leaf parsley leaves

1 Put the tongues in a pan of cold water and bring to the boil. Simmer, uncovered, for $1^1/_2$–2 hours or until tender. Remove from the heat and set the tongues aside in the cooking liquid.

2 To prepare the sweetbreads, put them in a large bucket or bowl filled with cold water and leave to soak in the fridge for at least 2 hours. Bring a saucepan of water to the boil with a splash of vinegar and a little salt. Drain the sweetbreads, put them in the boiling water and bring back to the boil. Remove and refresh in iced water. Take off the tough outer coating and fatty membrane from the sweetbreads, leaving them clean. Refrigerate in a covered container until ready to cook.

3 Preheat the oven to 200°C/gas 6.

4 Set the rack of lamb in a roasting tin and roast for 15–20 minutes (for rare to medium-rare meat). Remove from the oven, cover loosely with foil and leave to rest in a warm place.

5 While the lamb is roasting, blanch the broad beans in rapidly boiling salted water for 1 minute. Drain, refresh in iced water and drain again. Set aside.

6 Dust the sweetbreads with seasoned flour. Heat 30g of the butter in a frying pan until foaming, then sauté the sweetbreads over a medium heat for 2–3 minutes on each side or until nicely coloured. Remove with a slotted spoon and set aside.

7 Drain the tongues and cut them in half lengthways. Sauté them in the same pan for 2–3 minutes on each side or until nicely coloured. Throw in the broad beans and samphire, return the sweetbreads to the pan and add the stock. Simmer together for 2–3 minutes. Add the rest of the butter to glaze, and season to taste.

8 To serve, divide the sweetbreads, tongues and vegetables among warmed large bowls and spoon the sauce around. Cut the rack into cutlets and put two on each serving. Garnish with mint and parsley leaves. Accompany with potatoes and butter.

LAMB RACK AND PAN-FRIED LAMB PATTIES
FLAVOURED WITH ROSE PETALS

SERVES 4

2 racks of lamb, each with 4 rib bones, chined and excess fat removed

plain yoghurt to serve

salt and pepper

MARINADE

1 tbsp very finely chopped raw papaya

1 tbsp very finely chopped garlic

1 tsp very finely chopped green chillies

1 tsp ground fennel

1 tsp black pepper

1 tsp sweet paprika

3 tbsp mustard oil

100ml single cream

3 tbsp double cream

2 tbsp gram flour

2 tbsp Pernod or Ricard

pinch of grated nutmeg

MINT CHUTNEY

200g mint leaves

2 tbsp roughly chopped red onion

2 tbsp lemon juice

1 green chilli

2 tsp vegetable oil

4 tbsp thick, full-fat plain yoghurt

TAMARIND VINAIGRETTE

4 tbsp fresh tamarind extract (made by soaking tamarind slab in water and passing through a sieve)

1 tbsp finely chopped red onion

½ tbsp each finely chopped red and green pepper

5 tbsp olive or vegetable oil

LAMB PATTIES

1 tbsp finely chopped raw papaya

15g fried brown onions

¼ tsp Kashmiri red chilli powder

¼ tsp garam masala powder

small pinch of ground cardamom

½ tsp each ginger and garlic pastes, mixed

1 tsp finely chopped fresh ginger

1 green chilli, finely chopped

1 tbsp finely chopped coriander leaves

1 tbsp finely chopped mint leaves

1 tbsp gram flour, toasted in a pan until lightly browned

1 tsp dried rose petals

1 tbsp toasted pine nuts

2 tbsp thick, full-fat plain yoghurt

2 tbsp single cream

pinch of saffron strands

250g boned leg of lamb, finely minced

about 4 tbsp vegetable oil for shallow-frying

GARNISH

a few lightly sautéed slices of baby fennel bulb

fresh rose petals

mint leaves

sprigs of coriander

finely sliced red onions

olive oil for drizzling

1 Whisk all the marinade ingredients together and leave at room temperature for 30 minutes. Then rub the marinade all over the lamb racks. Set aside in the fridge to marinate for at least 2 hours before cooking.

2 Meanwhile, to make the mint chutney, drop the mint leaves into boiling water, lift out immediately with a slotted spoon and refresh in iced water. Drain well. Finely chop the mint in a food processor with rest of the chutney ingredients to make a very smooth consistency. Chill until required.

3 Combine the ingredients for the vinaigrette and whisk together with a little salt. Set aside until required.

4 To make the lamb patties, put all the ingredients except the minced lamb and oil for frying in a food processor. Blend to make a paste. Mix the lamb with the paste. Leave at room temperature for 30 minutes.

5 Preheat the oven to 200°C/gas 6.

6 Shape the mince mixture into six 5–6cm patties (you will have two left over, which can be frozen). Heat a non-stick frying pan and add a little of the vegetable oil. Fry the patties in batches over a medium heat until cooked and light golden on both sides. As they are cooked, remove and keep warm. Add more oil as needed.

7 Meanwhile, remove the lamb racks from the marinade, shake off the excess marinade and place the lamb in a roasting tin. Roast for 5–7 minutes for rare meat, basting with the excess marinade or juices from the meat halfway through. For medium meat, roast for a further 2–3 minutes, or 5 minutes more for well done. Remove the racks, baste with more of the juices and let rest in a warm place.

8 Toss all the garnish ingredients together, dressing them with a drizzle of olive oil. Carve the racks into 8 cutlets.

9 To serve, spoon a large dot of mint chutney and tamarind vinaigrette in the centre of each warmed plate, side by side. With the back of spoon, stretch them into a straight line in opposite directions. Place two cutlets on one side of the plate, one leaning on the other. Place a lamb patty at the top of the plate. Arrange the garnish on top of the patty. Serve with yoghurt.

224

ROAST BEST END OF DEVONSHIRE LAMB
WITH PAN-ROASTED POTATOES, SPINACH, TOMATO FONDUE AND A LIGHT LAMB JUS

SERVES 4

1 best end (rack) of lamb with 8 rib bones, French trimmed
olive oil
knob of butter
large sprig of rosemary
200g young spinach
salt and pepper

TOMATO FONDUE

1 small onion, chopped
2 garlic cloves, crushed
3 tbsp olive oil
300g whole plum tomatoes (about 4), skinned, deseeded and halved
3 sprigs of thyme, leaves stripped and finely chopped
4 small tomatoes, preferably 'English Breakfast' variety, blanched and skinned

ONION PURÉE

2 large onions, peeled and quartered
1 tbsp white breadcrumbs
15g butter
½ tsp chopped thyme leaves

LAMB SAUCE

800g lamb bones, chopped small
about 100ml olive oil
2 small onions, chopped small
1 head of garlic, cut crossways in half
1 carrot, chopped small
1 leek, chopped small
large sprig of thyme
large sprig of rosemary
1 tsp cumin seeds
½ cinnamon stick
200g ripe plum tomatoes, roughly chopped
2 tbsp tomato purée
400ml chicken stock
100ml veal glacé (optional)

BASIL AND MUSTARD PURÉE

10g basil leaves
½ tsp thyme leaves
1 tbsp olive oil
1 tsp Dijon mustard

ROAST POTATOES

4 large baking potatoes such as King Edward (6cm deep and 5cm wide)
about 200g butter
2 garlic cloves
sprig of thyme

1 Preheat the oven to 200°C/gas 6.

2 To make the tomato fondue, sweat the onion and garlic with the olive oil in a heavy-based ovenproof pan until soft; do not colour. Add the plum tomatoes and thyme, season lightly and stir together. Transfer to the oven and roast for 15 minutes. Stir, then roast for another 15 minutes. Repeat until the tomatoes are dried out and thick in texture. You should have enough fondue to fill the small tomatoes. Set aside.

3 Lower the oven to 180°C/gas 4. Cut the tops off the small tomatoes and, using a teaspoon, remove and discard the seeds. Fill with the tomato fondue. Place on a baking tray, season and brush with olive oil. Roast for 10–15 minutes, then set aside.

4 For the onion purée, put the onions in a saucepan and cover with water. Bring to the boil and add a pinch of salt. Reduce to a simmer and cook for about 25 minutes or until soft and translucent. Drain in a colander, then purée in a blender. Pass through a sieve into a clean heavy-based pan. Add the breadcrumbs and butter, and cook, stirring from time to time, for 10–15 minutes, adding a little water if necessary to make a thin purée. Add the chopped thyme and season. Set aside.

5 For the sauce, put the lamb bones in a roasting tin and roast for 20 minutes or until golden, stirring occasionally. Meanwhile, heat some of the oil in a large saucepan, add the onions, garlic, carrot and leek, and fry until soft but not coloured. Add the thyme, rosemary, cumin seeds and cinnamon, and sweat for 5 minutes. Stir in the tomatoes and tomato purée, and cook for a further 10 minutes.

6 Transfer the roasted bones to the saucepan and add 100ml water, the chicken stock and veal glacé, if using. Bring to the boil, then reduce to a gentle simmer and cook for 30 minutes. Pass through colander or sieve, then through a fine sieve into a clean pan. Simmer for about 5 minutes or until reduced to a sauce consistency. Set aside.

7 Place all the ingredients for the basil purée in a small blender and blend to a fine purée. Set aside.

8 To make the roast potatoes, use a deep 6cm round cutter to cut a big round chunk from each potato. Melt 150g of the butter in a small, heavy-based pan with the garlic and thyme. Add the potatoes (the butter should come about halfway up the side of the potatoes, so add more butter if necessary). Season with salt and pepper. When the potatoes are starting to colour underneath, turn them over. Fry for 20 minutes or until tender and golden. Remove from the heat and set aside in the pan.

9 Raise the oven temperature to 220°C/ gas 7.

10 Season the lamb joint with salt and pepper. Put a little olive oil in a small, heavy roasting tin and put into the oven to heat. Remove from the oven, add a little butter and place the lamb fat-side down in the tin. Add the rosemary. Return to the oven and roast for 5 minutes. Turn the lamb over and roast for another 5 minutes, for medium rare. For medium-well done, roast for a further 5 minutes. Brush the lamb with the basil paste and leave to rest in a warm place for 15 minutes.

11 Meanwhile, put the potatoes and tomatoes in the oven to warm through while you cook the spinach. Heat a little olive oil in a large pan, then add the spinach and cook briefly until it just wilts. Season with salt and pepper. Reheat the lamb sauce and onion purée.

12 For each serving, place a 6cm round cutter in the centre of the plate. Spoon some of the spinach into the cutter. Place a roasted potato on top and remove the cutter. Set a stuffed tomato on top of the potato to create a tower. Carve the lamb into eight cutlets and serve two per serving leaning against the spinach, on either side of it. Drizzle the sauce around and spoon the onion purée to the side or serve it in a separate dish. Serve immediately.

ROAST SADDLE AND SLOWLY BRAISED
SHOULDER OF SPRING LAMB
WITH FRIED NEW POTATOES,
NORFOLK ASPARAGUS AND YOUNG CARROTS

SERVES 8

BRAISED SHOULDER OF LAMB
1 tbsp olive oil
25g butter
1 shoulder of spring lamb, blade end,
    about 900g
about 800g duck or goose fat
salt and pepper

CHICKEN MOUSSE
110g skinless boneless chicken breast, diced
½ egg white, lightly beaten
140ml double cream

SADDLE OF LAMB
1 saddle of lamb on the bone, with fillet
    underneath and without the chump ends,
    about 1.25kg (ask the butcher to remove
    the tough outer skin)
225–250g large leaf spinach, picked from
    the stalks
3 tbsp sunflower oil
25g butter

GRAVY
1 large onion, chopped
6 garlic cloves, chopped
2 carrots, chopped
2 celery sticks, chopped
2 large glasses of white wine
chicken stock
redcurrant jelly (optional)

VEGETABLES
2 tbsp olive oil
40g butter, plus a large knob
275g new potatoes, peeled and cut
    into small even-sized dice
2 garlic cloves, roughly chopped
sprig of mint
about 16 young carrots, scraped
16–24 asparagus spears

1 This recipe needs to be started well in advance. Preheat the oven to 140°C/gas 1.
2 Start by braising the shoulder of lamb. Heat a frying pan over a high heat, then add the olive oil and butter. Add the lamb and turn to sear and lightly brown all over, seasoning with salt and pepper as you do so. Transfer the lamb to a deep saucepan and add enough duck or goose fat just to cover. Bring up to a gentle tremble on a medium heat, then cover the pan with a lid or foil. Transfer to the oven and cook for $1^1/_2$ hours. Lower the oven temperature to 120°C/gas $^1/_2$ and cook for another $1^1/_2$ hours. The lamb should be meltingly tender.
3 Carefully lift the lamb out of the fat and set it on a trivet to drain. When the lamb is cool enough to handle, shred about 275g of the meat with your fingers into a bowl, discarding any fat or gristle; cover and set aside in the fridge. (The rest of the meat can be frozen and used for other dishes, such as the base of a cottage pie; the duck or goose fat can also be used again.)

4 To make the chicken mousse, purée the chicken breast in a food processor. With a spatula, push the mixture back towards the blades, then add the egg white and process again. Remove the puréed chicken from the food processor. If you want a finer mixture, push the purée through a sieve into a bowl (this is best done a little at a time using the back of a ladle). Don't use too fine a sieve or it will take a long time.

5 Slowly pour the double cream into the chicken purée, beating carefully with a spatula to reach a dropping consistency. Add the shredded braised lamb, season with salt and pepper, and mix thoroughly. Cover and set aside in the fridge.

6 To prepare the saddle of lamb, use a sharp filleting knife to very carefully remove the whole central bone from the saddle (your butcher can do this for you, but you must emphasise to him that you want it with no holes through the middle of the saddle). Take off the little 'under' fillets of lamb. Set these aside to use later when assembling the dish.

7 Lay the saddle on your worktop, fat side down, and very carefully ease the loins away from the fat, leaving on the work surface a rectangular piece of lamb fat all in one piece. Working really carefully, using a very sharp knife, remove layers from the fat to leave as thin a layer as you can. The aim is to end up with a really, really thin layer of fat measuring about 32.5 x 23cm. Trim off any fat or sinew from the loins, then lay them lengthways, side by side, in the centre of the piece of fat.

8 Quickly blanch the spinach in boiling salted water for 2 minutes. Drain in a colander and refresh immediately under cold running water. Pat dry, spreading out the leaves on a clean tea towel. Lay the spinach leaves over the loins to cover them both completely. In the gap between the two loins, put the lamb and chicken mousse mixture. Place the 'under' fillets of lamb on top of this. Roll up the whole joint in the thin layer of fat and tie very tightly at 2.5cm intervals with butcher's string. Keep in the fridge until about 30 minutes before you are ready to cook.

9 Roughly chop the bones from the saddle of lamb and put them in a large saucepan with the vegetables, wine and enough stock to cover everything. Bring to the boil, then lower the heat and simmer very gently for about 4 hours, skimming off any scum as it comes to the surface. Strain through a sieve into a clean saucepan and boil to reduce by at least two-thirds, tasting until the gravy reaches the required depth of flavour. Pass through a very fine sieve and set aside. Stir in a little redcurrant jelly to sweeten when reheating, if wished.

10 Preheat the oven to 190°C/gas 5.

11 Heat a very large, heavy-based frying pan until hot. Add the sunflower oil and butter and allow to foam, then put the saddle in the pan and turn to brown all over. Lift the saddle onto a rack set in a roasting tin and season well. Roast for 25–35 minutes, depending on the thickness of the meat. When the lamb has finished cooking, remove from the oven and leave to rest for about 10 minutes.

12 Cook the vegetables while the meat rests. Heat the oil and the 40g butter in a frying pan over a medium heat, add the potatoes, garlic and mint, and season. Fry the potatoes, keeping them moving in the pan as they start to colour. When the potatoes are tender, drain in a sieve or on kitchen paper.

13 Meanwhile, plunge the carrots and asparagus into boiling salted water and cook for 2–3 minutes, then drain well and toss with a knob of butter and salt and pepper to taste. Reheat the gravy.

14 To serve, snip the string off the lamb and carve into 2.5cm-thick slices. (When carved the meat should be perfectly pink inside.) Arrange on the plates surrounded with the vegetables and add a drizzle of gravy.

RUMP OF LAMB 'SOUS-VIDE'
GOAT'S CHEESE, DEHYDRATED TOMATOES, DRIED SEEDS AND YOUNG SALAD SHOOTS

SERVES 4

2 rumps of lamb, each 250g (ask your butcher to trim and clean, and give you the trimmings)
100ml olive oil, plus extra for frying and drizzling
pared zest of 1 lemon
pared zest of 1 orange
5 sprigs of lemon thyme, coarsely chopped
2 sprigs of rosemary, coarsely chopped
4 bay leaves, coarsely chopped
250ml chicken stock
salt and white pepper

TOMATOES

8 very ripe, medium-sized vine tomatoes
sea salt
1 garlic clove, crushed
25g lemon thyme
3 tbsp extra virgin olive oil

TO SERVE

25g each pumpkin, sesame and sunflower seeds
50g pine nuts
200g young salad shoots or salad leaves
100g goat's cheese (log-shaped and ash-coated is good), left at room temperature for 2 hours

1 Season the lamb rumps with salt and white pepper. Heat a little oil in a frying pan, add the lamb and fry over a high heat for about 1 minute on each side to caramelise the surface of the meat. Leave to rest and cool.

2 Mix the 100ml olive oil with the lemon and orange zests and the chopped herbs in a large glass bowl. Put the lamb in and roll it around in the marinade, then cover and leave to marinate in the fridge for 24 hours.

3 Meanwhile, prepare the tomatoes. Preheat the oven to its lowest temperature. Make 2–3 slits in the skin of each tomato, being careful not to go through to the flesh. Halve the tomatoes widthways. Crush a generous sprinkling of sea salt with the garlic and thyme using a pestle and mortar. Roll the tomatoes in the mix. Lay the tomatoes cut-side up on a baking tray lined with baking parchment and drizzle with the oil to coat, then bake for 4–6 hours. The tomatoes will become dense and a bit wrinkly, but should still be softish inside and have a vibrant colour.

4 Transfer the lamb with its marinade to an airtight vacuum-sealed bag (see note below). Fill a large pan with water and heat it to 62°C. Put the bag in the water and cook the lamb for $1^1/_2$ hours, keeping the water temperature at a steady 62°C. The meat should now be really tender and pink inside.

5 While the lamb cooks, put the reserved lamb trimmings in a dry frying pan and fry over a high heat until caramelised. Drain, pat dry and transfer to a small pan. Pour over the chicken stock, cover with a lid and simmer gently for 45 minutes, to extract all the flavour from the lamb. Strain and keep this gravy warm.

6 Meanwhile, toast all the seeds and pine nuts in a dry frying pan on top of the stove. Set aside.

7 When the lamb is cooked, open the bag carefully, remove the lamb and pat it dry with kitchen paper. (Discard the marinade.) Heat a little oil in a non-stick frying pan. Season the fat side of the lamb with salt, then put the lamb in the pan and fry over a high heat to add colour only and caramelise the fat – it doesn't need more cooking. Remove and leave it to rest on a board for 30 seconds.

8 To serve, mix the seeds and nuts with the salad shoots. Sprinkle over a little salt and a drizzle of olive oil, then toss gently together with enough of the warm gravy to moisten. Put 2 tomatoes on each plate. Cut the goat's cheese into 1cm slices and put two slices on each plate. Carve each rump of lamb into four to give you eight slices in total. For each serving arrange one slice of lamb on the goat's cheese and another on the plate. Scatter the dressed salad shoots over the lamb.

Note: Sous-vide, which means 'under vacuum', is a great technique for cooking meat as well as fish and vegetables, and is widely used in restaurants. The meat is slowly poached in a sealed bag at an exact temperature so texture, moisture and flavour are kept intact. I shrink-wrap the meat using a vacuum-sealing machine, then poach in a Clifton water bath, both of which are specially designed for the professional kitchen.

SLOW-COOKED SHOULDER OF MOUNTAIN LAMB
WITH LEEK-WRAPPED LOIN AND CHAMP

SERVES 4

1 shoulder of lamb on the bone, about 1.5kg,
    trimmed of excess fat and sinew, and
    bone fully cleaned
few sprigs each of rosemary and thyme
olive oil
mirepoix of finely diced vegetables
    (2 carrots, 2 celery sticks and 1 large onion)
½ bottle (75cl) dry white wine
200ml white wine vinegar
1 best end (rack) of lamb, meat removed
    from the bones in one piece and
    bones reserved
½ onion, finely chopped
2 garlic cloves, roughly chopped
250g button mushrooms, sliced
1 large leek, leaves separated
knob of unsalted butter
salt and pepper

ONION SOUBISE

2 onions, finely sliced
2 shallots, finely sliced
1 garlic clove, chopped
½ tsp thyme leaves
olive oil
knob of unsalted butter

CHAMP

1kg floury potatoes, such as Kerr's Pink,
    King Edward or Desirée
300ml full-fat milk
60g unsalted butter
6 spring onions, finely chopped
2 tbsp chopped chives
1 banana shallot, finely chopped

GARNISH

1kg broad beans in their pods, shelled
500g peas in their pods, shelled
50g unsalted butter

1 Prick the shoulder of lamb all over with the rosemary and thyme sprigs, then coat lightly in olive oil. Leave to marinate in the fridge for 24 hours.

2 The next day, preheat the oven to 190°C/gas 5.

3 Season the lamb and sear in hot olive oil in a heavy frying pan until well coloured on all sides. Meanwhile, heat a little olive oil in a large flameproof casserole that has a tight-fitting lid. Add the vegetable mirepoix and sweat over a low to medium heat for 8–9 minutes or until softened but not coloured, stirring frequently.

4 Sit the lamb on the mirepoix. Pour over the wine and wine vinegar, and bring just to the boil. Cover the casserole with two layers of foil and tie with string, then put on the lid. Transfer to the oven to cook for 1 hour. Lower the temperature to 130°C/gas ½ and cook for a further 3 hours, removing the lid and foil for the last 30 minutes. When cooked, remove from the oven and set aside.

5 While the lamb shoulder is in the oven, season the loin from the best end of lamb, then sear on all sides in a little hot olive oil in a heavy frying pan. Remove from the pan and set aside to rest.

6 Clean the pan, then heat a little more olive oil and sweat the onion until softened but not coloured. Add the garlic and soften briefly, then add the mushrooms and cook for 2–3 minutes. Tip into a blender and blitz until finely chopped.

7 Blanch 4 large leek leaves in boiling water for 10 seconds. Drain and refresh in iced water, then drain and dry. Lay two large (catering-size) sheets of cling film on top of each other on a board and smooth out any wrinkles. Lay the leek leaves next to each other on the cling film, overlapping them slightly so they form a rectangular sheet of leaves. Spread the mushroom stuffing evenly over the leeks. Place the seared loin of lamb at one of the narrow ends and roll up to encase the meat in the sheet of leeks. Now roll the parcel in the cling film and tie the ends tightly with string. Keep in a cool place until ready to cook.

8 To make the onion soubise, sweat the onions, shallots, garlic and thyme in a little olive oil in a heavy pan for 8–9 minutes, stirring frequently. When the mix is soft and juicy but not coloured, remove the pan from the heat, cover and leave to cool slightly. Blitz in a blender with the knob of butter, then pass through a fine sieve into a clean pan. Set aside.

9 Next, make the champ. Cook the potatoes in their skins in a pan of simmering salted water for 20–30 minutes or until just tender (the flesh should offer no resistance when pierced in the centre with the tip of a small, sharp knife). Drain the potatoes and remove the skins, then lightly mash the flesh. In a small pan, combine the milk and butter, and bring to the boil. Add the spring onions, chives and shallot, remove from the heat and allow to infuse for about 1 minute. Stir this into the mashed potatoes and season. Keep warm.

10 While the potatoes are simmering, prepare the garnish and sauce. Blanch the broad beans and peas in separate pans of boiling salted water until tender. The beans should take 3–4 minutes, the peas 1–2 minutes. Drain and refresh both vegetables in iced water, then drain again. Remove the outer skins from the beans. Set the garnish vegetables aside.

11 Lift the shoulder of lamb off the mirepoix, cover and keep warm. Tip the contents of the casserole into a fine sieve and strain the liquid into a bowl; discard the solids. Deglaze the casserole with enough water to cover the bottom, then add this liquid to the strained cooking liquid in the bowl.

12 Heat a little olive oil in a frying pan until almost smoking. Add the bones and any trimmings from the best end of lamb, season and fry for 3–4 minutes or until well coloured and almost caramelised. Add the liquid from the lamb shoulder and reduce by half, then pass through a sieve lined with wet muslin into a clean pan. Add a knob of butter, season to taste and set aside.

13 Steam the lamb parcels above boiling water for 3 minutes. Reheat the broad beans with the butter and a spoonful of water for 1–2 minutes, then add the peas and toss with the beans until hot. Reheat the onion soubise and champ, if necessary.

14 To serve, cut the lamb parcels into portions and carefully remove the cling film. Divide the shoulder of lamb into chunks with a spoon and put some chunks on top of the peas and beans on one side of each warmed plate. Put a spoonful of onion soubise on the opposite side and top with the leek-wrapped loin of lamb. Spoon the champ in quenelles on the plates, then drizzle a little sauce over both types of lamb and around the plate.

BRYN WILLIAMS

WELSH LAMB STEW

SERVES 4-6
1kg boned shoulder of lamb, diced
about 2 tbsp olive oil
1.25–1.5 litres lamb stock
1 large potato, about 350g
1 medium leek
1 medium carrot
½ swede
salt and pepper
crusty bread to serve

1 Season the diced lamb with salt and pepper. Heat the olive oil in a heavy-based pan and brown the meat, stirring occasionally, for about 10 minutes. Cover with the stock, bring to the boil and skim off any surface scum if necessary. Simmer very gently for 40–45 minutes or until the meat is almost tender.
2 While the meat is cooking, cut all the vegetables into rough dice.
3 Stir the potatoes into the stew and cook for 5 minutes. Add all the remaining vegetables and cook for a further 20–30 minutes. When the vegetables are tender, the stock should be reduced to a thickened gravy.
4 Serve the stew with fresh crusty bread.

234

NEW SEASON LAMB
WITH A HERB AND MUSTARD CRUST
AND SCALLION CRUSHED POTATOES

SERVES 4
4 boneless loins of lamb, each 150g
4 tbsp light olive oil
6 tbsp fresh breadcrumbs
1 tsp roughly chopped thyme
1 tbsp chopped parsley
1 tbsp smooth strong Dijon mustard
1 tbsp wholegrain Dijon mustard
salt and pepper

SAUCE
300ml good brown lamb stock,
  made from bones and trimmings

pinch of thyme leaves
1 tsp chopped parsley
1 tsp wholegrain Dijon mustard
15g butter

SCALLION CRUSHED POTATOES
700g new potatoes, peeled
85g butter
4 spring onions (called scallions in
  Ireland), finely chopped

GARNISH
seasonal vegetables, such as new carrots,
  braised lettuce and broad beans

1 Preheat the oven to 200°C/gas 6.

2 Season the lamb with salt and pepper. In a heavy frying pan, heat 3 tbsp of the olive oil until it is nearly smoking. Add the lamb and cook over high heat until well browned all over. This should take about 5 minutes; the loins should still be rare inside. Place on a wire rack and allow to cool to room temperature.

3 Pour the breadcrumbs on to a baking sheet and drizzle with the remaining olive oil. Mix gently with your fingers. Put into the oven and toast until lightly browned, stirring two or three times. When browned, allow to cool, then add the herbs.

4 For the sauce, reduce the lamb stock until it has a light sauce consistency.

5 To prepare the scallion crushed potatoes, cook the new potatoes in boiling salted water until tender, then drain. Melt the butter in a saucepan over a moderate heat, add the spring onions and a little salt and cook gently for 1 minute. Add the potatoes and crush gently with a fork. Keep warm.

6 While the potatoes are cooking, finish the lamb. Mix the two mustards together and brush over the top of each loin. Dip the mustard-coated part of the loin into the breadcrumbs and gently press the crumbs on to the mustard. Set the loins on a baking sheet, crumb side up. Place in the top of the oven and roast for 4–5 minutes for medium rare, or 8 minutes for medium well done. Remove from the oven and allow to rest in a warm place while you cook the vegetables and finish the sauce.

7 Bring the sauce to the boil, then remove from the heat and stir in the herbs, mustard and butter. Check for seasoning.

8 To serve, spoon the vegetable garnishes and scallion crushed potatoes on to the warmed plates. Slice each loin into three thick slices and place on the potatoes. Spoon the sauce over or around.

ROAST BEST END OF LAMB
WITH TOMATO FONDUE, FONDANT POTATO
AND ONION PURÉE, WITH AN OLIVE SAUCE

SERVES 4
1 best end of lamb (8 cutlets minimum)
vegetable oil
200g spinach
unsalted butter
salt and pepper

OLIVE SAUCE
1kg lamb bones, chopped small
75g diced onion
75g diced leek
75g diced carrot
½ head of garlic
50ml olive oil
5g thyme
5g rosemary
150g ripe plum tomatoes
40g tomato purée
700ml chicken stock
200ml veal glace
1 tsp black olive tapenade or to taste

TOMATO FONDUE
400g plum tomatoes
30g chopped onion
1 tsp finely chopped garlic
40ml olive oil plus extra for brushing
1 tsp finely chopped thyme

ONION PURÉE
4 large onions, each cut into 4
sprig of thyme
1 bay leaf
50g white breadcrumbs
30g butter
pinch of chopped thyme

FONDANT POTATOES
2 large baking potatoes
50g butter
1 garlic clove, crushed
sprig of thyme

1 First make the olive sauce. Preheat the oven to 180°C/gas 4. Roast the bones lightly for 20–30 minutes.

2 Meanwhile, sweat the onion, leek, carrot and garlic in the olive oil, without colouring. Add the thyme and rosemary and sweat for a further 5 minutes. Stir in the tomatoes and tomato purée and cook for 10 minutes.

3 Transfer the roasted bones to a saucepan and add the sweated vegetables, stock, veal glace and 300ml water. Bring to the boil, then reduce to a simmer and cook for 30 minutes. Pass through a colander set in a bowl and then through a fine sieve into a clean saucepan. Reduce to a sauce consistency and pass through muslin. To finish, whisk in tapenade to taste and pass through a fine sieve. Reserve for later use.

4 Next prepare the tomato fondue. Cut the tomatoes in half and squeeze out the seeds. In a thick-bottomed copper pan sweat the onion and garlic in the olive oil, without colouring. Add the thyme and then the tomatoes halves. Season lightly and stir together. Place the pan in the oven and cook for 10 minutes, then stir again. Replace in the oven and cook for a further 10 minutes. Repeat the process until the tomato fondue is dry. Leave to cool, then put to one side and reheat when needed.

5 Turn the oven up to 200°C/gas 6. For the onion purée, put the onions in a saucepan, cover with water and add the thyme sprig and bay leaf. Bring to the boil, then reduce to a simmer and cook until the onions are completely soft. Drain well in a colander. Discard the herbs, then place the onions in a blender or food processor and blend until a fine purée.

6 Measure 200g of the onion purée and place in a thick-bottomed pan. Add the breadcrumbs and butter and cook gently for 15 minutes. Stir in the chopped thyme and some salt and pepper. Adjust the texture if necessary, adding a little liquid if the purée is too thick or cooking longer to thicken. Put into a piping bag and keep in a warm place until needed.

7 While the onion purée is cooking, season the best end with salt and pepper. Sear it all over in a little vegetable oil in small roasting tray on top of the cooker, then turn it fat side down and place in the oven. Roast for 5 minutes, then turn it over and roast for a further 4 minutes. Remove from the pan and leave to rest for 15 minutes. Reheat in the oven for 5 minutes before serving.

8 Prepare the fondant potatoes while the lamb is in the oven. Peel the potatoes and cut each one in half. Using a 4cm round cutter, cut out a cylinder from each half and block them off to an even height.

9 When the lamb has finished roasting, turn the oven down to 170°C/gas 3. Melt the butter in a small thick-bottomed pan (preferably copper) and add the potatoes, garlic, thyme and a seasoning of salt and pepper. Colour the base of each potato cylinder well before turning them over. Add a splash of water and cover the pan with a buttered paper. Place the pan in the oven and cook for 15 minutes or until the potatoes are soft in the middle.

10 Meanwhile, stir fry the spinach with a little butter, salt and pepper, and reheat the tomato fondue and olive sauce.

11 To serve, pipe the onion purée in a square around each warm plate. With the 4cm cutter used to cut the potatoes, dress the spinach in the middle of the plate, then place the fondant potatoes on top and on this put the tomato fondue. Slice the best end into eight cutlets and place two on each plate, on either side of the fondant potato. Spoon the sauce around, but within the onion purée.

LANCASHIRE HOT POT
WITH BRAISED RED CABBAGE

SERVES 4
1 middle neck of lamb, about 1kg
plain flour
vegetable oil
1 Spanish onion, thinly sliced
2 carrots, thinly sliced
1 garlic clove, thinly sliced
1 tbsp thyme leaves
1 tbsp chopped rosemary
3 Maris Piper potatoes, peeled
butter
salt and pepper

LAMB STOCK
1 large carrot, cut into 3 pieces
1 onion, cut into quarters

2 garlic cloves, peeled
sprig of rosemary
sprig of thyme
1 bay leaf
pinch of rock salt
1 tbsp tomato purée

BRAISED RED CABBAGE
1 small red cabbage, cored and sliced
1 red onion, diced
150g unsalted butter, diced
200ml red wine vinegar
50g clear honey
100g Demerara sugar
1 bay leaf
sprig of thyme

1 Preheat the oven to 200°C/gas 6. Remove the meat from the middle neck of lamb and set aside. To make the lamb stock, chop the bones and put them in a roasting tray. Roast until lightly browned.

2 Meanwhile, cook the carrot, onion and garlic in a little hot olive oil in a heavy-bottomed pot until lightly browned. Add the herbs and salt, then stir in the tomato purée and cook for a couple of minutes. Add the roasted bones and cover with 2 litres water. Bring to the boil, then turn down to a simmer and cook for 1 hour, skimming off any fat regularly. Pass the liquid through a fine sieve into a clean pan. Return to the heat and reduce until you have 1 litre of stock. Turn the oven to 150°C/gas 2.

3 To make the hot pot, cut the lamb into 2mm thick slices. Dust them with flour and quickly fry in hot oil until lightly coloured on both sides. Remove and set aside. In the same oil, quickly fry the onion, carrots and garlic until lightly browned.

4 Layer the lamb and vegetables in a heavy casserole dish, filling it to 1cm from the top. Season each layer with salt, pepper and herbs, and spoon liberal amounts of stock between each layer.

5 Evenly slice the potatoes about 1mm thick and arrange neatly all over the top of the dish. Put a few small knobs of butter on the potatoes, cover with a tight-fitting lid and cook in the oven for 1¹/₂ hours. Remove the lid and cook for a further 45 minutes.

6 Meanwhile, make the red cabbage. Mix together all of the ingredients, seasoning well with salt. Put into a roasting tray and cover with foil. Place in the oven and cook for about 1¹/₂ hours, stirring regularly, until most of the liquid has gone.

7 Serve the hot pot from the casserole on to warm plates with the cabbage.

ROAST LOIN AND BRAISED SHOULDER OF
SALT-MARSH LAMB
WITH CAPER JUS

SERVES 4

1 shoulder of salt-marsh lamb, about 2–3kg
vegetable oil
1 large onion, chopped
1 large carrot, chopped
2 sprigs of rosemary
250ml white wine
2 litres chicken stock
1 litre veal stock
2kg Desiree potatoes, peeled and finely sliced

1 best end of salt-marsh lamb, with 8 cutlets
salt and pepper

TO FINISH

selection of summer vegetables, such as
   baby carrots, broad beans and baby leeks
200g girolles or other wild mushrooms
   as available
olive oil
1 tsp capers

1 Preheat the oven to 140°C/gas 1.

2 Heat a little vegetable oil in a heavy-bottomed pan that can go into the oven. Sear the shoulder of lamb on all sides over a moderate heat. When coloured, remove the lamb from the pan and replace with the chopped onion and carrot and a sprig of rosemary. Cook for 4–5 minutes or until golden brown.

3 Add the white wine and reduce by half. Put the shoulder of lamb back in the pan on top of the vegetables and cover with the chicken and veal stocks. Bring to the boil. Cover the pan, then place in the oven and cook for 1 hour. Remove from the oven and leave to cool.

4 When cooled, pick the meat from the bone into small pieces. Strain the stock and discard the vegetables. Bring the stock back to the boil and skim.

5 Arrange some of the potato slices on the bottom of a 20 x 15cm square baking dish to create a thin layer. Season with salt, pepper and the remaining rosemary, chopped. Add a layer of picked lamb shoulder, then build up a further two layers of potato slices and lamb. Cover the layers with enough of the hot lamb stock to moisten. Place in the oven. Cook for 30 minutes or until the potatoes are tender and the liquid has been absorbed. Remove and keep hot. Turn the oven to 180°C/gas 4.

6 Season the best end of lamb, then sear, fat side down first, in a little vegetable oil in a heavy-bottomed pan. Turn to sear all over. Place in the oven and roast for 6–8 minutes. When cooked, leave to rest for 15 minutes.

7 Meanwhile, reduce 150ml of the lamb stock to a sauce consistency. Cook the summer vegetables in a little of the remaining lamb stock until tender; drain. Pan-fry the mushrooms in a little olive oil, then season.

8 To assemble, cut out four cylinders from the potato and lamb layers and place one on each warm plate. Carve the best end of lamb into cutlets and position to the side of the potato cylinder. Arrange the vegetables and mushrooms around the meat. Add the capers to the reduced lamb stock and pour over the dish. Serve immediately.

240

CANON OF LAMB
WITH BLACK PUDDING, MINTED PEA PURÉE, AND WILD GARLIC POTATO CAKES, GARNISHED WITH LAMB SWEETBREADS AND ROSEMARY GRAVY

SERVES 4

4 boneless loins of lamb, each about 150g

about 6 tbsp rapeseed oil

200g black pudding, preferably Pat
  O'Doherty's

100g caul fat, soaked in salted water for
  4 hours, rinsed and dried

800g floury potatoes, such as Dunbar
  Standards, peeled

100g wild garlic leaves, finely chopped
  (see note page 242)

200g freshly shelled peas

leaves of 4 sprigs of mint

200g lamb sweetbreads

salt and pepper

GRAVY

300ml red wine

1 tbsp roughly chopped rosemary leaves

1 tbsp roughly chopped thyme leaves

2 garlic cloves, roughly chopped

300ml brown beef stock

4 tbsp redcurrant jelly

60g chilled salted butter, diced

1 Season the lamb. Heat 2 tbsp oil in a heavy frying pan until very hot. Add the lamb and sear over a high heat for about 2 minutes until browned on all sides. The meat should still be very rare inside. Place the loins on a wire rack and allow them to cool to room temperature.

2 Remove the skin from the black pudding. Soften the pudding in a bowl, then spread a thin layer on top of each lamb loin. Wrap each loin in caul fat, then in cling film, and put in the fridge to firm up.

3 To make the potato cakes, finely grate the potatoes into a bowl. Season and add the chopped garlic leaves. In a heavy frying pan, heat 1 tbsp oil until it is just beginning to smoke. Press one-quarter of the potato mixture into a 10cm round, add to the hot pan and cook over a medium heat until golden brown on each side. This should take 8–10 minutes in total. Repeat with remaining mixture to make four cakes altogether, adding more oil as needed, and placing them on a baking tray as they are cooked.

4 Meanwhile, cook the peas in boiling salted water for about 5 minutes or until soft but still vibrant green. Drain and purée in a blender until smooth. Add the mint and purée a little more. Rub the purée through a very fine sieve into a clean saucepan, to remove the pea skins. Set the potato cakes and pea purée aside in a warm place.

5 For the gravy, pour the red wine into a pan and add the rosemary, thyme and garlic. Bring to the boil and reduce by two-thirds. Pour in the stock, bring back to the boil and reduce by three-quarters. Add the redcurrant jelly and stir until melted, then strain the gravy into a clean pan. Finish by whisking in the chilled butter, a piece at a time, for a high gloss. Set the gravy aside.

6 Blanch the sweetbreads in boiling salted water for 2 minutes. Drain and refresh in iced water, then lift the sweetbreads out and remove the outer skin with a very sharp knife. Set the sweetbreads aside in the iced water.

7 When you are ready to serve, preheat the oven to 200°C/gas 6.

8 Remove the cling film from the lamb and sear the loins in a very hot pan, rolling them over, for about 2 minutes or until the caul fat is browned on all sides. Transfer the loins to a baking tray and roast on the top shelf of the oven for 5–8 minutes, according to how well done you like your lamb. Remove and allow to rest for 2–3 minutes. Turn the oven temperature down to 160°C/gas 3.

9 While the lamb is roasting and resting, heat 2 tbsp oil in a heavy frying pan. Drain, dry and season the sweetbreads, then pan-fry over a medium heat for 3–5 minutes or until lightly browned. At the same time, quickly reheat the potato cakes in the oven, and the pea purée and gravy on top of the stove.

10 To serve, carve the lamb into neat slices. Put a potato cake on each plate and top with slices of lamb. Garnish with the sweetbreads and pea purée, and pool the gravy on the side of the pancake.

Note: When wild garlic is out of season, you can use 100g sorrel or spinach leaves with 2 crushed garlic cloves.

STUART GILLIES

ROASTED LOIN OF SUCKLING PIG WITH MUSTARD SAUCE

SERVES 8-10

1 boneless loin from a 10-12 week old suckling pig, about 3kg, flap removed and trimmed
about 450g sea salt (150g per kg of pork)
bunch of flat-leaf parsley, roughly torn
bunch of basil, roughly torn
150g wild garlic leaves, roughly torn
50ml olive oil
salt and pepper

VEGETABLE GARNISH

16 baby carrots, peeled
caster sugar
about 300g unsalted butter
10 Charlotte potatoes, about 7.5cm each, peeled
½ head of garlic, cut in half crossways
2 tbsp olive oil
500g baby spinach leaves
bunch of flat-leaf parsley, coarsely chopped

MUSTARD SAUCE

500ml home-made chicken stock
2 shallots, shredded or finely sliced
200ml double cream
25g coarse grain mustard
30g Dijon mustard

1 Weigh the loin and the amount of salt you need, then spread the salt out on a tray. Press the loin skin-side down into the salt. Cover with cling film and leave in the fridge for 12 hours.

2 Carefully rinse off all the salt and pat thoroughly dry. Lay the loin, skin-side up, on a board. Using a razor-sharp knife, Stanley knife or scalpel, score the skin carefully all the way along at 5mm intervals. Turn the loin over and stuff with the parsley, basil and wild garlic, then roll up tightly and tie with string. Place the loin skin-side up on a rack in a roasting tin and return, uncovered, to the fridge.

3 Cook the carrots in boiling salted water with a pinch of sugar for about 5 minutes or until just tender. Drain, refresh in iced water and drain again. Set aside.

4 To make the mustard sauce, boil the stock with the shallots until reduced by half, then pass through a fine sieve into a clean pan and bring to the boil again. Whisk in the cream and bring back to the boil, then reduce the heat and whisk in both of the mustards. Cook over a low heat until reduced to a pouring consistency, then remove from the heat. Cover and keep warm, stirring now and again.

5 Melt the butter in a wide, shallow, heavy saucepan. Add the potatoes. They should all be immersed in the butter, so add more butter if necessary. Add the garlic and seasoning, and bring the butter up to a brown foam. Cook the potatoes in the foam for about 25 minutes or until they are a deep golden brown and tender in the middle, shaking the pan gently every few minutes. Remove the pan from the heat and keep the potatoes warm in the butter.

6 Preheat the oven to 220°C/gas 7.

7 Drizzle the pork with the olive oil, then sprinkle with fine salt and rub well into the skin. Roast for 25–30 minutes or until the skin starts to firm and blister. Remove from the oven and leave to rest somewhere warm. Leave the oven on.

8 While the meat is resting, reheat the carrots in the olive oil without colouring, then add the spinach and chopped parsley, and toss until hot. Lift the potatoes out of the butter with a slotted spoon and put them in a small, heavy pan. Pour over 2 tbsp of the butter they were cooked in and put the potatoes into the oven to reheat for about 2 minutes. Gently reheat the mustard sauce without boiling.

9 Remove the string from the pork and carve the meat into equal slices, allowing two per person. Reheat in the oven on a non-stick mat or foil for 2 minutes.

10 To serve, check the potatoes for seasoning, then place on the side of the warmed plates. Put the other vegetables next to them, then place the pork in the middle, resting the slices on the potatoes. Pour over a little of the mustard sauce, and serve the rest on the side.

PLATE OF AGED MUTTON
POTATOES AND BROAD BEANS, WITH
CAPER AND HERB RELISH

SERVES 4

RACKS OF MUTTON

2 racks of mutton, preferably aged
   Herdwick, each with 6 rib bones, chined
   and trimmed of all fat
large sprig each of thyme and rosemary
4 garlic cloves, sliced
about 450ml organic rapeseed oil
salt and pepper

MUTTON 'PARK RAILINGS'

100ml organic rapeseed oil
2 onions, very finely diced
2 carrots, very finely diced
½ head of celery, very finely diced
2 leeks, very finely diced
1 head of garlic, smashed
½ bottle (75cl) dry white wine,
preferably English
1 breast of mutton, preferably aged
   Herdwick, trimmed of all skin
plain flour for coating
3 medium eggs, beaten
200g home-made fresh white breadcrumbs,
   seasoned with salt and pepper
vegetable oil for frying

RELISH

75g can anchovies, chopped
2 tbsp extra-fine capers, plus a little
   of their vinegar
150ml organic rapeseed oil
½–¾ tsp English mustard powder
squeeze of lemon juice
2 tbsp each very finely shredded flat-leaf
   parsley, basil and mint

TO SERVE

12–16 small new potatoes, preferably
   Maris Bard, scraped
few sprigs of mint
750g fresh broad beans, podded
butter
100ml mutton jus, made as duck jus
   (page 65), but using mutton bones and
   white wine, or 100ml gravy leftover from
   a lamb roast, warmed for serving

1 Put the racks of mutton in a strong plastic bag with the herbs and sliced garlic. Add enough rapeseed oil (about 400ml) to cover the meat. Seal and shake the bag, then leave in the fridge overnight. The next day, cut each rack in half so you have 4 racks, each with 4 bones.

2 Preheat the oven to 180°C/gas 4.

3 Heat 100ml rapeseed oil in a large, heavy flameproof casserole until hot. Add the diced vegetables and the smashed garlic, and brown over a medium to high heat. Pour in the wine and stir well, then place the breast of mutton on the vegetables. Add enough cold water to cover the meat. Bring to a simmer, then cover the casserole and transfer to the oven. Braise for 2 hours or until the meat is meltingly tender.

4 Take the breast out of the liquid, and twist and pull out the bones while the meat is still warm. Put the meat between two sheets of greaseproof paper, put heavy weights on top to flatten it and leave for 3–5 hours. After pressing, cut the meat into eight long strips (traditionally called park railings), each about 12cm long and 1.5cm wide.

5 Make the relish by stirring together all the ingredients except the herbs.

6 Cook the potatoes with the mint in a pan of gently simmering salted water for 10–12 minutes or until tender. Drain and set aside. Plunge the broad beans into well-salted boiling water to blanch for 2 minutes. Drain and refresh in iced water, then drain again and peel off the skins. Set aside.

7 Preheat the oven to 220–230°C/gas 7–8.

8 Season the racks of mutton. Heat a heavy ovenproof frying pan until hot, add a splash of oil and caramelise the racks quickly and evenly all over. Transfer to the oven to finish cooking for 8–10 minutes. Remove the racks from the oven, cover them loosely with foil and leave to rest in a warm place for 10–15 minutes so they will be evenly pink.

9 Meanwhile, coat the park railings in flour, beaten egg and breadcrumbs. Pour vegetable oil into a deep frying pan to a depth of 2.5–5cm (enough to cover the railings). Heat the oil until hot, then fry the railings for 2–3 minutes or until crisp and golden. At the same time, reheat the potatoes and broad beans together in a pan with a little butter, a drop of water and seasoning to taste. Mix the herbs into the relish and taste for seasoning.

10 To serve, carve one rack into three double cutlets and the other rack into one double cutlet and four single cutlets. Slot the bones of each double cutlet with a single cutlet on each plate, then criss-cross two park railings in front. Spoon the broad beans and potatoes on the left, and the caper relish on the right. Finish with a cordon of warm mutton jus.

PORK CUTLETS
WITH CELERIAC AND APPLE MASH

SERVES 4
4 thick pork cutlets, preferably organic
    Saddleback, with bone and untrimmed
25g unsalted butter, melted
8 sage leaves
salt and pepper

MASH
1 celeriac, 500-700g, peeled and cut
    into cubes
sprig of thyme
150ml full-fat milk
3 Bramley's cooking apples, peeled and
    cut into cubes
unsalted butter

1 To make the mash, put the celeriac in a heavy saucepan with 150ml water, the thyme, milk and seasoning. Cook for 20–30 minutes or until tender. At the same time, cook the apples with a little butter in a separate pan over a gentle heat for about 20 minutes or until soft, then blitz to a purée in a blender.
2 Drain the celeriac, return to the hot pan and mash roughly. Immediately add the apple purée and toss together. Cover the pan and leave in a warm place while you cook the pork cutlets.
3 Brush the cutlets well with melted butter. Place a sage leaf on both sides of each cutlet and brush with more butter so the sage leaves stick to the meat, then season with salt and pepper. Pan-roast in a heavy pan over a high heat until the internal temperature of the pork reaches 70°C when tested with a meat thermometer. Cooking should take 5–6 minutes in total, turning the cutlets halfway. At the end of cooking the meat should be coloured on the outside but pink inside. Strain the pan juices and reserve, then let the meat rest in the pan in a warm place for 10 minutes.
4 To serve, place a pork cutlet on each plate, spoon the mash alongside and drizzle over the strained juices from the pork.

POT ROAST PORK BELLY
COOKED IN CIDER
SERVED WITH ITS OFFAL AND CRACKLING, WITH SUMMER VEGETABLES

SERVES 4

1 piece of pork belly on the bone, with skin,
    1.5–2kg
1 large onion, roughly chopped
2 celery sticks, roughly chopped
2 carrots, roughly chopped
3 garlic cloves, halved
few sprigs of thyme
500ml dry cider
½ tbsp plain flour
1 litre hot beef or chicken stock
2 shallots, roughly chopped
about 100g unsalted butter
vegetable oil
1 pig's kidney, about 150g, cored and cut
    into rough 1cm dice
250–300g runner beans, very thinly sliced
    on the diagonal
500g fresh young broad beans, podded
    (about 200g podded weight)
salt and pepper

1 Preheat the oven to 180°C/gas 4.
2 Cut the bones out of the pork belly and place them in a flameproof casserole with the onion, celery, carrots, garlic and thyme.
3 Cut the meat into four equal servings. Remove the skin from each one using a razor-sharp knife or a Stanley knife. Score parallel lines in the skin, keeping them as close together as possible and cutting right through into the fat beneath. Blanch the skin in boiling water for 3–4 minutes, then drain and dry well. Set aside.
4 Score the fat on the pieces of pork in a criss-cross pattern, then season. Heat a heavy frying pan and cook the pieces of pork on a fairly high heat for 3–4 minutes on each side until nicely coloured. Place the pork fat-side up on top of the vegetables and bones in the casserole and pour in half the cider. Cover with a lid and cook in the oven for 1 hour, basting the meat every so often.
5 Season the blanched pork skin with salt, place on a baking tray and roast in the oven with the pork.

6 Remove the lid from the pork and drain off about two-thirds of the cooking liquid. Continue cooking the pork, uncovered, for a further 30 minutes or until the liquid has evaporated and the pork is crisping up. Check the crackling on the baking tray and continue cooking if it isn't yet crisp.

7 Lift the pork from the casserole and keep hot. Drain off all the fat from the pot, leaving behind the vegetables and bones. Place the pot over a low heat. Dust the vegetables and bones with the flour and stir well. Gradually stir in the rest of the cider and the stock, then bring to the boil and simmer for 15–20 minutes. Strain into a saucepan. Skim off any fat, and simmer until the sauce has reduced to about 250ml. Remove from the heat.

8 Gently cook the shallots in another saucepan with 50g butter for 1–2 minutes, then pour in the reduced sauce and stir to mix. Heat a little vegetable oil in a frying pan, season the kidney and fry for 2–3 minutes or until nicely coloured. Drain the kidney on kitchen paper and add to the sauce. Taste for seasoning and keep hot.

9 Cook the runner beans in boiling salted water for 3–4 minutes or until just tender. Drain, toss in a little butter and season to taste. Now cook the broad beans in boiling salted water for 3–4 minutes or until tender; drain and cool a little, then remove the outer skins if they are tough. Toss the beans in a little butter and season to taste.

10 To serve, place the runner beans in the centre of four plates. Slice each piece of pork into four or five pieces and place on the beans. Drizzle the sauce over, and scatter the broad beans around the edge. Break the crackling into shreds where it has been scored, and pile on top of the sliced pork.

SLOWLY BRAISED BELLY AND ROASTED LOIN CHOP OF PORK
WITH CRACKLING

SERVES 8

½ boned short pork belly, skin on, trimmed
   to weigh about 1.5kg
300ml vegetable oil
2 carrots, cut into 2cm pieces
4 celery sticks, cut into 2cm pieces
1 white onion, cut lengthways into eighths
1 head of garlic, cut crossways in half
1 leek, cut into 2cm pieces
6 ripe tomatoes, halved
small bunch of thyme
small bunch of rosemary
1 bay leaf
2.2 litres hot home-made chicken stock
20g salted butter

2 pork loins, each with 4 rib bones,
   preferably Middle White or another
   traditional English breed, chined and
   fully trimmed
40g unsalted butter
1 Duchy cabbage, leaves cut into forty-eight
   6cm squares
salt and pepper

1 Soak the pork belly in cold water for about 1 hour. Remove and dry very well, then season all over with salt. Heat 150ml of the oil in a large, heavy roasting tin over a medium-high heat until you can see a light haze rising. Gently place the pork belly skin-side down in the pan, taking care because the oil may spit a little. Cook for 5–8 minutes or until the skin has a nice colour, then turn the joint over and cook for another 5 minutes or until the meat is golden brown. Transfer the joint to a wire rack, placing it skin-side up.

2 Keep the roasting tin on the stove over a medium heat, and add the carrots, celery, onion, garlic and leek. Cook until well coloured, then add the tomatoes and cook until soft. Place the pork belly skin-side up on the vegetables. Add the herbs and 2 litres chicken stock, and bring to the boil. Turn the heat down to a very gentle murmer (almost not moving), cover the tin with a lid and cook for 3–3¹/₂ hours. Check the meat is done by piercing it in the middle with the tip of a sharp knife – it should slide in effortlessly. Remove the meat from the tin and leave to cool, then keep covered in the fridge.

3 Strain the cooking liquid through a fine sieve lined with muslin into a heavy saucepan. Simmer until reduced to about 500ml, skimming frequently. Season this sauce with salt if necessary, and set aside.

4 Preheat the oven to 190°C/gas 5.

5 Heat 50ml of the remaining oil in a clean, heavy roasting tin over a medium heat. Add the salted butter and heat until it starts to foam. Season the loins of pork well with salt, then sear until golden brown on all sides, turning regularly. Transfer the tin to the oven and roast for about 35 minutes or until the loins are glazed and moist. Turn them every 8 minutes or so, and baste with a spoonful or two of the remaining hot chicken stock. Remove from the oven and allow to rest in warm place.

6 Turn the oven up to 210°C/gas 6$^1/_2$. Remove the skin from the pork belly, taking a little of the fat beneath, and leaving a 2mm-thick layer of fat attached to the meat. Cut the skin into 2 x 4cm rectangles using a razor-sharp knife or a Stanley knife and set aside.

7 Cut the belly into eight 7 x 4cm rectangles. Heat 50ml of the remaining oil in a heavy frying pan until you can see a light haze rising. Carefully place the belly fat-side down in the pan and cook over a medium-high heat for about 5 minutes or until a deep golden colour. Place fat-side up on a tray and transfer to the oven to cook for 6 minutes.

8 Meanwhile, heat the remaining oil in a heavy frying pan. Season the pork skin, then put it skin-side down in the hot oil and fry over a medium-high heat until crisp. This will take 4–5 minutes, turning halfway. Remove the crackling with a slotted spoon, drain on kitchen paper and keep hot.

9 Heat the unsalted butter in another pan until it melts and starts to bubble. Add the 48 cabbage leaf squares, season with salt and cook for 2–3 minutes or until tender. Season with a good few twists of pepper, then transfer to kitchen paper using a slotted spoon and keep hot.

10 Reheat the sauce. Cut each piece of pork belly in half widthways. Carve the loins into single chops, and season the cut flesh with a little sea salt.

11 To serve, sit two pieces of pork belly on each plate and arrange six squares of cabbage in front. Rest a chop against the cabbage and garnish with the crackling, either left as it is or cut into pieces. Spoon a little of the sauce over and around, and serve the rest in a jug.

ROAST RACK OF PORK
WITH CRACKLING, ROSEMARY AND GARLIC, GOOSEBERRY PURÉE, WILTED SPROUTING BROCCOLI AND OLIVE OIL MASHED POTATOES

SERVES 6-8

1 rack of pork with at least 3 rib bones, about 1.5kg, chined and rind finely scored

2–3 garlic cloves, thinly sliced

sprigs of rosemary

450g purple sprouting broccoli, preferably Norfolk-grown

salt and pepper

GOOSEBERRY PURÉE

250g gooseberries, topped and tailed

about 50g caster sugar

2 elderflower blossoms (if available)

OLIVE OIL MASH

200ml milk

2 garlic cloves, finely chopped

2 sprigs of thyme

sprig of rosemary

1kg floury potatoes such as Desirée, peeled and chopped

about 175ml olive oil

1 Preheat the oven to 220°C/gas 7. Weigh the pork and calculate the cooking time, allowing 45 minutes per kg, then adding 20 minutes extra.

2 Make incisions about 2.5cm apart through the rind and into the flesh of the pork using a sharp knife, then push a slice of garlic and a small sprig of rosemary into each cut. Place the pork in a roasting tin and splash the rind with cold water before liberally sprinkling with salt.

3 Roast the pork, without opening the oven door, for 25 minutes. During this time, the crackling should start to bubble. Turn the oven down to 190°C/gas 5 and continue to roast for the remainder of the calculated cooking time. You should have good crackling and moist succulent meat. Check with a skewer to be sure the meat is cooked properly – the juices should run pink but not bloody. Remove the pork from the oven and allow to rest for 5 minutes in a warm place before carving.

4 While the pork is roasting, prepare the accompaniments. To make the gooseberry purée, put the gooseberries in a saucepan and add enough caster sugar just to cover and the elderflower blossoms, if using. Pour in enough cold water just to cover the gooseberries and sugar. Cover the pan and cook over a moderate heat for about 15 minutes or until the gooseberries are soft. Remove the elderflower blossoms and blitz the cooked gooseberries in a blender. Pass the purée through a fine sieve into a clean pan. Taste and add more sugar if needed. Set aside (reheat gently to serve).

5 For the olive oil mash, pour the milk into a saucepan, add the garlic, thyme and rosemary, and bring to the boil. Remove from the heat, cover and leave to infuse while you cook the potatoes.

6 Put the potatoes in a saucepan of salted water, bring to the boil and cook for about 15 minutes or until soft. Drain in a colander, then return to the pan and dry out by shaking the pan over a low heat. Push the potatoes through a sieve with the back of a ladle into a bowl, or use a potato ricer.

7 Strain the milk into another pan, add 100ml of the olive oil and slowly bring to the boil. Vigorously whisk the hot milk and olive oil into the potatoes to create a mash with a fairly runny consistency. (You can use an electric mixer, but not a food processor as this will make the potatoes too sticky and glutinous.) Adjust the consistency by adding more warm olive oil or milk, or both. Taste and season, and keep hot. (If preparing ahead, allow to cool, then gently reheat by stirring in a saucepan over a low heat.)

8 To prepare the broccoli, trim any tough stalks, much as if you were preparing asparagus. Bring a large saucepan of salted water to the boil and drop in the broccoli. Cook for a few minutes only, until the stalks are just tender (test with the point of a knife). Drain the broccoli immediately and give it a good grinding of salt and pepper.

9 To serve, carve the rack of pork and serve with the slightly warmed gooseberry purée, olive oil mash and sprouting broccoli.

MARK BROADBENT

CRACKLED PORK
WITH BEETROOT, CELERY LEAF AND HORSERADISH

SERVES 4
½ pork belly on the bone, preferably Middle
    White, skin scored
250g Maldon sea salt
2kg goose fat, duck fat or lard, or 2 litres
    grapeseed oil
6 small, raw beetroots
red wine vinegar
250g unsalted butter
150g celery leaves
200ml pork jus, made as duck jus,
    but using pork trimmings and
    bones and white wine, or 200ml
    gravy leftover from a pork roast,
    warmed for serving
salt and pepper

HORSERADISH SAUCE
100g fresh horseradish, peeled and
    finely grated
½ tbsp Dijon mustard
juice of ½ lemon
2 generous tbsp crème fraîche

1 Rub the skin of the pork belly with the sea salt, working it into the scored cuts. Leave uncovered in the fridge for 8 hours or overnight.

2 The next day, preheat the oven to 120°C/gas $^1/_4$.

3 Rinse the salt off the pork. Bring the fat to the boil in a large flameproof casserole. Lower the pork into it until submerged, then cover the pot and place in the oven to braise for $2^1/_2$–3 hours or until tender.

4 Remove from the oven. Leave the pork belly in the fat until lukewarm, then lift out and place skin-side down on a board. Twist and pull out all the bones, then cut away any gristle and excess fat. Now turn the pork skin-side up and sandwich between two sheets of greaseproof paper. Place a chopping board on top and press down lightly, then chill in the fridge overnight. Strain the fat and reserve.

5 The next day, put the beetroots in a saucepan of cold salted water, add a healthy splash of wine vinegar and bring to the boil. Simmer for up to 1 hour or until just cooked. Allow the beetroots to cool in the liquid, then lift out and peel with a vegetable peeler. Strain and reserve the cooking liquid.

6 Make the horseradish sauce by mixing all the ingredients together with salt and pepper to taste. Cover and chill for at least 2 hours before serving.

7 Preheat the oven to 230°C/gas 8.

8 Cut the pressed pork into four neat rectangular blocks, about 8.5 x 6.5cm (leftover pork can be immersed in goose or duck fat and kept as 'confit' in the fridge for up to a month). Heat a flameproof casserole or heavy ovenproof frying pan until hot. Add enough of the reserved strained fat to cover the bottom and heat until the fat is hot, then put in the pork skin-side down. Transfer to the oven and roast for 20 minutes or until the skin is crackled. Remove the pork and drain on kitchen paper. Keep hot.

9 Cut the beetroots in half lengthways. Heat through in a pan with a spoonful of the reserved cooking liquid, half the butter, and salt and pepper to taste.

10 Blanch the celery leaves in boiling salted water for 1–$1^1/_2$ minutes. Drain and refresh in iced water, then drain again and squeeze out the excess water. Reheat the leaves with the remaining butter and seasoning.

11 To serve, put the celery leaves in the middle of each large bowl or plate. Set the pork on top to one side and place the beetroot halves next to it. Drizzle over a little jus, and top the beetroot with a quenelle of horseradish cream.

SLOW ROAST PORK
WITH KENTISH APPLE TART
LEEKS AND CAULIFLOWER CREAM

SERVES 4
1 piece of pork belly, 1–1.2kg
vegetable oil
coarse sea salt
salt and pepper

GRAVY
knob of butter
1 carrot, roughly diced
1 large onion, roughly diced
2 celery sticks, roughly diced
sprig of thyme
1 bay leaf
2 Bramley's apples, roughly diced
100ml Calvados (optional)
300ml chicken stock
300ml veal or beef gravy/glace
    (or canned beef consommé)

APPLE TARTS
2 English onions, sliced
Demerara sugar
a few sage leaves, chopped
2 apples, peeled, halved and cored
4 puff pastry discs, each about
    11cm diameter

CAULIFLOWER CREAM
1 cauliflower, cut into florets
milk to cover
25g butter
squeeze of lemon juice

SMOKY LEEKS
100g streaky smoked bacon, diced
    or cut into strips
3 medium leeks, sliced or shredded
knob of butter

1 Preheat the oven to 160°C/gas 3.

2 Season the meat side of the pork belly with salt and pepper. Place the pork skin side up on a rack in a roasting tray. Brush the rind with oil and scatter coarse sea salt liberally over the top. Roast the joint for 2–2¹/₂ hours or until completely tender.

3 Meanwhile, make the gravy. Melt the knob of butter in a saucepan. Once sizzling, add the chopped carrot, onion and celery along with the thyme and bay leaf. Cook over a moderate heat, stirring from time to time, until the vegetables are a rich golden brown and beginning to soften. Add the diced apples and continue to cook for 5–10 minutes.

4 Pour in the Calvados, if using, and boil until reduced by three-quarters. Add the stock and gravy (or consommé) and bring to a simmer. Leave to simmer, skimming from time to time, until reduced to about 400ml, then reserve. (If using consommé, the gravy will need to be thickened with cornflour before serving.)

5 Next make the apple tarts. Place the sliced onions in a large saucepan or frying pan with 1 tbsp of water and cook slowly on a moderate heat until softened and the natural sugars begin to caramelise the onions. To help speed up the caramelisation, you can add 1 tsp of Demerara sugar to the onions. Once at a golden caramelised stage, remove from the heat and season with salt and pepper. Allow to cool, then stir in the chopped sage.

6 Butter four 9cm non-stick moulds and dust them with Demerara sugar. Place an apple half, flat side down, in each mould. Spoon the caramelised onion on top of the apple. Cover with the puff pastry discs, ensuring they are firmly pressed in and neatly edged. Pierce the pastry with a skewer to release steam during baking. Set aside until ready to cook.

7 For the cauliflower cream, place the cauliflower florets in a saucepan with just enough milk to cover. Bring to a simmer and cook for 15–20 minutes or until the cauliflower is completely tender. Spoon the florets with just a trickle of milk into a liquidiser and blitz until smooth. Add the butter and season with salt, white pepper and lemon juice. Quickly blitz again until completely emulsified and smooth. If the cauliflower creeam is slightly grainy, simply push it through a fine sieve. Set aside in a saucepan, and reheat for serving.

8 Once the pork is cooked, remove it from the oven. Lift the joint on to a board and leave to rest in a warm place. Turn the oven up to 180°C/gas 4 and bake the apple tarts for 15–20 minutes or until the pastry is golden brown. When baked, allow to rest for about 30 seconds before removing from the moulds.

9 While baking the tarts, prepare the smoky leeks. Warm a large frying pan or wok, then add the streaky bacon and fry over a moderate heat until just beginning to colour, leaving the pieces tender. Add the leeks and butter, and season with a twist of pepper. Stir the leeks for several minutes until softened. Remove from the heat and set aside. Reheat for serving.

10 Pour away any fat from the roasting tray and place it over a moderate heat. Add the gravy. This will now collect any residue, adding a natural pork edge. Simmer for several minutes, stirring well, then pass through a fine sieve. Keep hot.

11 To serve, cut the rind from the joint, cutting or breaking it into crisp bites. Carve the pork into slices or four large pieces. Arrange the pork, apple tarts and smoky leeks on the warm plates, and offer the cauliflower cream and gravy separately.

CASSEROLE OF
NORFOLK SAUSAGES
WITH MASH

SERVES 4

12 Norfolk sausages or other meaty
   pork sausages
2 English onions, thinly sliced
55ml olive oil
175g smoked streaky bacon, finely chopped
24 button mushrooms
1 small glass of red wine
600ml good beef stock
2 baking apples, peeled and diced
   (I use local Bramley's for this)
salt and pepper

MASH

3 decent sized baking potatoes,
   such as Norfolk Pinks or Maris Piper
75g salted butter
2 garlic cloves, crushed
150ml milk
6 tbsp whipping cream
sprig of rosemary
sprig of thyme
a good grating of nutmeg

1 Preheat the oven to 180°C/gas 4.

2 First, for the mash, put the potatoes into the oven to bake for 1–1½ hours, depending on the size of the potatoes.

3 Heat a deep-sided roasting tray on top of the cooker and colour the sausages all over. Remove and set aside, then fry the onions in the olive oil until they just start to caramelise. Add the bacon and mushrooms and continue frying for a couple of minutes. Next add the red wine and, over a high heat, reduce by half. Put the sausages back into the roasting tray and cover with the stock. Bring back to the boil, then place in the oven and cook for 30 minutes (if the sausages are cooking too quickly, cover with foil). Add the diced apple and cook for a further 10 minutes. You should now have a stew consistency with plenty of sauce.

4 While the sausages are in the oven, finish the mashed potato. Combine the butter, garlic, milk, cream and herbs in a saucepan and bring to the boil. Once boiling remove from the heat and leave for 20 minutes for the flavours to develop.

5 Take the baked potatoes from the oven and scoop out the flesh. Pass through a sieve or potato ricer set over a saucepan. Strain the milk and cream mixture, then gradually add to the potato, beating really well with a wooden spoon. Do not pour in the liquid in one swoop, as different varieties of potato vary in how much they will absorb; you want the potato to hold its shape on the plate rather than spread. Taste and season, then add the nutmeg.

6 To serve, spoon the mashed potato on to the centre of the warm plates, top with the sausages and spoon over the sauce, ensuring that each serving has plenty of bacon, apple and mushrooms.

LOIN OF PORK
WALNUT CRUST AND APPLE JUICE REDUCTION

SERVES 4

240g walnut bread
60g walnut halves
1 garlic clove, crushed
20ml walnut oil
4 small potatoes, peeled
250ml chicken stock
1 garlic clove, crushed
sprig of thyme
1 bay leaf
melted butter
75cl bottle Heron Valley apple juice
4 noisettes of pork cut from the boned loin, each 100g, excess fat trimmed
vegetable oil
sprigs of watercress to garnish
salt and pepper

BONED, SPICED AND BRAISED PORK BELLY

1.5kg pork belly, boned and skinned
20g crushed mixed spices (coriander seeds, cinnamon stick, cloves, juniper and allspice berries)
100g unsalted butter
50ml olive oil

1 large carrot, chopped
1 large onion, chopped
2 celery sticks, chopped
1 apple, cored and chopped
2 garlic cloves, crushed
2 sprigs of thyme
1 bay leaf
2 litres chicken stock

APPLE PURÉE

1 Granny Smith apple, peeled, cored and chopped
1 tsp apple juice
sprig of tarragon, blanched and chopped
sugar to taste

CHOUCROUTE OF SAVOY CABBAGE

450g Savoy cabbage, outer leaves and core removed, the rest shredded
4 shallots, diced
1 garlic clove, crushed
1 tsp white wine vinegar
120ml sweet white wine
60g unsalted butter
120g smoked bacon, diced and blanched
60g parsley, chopped

1 Preheat the oven to 180°C/gas 4.

2 First prepare the pork belly. Season the inside of the pork with salt and pepper and sprinkle evenly with the spices. Roll the pork into a sausage and secure tightly with string. Melt the butter with the oil in a deep roasting tray until just smoking. Add the pork belly and colour golden brown on all sides. Remove the belly and reserve.

3 Add the vegetables to the tray and cook until golden brown. Add the apple, garlic and herbs. Put the belly back into the tray and pour in the stock. Cover with foil and transfer to the oven to cook for 1 hour.

4 Remove the foil and continue to cook for 1–1¹/₂ hours, turning and basting regularly, until the pork is soft to the touch. Remove from the oven and leave to cool for at least 1 hour. Then lift the belly from the liquid and reserve. Pass the liquid through a fine sieve into a saucepan and reduce by one-third. Check seasoning. Set the belly and sauce aside. Before serving, slice the belly into four equal portions (remember to remove the string).

5 Blitz the walnut bread in a food processor until fine crumbs are obtained. Add the walnut halves, garlic, walnut oil, and some salt and pepper. Whiz again to make fine moist crumbs. Reserve.

6 To make the apple purée, cook the apple gently with the apple juice until tender. Crush with a fork to a coarse purée. Add the tarragon and sugar to taste. Set aside.

7 Put the potatoes in a small, shallow baking pan, half cover with the stock and add the garlic, thyme and bay leaf. Brush the tops with a little butter. Bring to the boil, then transfer to the oven and cook until the potatoes are golden and tender.

8 Meanwhile, reduce the bottle of apple juice by half by boiling rapidly, and make the choucroute. Add the cabbage to a saucepan of boiling salted water and cover with a lid. When the water starts to boil again, remove from the heat and drain in a colander. Refresh under cold running water, then drain on a kitchen cloth. Set aside.

9 Combine the shallots, garlic and vinegar in a shallow sauté pan and reduce down on a high heat until syrupy. Add the wine and reduce by two-thirds. Add the butter and, when it has melted and blended in, add the bacon. Fry the mixture until velvety and syrupy. Now add the cabbage and carry on cooking for a further 2 minutes, stirring constantly. Sprinkle with the chopped parsley and keep hot.

10 While the choucroute is being cooked, place the pork belly in a roasting tray, cover with the reduced sauce and gently heat through in the oven for 5–10 minutes. Keep basting to give a beautiful glossy and sticky texture.

11 Season the pork noisettes, then sear on both sides in a little vegetable oil in a hot pan that can be put into the oven. Sprinkle the pork with the walnut crust and cook in the oven for 5 minutes.

12 To serve, on each plate place a spoonful of choucroute and next to it a piece of pork belly. Spoon a little apple purée on the belly. Place a potato between the cabbage and belly. Carefully position the pork on the cabbage. Garnish with a sprig of watercress and serve with a jug of hot apple juice.

A nice addition is a beetroot-cider vinegar reduction: simmer 2 large grated raw beetroots with 500ml cider vinegar, 500ml water and 160g sugar for 20 minutes. Pass through a fine sieve, then reduce until syrupy. Spoon this randomly around each plate before serving.

262

A PLATE OF SCOTTISH PORK

SERVES 6-8

PORK BELLY
1 large onion, sliced
250g salt
200g golden caster sugar
8 juniper berries
1 bay leaf
1 tbsp black peppercorns
4 cloves
1 small piece of nutmeg
4 sprigs of thyme
1 Lombok chilli, slit lengthways in half
1 piece of pork belly on the bone,
   about 1.5kg, skin on
1 onion, chopped
4 celery sticks, chopped
2 carrots, chopped
2.5 litres chicken stock

GLAZE FOR BELLY
4 tbsp dark muscovado sugar
good pinch of ground cloves
1 tsp picked thyme leaves

PORK LOIN
1 tbsp olive oil
1 boned pork loin, about 650g, trimmed
salt and pepper
1 banana shallot, diced
½ fennel bulb, diced
2 celery sticks, diced
1 medium carrot, diced
250ml dry cider
200ml chicken stock
½ Granny Smith apple, peeled and diced

1 To prepare the pork belly, take a pan that's big enough to hold the pork and put in 2 litres of water, the sliced onion, salt and sugar. Bring to the boil and stir until the salt and sugar have dissolved. Take off the heat and add all the spices (except the chilli) and thyme, then allow to cool. When completely cold, add the chilli.
2 Immerse the pork belly in the spiced brine, making sure that it is completely submerged. Cover and keep in the fridge for 10 hours. Then remove the pork and place on a wire rack to drip dry.
3 Preheat the oven to 180°C/gas 4. Set the pork in a flameproof casserole. Place over a medium heat and add the chopped onion, celery, carrots and chicken stock. Bring to the boil, then transfer to the oven. Braise for 2 hours.
4 Take the casserole out of the oven, remove the pork and allow to cool slightly. Turn the oven up to 200°C/gas 6.
5 Combine all the ingredients for the glaze. Remove the skin from the pork and score the remaining fat in a criss-cross pattern. Press on the glaze. Place the pork glazed-side up in a roasting tin and add about 200ml of the stock from the casserole. Put the tin in the oven and roast for about 20 minutes, basting frequently, until the glaze is dark and sticky. When the belly has finished cooking, remove from the oven and keep warm. Lower the oven to 180°C/gas 4.

6 While the belly is cooking, prepare the loin (if you have a double oven, you can cook it while the belly cooks). Take an ovenproof pan that's big enough to hold the pork loin and set over a high heat. Add the olive oil. Season the pork loin and place it in the pan. Fry until golden brown on all sides. Remove from the pan and keep in a warm place.

7 Turn the heat down and allow the pan to cool slightly, then add the diced vegetables. Sweat in the juices left by the pork, but do not allow to colour. Add the cider and pull all the vegetables into the centre of the pan. Place the pork on top of the vegetables (so that it doesn't stew). Cover the pan with a lid and transfer to the oven. Cook for 30–35 minutes or until the pork reaches a core temperature of 52°C. Take the pan out of the oven, remove the pork and allow to rest somewhere warm for about 10 minutes.

8 Meanwhile, place the pan with the vegetables on the heat and add the stock. Reduce by about half until an intense flavour is achieved, then strain the liquid into a clean pan, pressing down on the vegetables in the sieve with the back of a spoon. Add the apple to the liquid and cook for about 1 minute.

9 To serve, slice the pork loin and divide among the warmed plates. Slice the belly pork into large chunks and add to the plates. Drizzle round the apple 'sauce'. Accompany with mashed potatoes.

JEREMY LEE

GROUSE AND ACCOMPANIMENTS

SERVES 4
4 grouse (ask the butcher to remove the intestines but leave the liver and heart)
75–90g unsalted butter
4 discs of white bread, about 4cm in diameter and 6mm thick
Madeira (optional)
salt and pepper

BREAD SAUCE
200ml full-fat milk
½ small onion, sliced
1 bay leaf
2 cloves
3 white peppercorns
5–6 scrapes of nutmeg
60g fresh, soft white breadcrumbs

FRIED BREADCRUMBS
40g unsalted butter
125g coarse breadcrumbs

GAME CHIPS
2–3 large potatoes (a good frying variety such as King Edward or Maris Piper), peeled
groundnut oil for deep-frying

TO SERVE
watercress
redcurrant jelly

1 To make the bread sauce, tip the milk into a saucepan and add the onion, bay leaf, cloves, white peppercorns and nutmeg. Heat the milk to just below boiling point. Remove from the heat, cover with a lid and let it sit quietly – the longer the better. Half an hour or so before serving, warm the infused milk, then strain it over the breadcrumbs. Stir gently, then cover and let sit for 10 minutes. Check the sauce for seasoning and consistency, adding a splash of milk if too thick or a few more breadcrumbs if too thin. Set aside.

2 Preheat the oven to 240°C/gas 7.

3 Liberally cover the grouse with butter and lightly salt them evenly all over. Heat a roasting tin in the oven, then add the birds and roast for 15 minutes. Remove from the oven and leave to rest for at least 15 minutes.

4 While the grouse roast rests, prepare the rest of the accompaniments. For the fried breadcrumbs, melt the butter in a frying pan over a gentle heat. Add the breadcrumbs and fry gently until they are a golden brown colour and crisp. Season with salt and pepper, then tip into a dish. Keep warm.

5 To make the game chips, slice the potatoes very thinly and rinse thoroughly until all trace of starch has vanished. Drain well, then dry the slices in a cloth. Heat the oil in a deep-fat fryer. Tip in a handful of the slices and fry until golden brown, stirring now and again to ensure they do not clump together. Remove and drain on kitchen paper. Add a little salt. Keep frying the game chips, then keep warm.

6 When the accompaniments are ready, remove the birds from the roasting tin and set aside. Set the tin over a gentle heat, add a little knob of butter and drop in the discs of bread. Fry gently, pushing the discs around the tin to pick up all residual grouse juices, until golden brown and crisp.

7 Remove the livers and hearts from inside the cooked birds and break them with a fork into a coarse paste. Season with a little salt and pepper. If a bottle of Madeira is handy, a spoonful would be very welcome. Spread this paste over the toasts and sit the birds on top.

8 Warm the bread sauce. Place the grouse, on their toasts, on individual warmed plates or all together on a big serving dish. Pile a big clump of watercress alongside the birds. Heap the game chips, fried breadcrumbs, redcurrant jelly and bread sauce in pretty bowls, and serve swiftly.

266

REGGIE JOHNSON'S CHICKEN
WITH SUMMER LEEKS AND MORELS

SERVES 4

1 organic chicken, about 1.5kg
olive oil
4 shallots, chopped
2 garlic cloves, chopped
100g small button mushrooms
sprig of thyme
1 bay leaf
splash of Pedro Eminent sherry
handful of tarragon
2 bunches of young English leeks,
    about 250g total weight
200g fresh morels
200g crème fraîche

100ml double cream
chervil to garnish

CHICKEN STOCK

olive oil
2 carrots, diced
3 celery sticks, diced
2 leeks, diced
2 onions, diced
knob of unsalted butter
1 bay leaf
sprig of thyme
1 tsp coriander seeds
1 tsp fennel seeds
50g dried morels, rehydrated in water

1 Joint the chicken and set aside the legs, thighs and breasts. Use the remainder of the chicken carcass to make the stock.

2 Roast off the chicken carcass and trimmings in a little oil in a hot pan until golden. Meanwhile, sweat the carrots, celery, leeks and onions in the butter in a saucepan until soft and coloured. Add the bay leaf, thyme and coriander and fennel seeds. Add the chicken carcass and pour in enough water to cover. Bring to the boil, then reduce the heat and simmer for 1 hour.

3 Strain the stock into a clean pan. Add the dried morels and continue to simmer gently until required.

4 Heat 2 tbsp oil in a large pan and fry the chicken pieces until coloured on all sides. Remove and set aside. Add half the shallots, the garlic and button mushrooms to the pan and cook for a few minutes to soften. Stir in the thyme and bay leaf, then add the sherry. Pour in 300ml of the chicken and morel stock and add half the tarragon leaves. Bring to the boil. Return the chicken pieces to the pan and cook for a further 10 minutes or until the chicken is tender.

5 Meanwhile, blanch the leeks in boiling water for 2 minutes. Drain.

6 Heat 1 tbsp oil in a pan and sauté the fresh morels with the remaining shallots for 2–3 minutes, to soften. Stir in the crème fraîche and cream and heat gently for a further few minutes.

7 Add the leeks and morels in cream to the chicken. Season with salt and pepper and add the remaining tarragon leaves. Warm through.

8 To serve, transfer the chicken, leeks and morels to four warm serving bowls and garnish with chervil. Serve with a glass of Pedro Eminent.

TANDOORI CHICKEN
WITH BLACK LENTIL SAUCE AND HERB PULAO
MANGO-APPLE-ROCKET SALAD AND PESHAWARI NAAN

SERVES 4
4 chicken breasts on the bone, skin removed
mixture of melted butter and oil for basting
1½ tsp lime juice
1 tsp chaat masala
salt
4 Peshawari naan to serve

FIRST MARINADE
1 tbsp ginger-garlic paste
1 tsp red chilli powder
2 tbsp lemon juice

SECOND MARINADE
250g thick plain yoghurt
1 tsp garam masala
100ml vegetable oil
½ tsp ground cinnamon
½ tsp red chilli powder
a pinch of edible red colouring (optional)

BLACK LENTIL SAUCE
200g black lentils
4 tbsp vegetable oil
1 tbsp finely chopped fresh ginger
2 garlic cloves, peeled
2 green chillies
1 tsp cumin seeds
1 tbsp ginger-garlic paste

½ green chilli, chopped
2 tbsp tomato paste
½ tsp each red chilli powder, ground
    coriander, ground turmeric, garam
    masala and fenugreek leaf powder
30g butter
2 tbsp single cream
1 tbsp chopped coriander leaves

HERB PULAO
15g butter
2 tsp vegetable oil
100g sliced onions
2.5cm cinnamon stick
2 black cardamoms
1 blade mace
500g Basmati rice, washed and soaked
    for 10–20 minutes
3–4 tbsp puréed spinach, coriander
    and mint
2 tbsp mascarpone cheese or cream

MANGO-APPLE-ROCKET SALAD
20g baby rocket leaves
1 Granny Smith apple, cut into julienne
1 green mango, cut into julienne
vinaigrette made with lime juice

1 Make three or four deep incisions in each chicken breast, without cutting all the way through. Mix together the ingredients for the first marinade with 1 tsp salt. Rub all over the breasts, then leave in the fridge for 20 minutes so the juices can drain.
2 Mix the ingredients for the second marinade with 1 tsp salt. Add the chicken and turn to coat, then leave in a cool place for 2–3 hours.
3 Meanwhile, make the black lentil sauce. Put the lentils, 2 tbsp oil, the ginger, garlic and whole chillies in a pan and cover with water. Bring to the boil, then simmer gently until the lentils are soft. Discard the garlic and chillies.
4 Prepare the seasoning by sautéing the cumin seeds, ginger-garlic paste and chopped chilli in the remaining oil until soft. Stir in the tomato paste and spices.

5 Add the cooked lentils to the seasoning and simmer for 10–15 minutes. Add the butter, cream and coriander with salt to taste. Blend with a hand blender to give a sauce consistency. Set aside, and reheat for serving.

6 Preheat a tandoor until moderately hot or preheat the oven to 200°C/gas 6.

7 Next make the pulao. Heat the butter and oil in a saucepan and fry the onions with the cinnamon, cardamom and mace until golden brown. Add the rice and 1 litre of water with 1 tsp salt. Bring to the boil, then cover the pan tightly and cook until the rice is tender and all liquid has been absorbed. Add the spinach purée and cheese or cream just before serving.

8 While the rice is cooking, skewer the chicken breasts and cook in the tandoor for 10 minutes. If using an oven, place the breasts on a non-stick baking tray and cook for 3 minutes; reduce the oven heat to 160°C/gas 3 and cook for a further 15 minutes.

9 Baste the chicken breasts with the butter and oil mixture and cook for a further 5 minutes. Remove from the tandoor or oven, baste the chicken again and sprinkle with the lime juice and chaat masala. Keep hot.

10 Toss all the ingredients for the salad together.

11 To serve, ladle the sauce on to four large round plates and spread out to cover. Place a large quenelle of herb pulao in the centre of each plate, set a tandoori chicken breast on the rice and garnish with the rocket and mango salad. Serve with naan.

TOM LEWIS

ROASTED BREAST OF GROUSE
BALQUHIDDER CHANTERELLES AND SEASONAL VEGETABLES WITH SAGE AND ONION JUS

SERVES 4
8 breasts of grouse or 4 whole young grouse
olive oil
salt and pepper

SAGE AND ONION JUS
2 shallots, chopped
1–2 garlic cloves, chopped
butter
200ml game stock
4–6 sage leaves
1 tbsp white truffle oil (optional)

SEASONAL VEGETABLES
the best vegetables you can source to complement the greatest of all game birds, according to the season, for example baby carrots, fine green beans, runner beans and new potatoes

SAUTÉED CHANTERELLES
200g fresh chanterelles
good knob of butter
1 garlic clove, sliced

1 Preheat the oven to 230°C/gas 8.

2 Whether using just the breasts of older grouse or whole young birds, sear them on both sides, or all over, in a little hot olive oil in a roasting tin. Then place in the oven. Roast breasts for 2–4 minutes and whole birds for 12–16 minutes. Remove from the oven and leave to rest for 10 minutes before serving.

3 While the grouse are cooking, make the jus. Sweat the shallots and garlic in a little butter, then add the stock and reduce by half. Just before serving, season and add the sage. For a bit of decadence, finish with truffle oil.

4 Cook the seasonal vegetables in boiling salted water.

5 At the last minute, sauté the chanterelles in the butter with the sliced garlic and a touch of salt and pepper.

6 To serve, slice each breast at a 45° angle into three pieces, or carve the breasts and legs from the whole grouse. Arrange the grouse neatly on warm plates with the seasonal vegetables and chanterelles and drizzle over the jus.

ATUL KOCHHAR

MURG KI BIRYANI
CHICKEN COOKED WITH RICE

SERVES 4
500g skinned and boned chicken thighs, cut into 2.5cm pieces
5 tbsp vegetable oil
3 dried red chillies
500g Basmati rice, washed and drained
salt

MARINADE
6 medium onions, finely sliced
vegetable oil for deep frying
200g set plain yoghurt, whisked until smooth
1 tbsp ginger-garlic paste
1 tsp ground turmeric

APPLE RAITA
250g plain Greek yoghurt
1 tsp toasted cumin seeds
¼ tsp crushed red chilli
1 tbsp finely chopped mint
pinch of caster sugar
1 Granny Smith apple, cored and finely chopped

RICE SEASONING
5cm piece of cassia bark or cinnamon
6 green cardamoms
1 tsp cumin seeds
4 cloves
10 black peppercorns

TO ASSEMBLE
45g melted butter
2 tsp garam masala
1 tbsp finely chopped mint leaves
1 tbsp finely chopped coriander leaves
pinch of saffron strands, soaked in 100ml tepid milk
2 tbsp mixed whole almonds, cashew nuts and raisins, deep fried to a light brown colour
4 puff pastry discs, each 10cm diameter
milk to glaze
1 tbsp mixed sesame seeds and onion seeds

1 First make the marinade. Deep fry the onions until crisp and brown; drain on kitchen paper. Save 3–4 tbsp of the onions for the garnish; purée the remainder with the yoghurt in a blender or food processor to make a fine paste. Mix this paste with the ginger-garlic paste, turmeric and $1^1/_2$ tsp salt. Mix the chicken into the marinade, then set aside in a cool place for 2 hours.

2 Meanwhile, make the apple raita. Whisk the yoghurt with the spices, mint and sugar. Stir in the apple. Keep in the fridge until required.

3 Heat 2 tbsp oil in a heavy-bottomed pan and sauté the whole dried red chillies for 1 minute. Add the marinated chicken and cook on a low heat for 10 minutes or until almost cooked. Remove from the heat and keep hot.

4 While the chicken is cooking, heat the remaining 3 tbsp oil in a saucepan and add the rice seasoning ingredients. Sauté for a few minutes until the spices splutter. Add the rice and sauté for 2 minutes, then add 1.5 litres of water. Bring to the boil. Boil the rice for 12–15 minutes or until almost cooked. Drain the rice, then spread out on a tray in a 2.5cm thick layer to cool a bit. Pick out the cassia, cardamom, cloves and peppercorns and discard.

5 Preheat the oven to 180°C/gas 4.

6 Brush four individual biryani pots or ovenproof soup bowls with melted butter. Add the chicken in a single layer. Cover with half of the rice and sprinkle with garam masala, herbs and butter. Spoon the remaining rice evenly on this and sprinkle with the rest of the garam masala and butter and the saffron milk. Scatter over the fried nuts and raisins and the reserved crisp fried onions.

7 Cover the pots or bowls with the puff pastry discs and seal the edges. Glaze with milk. Sprinkle the pastry with the sesame and onion seeds. Bake for 8–12 minutes or until the pastry is golden brown.

8 Serve each pot, sitting on a napkin on a plate, with the apple raita.

CHICKEN BREAST
WITH ST ENODOC ASPARAGUS, BROAD BEANS WILD MUSHROOMS AND A SOMERSET CIDER BRANDY CREAM SAUCE

SERVES 4

4 free range 'Ark' chicken breasts, each 200g
12 asparagus tips
100g shelled broad beans
unsalted butter
200g mixed wild mushrooms
200g baby spinach leaves
salt and pepper

SOMERSET CIDER BRANDY SAUCE

25g shallots, sliced
2 garlic cloves, peeled
200g unsalted butter
5 sprigs of thyme
1 bay leaf
50ml Somerset cider brandy
500ml home-made chicken stock
50ml double cream

1 First make the sauce. Sweat the shallots and garlic in 20g of the butter, without colouring. Add the thyme and bay leaf and sweat for a further 2 minutes, then add the brandy and reduce down to nothing. Add the chicken stock and reduce by half, then add the cream. Whisk in the remaining butter in small pieces. Season the sauce with salt and pepper and set aside.

2 Season the chicken breasts, then wrap them individually in cling film to keep the shape tight. Heat a saucepan of water to 90°C and poach the chicken breasts for 12–15 minutes or until cooked. Remove and leave to rest for 10 minutes.

3 While the chicken is poaching, cook the asparagus and broad beans separately in boiling salted water until tender; drain and refresh in iced water. Cut the asparagus tips to the same length and peel the broad beans to remove their tough skins.

4 Unwrap the chicken breasts. Heat a knob of butter in a frying pan, add the chicken and slowly colour the skin until golden and crisp.

5 Meanwhile, pan-fry the mushrooms in a little butter with salt and pepper. Add the mushrooms to the sauce together with the asparagus and broad beans and reheat. Quickly pan-fry the spinach with a little butter, salt and pepper, then drain on a tray lined with kitchen paper.

6 To serve, slice each chicken breast into five rounds and arrange around the warm plates. Place the spinach in the middle. Add three asparagus tips to each plate, then spoon around the mushrooms and broad beans with some sauce.

ROAST DUCK
WITH CRISPY DUCK HASH AND BEER GRAVY
SPRING GREENS AND ORANGE CURD CARROTS

SERVES 4
4 ducks
goose fat (optional)
salt and pepper

BEER GRAVY
groundnut oil
2 large onions, sliced
1 tbsp brown sugar (preferably Muscovado)
250ml beer (preferably Shepherd Neame 'Spitfire')
300ml chicken stock
200ml veal or beef gravy/glace or canned beef consommé

CRISPY DUCK HASH
50g shallots, finely chopped
olive oil
3 large baking potatoes, baked until cooked
2 knobs of butter

ORANGE CURD CARROTS
675g carrots, thickly sliced or cut into barrel shapes
2 tbsp orange curd
knob of butter

SPRING GREENS
450g spring greens, stalks removed and leaves torn into pieces
large knob of butter

1 Preheat the oven to 150°C/gas 2. Remove the legs from the ducks and place in a roasting tin. Slow roast for 1–1^{1}/$_{2}$ hours or until completely tender. (Alternatively, for a richer flavour, submerge the duck legs in goose fat before roasting them for 1^{1}/$_{2}$–2 hours.) Remove the meat from the leg bones, discarding any skin and fat, and keep to one side for the hash.

2 Chop away the central leg carcass from each bird, leaving the two breasts attached to the breast bone. Reserve the breasts.

3 To make the beer gravy, trim all fat from the carcasses, then chop them and roast in some groundnut oil in a saucepan until well coloured. Add the sliced onions and continue to fry over a moderate heat to a rich golden brown. Stir in the sugar, then pour the beer on top. Bring to the boil and reduce by three-quarters before adding the chicken stock. Continue to boil until reduced by half.

4 Add the veal or beef gravy (if using consommé, you will need to thicken the sauce with cornflour once it is completed). Bring back to a simmer, then cook for a further 30 minutes, skimming off any excess fat. Strain. Should the gravy be too thin, simply boil to a sauce consistency, but take care not to allow the flavour to become too strong. Set aside. (The gravy can be made well in advance and refrigerated until needed.) Reheat for serving.

5 To cook the duck breasts, preheat the oven to 200°C/gas 6. Gently begin to fry the duck breasts, skin side down, on top of the stove. As they fry the fat will melt away, leaving a thinner and crisper finish. Continue to fry for 10–15 minutes or until all the breasts are a rich, golden brown colour. Turn skin side up and place in the oven to finish cooking for 6–10 minutes, depending on the size of the breasts. Once roasted, allow to rest in a warm place.

6 While the breasts are cooking, make the duck hash. Sweat the chopped shallots in a little olive oil until tender. Scoop the potato flesh from the skins and mix it with the cooked shallots and duck leg meat. Season with salt and pepper.

7 Divide the duck hash into four portions and press into buttered rectangular or round moulds to shape; or simply shape into cakes with your hands. Melt the butter in an ovenproof pan and pan fry the hash until golden brown on the base. Turn over and transfer the pan to the oven. Roast for 8–10 minutes or until warmed through and with a crispy edge.

8 Meanwhile, prepare the orange curd carrots. Cook the carrots in boiling salted water until tender. Drain off most of the water, leaving a few tbsp in the pan. Set aside. Just before serving, add the orange curd and butter and heat, stirring gently, until they are completely melted and each slice of carrot is glazed. Season to taste with salt and pepper.

9 While the carrots are cooking, plunge the spring greens into a large pan of boiling water and cook for a few minutes until tender. Drain well. Place the butter in the pan in which you cooked the greens. Once the butter has melted, stir in the spring greens and season with salt and pepper.

10 To serve, remove the duck breasts from the bone and cut each into three or four slices. Place the duck hash towards the top of each warm plate, with the carrots and spring greens on either side beneath. Arrange the duck breasts on top of the greens and offer the gravy separately.

DUCK TOURTE
WITH BRAISED ROOT VEGETABLES AND MUSHROOM SAUCE

SERVES 4

2 sheets of puff pastry 4mm thick
500ml duck fat
4 duck legs
4 garlic cloves, peeled
1 bay leaf
large sprig of thyme
6 black peppercorns
pinch of rock salt
4 tbsp chopped parsley
2 egg yolks, beaten
1 egg, beaten

MUSHROOM SAUCE

500ml white wine
20g dried wild mushrooms
2 shallots, sliced
1 garlic clove, peeled
sprig of thyme
4 white peppercorns
pinch of rock salt
500ml chicken stock
400ml double cream
1 tsp lemon juice

BRAISED ROOT VEGETABLES

1 large swede
1 small celeriac
2 large carrots
100g unsalted butter
500ml chicken stock

1 First make the tourte. Cut each pastry sheet into a 20cm disc, place on trays and refrigerate while you prepare the filling. Put the duck fat and legs, garlic, bay leaf, thyme, peppercorns and salt into a deep heavy-bottomed pan and cook over a very low heat, or in the oven at 130°C/gas ¹/₂, for 3–4 hours or until the meat is falling off the bone. It is important not to cook the duck legs too fast or too hot, otherwise the meat will dry out.

2 Take the meat off the bones, discarding any fat, skin, sinew and small bones. Put it in a bowl and mix with the parsley and a few spoonfuls of the duck fat used for cooking. Check the seasoning. Form the meat mixture into a disc 15cm in diameter and 4cm high on a tray and put into the fridge to set.

3 Place the duck filling in the centre of one of the pastry discs. Brush the exposed pastry around the filling with the beaten egg yolks, right up to the duck, then carefully cover with the other pastry disc. Smooth down over the filling and press the pastry edges all around to seal well. Neaten up the edges with a sharp knife. Refrigerate for 30–45 minutes.

4 Next make the sauce. Put the white wine, mushrooms, shallots, garlic, thyme, peppercorns and salt into a pan and reduce by two-thirds. In another pan, reduce the stock by two-thirds. Add the stock to the wine mixture together with the cream and bring to a simmer. Pass through a sieve, then add the lemon juice and stir well. Set aside. Reheat for serving.

5 Preheat the oven to 180°C/gas 4.

6 Using the point of a small, sharp knife mark curved lines from the top centre of the pastry out to the edges. Make sure you only cut the pastry and not all the way through. Brush the surface of the tourte evenly with beaten whole egg. Allow to dry, then brush again. Place on a baking tray and bake for about 30 minutes or until well risen and a deep golden brown.

7 Meanwhile, to prepare the root vegetables, cut all of them into a 2cm dice. Divide the butter among three pans and heat until foaming. Add the diced vegetables to the pans, keeping them separate. Season, then cook until well coloured, stirring regularly. Add the chicken stock, equally divided, and cook until tender. Take care not to overcook or the vegetables will lose their shape. Remove the vegetables and reserve. Reduce any liquid to form a shiny emulsion. Before serving, reheat the vegetables in this emulsion.

8 This is a centre of the table dish. To serve, simply put the vegetables into a bowl and the sauce into a jug and cut the tourte into four. Then let everyone dive in.

ROASTED DUCK BREAST
WITH RED CABBAGE AND
HOME-MADE MUSTARD FRUITS

SERVES 4
2–4 duck breasts, depending on size
butter
rock salt and pepper

MUSTARD FRUITS
2kg small, firm pears such as William's
 or whatever is in season
400g sugar
mustard essence

DUCK SAUCE
500g duck bones, chopped
1 shallot, sliced
1 garlic clove, peeled
olive oil
sprigs of thyme
1 bay leaf
black peppercorns
50ml Madeira
150ml veal stock
150ml brown chicken stock

SPICE BAG
½ cinnamon stick, broken
3 juniper berries
3 cloves
2 star anise

BRAISED RED CABBAGE
1 red cabbage, finely shredded
100g brown sugar
250ml Port
500ml red wine
duck fat
1 onion, sliced
2 apples, peeled, quartered and
 sliced crossways
sprig of thyme
1 bay leaf
4 tbsp redcurrant jelly

LAYERED POTATOES
2 large Desiree potatoes
olive oil

1 First make the mustard fruits. Peel the pears and cut in half lengthways. Leave the stalks and seeds. Place the pears in a container, add the sugar and stir to mix. Cover and let sit at room temperature for 12 hours.

2 The pears will have begun to release their juices. Drain the juice into a pan and bring to the boil. Simmer for 5 minutes.

3 Cover the pears with this syrup and leave for another 12 hours.

4 Once again, drain the syrup from the pears, bring it to the boil and simmer for 5 minutes. Pour back over the pears and leave for 12 hours.

5 Repeat this procedure two more times, then drain the syrup into a pan, bring to the boil and reduce to one-third. Add the pears to the syrup and caramelise for 20 minutes. Allow to cool.

6 Add 10 drops of mustard essence to the pears, then seal in glass jars and leave to mature for 2–3 weeks before using.

7 Next make the duck sauce. Preheat the oven to 180°C/gas 4, then roast the duck bones until well browned. Meanwhile, sauté the shallot and garlic in a little olive oil until golden brown. Add the herbs and peppercorns, and pour in the Madeira.

Bring to the boil and reduce to a glaze. Drain all the fat from the duck bones, then add them to the pan. Add the stocks and bring to the boil. Simmer, skimming regularly, until reduced to about 100ml. Pass through a muslin cloth and allow to cool. Keep in the fridge until needed; reheat before using.

8 For the red cabbage, first prepare the spice bag. Lightly toast the whole spices in a dry pan until fragrant. Allow to cool, then wrap in a piece of muslin. Put the red cabbage in a container with the sugar, Port, wine and spice bag, cover with cling film and place a heavy weight on top. Leave to marinate in a cool place for 24 hours.

9 Drain the cabbage in a sieve set over a bowl; reserve the liquid. Heat some duck fat and sweat the onion and apples with the thyme and bay leaf until soft. Add the cabbage and sweat down until tender. Add the reserved liquid and continue to cook until it evaporates to a glaze. Check the seasoning, then finish with the redcurrant jelly. Keep to one side, and reheat for serving.

10 Preheat the oven to 200°C/gas 6.

11 While the cabbage is cooking, prepare the potatoes. Peel them, then slice very thinly (1–2mm), preferably on a mandolin. Divide into four portions and 'tile' each portion evenly (lay the slices on top of each other, almost completely overlapping, so you end up with them resembling a deck of cards displayed in a cascade). Trim the edges of each cascade to make a neat rectangle roughly 15cm long, 7cm wide and 2cm thick. Season with salt and pepper on both sides.

12 Heat a little olive oil in a frying pan that can be put into the oven. Add the potatoes and colour a golden brown on both sides. At this point the potatoes will not be cooked through. Just before serving, add the hot duck sauce, cover with a buttered paper and finish cooking in the oven for 5 minutes or until the potatoes are tender.

13 Meanwhile, score the skin and fat on the duck breasts without cutting through into the meat. Heat a frying pan over a low heat and add the duck breasts, skin side down. Allow the fat to render down. Pour away the excess fat, then add the butter to the pan and cook for a further 3–4 minutes or until the duck is medium rare.

14 Remove the duck breasts from the pan and allow to rest for 4–5 minutes. Then place the duck breasts in the oven to finish cooking for 5 minutes.

15 To serve, spoon the cabbage on to the warm plates, place the potato and sliced duck on top and finish with some mustard fruits.

280

ROAST NORFOLK DUCKLING
WITH ORANGE SERVED
WITH BUBBLE AND SQUEAK

SERVES 4
1 duckling, about 1.8kg, with giblets
vegetable oil
1 carrot, chopped
1 celery stick, chopped
3 garlic cloves, chopped
2 sprigs of sage
1 tsp soft brown sugar
1 tbsp red wine vinegar
1 large glass of red wine
2 tbsp runny marmalade
a little butter
1 orange, peeled and segmented
salt and pepper

BUBBLE AND SQUEAK
3 large baking potatoes
450g peeled swede, cubed
350g peeled parsnips, chopped
1 Savoy cabbage, leaves separated,
    halved and centre stalk removed
225g salted butter
3 medium-sized English onions,
    thinly sliced
1 garlic clove, chopped

1 Begin by making a good stock. Take the wings from the duck, and chop the giblets, heart and any other bits, except the liver (keep this to use later). Heat a splash of oil in a decent-sized saucepan and gently fry the carrot, celery and garlic with the sage until softened. Add the giblets, wings and other bits from the duck and lightly brown these. Now add the sugar and red wine vinegar and deglaze the pan, then add the red wine and reduce a little. Cover with 600ml of water and bring to the boil, then simmer gently for about 1 hour.

2 While the stock is simmering, prepare the vegetables for the bubble and squeak. Preheat the oven to 200°C/gas 6 and bake the potatoes for 45 minutes to 1 hour. Meanwhile, bring the swede to the boil in salted water, then cover and cook until very tender; drain. Do the same with the parsnips. For the cabbage, blanch the leaves in a pan of boiling water for about 5 minutes, then drain and refresh under cold running water. Squeeze the cabbage to remove any liquid.

3 Heat a frying pan until hot, then add 50g of the butter and fry the onions until they start to colour. Add the garlic, followed by the blanched cabbage leaves and another 50g butter. Turn the heat down to very low and gently stew the cabbage in the onions until soft. Lightly season, then remove from the heat and set aside, ready to reheat for serving.

4 Scoop the flesh from the baked potatoes and push through a sieve or potato ricer, adding a knob of the butter. Push the swede and parsnips through a sieve or ricer, add the remaining butter to them and season. Combine the potato, swede and parsnip in a saucepan, then set aside.

5 Preheat the oven to 200°C/gas 6.

6 Set the duck on a trivet in a roasting tin and score the skin with a sharp knife, trying not to penetrate through into the meat. Season the skin really well. Place in the hot oven and roast for 45 minutes. Some fat will have run out of the bird and you can baste the duck with this. Then brush over the marmalade. Return to the oven and continue roasting for a further 40 minutes, basting occasionally with the fat and residue in the tin. Remove from the oven and allow to rest for a few minutes, then take the legs off the duck. Return these to the oven to finish cooking for a further 15 minutes, if necessary.

7 While the duck is roasting, strain the stock into another pan and reduce by half over a high heat, skimming off any fatty scum that comes to the surface. Then keep reducing the stock to achieve a gravy with the desired consistency and flavour.

8 To finish the bubble and squeak, gently heat through the potato, swede and parsnip mixture and the cabbage and onion mixture.

9 Fry the liver in a little butter, then quickly chop the liver and add to the gravy.

10 To serve, carefully take the duck breasts off the bone. Slice the breasts and arrange on four warm plates with the meat from the legs. Spoon the potato, swede and parsnip mixture on the plates and top with the cabbage and onions. Finally, add the orange segments to the gravy and spoon over the duck.

A classic case of necessity mothering invention, bubble and squeak – named for the sound it made while cooking – combined leftover boiled beef with potatoes and cabbage. This is a more refined, though no less tasty, version of the ultimate comfort food.

GLAZED BREAST OF DUCK
WITH CRISP SKIN, FENNEL PURÉE AND
BRAISED BABY FENNEL

282

SERVES 6

1 whole duck and 4 duck breasts,
  preferably Goosnargh duck
225ml duck fat
75g unsalted butter
18 baby fennel, trimmed
1 star anise, cracked
salt and white pepper

STOCK

150ml duck fat
1 carrot, cut into 2cm dice
4 celery sticks, cut into 2cm dice
1 onion, quartered
1 head of garlic, cut in half crossways
bunch of thyme
2 bay leaves
good pinch of rock salt
10 white peppercorns
20 coriander seeds
2 tbsp tomato purée
2 litres hot chicken stock

FENNEL PURÉE

75g unsalted butter
1 large fennel bulb, very finely sliced
hot chicken stock
50ml Pernod
100ml double cream
1 tbsp olive oil
1 tsp Dijon mustard

1 Remove the breasts from the whole duck and set aside with the other breasts.
Pull the legs off the carcass and chop them into 3cm pieces (including the bones).
Roughly chop the carcass and wings. Set all the chopped bones aside for the stock.

2 Carefully remove the skin from the duck breasts using a sharp knife, and remove any sinews from the flesh. Set the breasts aside. Lay the skin flat on a tray and freeze until completely solid, then cut into 2cm squares.

3 Melt 150ml duck fat in a pan, add the diced skin and cook over a medium heat, stirring occasionally, for about 20 minutes or until the skin is crisp. Remove the skin with a slotted spoon and drain on kitchen paper.

4 Warm the remaining 75ml duck fat in a bowl until it is the consistency of softened butter. Season with a pinch of salt and a few twists of white pepper. Brush each duck breast well with the duck fat on both sides, then roll into a sausage and wrap tightly in cling film. Twist the ends of the film and tie tightly in a knot, as close to the duck as possible. Keep in the fridge until needed.

5 Preheat the oven to 200°C/gas 6.

6 To make the stock, spread the chopped duck carcass and wings (not the legs) in a large tray and roast for about 20 minutes or until a deep golden brown, turning frequently. Set aside. Heat the 150ml duck fat in a large, heavy saucepan on top of the stove and sear the chopped legs until nicely browned on all sides. Add the carrot, celery, onion, garlic and herbs. Season with the salt, peppercorns and coriander seeds, and cook until the vegetables are deep brown. Add the tomato purée and cook for 5 minutes, stirring regularly, then add the roasted bones followed by the hot chicken stock. Bring to the boil and skim off any froth, then turn the heat down to a gentle simmer. Cook for $1^1/_2$ hours, skimming regularly.

7 Strain the stock through a colander, then strain again through a muslin-lined fine sieve into a clean pan. Bring to the boil and boil rapidly until reduced by about two-thirds. Remove 100ml of this reduced stock and reserve for the sauce, then continue to reduce the rest until you have a nice glaze that coats the back of a spoon. Remove from the heat and keep warm.

8 Next make the fennel purée. Melt the butter in a heavy pan, add the fennel and season with salt. Add the Pernod and reduce until all the liquid has gone. Continue cooking over a medium to high heat for about 10 minutes or until the fennel is very soft, keeping it moist by occasionally stirring in a spoonful or two of hot chicken stock. Add the cream and boil until reduced by two-thirds. Purée in a blender until very smooth. Keep the purée warm.

9 To cook the baby fennel, melt the 75g butter until it starts to foam. Quickly colour the fennel over a medium to high heat, then season with salt and add the star anise. Cook for about 7 minutes, gradually adding the reserved 100ml reduced stock. When the fennel is tender, lift it out and keep both the sauce and the fennel warm.

10 Heat a pan of water to 63°C. Drop in the duck breasts (still in the cling film) and cook for 26 minutes for medium rare, gently turning the duck and pushing it under the water. Use a thermometer to check that the temperature of the water stays constant throughout. If you like your duck more cooked, increase the cooking time by 8 minutes for each extra stage of doneness.

11 To serve, reheat the reserved glaze. Unwrap the duck breasts and slice each into four pieces. Brush the duck with the warm glaze and sprinkle with the crisp skin. Spoon the fennel purée on each plate and lay the slices of duck across it, then make a neat pile of baby fennel on top. Drizzle a little sauce over and around, and serve the rest separately in a jug.

HONEY ROAST CORNISH DUCKLING
WITH CABBAGE AND SMOKED BACON

SERVES 4

4 Gressingham duck breasts, each 180g
vegetable oil for frying
100g clear honey
1 tsp Chinese five spice powder
salt and pepper

DUCK SAUCE

1kg duck carcasses, chopped small
1 tsp Chinese five spice powder
1 large onion, cut into thick rings
1/2 head of garlic, cut in half crossways
15g thyme plus 5 large sprigs
700ml chicken stock
100g clear honey
3 tbsp sherry vinegar
300ml veal glacé
1 tsp white peppercorns
3 tbsp double cream

CABBAGE

350g Savoy cabbage, cut into strips,
  not too fine
1 shallot, chopped
20g unsalted butter
40g smoked back bacon slices, cut into
  fine strips
20g garlic purée

GARNISH

20 celeriac slices, cut into 1.5cm dice,
  blanched and deep-fried
20 garlic cloves, blanched and roasted

1 Preheat the oven to 220°C/gas 7.

2 To make the duck sauce, put the duck carcasses in a roasting tin and roast lightly for 20 minutes. Just before they finish roasting, sprinkle the bones with the Chinese five spice. Remove the tin from the oven and place on top of the stove. Add the onion and garlic, and fry to very lightly colour the onion. Add the 15g thyme. Remove from the heat and leave to cool slightly. Pour the chicken stock into the roasting tin and stir well to deglaze.

3 Heat the honey in a large saucepan and bring to a rolling boil. Cook for 3 minutes over a high heat, but be careful not to burn the honey or the sauce will be bitter. Add the vinegar and reduce to nothing. Add the contents of the roasting tin, together with the veal glacé, peppercorns, remaining sprigs of thyme and the cream. Bring to the boil and skim off the scum. Reduce the heat to a simmer and cook for 30 minutes. Strain through a colander into a bowl, then pass through a fine sieve into a clean saucepan. Simmer to reduce to a sauce consistency, then taste and adjust the seasoning and acidity. Set aside.

4 Before cooking the duck breasts, put them in the freezer for a few minutes to make it easier to score the skins. Then, using a very sharp knife, score the fatty skin in a criss-cross pattern, being careful not to cut into the meat. Season the meat side with salt and pepper. Heat a little vegetable oil a heavy-based frying pan. Place the breasts skin-side down in the hot oil and cook over a fairly high heat so the fat is rendered; be careful not to burn the skin. Once the skin is golden brown and crisp, turn the breasts over and sear the other side for 1 minute. Turn the breasts over again and crisp the skin a little more. Then turn each breast once more and finish cooking to your desired degree.

5 Mix together the honey and five spice. Remove the breasts from the pan, brush the honey over the crisp skin and leave to rest.

6 Meanwhile, cook the cabbage in boiling salted water for a few minutes, then drain and refresh in iced water. Drain again well and pat dry. Soften the shallot in the butter. Add the bacon. Tip in the cooked cabbage and let it dry out briefly in the pan. Add the garlic purée and cook for a minute. Season with salt and pepper to taste.

7 To serve, reheat the sauce. Spoon the cabbage down the centre of each plate. Cut the duck breasts into thin slices and lay them on the cabbage. Arrange the garlic and celeriac all around and drizzle with the sauce. (Any extra sauce can be frozen.)

MARK HIX

RABBIT AND CRAYFISH STARGAZY PIE

SERVES 4

back and front legs from 4 wild rabbits
   (reserve the saddles for another dish,
such as a salad)
3 tbsp plain flour
2–3 tbsp vegetable oil
2 onions, finely chopped
good knob of unsalted butter
1 glass of English white wine or cider
2 litres hot chicken stock
500g good-quality puff pastry
   made with butter
beaten egg
salt and pepper

CRAYFISH

1 tsp fennel seeds
12 black peppercorns
few sprigs of thyme
2 star anise
1 bay leaf
24 live freshwater crayfish
1 litre chicken stock

1 Season the rabbit legs and dust them with 1 tbsp of the flour. Heat the oil in a heavy frying pan until hot, then lightly colour the rabbit legs over a medium heat for 3–4 minutes on each side. Remove and drain on kitchen paper.

2 In a large saucepan, gently cook the onions in the butter for 2–3 minutes without colouring. Dust with the remaining flour and stir well over a low heat for a minute, then gradually add the wine and the hot stock, stirring to prevent lumps from forming. Bring to the boil.

3 Add the rabbit legs and season lightly. Cover with the lid. Simmer gently for about 1 hour or until the rabbit is tender. Remove the rabbit legs and leave to cool. The sauce should be fairly thick – if it's not, continue simmering for a while until it has reduced down by half.

4 To cook the crayfish, bring a large saucepan of water to the boil with the fennel seeds, peppercorns, thyme, star anise, bay leaf, and 1 tbsp salt. Simmer for about 5 minutes. Plunge the crayfish into the liquid, bring the water quickly back to the boil and simmer for 1¹/₂ minutes. Drain and leave to cool.

5 Pick out 4 similar-sized crayfish for the garnish and set aside. Peel the rest, including the large claws, first removing the head and then squeezing the shell between thumb and forefinger to crack it. Set the meat aside. Crush the shells a little, put them in a saucepan with the stock and simmer for 30 minutes. Strain the stock through a sieve into a clean pan. Boil to reduce to 4–5 tbsp. Mix into the rabbit sauce.

6 Once the rabbit legs are cool, remove the meat from the bones. Mix into the sauce with the crayfish meat. Spoon into a large pie dish or four individual dishes.

7 Preheat the oven to 200°C/gas 6.

8 Roll out the pastry on a floured surface until about 3mm thick. Cut out a lid that is about 2cm larger all round than the top of the pie dish. (Or, if you are using individual dishes, cut the pastry into quarters, roll out and cut out four lids.) Brush the edge of the pastry lid with a little beaten egg, then lay it on top of the dish, egg-washed side against the rim. Trim the edge and press down to seal. Cut four small slits in the pastry lid (or a small slit in the centre of each of the individual ones) and insert the whole crayfish, keeping the top half of the body above the pastry lid. Brush the pastry with more beaten egg.

9 Bake the pie for 30–35 minutes or until the pastry is golden (small pies will take about 25 minutes); cover the crayfish with foil if they start to colour too much. Serve with greens or mashed root vegetables such as celeriac or parsnip and/or small boiled potatoes with chopped herbs.

288

SADDLE OF RABBIT IN SAVOY CABBAGE
WITH MILD PISTACHIO KORMA SAUCE

SERVES 4

3 long, boned saddles of rabbit, with livers

about 100g spinach leaves

butter for greasing

1 small Savoy cabbage, leaves lightly
   blanched

salt and pepper

mixed micro leaves, or mustard cress mixed
   with coriander leaves, to garnish

MARINADE

3 tbsp thick, full-fat plain yoghurt

2 tbsp double cream

pinch each of ground mace and ground
   cardamom

½ tsp garam masala powder

½ tsp finely chopped fresh ginger

½ tsp finely chopped, deseeded green chilli

tiny pinch of saffron stands

2 tbsp fried brown onions, blended to
   a paste with little plain yoghurt

PISTACHIO KORMA SAUCE

500g onions, diced

½ tsp each ginger and garlic pastes

5 green cardamom pods

1 small mace blade

1 green chilli, stalk removed

1 small bay leaf

4 black peppercorns

150g plain yoghurt

30g butter

25g toasted cashew nuts

3 tbsp single cream

½ tsp garam masala powder

2 tsp pistachio paste

pinch each of ground mace and
   ground cardamom

TOMATO RICE

4 large tomatoes

180g long-grain rice

1 tbsp vegetable oil or butter

½ tsp black or brown mustard seeds

1 tbsp unroasted peanuts

1 tbsp desiccated coconut

1 green chilli, deseeded and chopped

¼ tsp ground turmeric

¼ tsp ground coriander

1 Mix all the marinade ingredients together.

2 Split the two natural halves of the rabbit livers, still keeping them whole. Remove any sinew from the livers, and trim the excess fat from the rabbit belly (the meaty side of the boned saddle). Rub the marinade well onto the livers and belly of the rabbit, then set aside for 30 minutes.

3 Wrap the livers separately in enough of the spinach leaves to cover and protect them. Butter a 30cm square piece of foil. Place enough of the cabbage leaves on the foil to cover it, then place a marinated saddle on top. Put a spinach-wrapped liver in the cavity. Roll the saddle around the liver into a sausage shape and wrap in the foil, twisting the ends to ensure a tight parcel. Repeat with the remaining saddles and livers. Leave in the fridge overnight.

4 To make the pistachio korma sauce, pour 300ml water into a large pan and add the onions, ginger and garlic pastes, cardamoms, mace, green chilli, bay leaf and peppercorns. Bring to the boil, then simmer for 25–30 minutes or until the onions are soft and mushy. Remove and discard the bay leaf and chilli, and pour the rest of the ingredients into a blender. Blend to a smooth purée. Whisk in the yoghurt. Return to the pan and simmer for 10–15 minutes. Add the butter and simmer for a further 5 minutes.

5 Meanwhile, pound the cashew nuts to a fine paste using a pestle and mortar. Mix the cashew paste with the cream, garam masala, pistachio paste and ground spices. Add this mixture to the sauce in the pan and simmer for 5–10 minutes. Taste and adjust the seasoning, then set aside to cool.

6 Preheat the oven to 200°C/gas 6.

7 Place the saddles of rabbit on a baking tray and roast them, turning a few times, for 12–15 minutes or until cooked (insert a small knife into the meat – the juices that run out should be clear). Remove the rabbit from the oven and let rest in the foil for 2–5 minutes before serving.

8 While the rabbit is roasting, make the tomato rice. Put the whole tomatoes in a blender and blitz, then strain the juice into a bowl. Boil the rice until cooked; drain if necessary. While the rice is cooking, heat the oil in a pan, add the mustard seeds and, when they crackle, add the peanuts and coconut. Sauté to colour lightly, then add the green chilli, turmeric and coriander. Add the strained tomato juice and cook for 10–15 minutes or until it thickens. Adjust the seasoning. Add the warm rice to the tomato mixture and mix lightly with a fork. Keep warm.

9 To serve, reheat the pistachio korma sauce. Set a 7.5cm metal ring on each warmed plate and spoon in the tomato rice, packing it in really tightly. Carefully remove the rings. Slice the saddles and arrange on the rice. Spoon the pistachio sauce around and garnish with the mixed leaves.

VENISON WELLINGTON
WITH PICKLED CABBAGE

SERVES 4

1 venison fillet, about 650g

3 tbsp mixed crushed juniper berries and
    crushed black peppercorns

olive oil

500g shallots, chopped

2 garlic cloves, chopped

⅓ bunch of thyme, leaves picked

1kg button mushrooms, chopped

200g foie gras, diced (optional)

handful of flat-leaf parsley, chopped

2–4 leaves of Savoy cabbage, stalk removed

1 sheet of ready-rolled puff pastry,
    about 500g

1 egg, beaten

PICKLED RED CABBAGE

500g red cabbage, cored and finely shredded

20g coarse rock salt

300ml red wine

100ml red wine vinegar

100ml Cabernet Sauvignon vinegar

20g sugar

1 star anise

¼ cinnamon stick

2 cardamom pods

3 black peppercorns, crushed

1 tsp crushed coriander seeds

1 tsp crushed fennel seeds

1 tsp crushed juniper berries

1 tsp freshly grated nutmeg

sprig of thyme

½ bay leaf

1 garlic clove, crushed

Venison sauce

250g venison bones, chopped

10ml vegetable oil

25g chopped carrots

25g chopped parsnips

1 celery stick, chopped

2 shallots, chopped

25g chopped leek

3 sprigs of thyme

1 bay leaf

2 garlic cloves, crushed

4 juniper berries, crushed

100ml red wine

50ml ruby Port

300ml veal stock

1 First make the pickled red cabbage. Toss the cabbage with the rock salt in a large bowl. Cover with cling film and keep overnight in the fridge. Next morning, rinse well and drain.

2 To make the marinade, put the wine, vinegars and sugar in a heavy pan and bring to the boil, stirring occasionally to dissolve the sugar. Tie all the remaining ingredients in a piece of muslin and add to the pan. Add the cabbage and stir, then leave to simmer gently for 30 minutes.

3 Remove from the heat and leave to cool. When it is cold, place the cabbage in a container, cover and keep in the fridge until needed.

4 Preheat the oven to 160°C/gas 3.

5 To make the venison sauce, roast the venison bones for 15–20 minutes, then leave to cool. Meanwhile, heat the oil in a heavy pan and caramelise all the vegetables with the thyme, bay leaf and garlic. Add the crushed juniper berries and roasted venison bones. Add the red wine, bring to the boil and reduce by half. Add the Port and reduce by half again. Add the veal stock and season, then leave to cook slowly at a slight simmer for 1 hour.

6 Pass the sauce through a fine sieve into a clean pan. Using a ladle, skim any fat or scum from the sauce. Place back on the heat and reduce by half. Then set the sauce aside until needed.

7 Season the venison fillet with the crushed juniper berries and peppercorns.

8 Heat a little olive oil in a non-stick frying pan until hot. Add the venison fillet to the pan and sear for 1 minute on each side, to colour. Remove from the pan and leave to rest for 15 minutes.

9 Meanwhile, heat 1 tbsp olive oil in a separate pan and sauté the shallots and garlic with the thyme for 1–2 minutes, to soften. Add the chopped mushrooms and fry for 2–3 minutes. Cook until excess liquid has evaporated. Add the diced foie gras and parsley and heat until the foie gras is cooked through. Set aside to cool.

10 Bring a saucepan of salted water to the boil and blanch the cabbage leaves for 1–2 minutes. Remove the leaves and refresh in iced water. Drain on kitchen paper to remove the excess water.

11 Place a large sheet of cling film on a flat surface. Arrange the cabbage leaves on the film to make a layer that is the same length as the venison fillet and about twice the width. Spread the mushroom mixture over the cabbage and set the venison on top. Wrap the cabbage and mushroom mixture around the venison, with the help of the cling film. Roll up tightly in the film to form a cylinder shape and secure, then place in the freezer to set for 20 minutes.

12 Roll out the puff pastry to two 10 x 20–25cm rectangles. Remove the cling film from the wrapped fillet and place it on one of the puff pastry rectangles. Lay the second pastry rectangle over the venison and press the edges together to seal. Place on a greased baking tray. Brush the pastry with beaten egg and leave to rest in the fridge for 20 minutes.

13 Preheat the oven to 180°C/gas 4.

14 Place the venison parcel in the oven and roast for 15–20 minutes.

15 While the venison is in the oven, reheat the pickled cabbage. Also warm enough sauce for four servings. If you want a more juniper flavour, add 2 crushed berries to infuse in the sauce for 10 minutes, then pass the sauce through a sieve.

16 To serve, slice the venison Wellington into four pieces and place on warm plates. Drizzle over the sauce and serve with the pickled cabbage.

FINNEBROGUE VENISON
WITH COLCANNON PIE AND WILD MUSHROOMS

SERVES 6-8
1 haunch of venison, about 2.5kg
30g butter
1 tbsp olive oil
salt, cracked black pepper and white pepper

COLCANNON PIE
300g puff pastry
2 medium potatoes, about 300g, peeled
    and very thinly sliced
1 large parsnip, very thinly sliced
1 large Savoy cabbage, finely sliced, blanched
    and well drained
egg wash (1 yolk beaten with a little cream)
100ml whipping cream
1 egg yolk

SAUCE
200ml red wine
2 tbsp sherry vinegar
200ml venison or brown chicken stock
½ tsp thyme leaves
2 tsp redcurrant jelly
½ tsp cracked black pepper
45g butter

GARNISH
wild mushrooms, such as chanterelles,
    ceps, horn of plenty (trompettes),
    shiitake and oyster
Savoy cabbage, shredded or chopped
butter

1 Preheat the oven to 190°C/gas 5. To make the colcannon pie, roll out two-thirds of the pastry and use to line a 24cm ovenproof frying pan or round baking dish.
2 In a large bowl, toss the potatoes, parsnip and cabbage together and season well with salt and pepper. Fill the pastry case with the potato mixture. Brush the edges of the pastry with egg wash, then top with the remaining pastry and press to seal. Brush the lid with egg wash and cut a 1cm hole in the centre. Bake the pie for 55 minutes.
3 Mix together the cream and egg yolk. Carefully pour into the hole in the lid. Bake for a further 5 minutes. Allow to cool slightly before cutting into wedges for serving.
4 While the pie is baking, prepare the venison. Trim the outside of the haunch to remove any sinew and fat. Work carefully to be sure you don't remove too much of the meat. Separate each large muscle one at a time and place them to one side. Reserve the trimmings and the very small muscles for stock, or another use.
5 Season the large muscles generously with salt and cracked black pepper. Heat the butter and oil in a large ovenproof frying pan or heavy roasting tray and fry the pieces of venison until they have a nice colour on all sides. Place in the oven and roast for 5 minutes for medium rare, or 8 minutes for medium to well done. Remove from the pan and allow to rest in a warm place while you make the sauce.
6 Pour off excess fat from the pan, then add the wine and vinegar. Bring to the boil, scraping the bottom of the pan to release any delicious juices and sediment. Reduce the liquid by two-thirds. Add the stock and boil until reduced and concentrated, but still a fairly light sauce consistency. Remove from the heat and whisk in the thyme, redcurrant jelly, pepper and butter. Add a little salt if necessary.

7 While you are reducing the sauce, sauté the mushrooms and cabbage, separately, in a little butter.

8 To serve, slice the venison. Spoon some of the sautéed cabbage and mushrooms on to each warm plate and top with a few slices of venison. Arrange a wedge of colcannon pie behind the meat and spoon a little sauce around.

NICK NAIRN

LOIN OF ROE VENISON
WITH POTATO CAKE, ROAST ROOTS
CREAMED CABBAGE AND GAME GRAVY

SERVES 4
4 tbsp goose fat
100g carrot, cut into 1cm dice
100g parsnip, cut into 1cm dice
100g celeriac, cut into 1cm dice
100g beetroot, cut into 1cm dice
sprig of thyme
1 garlic clove, lightly crushed
20g butter
4 pieces of roe deer saddle with rib bone
    still attached, each 120g
60ml red wine
30ml red wine vinegar
40ml fruit vinegar
200ml light brown chicken stock
250g Savoy cabbage, finely shredded,
    blanched for 2 minutes, refreshed
    and drained
4 tbsp double cream
salt and pepper

GAME GRAVY
600g venison rib bones
25g unsalted butter
200g venison trimmings, chopped
4 shallots, finely sliced
8 button mushrooms, sliced
1 garlic clove, crushed
1 bay leaf
sprig of thyme
6 white peppercorns, crushed
30ml red wine vinegar
120ml Port
120ml red wine
700ml brown chicken or game stock
1 tsp redcurrant jelly
1 tsp arrowroot

POTATO CAKES
400g peeled Golden Wonder potatoes
10 tbsp goose fat

1 Preheat the oven to 180°C/gas 4.

2 First make the game gravy. Roast the venison bones for 45 minutes. Meanwhile, heat a medium-sized saucepan, add the butter and venison trimmings and caramelise for 20 minutes. Add the shallots, mushrooms, garlic, bay leaf, thyme, and crushed peppercorns. Gently fry for 5–10 minutes or until golden brown.

3 Pour in the red wine vinegar, followed by the Port and red wine. Boil until a thick, syrupy glaze is achieved. Add the stock, redcurrant jelly and roasted bones and simmer for 45 minutes.

4 Pass through a fine sieve into a small, clean pan and boil again to reduce by half. Thicken with arrowroot, then check the seasoning and set aside. Reheat for serving. (This makes more gravy than you need for this dish; keep the rest in the refrigerator or freeze it.)

5 Next make the potato cakes. Grate the potatoes on the coarse side of a box grater, then place them in a clean tea towel and squeeze out the liquid. Put the potatoes in a bowl, add 2 tbsp of the goose fat and season with salt and pepper. Mix well.

6 Heat four 10cm blini pans. Add 2 tbsp goose fat to each, then divide the potato mix among them, pressing down gently. Cook until crisp and golden on the base, then carefully turn over and continue cooking until the other side is golden and the potatoes are tender. (Alternatively you can make one big cake in a 25cm non-stick frying pan and cut into quarters for serving.) Place in a low oven to keep warm.

7 Heat 2 tbsp goose fat in a heavy-bottomed frying pan and pan-roast the diced vegetables with the thyme and garlic for 15–20 minutes or until coloured and cooked through. Transfer to an ovenproof dish and place in the oven to keep warm.

8 Heat the remaining 2 tbsp goose fat with the butter in the frying pan, then sear the venison until it is well coloured and cooked medium rare. Remove the venison from the pan and place it somewhere warm to relax. This will allow the juices that have been drawn out of the centre to return.

9 Pour out the fat from the pan, return it to a high heat and deglaze with the wine and vinegars. Boil fast to reduce, then add the stock and reduce again by one-quarter to really intensify the flavours. Strain this jus and keep warm.

10 Reheat the cabbage, adding the cream, and season with salt and pepper.

11 To serve, place a pile of cabbage in the centre of each warm plate. Add the potato cakes on top and place the roasted vegetables around the outside. Position the venison on the potato cakes, and pour over the reduced jus. Drizzle the game gravy around the outside of the plates.

WILD BOAR
LANCASHIRE HOT POT

SERVES 4

900g boneless shoulder of wild boar, cubed
25g plain flour
vegetable oil for frying
2 onions, finely sliced
pinch of sugar
25g butter
2 carrots, sliced
2 celery sticks, peeled and chopped
300ml red wine
300ml beef stock
3 sprigs of thyme
2 bay leaves
splash of Worcestershire sauce
salt and pepper

TOPPING

450g Maris Piper potatoes, peeled
  and finely sliced
150g melted butter

1 Season the cubes of wild boar and toss in the flour, then brown all over in a little hot oil. Remove and set aside.

2 Add the onions and sugar to the same pan together with the butter and cook for 20 minutes or until the onions are golden. Stir in the carrots and celery and cook for a further 2 minutes.

3 Return the meat and stir in the remaining flour. Cook for 2 minutes. Now add the wine, stock, thyme, bay leaves and Worcestershire sauce. Bring to the boil, stirring all the time. Turn the heat right down and cook for 90 minutes.

4 Preheat the oven to 200°C/gas 6.

5 Blanch the potatoes in boiling water for 1 minute. Drain and refresh.

6 Divide the wild boar mixture among four individual pie dishes. Top each dish with a good layer of potato slices and brush with lots of melted butter. Season. Bake for 10 minutes, then finish under a hot grill. Serve with braised red cabbage.

PIGEON WITH AYRSHIRE BACON
SERVED WITH CARROT AND CABBAGE AND CHANTERELLE MUSHROOMS

SERVES 4

4 wood pigeons, oven-ready
2 carrots, peeled or scraped
1 small Savoy cabbage
8 rashers Ayrshire streaky bacon, very
    thinly sliced
2 tbsp sunflower oil
150g chanterelle mushrooms
100ml Port
40ml double cream
25g butter

GAME STOCK

1 carrot, diced
1 onion, diced
2 celery sticks, diced
1 tbsp tomato purée
2 garlic cloves, halved

1 Preheat the oven to 220°C/gas 7.

2 Remove the breasts from the pigeons, cover and place in the fridge. For the stock, pull the legs off the pigeon carcasses, and roughly chop up the legs and carcasses. Place in a roasting tin. Roast for 25–30 minutes to a golden brown; do not allow them to burn.

3 Remove the legs and carcasses and set aside. Add the diced carrot, onion and celery to the roasting tin and return to the oven to brown for 15–20 minutes. Stir the tomato purée into the vegetables. Cook for a few more minutes, then remove from the oven and deglaze the tin with a little water, mixing well and scraping the bottom of the tin with a wooden spatula.

4 Put the pigeon legs and carcasses in a large saucepan and add the liquid and vegetable mixture from the tin. Top up with enough water just to cover. Add the garlic. Bring to the boil, then simmer for about 50 minutes, skimming the surface occasionally. Strain the stock into a clean bowl and set aside.

5 Cut the carrots lengthways in half, then turn 90° and cut in half again. Turn 90° again and cut into matchsticks. Remove and discard the outer leaves of the cabbage; quarter the heart and cut out the stalk, then shred finely. Set the vegetables aside.

6 Remove the skin from the pigeon breasts, then wrap each breast in a rasher of bacon. Set a large frying pan over a high heat and add the sunflower oil. When it is hot, pan-fry the breasts for 2–3 minutes on each side or until coloured. Remove from the pan and allow to rest in a warm place.

7 Turn the heat down to medium and add the chanterelle mushrooms to the pan. Fry until golden. Remove and keep warm.

8 Add the Port to the pan and reduce to about half, scraping the bottom of the pan with a wooden spoon or spatula to pick up all the juices and caramelised pieces left by the pigeon and mushrooms. Pour in 150ml of the game stock, and again reduce by half. (Extra stock can be frozen.) Add the double cream. Toss the mushrooms back into the sauce and bring to the boil. Remove from the heat and keep warm.

9 Set a large saucepan over a medium heat and melt the butter with 4 tbsp water. Toss in the carrot matchsticks and the cabbage, and stir to coat with the buttery liquid. Put the lid on the pan and steam for about 5 minutes or until the cabbage and carrots are tender.

10 Meanwhile, warm the pigeon breasts in a hot oven for just a few minutes. (You don't want the meat to start cooking again, as pigeon is lean and should be pink.)

11 To serve, divide the carrot and cabbage mix among four warm plates. Carve each pigeon breast into two and lay two breasts on top of the carrot and cabbage on each plate. Spoon the mushrooms and sauce around. Accompany with mashed or fondant potatoes.

CLASSIC
FISH AND CHIPS

SERVES 4

4 large King Edward potatoes, peeled
   and cut into chips
vegetable oil for deep-frying
4 portions of haddock or cod fillet
seasoned flour
salt

BATTER

150g plain flour
75g cornflour
½ tsp caster sugar
1 tsp olive oil

1 Mix together all the ingredients for the batter with 225ml water and 1 tsp salt and leave to rest for about 20 minutes.

2 Heat a deep pan of oil to about 120°C. Blanch the chips in the oil, in batches if necessary, for 5–8 minutes or until soft but not coloured. Drain on kitchen paper.

3 Heat the pan of oil to 160–180°C. Dip the fish in seasoned flour to coat lightly, then dip into the batter. Shake off any excess batter, then fry in the hot oil until golden and crisp, and cooked in the centre. As the fish is cooked, remove and drain on kitchen paper, then keep warm in a low oven.

4 Add the blanched chips to the hot oil and fry until golden brown and crisp. Drain on kitchen paper and season with salt. Serve immediately with the fish, and Sarson's vinegar to sprinkle over.

BLACKSTICKS BLUE ROULADE
WITH CRISPY VEGETARIAN BLACK
PUDDING AND ONION JAM DRESSING

SERVES 4
65g butter
90g plain flour
400ml milk, warmed
7 eggs, separated
big handful of roughly chopped basil
100g Parmesan, freshly grated
400g ricotta
225g Blacksticks Blue cheese, crumbled
sprinkle of sun-blush tomatoes
salt and pepper

ONION JAM DRESSING
3 red onions, finely sliced
1 garlic clove, crushed
30g butter
125g sugar
100ml red wine vinegar
extra virgin olive oil

OTHER BITS
12 pieces of Ireland's vegetarian black
   pudding
vegetable oil
handful of baby spinach
30g butter

1 First make the onion jam dressing. Gently fry the onions and garlic in the butter until golden and caramelised. Add the sugar and vinegar and bring to the boil, then simmer for 40 minutes or until nice and thick, stirring from time to time. Season and thin with a little olive oil. Set aside.

2 Preheat the oven to 200°C/gas 6.

3 To make the roulade, melt the butter in a saucepan and stir in the flour. Cook for 3 minutes, then add the milk a little at a time, stirring constantly. Cook until thickened. Remove from the heat. Season well, then mix in the egg yolks.

4 In a bowl whisk the egg whites until stiff. Fold them gently and carefully into the yolk mixture, so you keep as much air as possible. Fold in the basil. Spread on a greased and lined 45 x 30cm baking tray. Sprinkle evenly with the Parmesan, then bake for 15 minutes or until springy and risen. Turn out on to a sheet of greaseproof paper or baking parchment and leave to cool.

5 Season the ricotta, then spread it evenly over the roulade base, leaving a gap at the top and bottom. Scatter over the crumbled cheese and tomatoes. Roll up and wrap in greaseproof and foil. If not eating straight away, chill for up to 2 hours.

6 When ready to serve, preheat the oven to 200°C/gas 6. Cut the roulade into eight pieces and heat through in the oven for 10 minutes. Then finish by glazing them under a hot grill.

7 Meanwhile, fry the black pudding in medium hot oil until crisp. Drain on kitchen paper. Quickly wilt the spinach in the butter and season well.

8 To serve, sit some wilted spinach in the centre of each warm plate and top with two pieces of roulade. Place three pieces of black pudding around and spoon some onion jam dressing in between.

CHAPTER FOUR **DESSERTS**

ENGLISH TRIFLE
WITH A SORBET OF NORFOLK
RASPBERRIES AND SUGARED NUTS

SERVES 6

SUGARED NUTS
25g pine nuts
25g whole peeled almonds
25g whole peeled hazelnuts
25g pecan nuts, chopped
100g icing sugar, sifted
4 tbsp Grand Marnier

SPONGE
3 medium eggs
90g caster sugar
75g self-raising flour
1 tbsp cornflour
40g unsalted butter, melted and
    slightly cooled

SUGAR SYRUP
250g caster sugar
350ml sparkling rosé wine,
    preferably English

RASPBERRY SORBET
450g raspberries
juice of ½ lemon, strained

ROSE AND RASPBERRY JELLY
450g (hulled weight) really ripe raspberries
4 gelatine leaves
150ml sparkling rosé wine,
    preferably English

ENGLISH CUSTARD
300ml whipping cream
150ml full-fat milk
1 vanilla pod, split lengthways
4 medium egg yolks
100g caster sugar
2 tbsp cornflour

TO FINISH
about 5 tbsp Marsala
½ small jar of raspberry or strawberry jam,
    preferably home-made
425ml whipping cream

1 The sugared nuts, sponge, sorbet and jelly can all be made a day in advance
(the nuts will keep for a few days in an airtight container). To make the sugared
nuts, place all the ingredients in a large, heavy-based, non-stick frying pan and,
over the lowest possible heat, gently melt the icing sugar. Stir occasionally, being
very careful once the sugar starts to caramelise. Turn the mixture onto a very
lightly oiled tray and allow to cool.

2 Preheat the oven to 180°C/gas 4. Grease a deep, 20cm round cake tin and line
the bottom with baking parchment.

3 To make the sponge, put the eggs and sugar into a large bowl set over a pan of hot
water and beat with an electric mixer until the mixture becomes pale and creamy.
The mixture will increase in volume considerably and should become thick enough
to leave a trail on the surface when the beaters are lifted out. Remove the bowl from
the pan and continue to whisk until the mixture is cold.

4 Mix the self-raising flour with the cornflour. Sift half of it onto the surface of the
egg mixture and fold in with a metal spoon. Carefully pour half the cooled butter
around the edge of the mixture and lightly fold in. Sift over the remaining sifted

flour mix and fold in, alternating with the remaining butter. Pour into the prepared tin. Bake for 20–30 minutes or until the sponge is well risen, firm to the touch and beginning to shrink away from the sides of the tin. Allow to cool in the tin for a few minutes before turning out onto a wire rack. Leave to cool completely.

5 For the sugar syrup, put the sugar and wine into a saucepan and heat to dissolve the sugar, then simmer gently for 2 minutes. Leave to get cold.

6 To make the sorbet, blitz the raspberries in a food processor or blender, then press the purée through a fine sieve into a jug. Stir in 150ml of the sugar syrup, tasting as you do so (you may not need to use this much, depending on the sweetness of the fruit). Finally, stir in the lemon juice. Churn in an ice cream machine until softly set, then transfer to a container and freeze.

7 To make the jelly, place the raspberries and 150ml of the sugar syrup in a saucepan and gently bring to the boil. Poach the fruit gently until really soft. Pass the mixture through a piece of muslin or jelly bag into a jug.

8 Soften the gelatine leaves in a dish of cold water for 5 minutes. Remove the softened leaves, squeezing out any excess water as you do so, then stir the gelatine into the still hot raspberry juice. Allow to cool at room temperature, still in the jug, until just about setting, then very slowly and gently stir in the wine, retaining as many bubbles as possible as you do so. (If you pour and stir too quickly, the mixture will get very frothy.) Chill for 3–4 hours or until set (you can leave it overnight).

9 Break up the sponge into pieces and place in the bottom of a large glass bowl, or divide among individual glasses. Douse with the Marsala, then spread over the jam and leave to soak. Carefully break up the jelly with a fork or whisk, then spoon it over the soaked sponge.

10 To make the custard, pour the cream and milk into a heavy-based saucepan. Scrape in the seeds from the vanilla pod and add the empty pod too. Bring slowly to the boil, then set aside to infuse. Whisk the egg yolks, sugar and cornflour together in a large bowl. Gently reheat the cream and milk mixture. As soon as it reaches boiling point, pour it onto the egg yolk mixture, whisking all the time. Pour back into the saucepan and stir over a low heat until the custard thickens enough to coat the back of the spoon. Immediately remove the pan from the heat and pass the custard through a fine sieve into a bowl. (If you are not using it immediately, push a piece of cling film tightly down on top of the custard, then place another piece over the top of the bowl; this will prevent a skin from forming.) Allow to cool and thicken a little before pouring over the jelly.

11 To finish, roughly chop the sugared nuts. Whip the whipping cream to very soft peaks and spread this over the top of the custard. Sprinkle over the sugared nuts (any left over will keep for another time). Serve with the raspberry sorbet.

SEASONAL BERRY CUSTARDS
WITH A BAKED OAT CRUMBLE AND
LAVENDER HONEY ICE CREAM

SERVES 4
9 medium egg yolks
250g caster sugar
1 vanilla pod, split lengthways
1 litre whipping cream
200g mixed seasonal berries
juice of ½ lemon
100ml lavender honey

CRUMBLE
100g plain flour
50g porridge oats
70g salted butter
50g caster sugar

1 Put the egg yolks and 200g of the caster sugar in a bowl. Scrape the vanilla seeds from the pod, add to the bowl and mix together with a whisk. Bring the cream to the boil with the empty vanilla pod. Add to the egg mixture and mix thoroughly. Discard the pieces of vanilla pod, then divide the custard equally between a bowl and a jug. Set the bowl of custard over another bowl of ice to cool rapidly, and chill in the fridge for 10–15 minutes. Set the jug of custard aside.

2 Preheat the oven to 170°C/gas 3.

3 Combine the berries, remaining caster sugar and the lemon juice in a saucepan. Poach gently for 3–4 minutes. Spoon the berries into four 12cm moulds or cups and pour the unchilled custard from the jug on top. Set the moulds in a roasting tin and pour warm water into the tin to come halfway up the sides of the moulds. Bake for 30 minutes or until the custards are just set – they should wobble like a jelly when the mould is tapped. Remove the moulds from the tin of water and leave to cool, then put in the fridge. Keep the oven on.

4 To make the crumble, put all the ingredients into a food processor and blitz quickly. Spread the mixture on a baking sheet. Bake for 10–15 minutes or until golden. Leave to cool.

5 For the ice cream, mix the chilled custard with the lavender honey and churn in an ice cream machine until thickened. Decant into a container and freeze.

6 To serve, top the chilled berry custards with the crumble and ice cream.

306

VANILLA AND GINGERBREAD CHEESECAKES
WITH FRESH RASPBERRIES AND RASPBERRY SORBET

SERVES 8
250g full-fat soft cheese
250ml double cream
125g crème fraîche
125g caster sugar
seeds scraped from 1 split vanilla pod
300g English raspberries

GINGERBREAD
125g strong rye flour
125g plain flour
4 tsp baking powder
2 tsp ground mixed spice
2 tsp ground ginger
125ml full-fat milk
250g perfumed honey

3 medium eggs
50g light muscovado sugar
grated zest of 1 small lemon
grated zest of 1 small orange
seeds scraped from ½ split vanilla pod

STOCK SYRUP
1 thick slice of lemon
300g caster sugar
15g liquid glucose

RASPBERRY SORBET
500g English raspberries
caster sugar for sprinkling
¼ tsp liquid glucose
juice of ½ lemon

1 First make the gingerbread. Preheat the oven to 160°C/gas 3. Grease and line a 900g loaf tin.
2 Sift the dry ingredients into a large bowl. Mix the milk, honey, eggs and sugar in another bowl with the citrus zest and vanilla seeds, then add to the dry ingredients and mix well until evenly combined. Spoon the mixture into the prepared tin. Bake for 45 minutes or until a skewer inserted in the centre comes out clean. Cool in the tin for about 30 minutes, then remove and leave to cool on a wire rack.
3 To make gingerbread crumbs (you need 100g), cut the gingerbread into 5mm-thick slices and leave to dry on a tray overnight. The next day, grind the slices to fine crumbs in a food processor. Store in a plastic container until ready to use. (The rest of the gingerbread can be eaten as a cake; wrapped in foil it will keep for a week.)
4 For the stock syrup, put the lemon slice in a heavy pan with the sugar, liquid glucose and 300ml water. Heat gently, stirring occasionally, until the sugar has dissolved, then bring to the boil and boil for 5 minutes. Cool. Remove the lemon slice, then pass the syrup through a fine sieve into a container. Cover and chill.
5 To make the sorbet, put the raspberries in a heavy pan, sprinkle lightly with caster sugar and 2 tbsp water, and cook over a low heat for about 5 minutes or until the raspberries soften down. Tip into a fine sieve set over a bowl and push the purée through to remove the seeds. Cover and chill in the fridge.

6 Set 100ml raspberry purée aside in the fridge for later. Combine the remaining purée with 250ml chilled stock syrup, the liquid glucose and lemon juice. Churn in an ice cream machine until thickened, then decant into a clean container and store in the freezer until ready to use.

7 For the cheesecakes, stand eight metal rings, each measuring 5.5cm tall and 4.5cm across, on a non-stick mat or baking sheet lined with cling film. Combine the cheese, cream, crème fraîche, sugar and vanilla seeds in a large bowl. Whisk together well until thick, then put the mixture in a plastic piping bag and pipe neatly into the rings. Make sure there are no gaps or air pockets and pipe right up to the tops, then smooth the tops with the back of a flat knife. Refrigerate for 2 hours or until set firm.

8 Meanwhile, make eight quenelles of sorbet using two spoons and place on a tray lined with baking parchment. Place in the freezer. Put the raspberries in a bowl with the reserved 100ml raspberry purée and 'muddle' with a fork. Set aside at room temperature.

9 About 5 minutes before serving, remove the cheesecakes from the fridge. One at a time, lift a cheesecake off the mat and dip both ends in gingerbread crumbs, then warm the ring in your hands for 30 seconds (or very quickly flash round the ring with a blowtorch). Now hold the ring over a plate and carefully lift it up so the cheesecake drops out onto the plate.

10 To finish, put a spoonful of muddled raspberries to the side of each plate and sprinkle a line of gingerbread crumbs between the cheesecake and the raspberries. Top each cheesecake with a quenelle of sorbet and serve immediately.

MARCUS WAREING

ALMOND PANNACOTTA
WITH POACHED PEARS AND TOASTED ALMONDS

SERVES 6

ALMOND PANNACOTTA
300ml full-fat milk
300ml whipping cream
60g demerara sugar
175g flaked almonds, chopped
3 large gelatine leaves, soaked in ice-cold
    water for 30 minutes

PEARS
250g caster sugar
pared zest of ½ lemon
½ cinnamon stick
3 William's pears

TO SERVE
125g flaked almonds
a little icing sugar

1 Take six metal rings, about 8cm in diameter and 1cm deep, and tightly cover one end of each ring with cling film like a drum skin. Stand the rings on their covered ends on a tray and chill in the fridge.

2 To make the pannacotta, mix the milk, cream and sugar in a saucepan and bring to the boil. At the same time, toast the almonds under a medium-hot grill until golden brown, turning them frequently to prevent them from burning. When the liquids have boiled, add the hot nuts and remove from the heat. Cover the pan tightly with cling film and leave to infuse until totally cold.

3 Strain the almond milk into a bowl through a very fine sieve (preferably lined with muslin). Discard the almonds, then weigh the liquid. If there is less than 460g, make up the difference with extra milk. If more, discard the excess.

4 Warm one-quarter of the almond milk in a clean saucepan. Remove the gelatine leaves from the water and squeeze out any excess water, then add to the warm almond milk and stir until melted. Strain through a fine sieve into the cold almond milk and stir until thoroughly mixed. Pour equal amounts of the almond milk into each of the prepared rings and return to the fridge to set. This should take 2–3 hours.

5 Meanwhile, prepare the pears. Mix the caster sugar in a saucepan with 500ml water, the lemon zest and cinnamon. Heat gently until the sugar has dissolved, then bring to the boil over a high heat. Quickly peel the pears and add to the pan, then cover the surface of the liquid with a sheet of baking parchment. Cook over a very low heat for about 20 minutes or until the pears feel quite soft when pierced with the tip of a sharp knife. Remove from the heat and leave the pears to cool in the syrup.

6 When the pears are cold, remove and drain. Cut each pear in half lengthways and carefully remove the core, then slice each half finely and fan out on a serving plate. Check that the pannacotta is set, then remove the cling film and stand each ring on a plate next to the fanned pears. Carefully release each ring by running a hot, sharp knife between the ring and the pannacotta, then gently lift off the ring.

7 To serve, lightly toast the flaked almonds under a medium-hot grill, turning them frequently to prevent them from burning. Sprinkle the hot almonds over the pears at the last minute, and dust lightly with icing sugar.

RICH CHOCOLATE MOUSSE
WITH BLOOD ORANGE SORBET

SERVES 8

BLOOD ORANGE SORBET
200g caster sugar
425ml freshly squeezed blood orange
    juice, strained
juice of 1 lemon

MOUSSE
2 medium eggs
100g caster sugar
175g bittersweet chocolate (minimum 64%
    cocoa solids), roughly broken in pieces
50g unsalted butter
freshly grated nutmeg
2 tbsp strong warm coffee (espresso is good)
175ml double cream

1 To make the sorbet, put the sugar and 275ml water in a saucepan and bring to the boil. When the sugar has dissolved, simmer for about 5 minutes to make a stock syrup. Remove from the heat and add the orange and lemon juices. Stir well, then strain through a sieve. Allow to cool completely before churning in an ice cream machine. Freeze in an airtight container.

2 To make the mousse, begin by making an Italian meringue. Separate the eggs and drop the whites into the bowl of an electric food mixer. (Keep the yolks for later.) Put the sugar and 2 tbsp water in a small saucepan and dissolve over a moderate heat, then bring to the boil. Put a sugar thermometer in the syrup. When the temperature reaches just below 110°C, turn on the food mixer and whisk the egg whites at high speed until stiff. When the syrup has reached 115°C, remove from the heat and pour it slowly and carefully over the egg whites while continuing to whisk. Keep whisking until the meringue has cooled a little, then turn the machine to its lowest speed.

3 Combine the chocolate, butter and a grating of nutmeg in a heatproof bowl set over a saucepan of hot water (make sure the base of the bowl does not touch the water and that the water does not boil). As soon as the chocolate and butter have melted, remove the bowl from the hot water and allow to cool a little, then beat in the egg yolks and coffee. Leave to cool a little more, then fold the meringue into the chocolate mixture.

4 Whip the cream until it reaches soft, floppy peaks. Fold into the chocolate and meringue mixture. Pour into small ramekins (6–7cm diameter) or a large dish (800–900ml capacity) and chill for about 1 hour.

5 Serve the chocolate mousse with the blood orange sorbet.

310

CARRAGEEN MOSS PUDDING
WITH APPLES, ROSEHIP SYRUP
AND OATCAKES

SERVES 6
25g dried carrageen moss, washed,
   plus extra to serve
100ml full-fat milk
250ml double cream
1 vanilla pod, split lengthways
6 egg yolks
100g caster sugar
3 large gelatine leaves, soaked in warm
   water for 10 minutes, then squeezed
10g agar-agar
250g buttermilk
170ml condensed milk

OATCAKES
75g dried dulse
250g plain white flour
2 tsp baking powder
1 tsp salt

250g jumbo oatmeal
100g ground almonds
100g demerara sugar
200g unsalted butter
6 large egg yolks

ROSEHIP SYRUP
200g dried rosehips
30g caster sugar

APPLE JELLY
300ml organic apple juice
2 Granny Smith apples, peeled and chopped
8g agar-agar

APPLE PURÉE
5 Granny Smith apples, peeled and sliced
5 Gala apples, peeled and sliced
25g caster sugar
organic apple juice

1 First make the dough for the oatcakes. Soak the dulse in cold water for about 10 minutes, then drain and chop finely. Sift the flour, baking powder and salt into a bowl, then stir in the oatmeal, almonds and sugar. Rub in the butter, then mix in the egg yolks and dulse. Divide the dough equally into four and form each quarter into a log shape. Wrap each log in cling film and chill for 1 hour.
2 Meanwhile, make the rosehip syrup. Bring the rosehips and sugar to the boil in a heavy pan with 100ml water. Cover and leave to infuse off the heat for 1 hour. Blitz in a blender, then pass through a fine sieve and leave to cool.
3 Next, make the apple jelly. Bring the apple juice and apples to the boil in a heavy pan. Simmer for 1 minute, then remove from the heat and leave to cool. Whisk in the agar-agar. Pass through a fine sieve and pour into six serving glasses. Leave to set.
4 Preheat the oven to 200°C/gas 6. Line a baking tray with baking parchment. Unwrap the logs of oatcake dough and cut them into about 40 slices that are eye-pleasingly thick. Place the slices on the baking parchment and bake for 10–15 minutes or until golden brown. Transfer to a wire rack to cool.
5 For the apple purée, put the apples and sugar in a heavy pan with enough apple juice to cover and cook over a low heat for 10 minutes. Blitz in a blender, then pass through a fine sieve and leave to cool.

6 To make the pudding, wash the carrageen. Put it into a heavy pan with the milk, cream and vanilla, and simmer for 2–3 minutes. Meanwhile, whisk the egg yolks and sugar in a bowl. Tip the carrageen and liquid into a sieve held over the bowl and let the liquid strain through. Whisk this liquid into egg yolk mixture. Pour into a clean pan and stir over a very low heat until thickened. Remove from the heat and stir in the agar-agar and squeezed gelatine. Continue stirring until the gelatine has melted, then leave for 3–4 minutes to allow the agar-agar to soften. Pass the custard through a fine sieve (to remove the agar-agar) into a bowl, then add the buttermilk and condensed milk and stir well. Leave to cool. Put into a siphon (if using).

7 To serve, pour rosehip syrup over the set apple jelly, then cover with apple purée and syphon or spoon the pudding on top. Finish with some crushed dried carrageen moss. Serve the oatcakes on the side.

MARK HIX

DORSET BLUEBERRY TRIFLE

SERVES 4
100–125g sponge cake
4 tbsp Somerset Pomona (a blend of apple
    juice and cider brandy)
100–125g blueberries

JELLY
3 large gelatine leaves
100g caster sugar
150g blueberries

CUSTARD
300ml single cream
½ vanilla pod, split lengthways
5 medium egg yolks
60g caster sugar
2 tsp cornflour

TOPPING
250ml double cream
60g caster sugar, plus an extra 2–3 tbsp
    for frosting
2 tbsp dry English white wine, preferably
    Coddington Bacchus
juice of ½ lemon
pinch of freshly grated nutmeg
1 medium egg white
50g blueberries

1 First make the jelly. Immerse the gelatine leaves one at a time in a shallow bowl of cold water and leave for a minute or so until soft. Meanwhile, bring 220ml water to the boil in a saucepan. Add the sugar and stir until dissolved, then add the blueberries and simmer gently for 3–4 minutes. With a slotted spoon, take out about one-third of the blueberries and set aside for later. Strain the blueberry and syrup mixture through a fine-meshed sieve, pressing the berries lightly to extract their juice. Discard the berries in the sieve. Drain and squeeze the gelatine leaves. Add them to the blueberry syrup and stir the gelatine has until melted. Allow the jelly to cool, but do not let it set.

2 Break the sponge into pieces and put into four individual glass serving dishes or one large dish. Pour over the Pomona and scatter over the blueberries, then pour over the cooled jelly; it should just cover the berries. Chill for an hour or so to set.

3 Meanwhile, make the custard. Put the cream into a small saucepan. Scrape the seeds from the vanilla pod into the cream and add the pod too. Bring to the boil, then remove from the heat and leave to infuse for about 10 minutes. In a bowl, mix together the egg yolks, sugar and cornflour. Take out the vanilla pod and pour the cream onto the egg mixture, mixing well with a whisk. Pour back into the pan and cook gently over a low heat for a few minutes, stirring constantly with a wooden spoon until the custard thickens. Do not let it boil.

4 Remove the pan from the heat and give the custard a final mix with a whisk. Transfer to a bowl and lay cling film over the surface of the custard to prevent a skin from forming. Leave to cool for about 30 minutes.

5 Once the jelly has set, spoon the cooled custard over it. Leave to set for 30 minutes.

6 Now prepare the topping. Put the cream, sugar, wine, lemon juice and nutmeg into a bowl and carefully whisk until fairly firm (this won't take too long as the lemon juice will thicken the cream). Fold the reserved cooked blueberries through the cream, then keep in the fridge until the custard has set.

7 To frost the blueberries for decoration, lightly whisk the egg white just to break it up, then put the blueberries through it and shake off the excess. Now put the blueberries through the extra 2–3 tbsp caster sugar until well coated. Leave them on a plate to dry for about 15 minutes.

8 Just before serving, spoon the cream mixture on top of the trifle and decorate with the frosted blueberries.

314

APPLE TASTING OF THE SOUTH EAST

SERVES 4

APPLE-BASIL GRANITA
100g caster sugar
leaves of 3 sprigs of basil
450ml freshly pressed Granny Smith apple
    juice, or other bottled apple juice

GINGER ICE CREAM
300ml full-fat milk
300ml double cream
2 tbsp chopped candied stem ginger
1 tbsp finely chopped fresh ginger
60g granulated sugar
5 medium egg yolks
pinch of salt

APPLE CONFIT
60g unsalted butter, melted
2 tbsp granulated sugar
¼ tsp ground cinnamon
¼ tsp ground star anise
2 Gala apples, peeled and thinly sliced
2 Cox's apples, peeled and thinly sliced
finely grated zest of 1 orange

APPLE CHARLOTTE
25g unsalted butter
2 Queen Cox, Royal Snow or Jupiter apples,
    peeled and chopped
½ vanilla pod, split lengthways
1 tbsp apple brandy
2 brioches, cut into 1 x 1 x 2.5cm sticks

CRUMB TOPPING
120g plain flour
60g soft unsalted butter
2 tbsp light muscovado sugar
60g pecan nuts, chopped
pinch of ground cinnamon
pinch of grated nutmeg
1 tsp vanilla extract

TO SERVE
apricot sauce
whipped crème fraîche
lavender flowers
custard sauce
raspberry sauce
4 shards of cinnamon sticks
Queen Cox cider, mulled with cloves
    and cinnamon

1 The granita, ice cream and apple confit all need to be made ahead. For the granita, put the sugar in a heavy-based saucepan with enough water (about 100ml) to cover. Bring to the boil and boil for a few minutes until syrupy. Measure and reserve 60ml of the sugar syrup (the rest can be used for another occasion). Drop the basil leaves into boiling water, lift out immediately and put into iced water. Drain, then purée with 3 tbsp of the measured sugar syrup in a small blender until smooth. Strain through a fine wire sieve or muslin. Reserve a spoonful of this basil syrup for later, and combine the remainder with the rest of the measured sugar syrup and the apple juice. Pour into a freezer container and freeze for 3–4 hours. Scrape the surface into shavings using a metal spoon or fork, then return the granita to the freezer. (The granita can be kept for about 1 week.)

2 To make the ice cream, boil the milk and cream with the stem and fresh ginger in a heavy-based pan. In a bowl whisk together the sugar, egg yolks and a pinch of salt until smooth. Slacken the yolk mixture with one-third of the hot milk mixture, whisking constantly. Whisk this back into the rest of the hot milk and cook over a low heat, stirring constantly, until thick enough to coat the back of a wooden spoon. Strain through a fine wire sieve into a bowl. Set the bowl over a bowl of iced water to chill. Pour into an ice cream machine and churn, then freeze until required.

3 Preheat the oven to 140°C/gas 1.

4 To make the apple confit, lightly brush the inside of a 500g loaf tin or similar-sized small ceramic terrine mould with a little of the melted butter. Mix the sugar with the ground spices. Place a layer of sliced apples on the bottom of the tin, brush with some of the butter and sprinkle with some of the spiced sugar and orange zest. Repeat the layers until the tin is full. Lay a piece of baking parchment on the top layer and place a foil-wrapped heavy weight (such as a brick) on top. Bake for 8–10 hours or until the liquid has lightly caramelised and the height of the apple confit has significantly reduced. Remove the confit from the tin and cool, then wrap in cling film and chill overnight.

5 Turn up the oven temperature to 200°C/gas 6.

6 For the apple charlottes, heat the butter in a frying pan, add the apples and vanilla, and sauté for 2–3 minutes. Pour in the brandy and remove from the heat. Remove the vanilla pod. Butter four 5cm-diameter dariole moulds. Line the moulds with overlapping slices of brioche sticks, then fill with the sautéed apples. Bake for 5–8 minutes or until the brioche is lightly coloured. Cool.

7 Reduce the oven temperature to 180°C/gas 4. To make the topping, in a bowl rub the flour and butter together to coarse crumbs. Stir in the remaining topping ingredients to make a rough dough. Break into small pieces onto a baking sheet and bake for 3–5 minutes or until just golden brown. Cool.

8 Turn the apple charlottes out of their moulds, upside down. Finish the charlottes with the crumb topping. Cut the apple confit into 4cm squares.

9 To serve, spoon a little apricot sauce on each rectangular serving plate and place a square of apple confit on top. (Any extra confit will keep, wrapped in the fridge, for up to 2 days.) Garnish with crème fraîche topped with a lavender flower. Dot a little custard and raspberry sauce around. Add another small spoonful of apricot sauce and place a charlotte on top. Add a scoop of ginger ice cream. Scoop the granita into four shot glasses and add a shard of cinnamon stick to each as a stirrer. Sit this on the plates along with a glass of warm mulled cider.

316

ICED WHISKY CREAMS
WITH PRUNES AND TEA SYRUP

SERVES 6
handful of prunes
vegetable oil
5 egg yolks
85g caster sugar
300ml double cream
3 tbsp Glengoyne whisky

TEA SYRUP
250g granulated sugar
1 Scottish blend tea bag
2 tsp lemon juice, strained
1 vanilla pod, split lengthways
1 tbsp Glengoyne whisky

1 You need to start this recipe a good day ahead. To make the tea syrup, put a saucepan over a medium heat. Add the sugar and 250ml water, and stir until the sugar has dissolved. Bring to the boil. Add the tea bag and boil for 5–6 minutes.
2 Strain the mixture through a fine sieve into a bowl. (Be careful to avoid splashing, as the syrup will be very hot.) Add the lemon juice, vanilla pod (scraping out some of the seeds into the syrup as you do) and whisky, then the prunes. Cool, then cover and chill. Keep for at least 24 hours before using. The flavour will improve over time. (You will only need about 150ml syrup, so save the rest in an airtight jar for another time, such as for mixing with fruit salad.)
3 For the whisky creams, lightly grease a small terrine or loaf tin with vegetable oil. Place the egg yolks in a heatproof bowl set over a pan of simmering water and beat with an electric mixer for about 5 minutes or until thick and pale. Remove from the pan and cool while you make the syrup.
4 Heat the sugar with 3 tbsp water in a small pan until dissolved, then boil the syrup for about 5 minutes or until it reaches the softball stage (116–118°C). To check without a sugar thermometer, tip a drop of hot syrup into a glass of cold water; if the syrup is ready, you should be able to roll it into a soft ball.
5 Beat the egg yolks on full speed as you slowly pour on the syrup in a continuous stream, then reduce the speed by half and beat for a further 5 minutes or until thickened. Set aside to cool to room temperature.
6 In a clean bowl, whip the cream with the whisky until it starts to thicken; don't over-whip. Combine the egg mix and whipped cream, then pour into the terrine or loaf tin. Freeze for about 12 hours.
7 When ready to serve, remove the vanilla pod from the tea syrup, then gently reheat the syrup. Remove the whisky cream from the freezer. Dip the terrine briefly into warm water to help release the contents. Dry the terrine, then invert and tip out the whisky cream onto a board. Cut into slices.
8 Place one or two slices of whisky cream on each plate and add a few prunes. Drizzle the hot syrup over and around. Serve at once, before the whisky cream melts.

318

STRAWBERRY SOUFFLÉ
WITH STRAWBERRY SORBET AND
WELSH SHORTBREAD

SERVES 4
500g strawberries, hulled
150g caster sugar, plus extra for dusting
1 vanilla pod, split lengthways
2½ tbsp cornflour
soft butter for the dishes
4 egg whites
sifted icing sugar to dust

SORBET
100g caster sugar
100ml boiling water
500g strawberries, hulled

SHORTBREAD
100g soft slightly salted butter
45g icing sugar, sifted
125g plain flour
pinch of salt

1 To make the jam base for the soufflé, blitz the strawberries and 100g sugar in a food processor to a purée. Rub through a fine sieve into a heavy-bottomed pan. Scrape in the vanilla seeds from the pod. Bring to the boil over a medium heat, whisking continuously. Stir the cornflour with about 60ml of water just to slacken, then whisk into the strawberry purée until the mixture thickens. Cool, then chill.

2 Brush the insides of four soufflé dishes that are 9cm diameter and 6cm deep with softened butter, then dust with caster sugar. Chill.

3 To make the sorbet, dissolve the sugar in the boiling water, then simmer for about 2 minutes to make a sugar syrup. Cool. Blitz the strawberries with the syrup to a purée, and rub through a fine sieve into a bowl. Cool, then chill. Place in an ice cream maker and churn for 15–20 minutes to a soft scoop texture. Scoop out four neat quenelles and freeze them on a plate. (The rest of the sorbet can be kept in the freezer for up to 2 weeks.)

4 To make the shortbread, beat the butter and icing sugar together, then gently mix in the flour and salt to make a dough. Roll into a cylinder about 5–6cm in diameter, wrap in cling film and chill for at least 2 hours.

5 Preheat the oven to 200°C/gas 6. Cut the chilled dough into 5-mm thick slices (12–14 slices) and place on a baking sheet. Bake for 10–12 minutes or until golden round the edges. Slide onto a wire rack to cool and crisp. Leave the oven on.

6 To finish the soufflés, whisk the egg whites with the remaining 50g caster sugar to soft peaks. Fold into the soufflé jam base. Divide the mixture among the four dishes, filling them to the top, then level with the back of a knife. Bake for 9–11 minutes or until risen above the rim by half.

7 Remove from the oven and immediately dust the tops with icing sugar. Set each soufflé on a large plate. Put a frozen scoop of sorbet and a piece of shortbread to the side. Serve straightaway.

TRIO OF RHUBARB
RHUBARB AND GINGER MOUSSE,
RHUBARB ICE CREAM,
AND RHUBARB AND WHISKEY COMPOTE

SERVES 6
600g young, sweet rhubarb, chopped
325g caster sugar
50g fresh ginger, peeled and grated
2½ large gelatine leaves
100ml whipping cream
2 medium egg whites
6 sprigs of mint to finish

ICE CREAM
4 medium egg yolks
100g caster sugar
500ml whipping cream
½ vanilla pod, split lengthways

TUILE BASKETS
40g plain flour
40g icing sugar
2 medium egg whites, broken up with a fork
35g unsalted butter, melted and cooled

COMPOTE
15g salted butter
2 sticks of rhubarb, chopped
2 tbsp light soft brown sugar
3 tbsp whiskey, preferably Bushmills
1 tsp lemon juice

1 Put the rhubarb in a heavy pan with 200g of the sugar and 2 tbsp water. Cook gently for 8–10 minutes or until the rhubarb is soft and pulpy. Allow to cool.

2 Dissolve 25g sugar in 4 tbsp water in a heavy pan over a low heat. Add the grated fresh ginger and bring to the boil. Remove from the heat and leave to infuse until cold, then strain the syrup and discard the ginger. Set the ginger syrup aside.

3 To make the ice cream, mix the egg yolks and sugar in a bowl. Pour the cream into a heavy pan, scrape in the vanilla seeds and drop in the pod. Bring to the boil, then slowly pour onto the egg yolk mixture and stir together. Return to the pan and stir over a gentle heat until the custard coats the back of the spoon. Cool and chill, then mix with one-third of the rhubarb pulp and churn in an ice cream machine. Once softly set, store in the freezer.

4 Preheat the oven to 150°C/gas 2.

5 For the tuile baskets, sift the flour and icing sugar into a bowl. Slowly add the egg whites, then the butter, and mix until evenly incorporated. Drop six spoonfuls of the mixture slightly apart on one or two baking sheets lined with a non-stick mat or baking parchment. Flatten with the back of the spoon to make six discs, each about 12cm in diameter. Bake for 5–6 minutes or until lightly browned. Remove from the oven. Lift each disc off the baking sheet and immediately mould around a ramekin. Leave until cold.

6 To finish the mousse, let the gelatine leaves soak in a bowl of cold water for about 10 minutes. Meanwhile, add the ginger syrup to the remaining rhubarb pulp, then purée in a blender. Turn the purée into a pan and heat until hot, then remove from the heat. Drain and squeeze the gelatine, then stir into the rhubarb until melted.

7 Whip the cream in a bowl until it holds a soft peak. Whisk the egg whites in another bowl until they hold a soft peak, then slowly add the remaining 100g sugar and keep whisking until the sugar is dissolved and the mixture is thick and glossy. Fold the cream into the cold rhubarb and ginger purée followed by the egg whites. When all is incorporated, spoon into six 7.5–10cm non-stick moulds. Chill for about 4 hours or until set.

8 To make the compote, gently melt the butter in a pan and sauté the rhubarb for 5–6 minutes or until soft. Add the sugar, whiskey and lemon juice, and heat for a few minutes. If you would like a smoother texture, purée the compote in a mini-food processor or with a stick blender.

9 To serve, warm the mousse moulds by holding them in a hot cloth, then turn each mousse out onto a plate. Lift the tuile baskets off the ramekins and set them on the plates. Put a scoop of ice cream in each basket. Add a spoonful of compote on the side of the plate. Top each scoop of ice cream with a sprig of mint.

CRANBERRY AND CLEMENTINE CRUMBLE
WITH STEM GINGER ICE CREAM

SERVES 4
250g cranberries
grated zest and juice of 8 clementines
150g caster sugar
100g preserving sugar with pectin added
12 clementine segments, all skin and
    pith removed
icing sugar for dusting
chopped dried cranberries and pistachios
    for decoration

LEMON CURD CREAM
100g caster sugar
125ml lemon juice
3 large egg yolks
50g unsalted butter, diced
125ml double cream

ICE CREAM
400ml double cream
200ml full-fat milk
1 vanilla pod, split lengthways
150g stem ginger with its syrup, grated
100g caster sugar
3 large egg yolks

CRUMBLE
75g ground almonds
75g plain flour
50g large jumbo oats
50g chopped walnuts
50g stem ginger with its syrup, grated
125g clear honey
75g unsalted butter, melted

1 First make the lemon curd cream. In a heatproof bowl, whisk the sugar, lemon juice and egg yolks until combined. Set the bowl over a pan of gently simmering water and whisk to the thick ribbon stage. Take the bowl off the pan and whisk in the butter a little at a time. Leave the lemon curd to cool, then chill for about 30 minutes. Whip the cream to the ribbon stage. Fold into the lemon curd and keep in the fridge.

2 Mix the cranberries in a large heavy pan with half the clementine zest and juice. Add both types of sugar and 50ml water, and stir over a very low heat until the sugar has dissolved. Cook very gently, stirring once or twice, for 40–45 minutes or until the consistency of jam. Leave to cool.

3 For the ice cream, bring the cream and milk to the boil in a heavy pan with the vanilla pod, half the ginger and syrup, and half the sugar. Put the egg yolks in a bowl with the remaining sugar and beat to the thick ribbon stage. Strain the hot liquid into the egg yolk mixture, whisking continuously, then pour back into the pan and cook over a low heat for 5 minutes, stirring all the time, until the custard is thick enough to coat the back of a spoon. Leave to cool, then churn in an ice cream machine, adding the remaining ginger and syrup just before the ice cream is ready. Continue churning until the ice cream has thickened, then decant into a clean container and place in the freezer.

4 Preheat the oven to 160°C/gas 3.

5 To make the crumble, combine all the dry ingredients, then mix in the ginger and syrup, honey and melted butter. Spread the mixture out as flat as possible on a baking tray. Bake for 20–25 minutes or until light golden in colour. Scrape the hot crumble onto a cold tray (it will break into pieces), spread out flat and leave at room temperature to dry out and cool.

6 Put the remaining clementine zest and juice in a heavy pan. Reduce to a syrup, then add the clementine segments and warm through.

7 To serve, place a spoonful of cranberry jam in the bottom of each of four dessert glasses, then add a spoonful of lemon curd cream, a clementine segment and a light sprinkling of crumble. Repeat these layers twice, finishing with crumble dusted with icing sugar. Place a large quenelle of ice cream on top and sprinkle with chopped cranberries and pistachios to decorate.

ALMOND AND RASPBERRY TART
WITH CLOTTED CREAM

SERVES 6-8
500g English raspberries
25g caster sugar
clotted cream to serve

PASTRY
120g soft unsalted butter
60g icing sugar, sifted
60g caster sugar
300g plain flour, sifted
1 large egg, beaten

ALMOND CREAM
100g unsalted butter
100g icing sugar, sifted
1 large egg, beaten
25g plain flour, sifted
100g ground almonds

1 Put 200g of the raspberries in a heavy pan, sprinkle lightly with the caster sugar and 1 tbsp water, and cook over a low heat for 3–5 minutes or until the raspberries soften down. Tip into a fine sieve set over a bowl and push the purée through to remove the seeds. Cover and chill.

2 To make the pastry, soften the butter in a bowl and beat in both types of sugar until smooth and creamy. Work in half the flour, then repeat with the other half. Gradually add the egg, then turn the dough out of the bowl and knead lightly. Wrap and chill for about 30 minutes.

3 Preheat the oven to 180°C/gas 4.

4 Roll out the pastry dough on a floured surface and use to line a fluted 23cm flan ring set on a baking sheet (or a loose-bottomed tart tin), leaving a 3cm overhang. Line with greaseproof paper and fill with baking beans, then bake blind for 12–15 minutes or until the pastry is crisp and golden. Remove from the oven, take out the paper and beans, and allow the tart case to cool. Leave the oven on.

5 Muddle the remaining raspberries with the raspberry purée by mixing them gently together with a fork, then spread evenly over the bottom of the pastry case.

6 For the almond cream, cream the butter and icing sugar together until light and fluffy. Beat in the egg, then fold in the flour mixed with the almonds. Pipe the almond cream on top of the raspberries, taking it right up to the rim. Bake for about 30 minutes or until just golden, then allow to cool.

7 To serve, trim off the overhanging pastry edge and cut the tart into wedges. Serve with clotted cream.

RASPBERRY SHORTCAKE

SERVES 4

125g soft unsalted butter
40g caster sugar
1 tsp finely grated orange zest
170g plain flour
40g blanched best-quality almonds, such
   as Marcona, freshly ground (quite fine but
   still with some texture)
40g toasted white breadcrumbs
   (see note below)
250ml double cream
a great bowl of raspberries
a small bowl of caster sugar
a little icing sugar for sifting

1 Beat the butter and sugar together well until pale. Pop in the orange zest and beat very well. Add the flour, ground almonds and breadcrumbs, and mix thoroughly into a soft dough.

2 Cut a large piece of baking parchment. Place the dough at one end of the paper, then roll it in the paper to make a sausage shape roughly 5cm in diameter. Seal the sausage in the paper and chill overnight.

3 Preheat the oven to 170°C/gas 3.

4 Line a large baking sheet with baking parchment. Cut the roll of shortcake dough into 3-mm thick slices (about the thickness of a £1 coin) and lay them on the baking parchment. Bake for 12–15 minutes or until golden brown. Let cool and become crisp. Choose the 12 best shortcakes and store the rest for another time.

5 When ready to serve, whip the cream to soft peaks. Apply a comma of cream onto each plate (this helps stop the shortcake sliding around) and sit a shortcake on top. Spoon on a generous spoonful of cream and heap with a few berries, then sprinkle a little caster sugar over. Apply another wee spoonful of cream and place another shortcake on it. Repeat with more cream, a few more raspberries and another little blob of cream, then place the last shortcake on top and add a dusting of icing sugar. (If your raspberries aren't quite sweet enough, layer the shortcakes with a mix of half cream and half custard instead of all cream, adding a touch of vanilla extract and a little lemon juice to taste.)

Note: For toasted breadcrumbs, chop up 70g bread (to include crusts) and spread on a baking sheet. Bake in a preheated 150°C/gas 2 oven for 30 minutes or until lightly toasted, then process to crumbs in a food processor.

RHUBARB AND GINGER POLENTA CRUMBLE
WITH SOURED VANILLA ICE CREAM

SERVES 4
200ml ginger wine
75g light soft brown sugar
strip of pared orange zest
250g young pink rhubarb, cut
    into 2.5cm bâtons

ICE CREAM
3 medium egg yolks
85g caster sugar
250ml full-fat milk
1 vanilla pod, split lengthways
200ml double cream
100ml crème fraîche

CRUMBLE TOPPING
50g blanched almonds
60g plain flour
40g polenta (medium ground)
50g caster sugar
pinch of salt
2 drops of pure vanilla extract
75g chilled unsalted butter, chopped

1 First make the ice cream. Mix the egg yolks and sugar in a bowl and set aside. Pour the milk into a saucepan, scrape in the vanilla seeds and drop in the pods. Infuse the milk with the vanilla by warming gently. Scald the cream in another pan.
2 Add the milk and cream to the egg yolks and sugar. Pour this mixture into a clean saucepan, place over a gentle heat and stir constantly until thickened. Remove from the heat, stir in the crème fraîche and pass through a sieve. Leave to cool, then churn in an ice cream machine until thickened. Decant the ice cream into a clean container and place in the freezer.
3 For the crumble topping, toast the almonds by tossing them in a heavy pan over a medium heat. Chop finely and mix with the flour, polenta, sugar, salt and vanilla extract. Rub in the butter. Spread out the crumble on a baking tray and chill for about 30 minutes. (This will firm up the crumble so that it will be more crisp when baked.)
4 Preheat the oven to 140°C/gas 1.
5 Bake the crumble for 40 minutes. Allow to cool, then crumble into pieces with your hands. Set aside.
6 Gently heat the ginger wine with the sugar and orange zest in a large, shallow pan until the sugar has dissolved. Add the rhubarb and poach gently for 3–4 minutes or until soft. Leave the rhubarb to cool in the liquid, then drain the rhubarb really well.
7 To serve, for each crumble stand an individual metal ring (about 7.5cm in diameter and 3.5cm deep) on a plate or in a wide, rimmed bowl. Pack in pieces of rhubarb until the mould is nearly full. Add a generous sprinkling of crumble, then remove the ring. Top each serving with a spoonful of ice cream, or place it alongside.

RASPBERRY TRIFLE

SERVES 8
4 great big handfuls of raspberries
handful of slivered or flaked almonds,
    lightly toasted
icing sugar for dusting (optional)

LITTLE SPONGE CAKES
4 large organic eggs, separated
125g caster sugar, plus 2 tbsp
225g plain flour, sifted
50g unsalted butter, melted and cooled

SYLLABUB
thinly pared zest and juice of 1 lemon
1 glass of white wine
2 tbsp dry sherry, plus extra for soaking
    the sponge
60g caster sugar
300ml double cream

CUSTARD
500ml full-fat milk
5 large organic eggs
50g caster sugar

1 Start the trifle 1–2 days ahead. Preheat the oven to 170°C/gas 3. Line two baking sheets with baking parchment.

2 To make the sponge cakes, put the egg yolks and 125g caster sugar into a bowl and beat with an electric mixer until thickened and pale, and the mixture will form a ribbon trail on its surface when the beaters are lifted out.

3 In a separate bowl, whisk the egg whites until stiff. Add the remaining 2 tbsp caster sugar and whisk until stiff peaks are formed again. Fold a spoonful of the whisked egg white into the egg yolk mixture, followed by a spoonful of flour and a little of the butter. Continue like this until all the egg white, flour and butter have been added. Heap little spoonfuls of the batter onto the lined baking sheets and bake for 15–20 minutes or until firm to the touch and golden brown (you'll make about 2 dozen sponges). Let cool. (The sponges can be very happily stored for several days in an airtight tin.)

4 The syllabub should be started a day ahead. Put the lemon zest and juice into a bowl with the wine and sherry. Cover and refrigerate overnight.

5 To make the custard (preferably also a day ahead), bring the milk to the boil in a good-sized pan. Stir the eggs and sugar together in a bowl. Pour the heated milk over the egg mix, stirring all the while, then pour back into the pan. Return the pan to a low heat and cook gently, stirring, until the custard is thickened and fully cooked. Take care that the custard doesn't get too hot or it could curdle. When done, strain and put to one side.

6 Now start to layer everything up (preferably the day before serving): place half the sponges in the bottom of a handsome bowl and liberally anoint with sherry. (The leftover sponges can be frozen or stored for another time.) Once happily plumped with the good stuff, tip in heaps of raspberries (keeping a few back). Pour over the custard, then cover with cling film and refrigerate.

7 Finish the syllabub just before serving. Stir the sugar into the chilled syllabub mixture until dissolved, then discard the lemon zest. Add the cream and beat gently to mix, then with vigour until soft peaks are achieved. Heap onto the custard and tumble the remaining raspberries on top. Scatter on the almonds and dust with icing sugar if you wish. Serve immediately.

MICHAEL CAINES

POACHED PEAR
IN MULLED RED WINE
WITH GINGERBREAD ICE CREAM AND CLOTTED CREAM

SERVES 4

GINGERBREAD ICE CREAM
600ml milk
25g milk powder
250g gingerbread, broken up

POACHED PEARS
1.5 litres red wine, such as Pinot Noir
300g caster sugar
1 strip of orange zest
1 tsp Chinese five spice powder
4 ripe pears, such as William's

TO SERVE
clotted cream

1 To make the gingerbread ice cream, pour the milk into a saucepan, stir in the milk powder and bring to the boil. Pour this onto the gingerbread in a bowl and leave to soak for 30 minutes. Blitz in a blender or food processor to a fine purée. Cool, then chill. Churn in an ice cream machine until softly set. Remove from the machine and place in a container in the freezer.

2 For the poached pears, pour the red wine into a saucepan and bring to the boil. Remove from the heat. Set the wine alight and allow the flames to die down. Add the sugar, orange zest and spice, and bring back to the boil. Leave to cool.

3 Peel the pears, leaving the stalks on, and place them in the cooled red wine syrup. (If you have time, leave the pears in the red wine syrup for 8 hours before cooking, as they will take on more colour.) Bring the syrup to a slow simmer and cook the pears for about 20 minutes or until soft through to the centre. Remove the pears from the syrup and set aside.

4 Strain 1 litre of the red wine syrup through a sieve into a clean saucepan. Bring to the boil, then simmer for 30–40 minutes to reduce to a syrupy consistency.

5 To serve, cut the pears in half and remove the cores. Place the pears on plates with some of the reduced syrup and serve with a scoop of the ice cream and clotted cream.

330

TOFFEE APPLE SUNDAES

SERVES 6

CARAMEL ICE CREAM
250g caster sugar
1 vanilla pod, split lengthways
200ml double cream
8 medium egg yolks
350ml full-fat milk

BUTTERSCOTCH SAUCE
400g light soft brown sugar
1 vanilla pod, split lengthways and seeds
  scraped out
500ml double cream
140g chilled unsalted butter, diced
4 tbsp liquid glucose

APPLE COMPOTE
1kg Bramley's apples, peeled and cut
  into large segments
juice of ½ lemon
100g caster sugar

TOFFEE APPLE SLICES
350g caster sugar
2 dessert apples, cut lengthways
  into 8 thin slices

TO SERVE
500ml plain yoghurt, preferably Ann
  Forshaw's Goosnargh yoghurt

1 First make the ice cream. Put the sugar in a heavy pan and heat gently, without stirring, until melted and golden brown. Scrape the seeds from the vanilla pods into the pan. Cut the pod into small pieces and add them too. Stir gently with a wooden spoon until the caramel is a deep mahogany colour. Wait a moment longer, until you think the caramel smells slightly burnt, then stir in the cream with a long-handled wooden spoon. Take care, as the mix will bubble furiously. Lower the heat and stir quickly to quell the bubbles. Remove from the heat.

2 Beat the egg yolks in a heatproof bowl. Heat the milk in a pan, then beat into the egg yolks. Stir this into the caramel-cream mixture. Cook gently as if making a custard sauce, until just below boiling point, then strain through a fine sieve into a cold bowl. Cover the surface with cling film to prevent a skin from forming and leave to cool. When cold, churn in an ice cream maker until thickened. Decant into a clean container and place in the freezer.

3 Next make the butterscotch sauce. Put the sugar in a heavy pan and heat gently, without stirring, until melted and golden brown. Add the vanilla pod and seeds, and stir gently with a long-handled wooden spoon until you have a deep mahogany coloured caramel. Wait a moment longer, or until you think the caramel smells slightly burnt, then stir in the cream. Take care, as it will bubble furiously. Lower the heat and stir quickly to quell the bubbles. When all the cream has been incorporated, stir in the diced butter a little at a time until you have a smooth, creamy sauce, then stir in the liquid glucose. Remove from the heat and cover the surface of the sauce with cling film to prevent a skin from forming. Leave to cool, then keep in the fridge.

4 Put the apples, lemon juice and sugar for the compote in a heavy saucepan. Cover and cook over a medium heat, stirring occasionally, until the apples soften but still

retain some shape and texture. The compote should be slightly tart, not sweet. Leave the compote to cool, then chill.

5 For the toffee apple slices, line a baking sheet with baking parchment and have ready two bowls of iced water. Dissolve the sugar in 350ml water over a low heat in a heavy pan. Bring to the boil and boil until the caramel reaches the hard-crack stage (145°C on a sugar thermometer). Remove from the heat and stop the cooking by immersing the base of the pan in one of the bowls of iced water. Remove the pan immediately or the caramel will set solid. Using a fork, dip the apple slices one at a time into the caramel, then lift out and plunge into the second bowl of iced water to set the caramel. Remove and leave to set on the parchment. If the caramel sets before you've dipped all the apple slices, return the pan to a gentle heat to loosen it.

6 Chill six large 'old-fashioned' glasses or sundae coupes in the freezer until ice-cold.

7 To serve, gently reheat the butterscotch sauce. In each glass, make alternate layers of apple compote, butterscotch sauce and yoghurt. Repeat the layers, then top with ice cream and toffee apple slices.

SAT BAINS

RASPBERRY SPONGE
WITH RASPBERRIES, GOAT'S MILK ICE CREAM AND BLACK OLIVE AND HONEY

SERVES 8

RASPBERRY OIL
150ml light olive oil
50g freeze-dried raspberries

BLACK OLIVE AND HONEY TUILE
50g pitted black olives, rinsed
50ml clear honey, warmed

GOAT'S MILK ICE CREAM
500ml goat's milk
100g clean, fresh hay, well washed (optional)
5 egg yolks
40g caster sugar

SPONGE
3 organic eggs
160g golden caster sugar

125ml semi-skimmed milk
160g plain flour, sifted
20g baking powder
60g ground almonds
20 raspberries

RASPBERRY JELLY
400g raspberries
50g caster sugar
1½ gelatine leaves

TO SERVE
about 2 tbsp raspberry vinegar
raspberry jam
about 150g raspberries
lemon curd
3-4 sprigs of mint

1 The raspberry oil is best made a week ahead (freeze-dried raspberries are available in healthfood shops). Blitz the olive oil and raspberries in a blender to extract the maximum flavour, then strain through a sieve and set aside.

2 Preheat the oven to the lowest setting. Lay a non-stick mat on a baking sheet, or line the sheet with baking parchment.

3 For the black olive tuile, blend the olives and honey in a small blender to a paste, then sieve if you like, pressing all the paste through. Spread the paste very thinly on the mat or parchment. Leave in the oven to dry out for 5–6 hours. The tuile will seem slightly soft and pliable, but will become very brittle when it cools.

4 Meanwhile, make the ice cream. Heat the milk in a large pan. If using the hay, throw it in, then remove from the heat and leave to infuse at room temperature for 1 hour; strain. Whisk the egg yolks and sugar in a bowl until the mixture leaves a ribbon trail when you lift the beaters. Add the milk, whisking it in, then pour into a saucepan. Heat slowly, stirring all the time and without allowing it to boil, to 86°C (check with a digital thermometer). The custard will be smooth and thickly coat the back of a wooden spoon. Strain into a bowl and chill. When cold, churn in an ice cream machine to the soft scoop stage. Transfer to a container and freeze overnight.

5 Preheat the oven to 190°C /gas 5.

6 To make the sponge, whisk the eggs and sugar with an electric mixer until the mixture leaves a ribbon trail when you lift the beaters. With the machine running, pour in the milk, then add the combined sifted flour, baking powder and ground almonds. Slowly pour in the raspberry oil. The mixture will be like a soft batter.

7 Pour the mixture into a 20cm square cake tin that is 4cm deep (it's only necessary to line the tin if it isn't non-stick). Drop the whole raspberries all over so they softly sink into the sponge. Bake for 35–40 minutes or until firm to the touch. Cool for a few minutes in the tin, then turn out onto a wire rack to cool completely.

8 To make the raspberry jelly, tip the raspberries and sugar into a bowl, cover with cling film and set over a pan of gently simmering water. Poach the raspberries with the sugar for 20 minutes or until the raspberries have collapsed. Strain the juice through a piece of muslin into a bowl. You should have 300ml raspberry juice. Soak the gelatine in cold water, then squeeze and stir into the warm juice until melted. Leave at room temperature for about 1 hour or until softly set but still runny.

9 Cut the sponge into eight squares. Dip the sponge squares into the jelly and leave for a few minutes to absorb it, then set the sponge on a tray. Chill for 2 hours.

10 To serve, sit the cake squares on serving plates. Drizzle all over with the raspberry vinegar (or spray on using an atomiser), then lightly spread a little raspberry jam on the tops. Fill half of the raspberries with raspberry jam and half with lemon curd, then equally dot the raspberries around each plate. Tear up the sprigs of mint and scatter them over. Add quenelles of the ice cream on the side. To finish, crack the tuile sheet into pieces and lay them on top of the ice cream.

334

PERRY JELLY
AND SUMMER FRUITS
WITH ELDERFLOWER ICE CREAM

SERVES 4
4 large gelatine leaves
500ml perry (sparkling pear cider)
75g caster sugar
125g mixed berries, such as blueberries,
   raspberries and wild strawberries

ELDERFLOWER ICE CREAM
300ml full-fat milk, preferably
   Channel Island milk
6 medium egg yolks
100g caster sugar
300ml Jersey or clotted cream, or
   a mixture of the two
200ml elderflower cordial

1 First make the ice cream. Bring the milk to the boil in a heavy saucepan, then remove from the heat. Whisk the egg yolks and sugar together in a bowl, pour in the milk and whisk well. Return to the pan and cook over a low heat for about 5 minutes, stirring constantly with a whisk. Do not boil. Remove from the heat and whisk in the cream and elderflower cordial. Leave to cool, then churn in an ice cream machine until thickened. Decant into a clean container and place in the freezer.

2 To make the perry jelly, immerse the gelatine leaves one at a time in a shallow bowl of cold water and leave for a minute or so until soft. Bring 100ml of the perry to the boil in a medium saucepan, add the sugar and stir until dissolved. Drain and squeeze the gelatine leaves, then add to the hot perry and stir until melted. Remove from the heat, add the rest of the perry and stir well. Put the pan of jelly somewhere cool, but do not let it set.

3 Divide half the berries among four individual savarin moulds or individual jelly moulds, or use one large mould. Pour in half the cooled jelly. Chill for an hour or so to set, then top up with the rest of the berries and unset jelly. (This ensures the berries stay suspended and don't float to the top.) Return to the fridge to set.

4 To serve, turn the jellies out onto individual plates and sit a ball of elderflower ice cream in the middle of each one.

EARL GREY TEA CREAM
AND ECCLES CAKES

SERVES 6

ECCLES CAKES
225g plain flour
pinch of salt
160g chilled unsalted butter, plus 25g
    soft unsalted butter
100g caster sugar
200g currants
50g chopped candied peel
freshly grated nutmeg
milk and granulated sugar, to finish

EARL GREY TEA CREAM
95g egg yolks, from 5–6 large eggs
80g caster sugar
260ml full-fat milk
260ml double or whipping cream
7 Earl Grey tea bags

MILK FOAM
600ml full-fat milk
100ml condensed milk
100ml whipping cream

1 First make the pastry for the Eccles cakes. Sift the flour and salt into a bowl. Dice half the chilled butter and rub into the flour, then add just enough cold water (about 4–5 tbsp) to bring everything together into a soft dough. Cover the bowl with cling film and chill for 30 minutes.

2 On a lightly floured surface, roll out the dough into a rectangle measuring about 20 x 10cm. Cut the remaining chilled butter into thin slices. Cover the middle third of the dough with one-third of the butter slices, then fold the unbuttered thirds of dough over the buttered third, first one and then the other, making a square. Wrap and refrigerate for 15 minutes.

3 Repeat step 2 twice more, turning the block of dough 90° each time, and chilling between each rolling. Repeat two more times, but without any butter, then chill again for at least 30 minutes.

4 Make the Earl Grey tea creams while the pastry is chilling. Preheat the oven to 150°C/gas 2. Set six shallow 150ml teacups or ramekins in a roasting tin.

5 Whisk the egg yolks and half the sugar in a large bowl. Put the milk, cream and tea bags in a heavy saucepan with the remaining sugar and bring just to the boil over a medium-high heat, stirring occasionally. Immediately the liquid reaches the boil, strain it slowly through a fine sieve over the egg yolks and sugar. (Don't let the liquid boil or leave the bags to steep, or the creams will taste like stewed tea.) Whisk well until evenly combined, then strain the mixture slowly through the sieve into a large measuring jug. Skim to remove any foamy bubbles.

6 Pour the mixture slowly into the cups so that each one is two-thirds full. Skim off any more bubbles. Pour hot water into the roasting tin to come halfway up the sides of the cups. Bake for 25–30 minutes. The creams should be only just set, with a slight wobble in the centre. Remove the cups from the water and leave to cool, then cover and refrigerate for at least 4 hours or overnight.

7 Boil the milk for the foam until reduced to 200ml. Pour into a bowl and leave until cold. Whisk the reduced milk with the condensed milk and cream, then pour into the siphon (see note below). Charge the siphon with two cartridges and release a little gas, then shake well. Keep the siphon in a bowl of iced water until ready to use.

8 Finish making the Eccles cakes about an hour or so before serving, because they are best served warm. Preheat the oven to 240°C/gas 8. Line a baking tray with baking parchment,

9 For the filling, cream together the 25g soft butter and the caster sugar, then add the currants, candied peel and nutmeg. Roll out the pastry on a lightly floured surface until 4mm thick. Cut out twelve 7cm discs. Spoon a little of the filling in the centre of each disc. Brush the edges with a little water, then pull the edges into the centre and pinch them together to seal.

10 Turn the cakes over, place on the prepared tray and push down lightly with the palm of your hand to flatten a little. With a small sharp knife, make three short incisions in the top of each cake. Brush with a little milk and sprinkle liberally with granulated sugar. Bake for 10–12 minutes or until the edges have turned golden brown. Remove from the oven and leave to cool for a few minutes.

11 To serve, cover the top of each Earl Grey tea cream with milk foam, and place a warm Eccles cake on the saucer.

Note: You need a whipped cream dispenser (an iSi siphon) and two N_2O cartridges.

338

MUSCOVADO AND HAZELNUT TART
WITH YOGHURT SORBET

SERVES 6-8
150g dark muscovado sugar
120g plain flour, sifted
50g soft salted butter
100g whole hazelnuts, toasted
1 large egg
½ tsp baking powder
150g soured cream

YOGHURT SORBET
50g caster sugar
500ml good-quality plain yoghurt
juice of ½ lemon, strained

TO FINISH
1 tbsp dark muscovado sugar
1 tbsp whole hazelnuts, toasted

1 To make the yoghurt sorbet, add the sugar to 120ml boiling water in a small pan and bring back to the boil, stirring to dissolve the sugar. Boil for a few seconds, then remove from the heat and leave to cool.

2 When the sugar syrup is cold, mix into the yoghurt with the lemon juice. Taste and adjust with more lemon juice, if necessary. Churn in an ice cream machine for about 15 minutes or until softly set, then transfer to a container and freeze.

3 Preheat the oven to 200°C/gas 6.

4 To make the tart, put the sugar, flour, butter and nuts in a food processor and blitz to a coarse breadcrumb texture. Remove half the mixture from the food processor and spread it over the bottom of a 20cm round non-stick tin that is 5cm deep (not loose-bottomed). Pat the mixture down gently with the back of a spoon as you would for a cheesecake base, without pressing too firmly.

5 Tip the other half of the mixture into a bowl. Add the egg, baking powder and soured cream, and beat to a batter. Pour this over the crumb base. Scatter over the 1 tbsp muscovado. Bake for about 25 minutes or until just firm. To check if done, push a skewer into the centre; it should come out clean.

6 Use a Microplane grater to shave the toasted hazelnuts into fine powdery shavings. Serve the tart at room temperature in wedges, with the hazelnut shavings scattered over and with a spoonful of yoghurt sorbet at the side.

340

CRANACHAN
WITH OATMEAL PRALINE

SERVES 8
3 large free-range egg yolks
25g caster sugar
35g clear honey (2½ tbsp)
5 tbsp whisky
150g crème fraîche
100g mascarpone cheese
2/3 long gelatine leaf
2 tsp lemon juice
raspberries to serve

OATMEAL PRALINE
100g caster sugar
50g pinhead oatmeal

JELLY
250g raspberries
3 tbsp caster sugar
4 tsp lemon juice
2/3 long gelatine leaf

1 First make the oatmeal praline. Line a baking sheet with baking parchment. Place a frying pan over a medium heat and sprinkle in the sugar. Allow the sugar to melt without stirring, then turn up the heat. As the sugar begins to caramelise, mix in the oats and stir. Carefully tip the contents onto the lined baking sheet and leave to cool completely. Once cold, break into pieces with a rolling pin, and grind in a pestle and mortar to a coarse powder. (This can be done ahead. If you don't use all the praline, it can be stored in an airtight container for future use.)

2 To make the jelly, set a medium-sized heavy pan over a gentle heat and add the raspberries, sugar, lemon juice and 6 tbsp water. Bring to the boil and simmer for 3 minutes or until the raspberries have softened. Meanwhile, soften the gelatine in a small bowl of cold water.

3 Remove the pan from the heat and rub the raspberry mixture through a fine sieve into a clean pan, to remove the seeds. You should get about 200ml of raspberry purée. Gently reheat the purée, then remove from the heat. Drain and squeeze the gelatine, add to the hot raspberry purée and stir until the gelatine has melted. Leave to set to a very soft jelly.

4 Put the egg yolks and sugar in a large heatproof bowl and whisk to combine. Mix in the honey and 3 tbsp of the whisky. Set the bowl over a pan of simmering water and beat with an electric mixer for 5–6 minutes or until the mixture starts to thicken – when you lift the beaters out of the mixture in a circular motion, you should be left with a distinct trail on the surface. (If you have a thermometer, the mix should be at 80°C.) When ready, take the bowl off the pan and allow to cool.

5 In another bowl mix the crème fraîche and mascarpone together. Soak the gelatine as before. Gently warm the remaining whisky in a small pan (don't allow it to get too hot). Lift the gelatine from the soaking water, squeeze it gently and add to the whisky. The gelatine should melt almost at once. Fold the whisky into the mascarpone mixture, then add the cooled egg yolk mixture and the lemon juice. Carefully fold the whole lot together. Cover and keep in the fridge.

5 To serve, add a handful of raspberries to the softly set jelly. Put a couple of spoonfuls of jelly in the bottom of eight dessert glasses. Add a couple of spoonfuls of mousse on top, then sprinkle with some oatmeal praline. Add more jelly, then more mousse and another sprinkling of praline. Finish with a few raspberries.

MATT TEBBUTT

MONMOUTH PUDDING

SERVES 4
90g fresh breadcrumbs
light soft brown sugar
450ml full-fat milk
grated zest of 1 lemon
25g unsalted butter
4 tbsp caster sugar

3 large eggs, separated
100g fresh seasonal soft fruit, such
as raspberries, strawberries, cooked
gooseberries, blackcurrants and
redcurrants, or your favourite
home-made jam

1 Preheat the grill to hot.

2 Spread the breadcrumbs on a baking tray and sprinkle with a little brown sugar. Put the tray under the grill and toast the breadcrumbs for a few minutes, turning them frequently. Remove and set aside.

3 Put the milk in a medium saucepan with the lemon zest, butter and 1 tbsp of the caster sugar. Bring to a simmer. Stir in the toasted breadcrumbs. Leave to stand off the heat for 30 minutes.

4 Preheat the oven to 200°C/gas 6.

5 Stir the egg yolks into the milk and breadcrumb mixture. Pour into a 900ml baking dish and scatter over the soft fruit or spread jam on top.

6 Whisk the egg whites until they form firm peaks. Fold in the remaining caster sugar, and whisk until stiff again. Spoon the meringue over the fruit to cover it completely. Bake for 10–15 minutes or until the meringue is lightly golden. Serve the pudding warm, straight from the dish.

342

COX'S APPLE TART

SERVES 4
250g puff pastry, thawed overnight in
    the fridge if frozen
6 Cox's apples
squeeze of lemon juice
caster sugar for sprinkling
vanilla ice cream or clotted cream
    to serve

APPLE COMPOTE
80g unsalted butter
600g Granny Smith apples, peeled
    and chopped
80g caster sugar
1 vanilla pod, split lengthways

VANILLA BUTTER
1 vanilla pod, split lengthways
100g soft unsalted butter

1 To make the apple compote, melt the butter in a stainless steel saucepan. Add the apples and sugar. Scrape the seeds from the vanilla pod into the mixture, then drop in the pod. Cook on a moderate heat for about 20 minutes to make a thick compote, stirring from time to time. If the texture is too runny, leave to cook a little longer.

2 Remove the vanilla pod, then put the apple compote into a blender and blend to a fine pulp. Rub through a fine sieve into a container and set aside.

3 Roll out the pastry on a lightly floured surface to a 50 x 14cm rectangle. Using a 12cm cutter (or by cutting around a plate), cut out four discs. Place the discs on a baking tray and let rest in the fridge for 10 minutes.

4 To make the vanilla butter, scrape the seeds from the vanilla pod and mix them with the soft butter. Set aside.

5 Preheat the oven to 220°C/ gas 7.

6 Peel the Cox's apples. Slice off four even-sized apple circles, brush these with lemon juice and set aside. Core the apples, then cut them in half lengthways and slice each half thinly.

7 Remove the pastry discs from the fridge and prick them all over with a fork. Spoon some apple compote into the middle of each pastry disc, then fan the apple slices on top so they overlap tightly over the compote and pastry, starting from the middle like the spokes of a wheel. Finish by placing the reserved apple circles in the middle of each tart to cover the centre.

8 Lightly brush the apple slices with some of the vanilla butter, then sprinkle with a little caster sugar. Bake for 10 minutes, then remove and brush with more of the vanilla butter. Bake for a further 8–10 minutes or until the apples are golden. Remove from the oven and leave to rest for 10 minutes.

9 Serve the tarts with vanilla ice cream or clotted cream. (The tarts can be made and baked in advance and eaten cold, or reheated to serve hot.)

CUSTARD TART
WITH GARIBALDI BISCUITS

SERVES 4

GARIBALDI BISCUITS
100g butter, melted
100g icing sugar, sifted
100g plain flour
100g egg whites
200g currants

PASTRY
225g plain flour
pinch of salt
grated zest of 1 lemon
150g butter
75g caster sugar
1 egg yolk and 1 whole egg,
    beaten together

CUSTARD FILLING
9 free range egg yolks
75g caster sugar
500ml whipping cream
freshly grated nutmeg

1 First, make the garibaldi biscuits. Mix together the butter, icing sugar and flour using a wooden spoon until the mixture is smooth. Slowly add the egg whites, stirring, until they are completely incorporated, then fold in the currants. Bring together into a ball, wrap in cling film and chill for at least 1 hour.

2 Roll out the dough on a lightly floured surface to 5mm thick. Cut into 3 x 7cm rectangles with a small sharp knife. Place on a baking tray lined with greaseproof paper, ensuring the biscuits are not touching each other. Put the tray into the fridge to rest for 30 minutes.

3 Preheat the oven to 180°C/gas 4. Bake the biscuits for 8–10 minutes or until golden brown. Remove and cool on a wire rack. Keep in an airtight tin.

4 To make the pastry, rub together the flour, salt, lemon zest and butter until the mixture resembles breadcrumbs. Add the sugar, then slowly add the eggs, mixing until the pastry forms a ball. Wrap tightly in cling film and refrigerate for 2 hours.

5 Preheat the oven to 170°C/gas 3.

6 Roll out the pastry on a lightly floured surface to 2mm thickness. Use to line an 18cm flan ring placed on a baking sheet. Line with greaseproof paper and fill with baking beans, then bake blind for about 10 minutes or until starting to turn golden brown. Remove the paper and beans and cool. Turn the oven down to 130°C/gas 1/2.

7 For the filling, whisk together the yolks and sugar. Add the cream and mix well. Pass the mixture through a fine sieve into a saucepan and warm to tepid.

8 Fill the pastry case with the custard, to within 5mm of the top. Carefully place in the middle of the oven and bake for 30–40 minutes or until the custard appears set but not too firm. Remove from the oven and cover the surface liberally with grated nutmeg. Allow to cool to room temperature.

9 Before serving, warm the biscuits through in the oven for 5 minutes. Cut the tart with a sharp knife and serve with the biscuits.

TOST WY OF BARA BRITH
WITH BAKED PLUMS AND
YOGHURT ICE CREAM

SERVES 4
9 plums, halved and stoned
1 tbsp honey
sprig of lemon thyme
1 vanilla pod, split lengthways

YOGHURT ICE CREAM
150ml milk
60g sugar
6 egg yolks
250g fresh plain yoghurt

PEPPER TUILES
150g unsalted butter
250g caster sugar
200ml canned coconut milk
1 tbsp cracked black pepper
100g plain flour

TOST WY
3 eggs
3 tbsp milk
4 slices of Bara Brith, cut 1cm thick,
  crusts removed
unsalted butter

1 First make the yoghurt ice cream. Combine the milk and sugar in a pan and bring to the boil. Pour the hot liquid onto the egg yolks and whisk. Return to the pan and put back on to the heat to thicken. When the custard coats the back of a spoon remove from the heat and leave to cool. When cold add the yoghurt and mix well. Churn in an ice cream machine, then keep in the freezer until needed.
2 Next make the pepper tuiles. Whisk together the butter, sugar and coconut milk until smooth, then mix in the pepper. Fold in the flour. Chill for 1 hour.
3 Preheat the oven to 180°C/gas 4.
4 Spread the tuile mixture very thinly (2–3mm) over a non-stick baking sheet. Bake for 8–10 minutes or until golden. Leave to cool on the sheet. When cold, remove and break into mouth-size pieces. (This will make more tuiles than you need for this recipe, but they will keep for a week.)
5 Create a foil envelope and in it place the plums, honey, lemon thyme and vanilla pod. Seal the package so it is airtight, then place on a baking tray in the oven and bake for 10–12 minutes. Remove from the oven, but do not open the bag, to ensure the contents keep warm.
6 To make the tost wy, whisk together the eggs and milk in a wide, shallow dish. Place the slices of Bara Brith in the mixture, turning them to coat, then fry them in a little bit of unsalted butter in a non-stick pan until the egg mixture has cooked and both sides are golden brown.
7 To serve, place a slice of tost wy on each plate and position some of the warm plums on top. Drizzle some of the plum juice over the plate. Place a scoop of yoghurt ice cream to the side and put some tuiles on it.

346

PASSION FRUIT BHAPA DOI
WITH DARK CHOCOLATE MOUSSE AND PISTACHIO KULFI

SERVES 4

PISTACHIO KULFI
200ml milk
good pinch of ground cardamom
40g granulated sugar
30g pistachio nuts, lightly toasted and ground
2–3 drops screwpine flower essence

BHAPA DOI
150ml condensed milk
200g plain Greek yoghurt
30ml passion fruit purée (sieved pulp)
2 passion fruits, cut in half and pulp
   scooped out
raspberry coulis
raspberries

DARK CHOCOLATE MOUSSE
125g dark chocolate (55% cocoa)
60g egg yolks
280ml double cream
30g ground pistachio nuts
20ml Cointreau or other orange liqueur

PASSION FRUIT CHUTNEY
200ml passion fruit purée (sieved pulp)
60g palm sugar
3⁄4 tsp crushed red chillies
1 tsp salt
1⁄4 tsp cornflour mixed with water
1⁄2 tsp lime juice

1 First make the pistachio kulfi. Put the milk and cardamom in a heavy-bottomed saucepan and bring to the boil, then turn down the heat. Reduce the milk, stirring constantly, until it is about one-third of the original quantity and has a granular consistency. Remove from the heat, add the sugar and toasted nuts and mix well. Return to a low heat and stir until the sugar has dissolved. Allow the mixture to cool, then stir in the essence. Chill in the refrigerator.

2 Churn in an ice cream machine for 30–45 minutes or until softly set (this will produce a good texture), then spoon into two 8cm conical moulds (or four smaller moulds) and freeze until firm. Alternatively, just spoon the mixture into conical moulds and freeze it.

3 Preheat the oven to 140°C/gas 1.

4 Next make the bhapa doi. Whisk the condensed milk and yoghurt with the passion fruit purée, mixing well. Line four ramekins with muffin papers and spoon some passion fruit pulp into each. Pour in the yoghurt mixture.

5 Set the ramekins in a baking tray and pour enough hot water into the tray to come one-quarter of the way up the sides of the ramekins. Place the tray in the oven and bake for 30–40 minutes. Remove the ramekins from the tray and allow to cool, then place in the refrigerator to chill.

6 To make the mousse, melt the chocolate in a heatproof bowl set over a pan of simmering water. Remove the bowl and stir the chocolate until smooth, then set

aside. Set another bowl with the egg yolks on the pan of hot water and whisk to a ribbon consistency. Remove from the pan of hot water.

7 Whip the double cream to soft peaks, then fold in the melted chocolate and whisked egg yolks. Mix in the ground pistachios and liqueur. Leave to set in the refrigerator for 2–3 hours.

8 For the passion fruit chutney, heat together the passion fruit purée, sugar, chilli flakes and salt. Reduce to three-quarters of the original quantity. Add the cornflour and stir until thickened. Remove from the heat and allow to cool, then add the lime juice. Chill before serving.

9 To serve, turn out the bhapa doi on to four square plates and peel off the muffin papers. Turn out a kulfi (or half of a larger kulfi) alongside and add a large quenelle or ball of mousse. Drizzle with raspberry coulis and passion fruit chutney. Finish each plate with 3–5 raspberries on the bhapa doi.

TIVERTON
STRAWBERRY SHORTCAKE
WITH BASIL CARAMEL

SERVES 6

SHORTBREAD
55g unsalted butter
45g icing sugar, sifted, plus extra for rolling
20g basil leaves, chopped
½ egg, beaten
100g plain flour
¾ tsp baking powder

BASIL AND LEMON MOUSSE
150g caster sugar
15g basil leaves, chopped
375ml double or whipping cream
1½ gelatine leaves, soaked in cold water
   for at least 10 minutes
juice of 2½ lemons

BASIL CARAMEL
100g glucose
150g fondant
handful of basil leaves

GARNISH
400g small strawberries
50ml strawberry coulis
10g icing sugar

1 First make the shortbread. Beat the butter with the icing sugar using an electric mixer until pale in colour. Add the basil and egg and mix well, then gradually add the flour and baking powder. When ready, the mixture will pull away from the sides of the bowl. Remove and chill for 2 hours before using.

2 Preheat the oven to 180°C/gas 4. Roll out the shortbread dough on a sugared surface to about 5mm thick. Cut out six oblong-shaped pieces, each 10cm long and 5cm wide. Place on greaseproof paper-lined baking trays and bake for 6–8 minutes or until golden brown. Remove from the oven. You may need to trim the edges to straighten the sides and make them equal, mainly for presentation. Leave to cool completely and reserve until needed.

3 Next make the mousse. Mix 50g of the sugar with 5 tbsp water in a pan. Bring to the boil and simmer for 10 minutes. Remove from the heat and add the basil. Cover with cling film and leave to cool.

4 Whip the cream until starting to thicken. Add the remaining sugar, then whip until thick but not stiff.

5 Gently squeeze the gelatine leaves dry, then melt in a little of the warmed basil stock. Add to the rest of the basil stock together with the whipped cream and lemon juice, mixing well. Pour into six oblong metal moulds, each 10cm long, 5cm wide and 5cm deep. Place in the freezer to set.

6 Make the basil caramel by heating the glucose and fondant to 168°C (a clear caramel). Add the basil, then pour on to two greaseproof paper-lined baking trays. When the caramel is completely cold and set, blitz to a fine powder in a food processor. Pass through a sieve, then spread out evenly on two baking trays. Re-cook the basil caramel in a 200°C/gas 6 oven until it melts together to form a thin, glass-like sheet. Leave to cool. Once cool break into irregular shapes.

7 To serve, place a shortbread biscuit in the centre of each of six plates. Turn out a mousse on to each biscuit. Glaze the strawberries by rolling them gently in the coulis and icing sugar, then arrange attractively on each mousse. Carefully place the basil caramel around to enclose the mousse and give an effect of stained glass.

Though Scottish shortbread is the most famous variety, there are many regional variations on this light, rich and crisp biscuit. Summer makes a welcome appearance when shortbread is combined with the strawberries for which Devon is renowned.

LEMON MERINGUE PIE

SERVES 6

SWEET PASTRY
140g plain flour
60g chilled butter, diced
30g caster sugar
1 egg yolk

LEMON CURD
1 tbsp cornflour
finely grated zest and juice of
    2 medium lemons

150g butter
120g caster sugar
3 egg yolks
1 egg

MERINGUE
3 egg whites
90g caster sugar

1 Prepare the sweet pastry by rubbing together the flour, butter and sugar until the mixture looks like fine breadcrumbs. Mix in the egg yolk, then slowly add enough cold water to make a smooth dough. Wrap the dough and chill for about 30 minutes.
2 Preheat the oven to 190°C/gas 5.
3 Roll out the pastry dough on a lightly floured surface so it is big enough to line a 23cm flan ring or loose-bottomed flan tin that is 2.5cm deep. Place the ring or tin on a baking sheet and line with the pastry. Trim the edges. Line the pastry case with a piece of greaseproof paper, then tip in some dried baking beans. Bake blind for 15 minutes or until the pastry is cooked and the edges are lightly coloured, removing the paper and beans for the last few minutes of baking.
4 Reduce the oven to 160°C/gas 3.
5 To make the lemon curd, blend the cornflour with the lemon juice. Melt the butter in a saucepan. Add the lemon zest and sugar, and bring to the boil. Whisk in the cornflour mixture and cook, stirring, for 1–2 minutes to cook the cornflour. Remove from the heat and allow the mixture to cool slightly. Beat in the egg yolks and the whole egg. Return the pan to a very low heat to thicken the curd, stirring occasionally – if the heat is too high the eggs will scramble. Spoon the lemon curd into the pastry case while it is still warm, then leave to cool while you make the meringue.
6 Whisk the egg whites in a very clean bowl. Just before they reach soft peak stage, gradually add the caster sugar, whisking between each addition, and whisk until soft peaks are formed.
7 Spoon the meringue over the cooled lemon curd, making sure you completely cover the surface. Bake for 20–30 minutes or until the meringue is set and slightly coloured. Serve the pie warm.

CARAMELISED
VANILLA EGG CUSTARD
WITH MARINATED DEVON SUMMER
FRUITS AND A MINT BROTH

SERVES 4
5 egg yolks
50g caster sugar
850ml milk
3 vanilla pods, split lengthways
500ml whipping cream
Demerara sugar

MARINATED SUMMER FRUITS
100g each strawberries, raspberries,
    redcurrants, blackcurrants and
    blackberries
caster sugar
chopped mint

MINT BROTH
300ml milk
30ml crème de menthe

1 First make the custard mixture. Cream the egg yolks with the sugar. Pour the milk into a saucepan and scrape in the seeds from the vanilla pods; add the pods too. Bring just to the boil. Add the hot milk to the creamed eggs and sugar, stirring. Then add the cold cream. Pour into a bowl, cover and leave in the refrigerator for 12 hours to infuse. Then lift out the vanilla pods.

2 Preheat the oven to 100°C/gas low. Warm four 6 x 4cm metal rings, then wrap a double layer of cling film around the bottom half. Place the rings in a baking tray and fill them three-quarters full with the custard. Pour hot water into the tray around the rings (no higher than the cling film). Cook in the oven for 45 minutes or until the custard has set. Remove from the oven and leave to cool.

3 For the marinated fruits, remove the stalks and hulls from the fruits and cut the strawberries into four. Rinse the fruit in cold water and drain well in a colander. Put 100g of the fruit in a mixing bowl and, using a fork, mash well with some caster sugar. Add the rest of the fruit and some freshly chopped mint and leave to stand for 5 minutes. Taste and add a little more sugar if the fruit is too sharp.

4 While the fruit is marinating, put the milk and crème de menthe in a small saucepan and warm to 80°C.

5 Sprinkle the top of the custards with a thin, even layer of Demerara sugar. Peel off the cling film from the bottoms, then place a custard on each plate and remove the ring. Quickly melt and caramelise the sugar using a blow torch.

6 Dress the marinated fruit on the plates around the custards. Froth the mint broth using a hand blender to create a cappuccino effect, then spoon over the fruit and around the plate. Serve immediately.

RED FRUIT SOUP
WITH ROSEMARY SYRUP
AND LEMON MADELEINE

SERVES 4
600g red fruits (strawberries, raspberries, redcurrants)
50g icing sugar, sifted
25ml crème de framboise

ROSEMARY SYRUP
50g brown sugar
75g clear honey
200g white wine
25g powdered pectin
1 tsp chopped rosemary

LEMON MADELEINES
125g egg yolks
100g caster sugar
grated zest of 1 lemon
100g plain flour
5g baking powder
125g butter, melted

1 Mix together the red fruits, icing sugar and framboise. Cover with cling film and leave to macerate for at least 3 hours, to extract as much juice and flavour as possible.
2 For the rosemary syrup combine all the ingredients with 150ml water in a saucepan and bring to the boil. Skim off any scum and reduce by half. Pour into a bowl, then allow to cool. Chill to set to a jelly.
3 Next make the mixture for the madeleines. Beat the egg yolks and sugar together until pale in colour. Add the lemon zest. Gradually add the flour and baking powder and mix well. Slowly add the melted butter, mixing until incorporated. Leave to rest for 30 minutes.
4 Meanwhile, blitz the red fruits in a blender or food processor. Pass through a sieve and check the soup for sweetness; it may need a little extra icing sugar. Reserve.
5 Preheat the oven to 190°C/gas 5.
6 Spoon the madeleine mixture into a large madeleine tin with eight depressions. Bake for 10 minutes or until lightly golden. Remove from the oven and keep warm.
7 To serve, ladle the soup into four chilled soup bowls. Place a spoonful of the rosemary jelly in the centre of each bowl and serve the madeleines on a side plate.

BUTTERMILK CREAM
WITH RHUBARB AND ROSE PETALS

SERVES 8

600ml double cream
2 vanilla pods, split lengthways
200ml condensed milk
4 gelatine leaves, soaked in cold water
  for at least 10 minutes
700ml buttermilk, at room temperature

CRYSTALLISED ROSE PETALS

30 organic rose petals
3 pasteurised egg whites, lightly whisked
sifted caster sugar

HAZELNUT SHORTBREAD

300g plain flour
100g caster sugar
75g hazelnuts, toasted and ground
225g unsalted butter, chilled and diced

RHUBARB

500g tender young rhubarb
200g sugar
200ml grenadine syrup
3 tbsp rose water

1 First prepare the crystallised rose petals. Brush the petals lightly with the egg white, then dust generously with sugar. Place on a tray and allow to dry overnight.

2 Next make the hazelnut shortbread. Place all the ingredients in a chilled food processor and process until it just comes together. (Over-processing will cause the butter to start to melt.) Tip out on to a clean work surface and, using the heel of your hand, quickly press together to make sure that all the ingredients are well mixed. Pat into a round, wrap tightly in cling film and chill for at least 1 hour.

3 Roll out the chilled dough to a round or rectangle just under 1cm thick. If round, cut into pie-shaped wedges; if a rectangle, cut into squares or other shapes as desired. Transfer to a baking sheet and chill again for at least 30 minutes.

4 Preheat the oven to 150°C/gas 2. Bake the shortbread for 25–30 minutes. Allow to cool and set slightly before removing to a wire rack to finish cooling.

5 For the buttermilk creams, heat the double cream with the split vanilla pods. As soon as it comes to the boil, remove from the heat and add the condensed milk. Gently squeeze dry the gelatine leaves, add to the hot cream and stir until melted.

6 When the cream mixture has cooled to near body temperature add the buttermilk. Strain through a fine sieve. Scrape the seeds from the vanilla pods and stir into the cream mixture. Carefully pour into eight 8–10cm ramekins or other moulds. Allow to set in the fridge for at least 4 hours.

7 Cut the rhubarb on a sharp angle into 2mm slices. In a wide pan, bring the sugar, 400ml water, grenadine syrup and rose water to the boil. Add the rhubarb and cook gently at a simmer for 2–3 minutes. Remove from the heat and allow to cool.

8 To serve, dip the moulds into hot water for a few seconds, then gently turn out a buttermilk cream on to the centre of each cold plate. Surround with a spoonful of rhubarb and its gorgeous sauce. Place two or three rose petals on top of the buttermilk cream and serve with the hazelnut shortbread.

STICKY TOFFEE
BREAD AND BUTTER PUDDING

SERVES 6

200g stoned Medjool dates
½ tsp bicarbonate of soda
6 slices of white bread, crusts off
75g softened butter
3 whole eggs
3 egg yolks
1 vanilla pod, split lengthways
75g caster sugar
500ml double cream
Demerara sugar
pouring cream to serve

SAUCE

100g butter
100g golden syrup
100g soft dark brown sugar
100ml double cream
100g stoned Medjool dates, finely
    chopped (optional)

1 Place the dates and bicarbonate of soda in a saucepan and just cover with water. Simmer gently until the dates break down.

2 Butter the bread, then cut each slice in half to make triangles or cut out rounds. Alternately layer the bread and dates in four buttered 150ml ramekins or a buttered 25 x 20cm baking dish, starting and finishing with a layer of bread.

3 Beat together the whole eggs, yolks, seeds scraped from the vanilla pod and caster sugar in a bowl. Heat the cream to scalding point, then pour on to the egg mixture, mixing well. Pour over the bread and dates. Leave to soak for at least 20 minutes.

4 Preheat the oven to 175°C/gas 4.

5 Set the ramekins or baking dish in a roasting tray of water. Bake for 16 minutes for the ramekins or 25 minutes for the large dish or until the custard has set.

6 To make the sauce, simply combine the butter, syrup and sugar in a saucepan and bring to the boil. When it's all smooth and dissolved, remove from the heat and stir in the cream and optional dates. Keep warm.

7 Sprinkle the top of the pudding evenly with Demerara sugar and caramelise under the grill. Serve a good portion of pudding with the sauce and pouring cream.

358

STRAWBERRY CHAMPAGNE TRIFLE

SERVES 4

3–4 punnets of early season English
   strawberries
100–150ml double cream, whipped
   to a soft peak, to serve

SPONGE BASE

3 eggs
100g caster sugar
1 tsp honey
125g plain flour, sifted
2 tsp baking powder
125g butter, melted and cooled
strawberry jam

CHAMPAGNE JELLY

175g sugar
300ml Champagne or sparkling wine
strip of lemon zest
strip of orange zest
5 gelatine leaves, soaked in cold water
   for at least 10 minutes

VANILLA CUSTARD

100g custard powder
1.2 litres milk
3 vanilla pods, split lengthways,
   or 1 tbsp vanilla essence
50g caster sugar

1 Preheat the oven to 180°C/gas 4.

2 First make the sponge base. In an electric mixer, whisk together the eggs, sugar and honey to a thick creamy consistency. Gently fold in the flour and baking powder, followed by the melted butter. Divide the mixture between two greased 18–20cm sponge tins lined with baking parchment, spreading evenly. Bake for 6–8 minutes or until firm with a spongy finish. Remove from the oven and leave to cool.

3 Once cold, sandwich the two sponge layers with strawberry jam and press into a 2 litre glass serving bowl.

4 To make the Champagne jelly, boil 200ml water with the sugar for a few minutes, then add the Champagne and lemon and orange zests. Simmer for a few more minutes, then remove from the heat. Gently squeeze dry the soaked gelatine, then stir into the liquid until completely melted. Leave to cool before passing through a sieve. Chill in the fridge to a thick pouring consistency.

5 Trim the strawberries, then lay them side by side on top of the sponge. Pour half of the jelly over the berries and refrigerate to set before topping with the remaining jelly. Return to the fridge to set.

6 For the custard, in a bowl mix the custard powder with enough of the milk to loosen. Put the remainder of the milk in a saucepan and scrape in the seeds from the vanilla pods. Add the pods too. Bring just to the boil, then pour a little of the hot milk on to the loosened custard powder, whisking constantly. Pour this mixture back into the pan and continue to whisk as the custard comes to the boil. At this point, add the sugar and simmer for a few minutes before straining into a bowl or jug. Cover closely with greaseproof paper or cling film and leave to cool.

7 Pour the custard on top of the set Champagne jelly and refrigerate to set.

8 When serving, top each portion with a dollop of whipped cream.

EVE'S PUDDING

SERVES 4

6 large Bramley's apples, peeled,
    cored and sliced
100g sultanas
50g sugar
1 punnet of blackberries
whipped cream or custard to serve

SPONGE MIX

100g caster sugar
100g margarine
2 large eggs
100g self-raising flour

1 Preheat the oven to 220°C/gas 7.

2 Place the apples in a buttered baking dish. Scatter on the sultanas. Sprinkle with the sugar and then with the blackberries.

3 To make the sponge mix, cream together the sugar and margarine. Beat in the eggs, then fold in the flour.

4 Cover the fruit with the sponge mix. Bake for 30–40 minutes or until the sponge is golden brown and cooked through. Serve hot with whipped cream or custard.

RHUBARB COMPOTE
WITH MANGO, VANILLA ICE CREAM WITH NUTMEG

SERVES 4
300g sugar
sprig of rosemary
300g rhubarb, cut into batons
splash of grenadine
3 Alfonso mangos, peeled, stoned and sliced
freshly grated nutmeg to finish

SABLÉ BISCUITS
125g icing sugar, sifted
125g unsalted butter
2 vanilla pods, split lengthways
250g plain flour

pinch of salt
2 eggs
100ml double cream

VANILLA ICE CREAM
600ml double cream
300ml milk
2 vanilla pods, split lengthways
4 egg yolks
175g caster sugar
pinch of freshly grated nutmeg

1 First make the paste for the sablé biscuits. Place the icing sugar, butter, seeds scraped from the vanilla pods, flour and salt in a bowl and rub together using your fingertips. Add the eggs and stir in the cream. Cover with cling film and put to chill in the fridge.

2 Meanwhile, make the vanilla ice cream. Put the cream and milk in a pan and scrape in the seeds from the vanilla pods. Add the pods too. Bring to a gentle simmer. In a bowl set over a pan of boiling water, whisk the egg yolks with the sugar until pale and fluffy. Pour the hot cream mixture over the egg mixture, whisking constantly. Pass the mixture through a sieve into a bowl set over iced water to cool. Once cooled, add the grated nutmeg, then churn in an ice cream machine.

3 Preheat the oven to 120°C/gas $^1/4$.

4 Roll out the sablé biscuit paste on a floured surface and cut into 9–10cm rounds using a metal ring. Place on a baking tray lined with non-stick silicone paper and bake for 12–14 minutes or until golden. Remove and allow to cool on a wire rack. (You will make more biscuits than you need for 4 servings; the rest can be kept in an airtight tin for 2–3 days.)

5 Make a stock syrup by heating the sugar and 300ml water, stirring to dissolve the sugar. Add the rosemary and cook for 8–10 minutes or until syrupy. Add the rhubarb pieces and grenadine and cook over a low heat for 5–6 minutes or until just tender. Remove from the heat and leave to cool.

6 To serve, place a sablé biscuit on each serving plate. Place the metal ring used to cut the biscuits on top and spoon the drained rhubarb inside. Arrange the mango slices on the rhubarb in a circular pattern, then remove the cutter and top with quenelles or scoops of ice cream. Dust with grated nutmeg.

BREAD AND BUTTER PUDDING

SERVES 4

1 loaf of crusty white bread, sliced
250g softened butter
4 whole eggs
2 egg yolks
250ml whole milk
500ml double cream
100g caster sugar
2 tsp ground cinnamon
150g mixed dried fruit
25g Demerara sugar
grated zest of 2 oranges

1 Lay out the sliced bread (with the crusts on or off, as you prefer) and leave overnight to dry out.
2 Preheat the oven to 150°C/gas 2.
3 Butter each slice of bread well. Whisk together the eggs and yolks, milk, cream, caster sugar and cinnamon. Layer the buttered bread in a deep baking dish, overlapping the slices slightly. Soak each layer with the custard mixture and sprinkle with dried fruit. Sprinkle the top with the Demerara sugar and orange zest.
4 Place the dish in a baking tray and add enough water to come one-quarter of the way up the side of the dish. Bake for about 45 minutes.
5 Serve on its own, or with ice cream or pouring cream.

WHITE CHOCOLATE MOUSSE
WITH RED RASPBERRY COULIS

SERVES 4
1 tsp powdered gelatine
4 tbsp milk
150g white chocolate, broken up
350ml double cream

RASPBERRY COULIS
200g frozen raspberries
juice of ½ lemon
4 tbsp caster sugar
2 tbsp icing sugar, sifted
1 tbsp Grand Marnier or other
    orange liqueur (optional)

GARNISH
raspberries
dark and white chocolate shavings

1 First make the coulis. Purée the berries and lemon juice in a blender. Pass through a sieve, pressing with the back of a spoon. Add the caster sugar, icing sugar, 120ml water and the liqueur. Mix well.

2 Place in a saucepan over a moderate heat and bring to the boil, stirring frequently. Reduce the heat and continue stirring for 1 minute. Remove from the heat and leave to cool.

3 In a glass measuring jug, sprinkle the gelatine over 4 tbsp water, then allow the mixture to soften for 1–2 minutes. Microwave on high for 20 seconds. Allow to stand for 2 minutes or until the gelatine granules are completely dissolved. (Alternatively, place the jug in a bowl of hot water and stir until the gelatine has completely dissolved.)

4 Put the milk in a small saucepan and bring to simmering point. Remove from the heat and add the chocolate. Stir until the chocolate has melted and the mixture is smooth. Add the gelatine to the chocolate mixture and mix well. Refrigerate for about 10 minutes or until slightly thickened but not set.

5 Whip the cream until peaks will hold their shape. Fold the white chocolate mixture into the whipped cream.

6 Beginning with the raspberry coulis, make alternate layers of coulis and mousse in tall parfait glasses. Chill for 1–2 hours.

7 To serve, garnish with fresh raspberries and dark and white chocolate.

364

BUTTERMILK PANNACOTTA
WITH POACHED STRAWBERRIES AND
WELSH SHORTBREAD BISCUIT

SERVES 4
350ml double cream
100g sugar
350ml buttermilk
3 gelatine leaves, soaked in cold water
   for at least 10 minutes

WELSH SHORTBREAD
200g unsalted butter

90g icing sugar, sifted
250g plain flour
pinch of salt

POACHED STRAWBERRIES
200g sugar
300ml white wine
500g strawberries, quartered

1 First make the shortbread. Mix the butter and icing sugar together, then gently mix in the flour and salt to make a dough. Roll into a cylinder, wrap in cling film and refrigerate for at least 2 hours.

2 Preheat the oven to 180°C/gas 4.

3 Cut the chilled shortbread dough into 5mm thick slices and place on a baking sheet. Bake for 10–12 minutes or until golden. Cool slightly on the baking sheet, then transfer to a wire rack to finish cooling. If you like, dust them with sugar.

4 Bring the double cream and sugar to the boil, stirring to dissolve the sugar, then pour on to the buttermilk. Gently squeeze the gelatine dry, add to the mixture and stir until completely melted. Pass through a sieve. Divide equally among four shot glasses and place in the fridge to set.

5 For the strawberries, dissolve the sugar in 200ml water and bring to the boil. Add the wine and bring back to the boil, then pour over the prepared strawberries. Cover with cling film and leave to cool.

6 To serve, put a shot glass of pannacotta on each plate with the shortbread to the side and add the strawberries with their juice.

CLASSIC SUMMER PUDDING
WITH MIXED SCOTTISH RED BERRIES
A VANILLA AND GLENTURRET ICE CREAM
AND A SHORTBREAD BISCUIT

SERVES 4

SUMMER PUDDING
1kg mixed red berries in equal quantities
   (strawberries, raspberries,
   blackcurrants, redcurrants)
250g caster sugar or more to taste
1½ gelatine leaves, soaked in cold water for
   at least 10 minutes
8 slices of white bread, crusts removed

SHORTBREAD
185g unsalted butter
90g caster sugar
235g plain flour
30g cornflour
good pinch of salt
1 tsp good quality vanilla essence

VANILLA AND GLENTURRET ICE CREAM
750ml double cream
450ml milk
2 vanilla pods, split lengthways
350g caster sugar
15 egg yolks
Glenturret whisky

TO SERVE
red berry coulis
redcurrants
icing sugar (optional)

1 First make the pudding. Put the berries in a thick-based pot, with the strawberries sprinkled with the sugar at the bottom. Very slowly warm through. When still undercooked, remove from the heat.

2 Gently squeeze dry the gelatine leaves, then add them to the warm berries and stir until completely melted. Taste the mixture: if it seems a bit tart, stir in extra caster sugar as required.

3 To mould the puddings you need four metal rings that are 4–6cm diameter and 3–4cm high. Set them on a tray lined with cling film.

4 Cut a disc from each of four of the bread slices to fit the rings. Dip the bread in the berry juices, then press into the bottom of the rings. Spoon in the berries, using a slotted spoon. Cut discs from the remaining bread to fit the top of the rings. Dip these in the rest of the berry juices, then press into place. Cover the puddings and chill in the fridge to set.

5 Preheat the oven to 160°C/gas 3.

6 To make the shortbread, beat the butter and sugar in a bowl until light in colour. Add the remaining ingredients and mix until it binds together. Put in the fridge to cool for 4–5 minutes. Then roll out until about 5mm thick and cut into circles. Place on a non-stick baking tray. Mark with a fork or leave plain. Bake for 5–8 minutes. Cool on a wire rack.

7 For the ice cream, mix the cream and milk in a large pan. Scrape the vanilla seeds from the pods into the pan, then add the pods too and bring slowly to the boil. In a bowl, whisk the sugar with the egg yolks until pale and thick. Pour a little of the hot cream on to the eggs, then pour back into the pan. Cook, whisking constantly, until the custard thickens and will coat the back of a spoon. Pass the custard through a sieve and leave to cool.

8 Churn the cold custard in an ice cream machine. When it starts to freeze add Glenturret to taste (a bloody good pour). When ready, transfer the ice cream to a freezerproof container and put into the freezer.

9 To serve, place a pudding (still in its metal ring) off-centre on each plate (ideally use square plates). Place the shortbread to the side. Lift the ring off the pudding. Pour a little coulis over the top of the pudding and garnish with a few redcurrants. Place the ice cream on top of the shortbread. Finish by sprinkling a little icing sugar over the pudding, if wanted.

Scotland may not be the first place people think of as a fruit-growing region, but wild berries abound, not only in temperate Tayside and Fife, but also in the harsher climes of Grampian and the Highlands, Arran and Ayrshire. The country's long summer days ensure these wild foods have plenty of time to ripen, and intensify their flavour. Too much heat, and they would simply shrivel.

BAKED EGG CUSTARD
WITH SUMMER FRUITS

SERVES 4
400ml double cream
175ml full fat milk
6 free range egg yolks
6 tbsp runny honey
freshly grated nutmeg
mint to garnish (optional)

RASPBERRY SAUCE
450g ripe, undamaged raspberries
juice of 2 lemons
juice of 1 orange
175g caster sugar
1 bottle red wine

RED FRUIT COMPOTE
450g raspberries
55g redcurrants, picked
55g blackcurrants, picked
85ml crème de framboise

1 Preheat the oven to 160°C/gas 3.

2 Heat the cream and milk together until almost boiling, then remove from the heat. Beat the egg yolks and half the honey together, then pour in the hot cream mixture. Strain into a jug.

3 Drizzle the remaining honey into four non-stick dariole moulds. Grate a little nutmeg on top of the honey, then pour in the custard. Sprinkle the top with a little more grated nutmeg.

4 Place the dariole moulds in a baking tray and pour in hot water to come halfway up the sides of the moulds. Place in the oven and bake for 50–60 minutes or until just set. Remove the moulds from the water and allow to cool. Keep in the refrigerator until half an hour before serving.

5 For the sauce, purée the raspberries with the two citrus juices in a blender until smooth. Pass through a fine sieve into a non-reactive saucepan. Discard the pips. Add the sugar and red wine and bring to the boil over a moderate heat. Reduce the heat and simmer until reduced to about 300ml. Skim off any scum that may come to the surface and discard.

6 Add the fruit and cook for 3 minutes. Remove from the heat and allow to cool, then add the framboise. Using a slotted spoon, spoon the fruit into four dariole moulds lined with cling film. Cover with the overhanging cling film, then weigh down with a light weight to compress the fruit. Leave overnight. Reserve the sauce in a cool place.

7 Turn the custards out on to four plates. Turn out the fruit compotes beside the custard, then add a swirl of the raspberry sauce.

370

COOKED CREAM
WITH A COMPOTE OF GOOSEBERRIES
AND ELDERFLOWER

SERVES 4
600ml double cream
55g caster sugar
1 vanilla pod, split lengthways
2–3 gelatine leaves, soaked in
   4 tbsp water for 10 minutes

GOOSEBERRY AND ELDERFLOWER COMPOTE
225g caster sugar
grated zest and juice of 1 lemon
2 tbsp elderflower cordial
2 heads of elderflowers, washed
450g gooseberries, trimmed

1 Place the cream, sugar and vanilla in a pan and bring to a near simmer. Once the sugar has dissolved, add the gelatine and its soaking water and stir until melted. Strain through a fine sieve, then pour into four individual glasses. Chill for 3 hours.
2 To make the compote, place the sugar, lemon zest and juice, cordial, 600ml water and the elderflowers in a saucepan and simmer gently for 20 minutes. Strain and return to the saucepan. Bring back to a simmer, then add the gooseberries and cook for about 10 minutes or until they are tender but still hold their shape. Remove the gooseberries to a sieve set over a bowl and return any juices to the pan.
3 Return the pan to the heat and simmer gently to reduce the liquid until you have a viscose syrup. Skim from time to time. Allow to cool, then spoon the gooseberries gently into the syrup. Chill for 2–3 hours.
4 To serve, spoon the gooseberries and syrup on top of the creams.

STEAMED
TREACLE SPONGE PUDDING
WITH CLOTTED CREAM ICE CREAM

SERVES 4
4 tbsp golden syrup
grated zest and juice of 1 orange
175g softened unsalted butter
175g light soft brown sugar
3 eggs, beaten
1 tsp black treacle
175g self-raising flour

CLOTTED CREAM ICE CREAM
300ml clotted cream
150ml milk
5 eggs yolks
115g caster sugar

1 First make the ice cream. Place the cream and milk in a saucepan and heat gently until on the point of boiling (just starting to tremble on top). Meanwhile, whisk the egg yolks with the sugar in a large bowl until well combined. Slowly add the hot cream mixture, continuing to whisk as you do so. Pour the mixture back into the saucepan and cook over a low heat, stirring constantly, until thick enough to coat the back of the spoon. Be careful not to let the mixture get too hot or it might split. Pass through a fine sieve and allow to cool completely.

2 Churn in an ice cream machine to a soft consistency. Transfer to an airtight container and put into the freezer for at least 2 hours. If more convenient, you can make the ice cream the day before. You may find if you freeze it for 24 hours or more, you will need to take it out of the freezer about 20 minutes before serving, otherwise it will be very solid and difficult to serve.

3 Butter the inside of a 1 litre pudding basin. Combine the golden syrup with the orange zest and juice, then pour this into the bottom of the basin. Set aside.

4 Beat the butter and sugar together really well until the mixture is pale, then slowly add the beaten eggs, beating well after each addition. Add the black treacle, followed by the flour, again beating well.

5 Spoon this mixture into the pudding basin and cover with greaseproof paper and foil, pleated across the middle; tie on with string and trim off excess all around. Steam the pudding for 2 hours, checking the water level at regular intervals.

6 To serve, run a knife around the rim of the basin and ease out the pudding on to a large serving plate. Give each portion a good spoonful of ice cream. For extra indulgence, serve with some custard too.

WELSH CAKES
WITH ROASTED APRICOTS
AND WELSH CAKE ICE CREAM

SERVES 4
12 apricots, halved and stoned
caster sugar
unsalted butter

WELSH CAKES
225g self-raising flour
½ tsp mixed spice
pinch of salt
85g caster sugar
115g butter or margarine
85g sultanas

1 large egg, beaten
milk if needed
lard for cooking

ICE CREAM
175g egg yolks
90g caster sugar
375ml whipping cream
125ml milk
1 vanilla pod, split lengthways
ground cinnamon
freshly grated nutmeg

1 First make the Welsh cakes. Sift the flour, spice and salt into a bowl and stir in the sugar, then rub in the butter until the mixture has a crumb-like texture. Add the sultanas and mix together, then mix in the egg using a fork. Gather into a dough. If too dry add a spot of milk.

2 Turn the dough on to a lightly floured board and roll out to about 5mm thick. Cut out four 8–10cm rounds and four 5cm rounds. Cut the remaining dough into rounds or other shapes of any size, re-rolling the trimmings as necessary (these cakes will be used for the ice cream).

3 Lightly grease a griddle with lard, then heat on a low heat. Start with a cake or two for the ice cream to test the heat of the griddle. Then lightly cook all the cakes for 20–30 seconds on each side or until golden brown. Leave to cool.

4 To make the ice cream, beat together the egg yolks and sugar in a bowl until pale. Pour the cream and milk into a saucepan and scrape in the seeds from the vanilla pod; add the pod too. Heat until the cream is just coming to the boil, then pour a little over the egg mix and whisk together. Pour this mixture into the rest of the hot cream mixture in the pan and cook, stirring, until thickened enough to coat the back of a wooden spoon. Take care not to let the custard boil. Remove from the pan and cool over ice, then strain.

5 Churn the custard in an ice cream machine. Just as it is ready, sprinkle in 300g crumbled Welsh cakes and finish with ground cinnamon and nutmeg to taste. Transfer to a container and freeze for about 2 hours to harden.

6 Roast the apricots in a frying pan with a touch of sugar and butter until soft.

7 To serve, spoon the warm apricots on top of the large Welsh cakes. Add the smaller Welsh cakes and top each serving with a scoop of ice cream.

HOT BLAIRGOWRIE
RASPBERRY SOUFFLÉ
WITH MALT WHISKY, HONEY AND OATMEAL ICE CREAM

SERVES 4

400g raspberries
1 tbsp lemon juice
100g caster sugar
2 tsp crème de framboise
7g cornflour (about 1 tsp)
icing sugar
170g egg whites (about 6)
pinch of cream of tartar

ICE CREAM

500ml double cream
½ vanilla pod
2½ tbsp clear honey
1 tbsp glucose
4 egg yolks
30g oatmeal
10g icing sugar, sifted
1½ tbsp Glengoyne malt whisky

1 First, prepare the custard for the ice cream. Pour the cream into a thick-based pan and place over a moderate heat. Split the vanilla pod lengthways and lightly scrape out the seeds into the cream. Add the vanilla pod too, and the honey and glucose. Bring the cream to a calm simmer, then remove from the heat and let stand for at least 10 minutes, to infuse.

2 Lightly whisk the egg yolks in a bowl. Pour some of the warm cream over the yolks and mix well, then return this mixture to the remaining cream and combine. Set the pan over a moderate heat and cook, stirring constantly (from side to side to ensure that the mixture in the centre of the pan is being moved as well as the edges) until the mixture starts to thicken and will coat the back of the spoon. Take care not to allow it to become too hot or the egg will curdle and the custard will become lumpy (if this happens, press through a fine mesh sieve to remove lumps). Immediately pass through a coarse sieve into a clean cold bowl. Cover the surface of the custard with cling film to prevent a skin from forming and leave to cool.

3 Press the raspberries through a fine sieve to produce 180g of purée. Put this into a thick-bottomed pan, add the lemon juice and reduce down to a thick jam, stirring from time to time and being careful not let it catch and burn.

4 Put 45g of the sugar in a separate pan. Melt it, then boil until it becomes a thick syrup (121°C on a sugar thermometer). To test without a thermometer, dip a teaspoon into the syrup and then quickly into cold water. You should be able to roll the cooling syrup into a ball between your fingers. Be careful as the syrup is hot! When it has reached the right point, stir the hot syrup into the raspberry jam.

5 Mix the framboise and cornflour together and stir into the jam over the heat. This will help the jam to thicken. Turn the jam into a small bowl, sprinkle the surface with icing sugar and cover closely with cling film. This can all be done the day before and kept in the fridge. Return the jam to room temperature before using.

6 Preheat the grill to moderate.

7 To finish the ice cream, spread the oatmeal on a baking tray, lightly dust with about one-third of the icing sugar and place under the grill. Cook for a couple of minutes, then turn the oatmeal and sprinkle with more icing sugar. Place back under the grill for another 2 minutes, then repeat the process. Alternatively, cook the oatmeal and sugar in a dry frying pan, stirring constantly. In the end, the oatmeal should be light, golden brown with a crisp, sugary crust. Allow to cool completely.

8 Churn the custard in an ice cream machine, stirring in the cool, caramelised oatmeal and whisky once the ice cream has thickened. Remove the ice cream to a clean container and place in the freezer. If making ahead of time (the ice cream can be kept in the freezer for 3 weeks), scoop four balls of ice cream and freeze them on a tray. Allow to soften in the fridge for 30 minutes before serving.

9 When ready to serve, preheat the oven to 180°C/gas 4. Whisk the egg whites with the cream of tartar until you can form soft peaks, then fold in the remaining caster sugar, taking care not to overmix. Lightly fold the whites into the jam, leaving thin traces of white visible in the mixture. Spoon into four buttered and sugared large ramekins, place these on a baking tray and bake for 10 minutes.

10 Transfer the ramekins to plates. Dust the hot soufflés with icing sugar, make a small hole in the top and place a ball of ice cream inside. Serve immediately.

HOT RHUBARB SOUFFLÉ
WITH CUSTARD AND GINGER ICE CREAM

SERVES 4

315g pink rhubarb, trimmed and cut
   into 2.5cm pieces
grated zest of ½ orange
25ml orange juice
20g cornflour, mixed with a little water
110g caster sugar
3 egg whites
sifted icing sugar

vanilla pouring custard made with
   425ml full fat milk, ½ vanilla pod,
   4 egg yolks and 75g caster sugar

GINGER ICE CREAM

150ml whipping cream
250ml milk
50g fresh ginger, peeled and grated
5 egg yolks
75g caster sugar

1 Put the rhubarb in a saucepan with the orange zest and juice and 75ml water. Gently heat until completely soft. Purée in a blender and pass through a fine sieve into a clean pan. Return to the heat, add the cornflour mixture and stir until the purée is very thick. Remove from the heat, place a sheet of cling film directly on top of the purée and set aside.

2 In another pan dissolve 75g of the sugar in 6 tbsp of water over a low heat. Boil to the soft ball stage (115°C on a sugar thermometer). Pour into the warm rhubarb purée and mix well, then gently heat. Transfer to a large bowl and cool completely.

3 Butter four 8.5cm ramekins well with softened unsalted butter, making the brush strokes go upwards so as not to hinder the rising of the soufflé. Chill until set, then repeat the buttering process. Dust well with caster sugar. Return to the fridge.

4 To make the ice cream, put the cream, milk and ginger in a large pan and bring slowly to the boil, stirring frequently. Meanwhile, whisk the egg yolks and sugar in a bowl until pale. Once the cream mixture has come up to the boil, pour over the egg yolks and sugar and whisk together. Strain the custard back into the pan and slowly heat until the custard thickens enough to coat the back of a spoon. Don't allow it to get too hot or it might split. Strain into a bowl and allow to cool completely. When cold, churn in an ice cream machine to a soft consistency, then transfer to an airtight container. Freeze for at least 2 hours. (The ice cream can be made the day before.)

5 Twenty minutes before serving, preheat the oven to 200°C/gas 6.

6 To finish the soufflés, whisk the egg whites until stiff, slowly adding the remaining 25g caster sugar to produce a meringue. Using a slotted spoon, quickly beat one-third of the meringue into the rhubarb purée, then gently fold in the remainder.

7 Spoon into the buttered ramekins. Level the tops and run your thumb around the edge, just inside the rim of the ramekin. Set the ramekins on a baking tray and bake for about 10 minutes or until the soufflés have risen about 2cm above the ramekins.

8 Transfer to plates, dust with icing sugar and add a blob of ginger ice cream alongside. Serve immediately, with the custard to be poured into the soufflés.

BLACK DAN'S
HONEY AND TOASTED OATMEAL CRANACHAN
WITH COMRIE STRAWBERRIES POACHED IN PERNOD AND CINNAMON

SERVES 4

3 tbsp oatmeal

150ml milk

3–4 tbsp Black Dan's honey or other
best quality runny honey

1 small vanilla pod, split lengthways

2 gelatine leaves, soaked in cold water
for 10 minutes

450ml double cream

POACHED STRAWBERRIES

500g strawberries

1 cinnamon stick

2½ tbsp caster sugar

3–4 thumb pours of Pernod

1 Toast the oatmeal in a dry pan for 2–3 minutes, stirring. Set aside.

2 Place the milk and honey in a saucepan and scrape in the seeds from the vanilla pod. Add the pod too, then heat until bubbles start appearing around the edge. Do not boil. Remove from the heat. Gently squeeze dry the gelatine, add to the hot milk and stir until completely melted. Stir in the cream. Pass through a sieve into a jug.

3 Divide the toasted oatmeal among four dariole moulds. Slowly pour in the honey cream mixture. Leave to set in the fridge for 4–5 hours.

4 To prepare the strawberries, combine all the ingredients in a heatproof bowl and cover with cling film. Set over a pan of boiling water and cook for 8–10 minutes. Every now and again, carefully tilt the bowl to swirl the juice over the strawberries. Remove from the hot water and leave to cool.

5 To serve, dip each mould into warm (not hot) water and count to five, then turn out on to a plate. Spoon the poached strawberries around the cranachan.

Cranachan is also known as 'cream crowdie' in Scotland, after the soft local cheese – crowdie – which was used instead of cream. This version is named in honour of Tom Lewis's gardener, Black Dan Campbell.

SPICE CAKE
WITH SUMMER FRUITS

SERVES 4
100g strawberries
100g raspberries
100g blueberries
50g caster sugar
sifted icing sugar

SPICE CAKES
500g caster sugar
200g plain flour
150g ground almonds
25g liquorice powder
25g ground cinnamon
25g ground star anise

25g ground ginger
25g ground cardamom
1 tsp bicarbonate of soda
500g unsalted butter, melted and heated
  to a light nut brown
100g honey
8 egg whites

LEMON CURD
75ml lemon juice
50g caster sugar
2 eggs
50g unsalted butter

1 For the spice cakes, mix together all the dry ingredients in a bowl. Add the butter and honey and mix well, then add the egg whites and mix again, to combine. Cover and leave in the fridge to chill for at least 1 hour.

2 Place half the strawberries, raspberries and blueberries in a pan with the caster sugar and cook on a gentle heat until the sugar has dissolved, stirring occasionally. Pass the fruit through a sieve and leave to cool. Once cool, gently stir in the remaining whole fruits. Set aside.

3 For the lemon curd, combine the lemon juice, sugar, eggs and butter in a bowl set over a pan of simmering water. Whisk until you reach the ribbon stage. Remove from the heat and allow to cool.

4 Preheat the oven to 180°C/gas 4.

5 Grease 8–9cm rings with butter or oil and place on a non-stick baking tray. Fill the rings with the spice cake mixture and bake for 9–11 minutes or until a cake will spring back when lightly pressed in the middle. Remove from the oven and allow to cool. Remove from the rings before serving. (This makes more than four cakes; the rest will keep in an airtight tin for up to a week.)

6 To serve, spoon the lemon curd on each plate and set a spice cake on top. Arrange the summer fruits alongside and dust the cake with icing sugar.

KENTISH APPLE MOUSSE
WITH TOASTED HONEY SYRUP APPLES

SERVES 4-6

ALMOND SPONGE BASE
75g unsalted butter, diced
75g caster sugar
75g ground almonds
2 tbsp plain flour
1 egg

ITALIAN MERINGUE
175g caster sugar
15g liquid glucose
3 egg whites

MOUSSE
4 large apples, peeled, cored and diced
butter
200ml apple juice
50ml Calvados
3 egg yolks
20g caster sugar
2 gelatine leaves, soaked in cold water
   for at least 10 minutes
150ml whipping cream, whipped to a soft peak

JELLY TOPPING
200ml sweet wine
75ml orange juice
juice of ½ lemon
75g caster sugar
1 whole clove
2 English apples, chopped
gelatine leaves (see method)

TOASTED HONEY SYRUP APPLES
300ml sweet cider
2 apples
squeeze of lemon juice
Demerara or caster sugar to glaze
50g raisins
75g clear honey

1 Preheat the oven to 180°C/gas 4. Butter a 20cm loose-bottomed cake tin and line the bottom with baking parchment.

2 First make the almond sponge. In a food processor blend together all of the ingredients until thoroughly mixed. Spread the mixture in the bottom of the cake tin. Bake for 9–10 minutes or until the sponge is firm to the touch. Remove from the oven and leave to cool.

3 Next make the Italian meringue for the mousse. Bring the sugar, glucose and 50ml water to the boil and boil until the syrup reaches the thread stage (110°C on a sugar thermometer). At this point, whisk the egg whites in an electric mixer until firm. As soon as the syrup reaches the hard ball stage (118–120°C), remove the pan from the heat. Turn the mixer to its lowest speed, then pour the syrup into the egg whites in a thin stream. Once all the syrup has been added, continue to whisk the meringue until only just warm. Reserve. (This will make twice as much meringue as you need for the mousse; divide the remainder and bake in a low oven until crisp outside with a soft centre.)

4 For the mousse, cook the diced apples gently in a little butter until softened, then purée in a blender or food processor until completely smooth.

5 Boil the apple juice and Calvados together until reduced by half. Meanwhile, in an electric mixer, whisk the egg yolks and sugar together to a creamy ribbon stage. Pour on the hot apple juice while whisking, then return the mixture to the saucepan. Cook gently, stirring constantly, until thick enough to coat the back of the spoon. It is important the custard does not boil. Remove from the heat.

6 Squeeze dry the gelatine leaves, then add to the custard and stir until completely melted. Cool until just warm, then stir in the apple purée. Fold in 100g of the Italian meringue and the softly whipped cream. Spoon the mousse into the cake tin and smooth the top. Chill in the fridge to set.

7 To make the jelly, put the wine, orange juice, lemon juice, sugar, clove and chopped apples in a pan and simmer until the apples have softened. Strain through a sieve and measure the finished quantity of liquor; you need 1 gelatine leaf for every 100ml liquor. Soak the gelatine in cold water for 10 minutes, then gently squeeze dry and add to the pan. Stir until completely melted. Leave to cool. Once the mousse has set, pour the cold jelly on top, then return to the fridge to set the jelly.

8 For the toasted honey syrup apples, pour the cider into a saucepan and bring to the boil. Meanwhile, peel, halve and core the apples, then cut each half into three or four wedges. Squeeze the lemon juice over the apples to prevent them from discolouring. Add the apples to the cider and bring back to a simmer. Cook for 1–2 minutes or until tender. Remove the apples from the pan and keep to one side. When needed, dip one side of each wedge in sugar and glaze to a rich golden brown under a preheated grill or with a blow torch.

9 Add the raisins and honey to the cider, return to the boil and reduce to a syrup consistency. Pass through a sieve, pushing through all the juices from the raisins. Allow to cool before serving.

10 Loosen the mousse from the tin by quickly blasting a blow torch around the sides or pressing and moving a warmed knife between the mousse and tin. Ease the ring away from the bottom of the tin.

11 To serve, cut the mousse into wedges and place on the plates with the toasted apples side by side. Drizzle the apples with the honey syrup.

382

LEMON CREAM TART
WITH FRESH STRAWBERRIES

SERVES 6-8
225g sweet shortcrust pastry
beaten egg yolk

LEMON CUSTARD FILLING
750ml whipping cream
grated zest and juice of 2 unwaxed lemons
½ vanilla pod, split lengthways
9 egg yolks
125g caster sugar

STRAWBERRY SAUCE
640g fresh strawberries
60g caster sugar
1 tbsp lemon juice

GARNISH
sifted icing sugar
mint sprigs

1 Roll out the pastry to about 5mm thick and use to line a 23cm flan ring set on a baking tray. Chill for at least 30 minutes.

2 Preheat the oven to 180°C/gas 4. Line the pastry case with greaseproof paper and fill with dried beans. Bake for 12–14 minutes or until golden brown. Remove the paper and beans, and bake for a further 1–2 minutes, just to allow any moisture left in the bottom to cook out. Remove from oven, brush the pastry lightly with egg yolk to seal and allow to cool.

3 To make the custard filling, place the cream, lemon zest and vanilla pod in a pan and bring just to the boil. Remove from the heat and leave to infuse for 30 minutes.

4 Add the lemon juice to the cream. Whisk together the egg yolks and sugar in a bowl. Strain the cream mixture over, whisking constantly.

5 Turn the oven to 160°C/gas 3. Pour the custard filling into the pastry case and place in the oven. Bake for about 30 minutes. Remove when the centre is still slightly wobbly, like a crème brûlée. Allow to cool to room temperature.

6 For the sauce, purée about 200g of the strawberries in a blender with the caster sugar and lemon juice, then pass through a sieve. Toss the remaining strawberries into the sauce.

7 To serve, slice the tart into wedges. If you want to brûlée the tart, sprinkle with icing sugar and use a blow torch to achieve a golden caramelised surface. Place a slice of tart in the centre of each plate and add a generous spoonful of strawberries and a drizzle of sauce. Decorate with a sprig of mint and a sprinkle of icing sugar.

DARTMOOR RASPBERRY MOUSSE
WITH ITS OWN JELLY
WITH DEVONSHIRE CLOTTED CREAM
AND RICE PUDDING ICE CREAM

384

SERVES 4

RASPBERRY MOUSSE
200g caster sugar
4 egg whites
200g raspberries
3 gelatine leaves, soaked in cold water for
   at least 10 minutes
200ml whipping cream, whipped until thick

RASPBERRY JELLY
200g raspberries
40g sugar
juice of ½ lemon
2 gelatine leaves

RICE PUDDING
200g pudding rice
200g caster sugar
50g desiccated coconut
1 litre milk
1 vanilla pod, split lengthways

CLOTTED CREAM CURD
3 eggs
6 egg yolks
100g caster sugar
200ml milk
200g clotted cream

TO SERVE
120g raspberries
raspberry coulis

1 To make the mousse, dissolve the sugar in 75ml water, then boil to the soft ball stage (120°C on a sugar thermometer). Whisk the egg whites until they form soft peaks. Slowly pour the sugar syrup on to the whites while whisking. Continue whisking the meringue until cold.

2 Purée the raspberries in a food processor, then pass through a sieve. Warm some of the purée. Gently squeeze dry the gelatine, add to the warm purée and stir until completely melted. Add to the rest of the purée. Leave in the refrigerator until starting to set, then fold in the meringue followed by the whipped cream. Pipe the mousse into four 6 x 6cm rings set on a tray lined with baking parchment and leave to set in the refrigerator.

3 To make the jelly, place the raspberries, sugar and lemon juice in a saucepan with 100ml water. Cover with cling film or a tight-fitting lid and bring to the boil, then remove from the heat. Drain in a sieve lined with a muslin cloth set over a bowl. Gather up the cloth and leave to hang over the bowl for about 2 hours so the clear juice filters through. Reserve the cooked raspberries.

4 Soak the gelatine in cold water for about 10 minutes, then gently squeeze dry. Warm a little of the juice, add the gelatine and stir to melt completely. Put the cooked raspberries in the bottom of four shot glasses. Fill up the glasses with the juice mixture and leave to set in the refrigerator.

5 Next make the rice pudding for the ice cream. Blanch the rice in boiling water for 2–3 minutes, then drain and refresh in running cold water. Put back into the saucepan and add the sugar, coconut and milk. Scrape in the seeds from the vanilla pod, then add the pod too. Bring to the boil, then cook for 30 minutes, stirring from time to time. The mixture should be boiling to reduce the cooking liquid. Tip the rice into a colander and leave to drain.

6 For the clotted cream curd, cream together the eggs, egg yolks and sugar. Bring the milk to the boil, then stir into the creamed mixture. Pour back into the saucepan and cook out well until very thick.

7 Put the clotted cream in a blender and add the curd. Blend well until smooth, then place in a bowl and allow to cool. Combine with the rice pudding (remove the vanilla pod first) and churn in an ice cream machine (do this just before serving, so as not to freeze the rice hard).

8 To serve, turn out each mousse at the end of an oval plate and dress the top with fresh raspberries. Place a shot glass at the other end of each plate and top the jelly with a ball of ice cream. Decorate the plate with a few raspberries and coulis.

Clotted cream is, along with jam and scones, an essential ingredient of afternoon tea. Very much a speciality of the South West, it's made by scalding milk with boiling water, then leaving it to cool overnight. By morning, it's crusty, creamy and sweet. Combine with fruit to counter its artery-clogging qualities.

STRAWBERRY KNICKERBOCKER GLORY

SERVES 4

CANDIED AND DRIED STRAWBERRIES
20 strawberries, hulled and thinly sliced
100–200g icing sugar, sifted

STRAWBERRY WAFERS
2 sheets of rice paper
200g caster sugar

SPICED STRAWBERRY COMPOTE
750ml raspberry liqueur
    (crème de framboise)
2 vanilla pods, split lengthways
pared zest of 1 orange, cut into julienne
pared zest of 1 lemon, cut into julienne

8 black peppercorns
750ml freshly squeezed orange juice,
preferably from blood oranges
25 strawberries, hulled

VANILLA ICE CREAM
600ml full-fat milk
750ml double cream
1 vanilla pod, split lengthways
7 medium free-range egg yolks
250g caster sugar

TO FINISH
strawberry confetti (see method below)
500ml double cream

1 Preheat the oven to 85°C/the lowest possible setting on a gas oven.
2 To make the candied and dried strawberries, lay half of the strawberry slices
in a single layer on a non-stick mat, non-stick baking sheet or baking parchment.
Dust with icing sugar. Dry the strawberries in the oven overnight until they are
crisp and candied. Dry the remaining strawberries in the oven in the same way,
but without dusting them with icing sugar.
3 The next day make the wafers, with the oven at the same temperature. Cut each
sheet of rice paper into three or four pieces, or simply tear them to give a more
natural look. Dissolve the sugar in 200ml water over a low heat, then increase the
heat and boil for 3–4 minutes or until reduced to a syrup. Pour the syrup into a
shallow tray. Place the rice paper in the syrup, then carefully lift it out, keeping the
shape of the paper. Place the rice papers on a non-stick baking sheet, or a baking
sheet lined with baking parchment, and sprinkle generously with candied and dried
strawberries (reserving some of each for making confetti and decorating later).
Bake for 3–4 hours or until crisp and rigid.
4 While the wafers are in the oven, make the compote. Put the raspberry liqueur
in a heavy stainless steel saucepan with the vanilla pods, orange and lemon zests,
and peppercorns. Boil until reduced to a syrup. Reduce the orange juice in a separate
pan to a syrup. Mix the two syrups together in one pan and add the strawberries.
Roll them in the syrup over a medium heat until they are just starting to collapse.
Take the pan off the heat.

5 With a slotted spoon, transfer the strawberries and a little of their syrup to a food processor. Reserve the remaining syrup in the pan. Pulse the strawberries until crushed but not puréed, then reduce in a clean pan over a gentle heat until a compote consistency (it should just drop off a spoon when shaken). Remove the orange and lemon zests and the vanilla pods from the sticky syrup. Cut the vanilla pods into fine julienne, the same size as the zest. Put the zest and vanilla julienne on a non-stick baking sheet.

6 When the wafers are done, remove them from the oven. Put the zest and vanilla julienne in the oven and leave to dry out overnight. When the wafers are cool, slide a palette knife under the rice papers and lift them off the baking sheet.

7 To make the vanilla ice cream, heat the milk, cream and vanilla pod in a heavy saucepan over a high heat, whisking to loosen the vanilla seeds. Leave to infuse off the heat for 30 minutes. Beat the egg yolks and sugar together in a bowl, then strain into the infused mixture and mix well. Leave to cool. Discard the vanilla pod. Churn in an ice cream machine until thickened, then decant the ice cream into a clean container and place in the freezer.

8 Before serving, chill four tall sundae coupes in the freezer until ice-cold. Break the reserved dried strawberries into tiny pieces (confetti). Whip the cream to almost a stiff peak, and spoon into a piping bag fitted with a 5mm tube.

9 To finish, fill the coupes with alternate layers of sticky syrup, ice cream, whipped cream and compote. Finish with a topping of whipped cream, zest and vanilla julienne, candied strawberries, confetti and wafers. Serve immediately.

Note: I always make a larger quantity of ice cream and spiced strawberry compote than I need for this dessert, because it's always good to have a tub of home-made ice cream in the freezer, and the chilled compote is great for breakfast, either on its own or poured over plain yoghurt.

388

LYTHE VALLEY
DAMSON CHEESECAKE

SERVES 8
100g caster sugar
1 vanilla pod, split lengthways
250g damsons, stoned

CHEESECAKE
250g digestive biscuits, crushed
175g butter, melted
750g ricotta
500g cream cheese
150g caster sugar
6 eggs
1 vanilla pod, split lengthways

SAUCE
150g caster sugar
1 vanilla pod
200g damsons, stoned
100ml damson gin

TO SERVE
200g mascarpone
75g icing sugar, sifted
1 vanilla pod, split lengthways
sprigs of mint

1 Put the sugar, seeds from the vanilla pod and 100ml water in a saucepan and heat gently until the sugar has dissolved. Remove from the heat and add the damsons. Leave to poach for at least 20 minutes, then drain.

2 Preheat the oven to 180°C/gas 4.

3 To make the cheesecake, combine the biscuits and butter and press over the bottom of a 20cm spring-sided cake tin (or use individual moulds).

4 Put the ricotta and cream cheeses, sugar and eggs in a food processor. Scrape in the seeds from the vanilla pod and whiz until smooth. Stir in the drained damsons. Spoon on top of the biscuit base. Bake for about 1 hour.

5 Remove from the oven and allow to cool, then chill. Remove the cheesecake from the tin before serving.

6 To make the sauce, slowly bring the sugar, vanilla pod and 100ml water almost to the boil, then simmer until the sugar dissolves. Remove from the heat and stir in the fruit and gin. The sauce can be served warm or cool.

7 To serve, whisk the mascarpone with the icing sugar and seeds scraped from the vanilla pod. Place a slice of cheesecake on each plate and top with lashings of sauce, mascarpone and a sprig of mint.

RHUBARB AND GINGER MOUSSE
WITH RHUBARB SAUCE

SERVES 8

900g fresh pink rhubarb, trimmed and cut into chunks
4 'balls' stem ginger in syrup, drained (keep the syrup)
200g + 3 tbsp sugar
4 egg whites
4 gelatine leaves, soaked in cold water for at least 10 minutes
300ml double cream

1 Put the rhubarb into a pan with 2–3 tbsp of water and simmer for 10–15 minutes or until soft and pulpy. Blitz with half the stem ginger in a blender until you have a nice, smooth purée (this is best done in two batches). Pass through a sieve. Measure out 600ml of purée and put it to one side. The remaining purée will be used to make a rhubarb and ginger sauce.

2 Dissolve the 200g sugar in a little water over a high heat and boil the resulting syrup down to the soft ball stage (115°C on a sugar thermometer). Remove from the heat. Whisk the egg whites in a bowl and, when they start to thicken up, slowly pour on the hot sugar syrup. Continue to whisk for 3 minutes or until doubled in bulk and a firm meringue is formed.

3 In a medium-sized saucepan, warm through the 600ml rhubarb purée (do not let it boil). Gently squeeze dry the gelatine leaves, then add to the purée and stir until completely melted. Pour the purée onto the meringue and fold in until fully incorporated and there are no streaks of white.

4 Whip the cream into a soft peak and fold it into the meringue mix. This is your mousse. Pour it into a large jug – this makes it easier to fill the moulds. Pour the mousse into eight dariole moulds that are 6cm deep and 6cm wide. Leave to set overnight in the fridge.

5 Take 8 tbsp of the remaining rhubarb and ginger purée and combine it in a pan with the remaining 3 tbsp sugar and 4 tbsp ginger syrup. Bring to the boil and boil for 1 minute, then remove from the heat. When cool, cover and chill. Cut the remaining ginger into fine shreds, cover and set aside.

6 To serve, dip the dariole moulds in hot water for 15–20 seconds, then turn out the mousses on to chilled plates. Spoon the rhubarb and ginger sauce around them and top with some shredded ginger.

ANGLO-INDIAN APPLE CRUMBLE

SERVES 6
2 tbsp raisins
1 tbsp apple brandy
450g Granny Smith apples, peeled and
    cut into 1cm chunks
2 tbsp toasted slivered or flaked almonds
50g dark muscovado sugar
1 tbsp plain flour
pinch of ground cinnamon
pinch of crushed black pepper

CRUMBLE
300g plain flour, sifted
pinch of salt
175g dark muscovado sugar
200g unsalted butter, at room temperature,
    cubed, plus knob of butter for greasing

TO SERVE
thick cream, custard or vanilla ice cream

1 Soak the raisins in the apple brandy in a large bowl for 30 minutes (or overnight).
2 Preheat the oven to 200°C/gas 6. Butter a 23–24cm round ovenproof dish.
3 To make the crumble, mix the flour, salt and sugar in another large bowl. Rub in the butter, adding a few cubes at a time, until the mixture resembles fine crumbs.
4 Add the apples and toasted almonds to the raisins and sprinkle over the sugar, flour, cinnamon and black pepper. Stir well, being careful not to break up the fruit.
5 Spoon the fruit filling into the buttered dish and sprinkle the crumble mixture on top. Bake for 35–40 minutes or until the crumble is browned and the filling is bubbling. Serve hot, with thick cream, custard or vanilla ice cream.

	JANUARY	FEBRUARY	MARCH	APRIL	MAY	JUNE
FRUIT & NUTS	Apples Pears Rhubarb, forced	Rhubarb, forced	Rhubarb, early	Rhubarb Strawberries	Cherries Elderflowers Raspberries Rhubarb	Cherries Elderflowers Gooseberries Redcurrants Strawberries, cultivated Tayberries
MEAT, GAME & POULTRY	Goose Hare Partridge, matured Pheasant Rabbit Venison	Goose Guinea Fowl Partridge Pheasant Rabbit	Pigeon Rabbit	Guinea fowl Lamb, Welsh Rabbit Wood pigeon	Duck Lamb, new season	Lamb, new season
VEGETABLES	Cabbage Carrots Cauliflower, Cornish Celeriac Kale Kohlrabi Leeks Shallots Spinach Squash Swede Turnips	Broccoli, purple sprouting Cabbage Carrots Celeriac Chicory Leeks Parsnips Salsify Shallots	Beetroot Broccoli, purple sprouting Calabrese Carrots Chicory Garlic Leeks Mint Nettles Onions Parsley Parsnips Radishes Seakale Sorrel Spring greens	Broccoli, purple sprouting Cabbage, spring Carrots Dandelion Garlic, wild Kale Leeks Mushrooms, wild (e.g. morels) Potatoes (Jersey Royal) Radishes Sorrel, wild Spinach Watercress	Asparagus Beans, broad Carrots Cauliflower Mint Mushrooms, wild (e.g. morels) Nettles Parsley Peas Potatoes, new Radishes Rocket Samphire Sorrel Spinach Watercress	Artichokes, globe Asparagus Aubergines Beans, broad Broccoli, calabrese Carrots Courgettes Cucumber Fennel, wild Horseradish Lettuce Peas Peppers Potatoes, new Radishes Samphire Watercress
CHEESE	Appleby Cheshire Stilton Wensleydale, blue	Cheddar, farmhouse Cheshire, blue Stilton Wensleydale, blue	Cotherstone Ewe's milk cheeses Stilton	Ewe's milk cheeses Goat's milk cheeses, fresh Single Gloucester	English soft cheeses Ewe's milk cheeses	Cheddar, farmhouse Ewe's milk cheeses Goat's milk cheeses, fresh
FISH & SEAFOOD	Cod John dory Lobster Oysters, native Scallops Turbot	Halibut Lemon sole, and other flat fish Mussels	Lobster Mackerel Mussels Salmon, wild Sardines Sea trout	Cockles Crab, brown Lobster Oysters, native Razor clams Salmon, wild	Crab, brown Haddock Lemon sole Prawns Sardines Sea bass Sea trout	Crab Grey mullet Hake Lobster Mackerel Salmon, wild Sardines Sea trout Whitebait

	JULY	AUGUST	SEPTEMBER	OCTOBER	NOVEMBER	DECEMBER

FRUIT & NUTS	Blackcurrants
	Blueberries
	Cherries
	Elderflowers
	Gooseberries
	Loganberries
	Raspberries
	Strawberries
		Apples
		Blackcurrants
		Blueberries, Dorset
		Cherries
		Cobnuts
		Gooseberries
		Greengages
		Loganberries
		Pears
		Plums
		  (Early Laxton,
		  Czare, and Opal)
		Sloes
		Strawberries, wild
			Apples (Worcester
			  Pearmain, James
			  Grieve)
			Blackberries
			Blackcurrants
			  and redcurrants
			Chestnuts
			Cobnuts
			Crabapples
			Damsons and
			  plums
			Elderberries
			Figs
			Greengages
			Pears
			Sloes
				Apples (especially
				  Cox's Orange
				  Pippins)
				Chestnuts
				Cobnuts
				Damsons and
				  bullaces
				Elderberries
				Figs
				Hazelnuts
				Quinces
				Rowanberries
				Walnuts
					Almonds
					Apples
					Chestnuts
					Cranberries
					Hazelnuts
					Medlars
					Pears
					Quinces
					Sloes
					Walnuts
						Almonds
						Apples
						Chestnuts
						Cranberries
						Hazelnuts
						Pears
						Pomegranates
						Quinces
						Walnuts

MEAT, GAME & POULTRY	Lamb, new season
	Venison
	Wood pigeon
		Grouse
		  (from the 12th
		  onwards)
		Hare
			Duck, wild
			Goose
			Grouse
			Lamb, autumn
			Rabbit
			Venison
			Wood pigeon
				Grouse
				Guinea fowl
				Lamb
				Partridge
				Pheasant
					Goose
					Grouse
					Mallard
					Partridge, grey
					Pheasant
						Duck, wild
						Goose
						Pheasant
						Turkey

VEGETABLES	Artichokes,
	  globe
	Aubergines
	Beans, broad,
	  French and
	  runner
	Cauliflower
	Cucumber
	Fennel
	Garlic
	Lettuce
	Peas
	Radishes
	Sage
	Samphire
	Shallots
	Sweetcorn
	Tomatoes
	Watercress
		Aubergines
		Basil
		Beans, French
		  and runner
		Beetroot
		Courgettes
		Cucumber
		Fennel
		Leeks
		Lettuce
		Mushrooms, wild
		  (e.g Scottish
		  girolles/
		  chanterelles)
		Peas
		Peppers
		Potatoes
		  (Pink Fir Apple
		  and Ratte)
		Samphire
		Squash
		Sweetcorn
		Tomatoes
			Beetroot
			Cauliflower
			Chard
			Cucumber
			Kale
			Mushrooms, wild
			  (e.g. ceps)
			Onion
			Pumpkin
			Salad leaves
			Spinach
			Sweetcorn
			Tomatoes
				Beetroot
				Broccoli
				Cabbage, red
				  and Savoy
				Cardoons
				Chicory
				Courgettes
				Jerusalem
				  artichokes
				Kale
				Marrows
				Mushrooms, wild
				  (e.g. ceps and
				  girolles/
				  chanterelles)
				Parsnips
				Pumpkins
				Salsify
				Squashes, winter
				Tomatoes
				Watercress
					Beetroot
					Brussels sprouts
					Cabbage
					Cauliflower
					Celery
					Jerusalem
					  artichokes
					Leeks
					Mushrooms, wild
					Parsnips
					Potatoes
					Pumpkins
					Swede
					Turnips
						Beetroot
						Brussels sprouts
						Cabbage, red
						Celeriac
						Garlic
						Jerusalem
						  artichokes
						Kale, curly
						Leeks
						Parsnips
						Pumpkins
						Spinach
						Swede
						Turnips

CHEESE	Goat's milk
	  cheeses
		Cheddar,
		  farmhouse
		Goat's milk
		  cheeses
			Cheshire,
			  farmhouse
			Double
			  Gloucester
					Ribblesdale	Stilton
						Wensleydale,
						  blue

FISH & SEAFOOD	Clams Crab Lobster Pike Pilchards Prawns Squid, Scottish Trout	Crayfish Dover sole Haddock Herring John dory Mullet, red Pilchards Salmon, wild Trout	Clams Dover sole Eel Mussels Oysters, native Pilchards Plaice Prawns Sea bass Trout, brown	Cod Crab, brown Dover sole Eels Mussels Oysters, native Squid Turbot	Halibut Herring Lobster Mackerel Sea bream	Carp Mussels Oysters Sea bass Skate Turbot

Sat Bains is Chef/Proprietor of Restaurant Sat Bains with Rooms.
Trentside, Lenton Lane, Nottingham,
Nottinghamshire NG7 2SA
(0115 9866 566; www.restaurantsatbains.com)

Galton Blackiston is Chef Patron at Morston Hall Hotel and Restaurant.
Morston, Holt, Norfolk NR25 7AA
(01263 741041; www.galtonblackiston.com,
www.morstonhall.com)

Mark Broadbent is Executive Chef at Bluebird.
Gastrodrome, 350 Kings Road, London SW3 5UU
(020 7599 1156; www.conran-restaurants.co.uk)

John Burton Race is Head Chef at The New Angel,
Dartmouth, Devon. *

Michael Caines is Executive Chef at Gidleigh Park and Director of Food & Beverage, ABode Hotels.
Gidleigh Park, Chagford, Devon TQ13 8HH
(01647 432367; www.gidleigh.com)
Michael Caines at ABode Exeter, Cathedral Yard, Exeter, Devon EX1 1HD
(01392 223638; www.michaelcaines.com/exeter)
Michael Caines at ABode Glasgow, 129 Bath Street, Glasgow G2 2SZ
(0141 572 6011; www.michaelcaines.com/glasgow)
Michael Caines at ABode Canterbury, High Street, Canterbury CT1 2RX
(01227 826684; www.michaelcaines/canterbury.com)
Michael Caines at ABode Manchester, 107 Piccadilly, Manchester. M1 2DB
(01612 005678; www.michaelcaines.com/manchester)
All ABode properties sit side-by-side with the Michael Caines concepts and house a selection from: Michael Caines Fine Dining, MC Champagne Bar, MC Cafe Bar, MC Vibe Bar, MC Boutique, MC Tavern

Richard Corrigan is the Chef/Owner of Lindsay House and Bentley's.
Lindsay House, 21 Romilly Street, London W1D 5AF
(020 7439 0450; www.lindsayhouse.co.uk)
Bentley's Oyster Bar and Grill, 11-15 Swallow Street, London W1B 4DE
(020 7734 4756; www.bentleysoysterbarandgrill.co.uk)

Stuart Gillies is Executive Chef at Boxwood Café.
The Berkeley, Wilton Place, Knightsbridge,
London SW1X 7RL
(020 7235 1010; www.gordonramsay.com/
boxwoodcafe)

Angela Hartnett is Chef Patron at Murano, Mayfair and
York & Albany, Gloucester Gate, Regents Park, both in London. *

Mark Hix is Chef Patron at Hix Oyster and Chop House, Smithfield Market, London. *

Atul Kochhar is Chef-Owner of Benares.
12a Berkeley Square, London, W1
(020 7629 8886; www.benaresrestaurant.com)

Jeremy Lee is Head Chef at Blueprint Café.
28 Shad Thames, London SE1 2YD
(020 7378 7031; www.conran-restaurants.co.uk/
restaurants/blueprint_cafe/home)

Tom Lewis is Head Chef at Monachyle Mhor.
Balquhidder, Perthshire FK19 8PQ
(01877 384622: www.monachylemhor.com)

Noel McMeel is Executive Head Chef at Castle Leslie and runs the Castle Leslie Cookery School.
Castle Leslie, Glaslough, County Monaghan, Ireland
(+353 (0) 47 88100; www.castleleslie.com)

details not available at the time of publication

Nick Nairn runs one of Britain's best cookery schools Nick Nairn Cook School.
Port of Menteith, Stirling FK8 3JZ
(01877 389900; www.nicknairncookschool.com, www.nairnsanywhere.com, www.nicknairn.tv)

Paul Rankin is Chef Patron at Cayenne.
7 Ascot House, Shaftesbury Square, Belfast BT2 7DB
(028 9033 1532; www.rankingroup.co.uk/cayenne.php)
Roscoff Brasserie, 7–11 Linenhall Street, Belfast BT2 8AA
(028 9031 1150; www.rankingroup.co.uk/roscoff.php)
Rain City, 3335 Malone Road, Belfast BT9 6RU
(028 9068 2929; www.rankingroup.co.uk/rain_city.php)
Branches of Café Paul Rankin are at Fountain Street, Belfast
(028 9031 5090); Arthur Street, Belfast (028 9031 0108);
Castlecourt Shopping Centre, Belfast (028 9024 8411);
Lisburn Road, Belfast (028 9066 8350);
Belfast International Airport (028 9445 4992);
High Street Mall, Portadown (028 3839 8818);
Junction One International Outlet Centre, Antrim (028 9446 0370); Bow Street, Lisburn (028 9262 9045);
Dundrum Town Centre, Dublin (00353 1 2963105).

Gary Rhodes is Head Chef at Rhodes Twenty Four Tower 42.
25 Old Broad Street, London EC2N 1HQ
(020 7877 7703; www.rhodes24.co.uk)
Rhodes W1, The Cumberland, Great Cumberland Place, London W1A 4RS (020 7479 3938; www.garyrhodes.com)

Simon Rimmer is Chef Patron at Greens Manchester.
43 Lapwing Lane, West Didsbury, Manchester M20 8NT
(0161 434 4259)
and Chef Patron at Earle in Hale.
4 Cecil Road, Hale, WA15 9PA (0161 929 8869)

Matt Tebbutt is owner and Head Chef at The Foxhunter.
Nantyderry, Abergavenny, Monmouthshire NP7 9DN
(01873 881101; www.thefoxhunter.com)

Marcus Wareing is Head Chef at Pétrus.
The Berkeley Hotel, Wilton Place, Knightsbridge, London SW1X 7RL (020 7235 1200; www.marcuswareing.com)

Bryn Williams is Head Chef at Odettes.
130 Regents Park Road, Primrose Hill, London NW1 8XL
(020 7586 8569; www.odettesprimrosehill.com)

Antony Worrall Thompson is Chef Patron at Notting Grill.
123a Clarendon Road, London W11 4JG
(020 7229 1500; www.awtonline.co.uk)
Kew Grill, 10b Kew Green, Richmond, Surrey TW9 3BH
(020 8948 4433)
Barnes Grill, 2-3 Rocks Lane, SW13 0DB
(020 8878 4488)
Windsor Grill, 65 Street Leonards Rd, Windsor SL4 3BX
(01753 859 658)
Greyhound Free House and Grill, Gallowstree Road, Rotherfield Peppard, Oxon RG9 56HT
The Lamb Free House & Kitchen, Satwell, Rotherfield Greys, Henley-on-Thames, RG9 4QZ (01491 628 482)

ACKNOWLEDGEMENTS

Great British Food is a compilation edition of *Great British Menu* and *Great British Menu Cookbook*.

Great British Menu was produced for Dorling Kindersley by:
Writer Paul Lay
Project Manager and Editor Norma Macmillain
Art Direction and Text Design Smith & Gilmour, London
DTP Designer Louise Waller
Production Controller Elizabeth Warmen
Operations Publishing Manager Gillian Roberts
Art Director Peter Luff
Creative Publisher Mary-Clare Jerram
Publisher – Special Projects Stephanie Jackson
Publisher Corinne Roberts
Senior Jacket Creative Nicola Powling
Jacket Editor Anna Stewart
Photographers Dan Jones (food), Noel Murphy (locations),
Chris Bairstow, Steve Sklair, Jessica North (chefs)

Great British Menu Cookbook was produced for Dorling Kindersley by:
Editor Laura Nickoll
Executive Managing editor Adèle Hayward
DTP Designer Traci Salter
Art Editor Nicola Rodway
Production Controller Luca Frassinetti
Operations Publishing Manager Gillian Roberts
Art Director Peter Luff
Publisher Stephanie Jackson
Project Manager and Editor Norma MacMillan
Art Direction and Text Design Smith & Gilmour, London
Photographers Dan Jones (food), Noel Murphy (locations), Adrian Reay,
Joff Wilson and Ross Blair (chefs)
Food Stylist Stephen Parkins-Knight
Recipe Consultants Angela Nilsen and Jeni Wright

Dorling Kindersley would also like to thank the following for their help with the original editions:

Great British Menu
Alex, Emma, Saskia, Brianne, Katrin and Jim at Smith & Gilmour; Stephen Parkins-Knight, food stylist, for preparing and presenting recipes for the camera; Noel Murphy for location photography, Dan Jones for food photography and Fabio Alberti for photographic assistance; Divertimenti for loan of props; Alan Kennedy, Rosie Rose, Derek Morrison, Bob Kennard, David and Christine Pugh, Anthony Buscomb, Denis Lynn, Willie Weston, Tony Batchelor and Neil Robson for their help with location photography; Jackie Baker, Sophie Seiden, Vanessa Land and Annina Vogel at Optomen Television; and Hilary Bird for the index

Great British Menu Cookbook
Alex, Emma, Helen, Jim, Katrin and Saskia at Smith & Gilmour; Nicola Moody, Raewyn Dickson, Ross Blair, Christopher Monk, Sam Knowles, Vanessa Land and Karen Taylor at Optomen Television; Roz Denny and Val Barrett for recipe testing; Bex Ferguson and Clemmie Jacques for assisting with the recipe testing; Country Cheeses and Sue Proudfoot (Whalesborough Farm), Kathy Hayward and Ken Hayward at Thornham Oysters, Roger Olver and Tanya Dalton at Cornish Duck Company, and Jackie Thompson and Paul Booker at Letheringsett Watermill for help with location photography; and Hilary Bird for the index